On Being the Church in the United States

American University Studies

Series VII
Theology and Religion
Vol. 170

PETER LANG
New York • Washington, D.C./Baltimore • San Francisco
Bern • Frankfurt am Main • Berlin • Vienna • Paris

Barry Penn Hollar

On Being the Church in the United States

Contemporary Theological Critiques of Liberalism

PETER LANG
New York • Washington, D.C./Baltimore • San Francisco
Bern • Frankfurt am Main • Berlin • Vienna • Paris

Library of Congress Cataloging-in-Publication Data

Hollar, Barry Penn.
    On being the church in the United States: contemporary theological
critiques of liberalism / Barry Penn Hollar.
        p.   cm. — (American university studies: Series VII, Theology and
religion; vol. 170)
    Includes bibliographical references.
    1. Liberalism (Religion)—United States—History—20th century.
2. Church and the world—History of doctrines—20th century.
3. Christianity and culture—History—20th century. 4. Niebuhr,
Reinhold, 1892–1971. 5. Hauerwas, Stanley, 1940–   . 6. Ruether,
Rosemary Radford. I. Title. II. Series.
BR517.H553   1994   230'.046—dc20   93-29225
ISBN 0-8204-2350-5   CIP
ISSN 0740-0446

Die Deutsche Bibliothek-CIP-Einheitsaufnahme

Hollar, Barry Penn:
On being the church in the United States: contemporary theological critiques
of liberalism / Barry Penn Hollar. - New York; San Francisco; Bern;
Baltimore; Frankfurt am Main; Berlin; Wien; Paris: Lang, 1994
    (American university studies: Ser. 7, Theology and religion; Vol. 170)
    ISBN 0-8204-2350-5
NE: American university studies / 07

The paper in this book meets the guidelines for permanence and durability of
the Committee on Production Guidelines for Book Longevity of the
Council on Library Resources.

To Quentin Clay Penn Hollar, my son,
with the prayer that he may know a more faithful church
than I have known.

Acknowledgments

There are many people without whose assistance and support this book would not have been possible. I am especially grateful to to the following:

My parents, Leonard and Thelma Hollar of Singer's Glen, Virginia, who provided a home environment during childhood for the discussion of issues related to faith and politics.

David Bailey Harned, my teacher and friend as an undergraduate at the University of Virginia, who was the first to instill in me a measure of confidence as a student and scholar.

David Little, my teacher at the University of Virginia, who taught me much and whose disagreement with me is always instructive.

James F. Childress who was my dissertation director and has been an excellent mentor and friend for many years.

My colleagues in the Department of Religious Studies at the University of Virginia with whom the ideas expressed here were first discussed and clarified. Especially Bill Boley, Joel Zimbelman, David Kelsay, Courtney Campbell, Linda Estelle, Richard Brown, and Thom Donlin-Smith.

Mike Duffy with whom I began doctoral studies and who has poured carefully over every letter of this work. He more than anyone else has provided the inspiration and the assistance to take what began as a dissertation and bring it to the form in which it is presented here.

Cathy Lauffer, a student at Shenandoah University, who has carefully and thoughtfully provided a last examination of the pages of this book.

Doris Harrison, Raymond Wrenn, and Kenneth Starr, members of the Board of Trustees of Shenandoah University, who made generous contributions to the University's Faculty Publications Fund which supported the publication of this book.

Most of all, I am grateful to my wife, Jayne Penn Hollar, who has supported me with her love and, especially during my doctoral studies, with financial support. She often worked a "double shift" that enabled me to devote myself to the work that is represented here. I hope in some way that this will contribute to a church and world in which women and men are more mutual partners in every dimension of life.

Permission to reprint from the following is gratefully acknowledged.

From John Rawls "Justice as Fairness: Political Not Metaphysical." Philosophy and Public Affairs, Vol. 14, Summer 1985. Baltimore: John's Hopkins University Press, 1985. Reprinted by permission of the publisher. All rights reserved.

Reprinted with permission of Macmillan Publishing Company, a Division of Macmillan, Inc. from THE CHILDREN OF LIGHT AND THE CHILDREN OF DARKNESS By Reinhold Niebuhr. Copyright 1944 Charles Scribner's Sons; copyright renewed (c) 1972 Ursula M. Niebuhr.

Table of Contents

xii

Introduction:

The Church in a Liberal Political Culture

Four Options for the Church in a Liberal Culture

REINHOLD NIEBUHR, Stanley Hauerwas, and Rosemary Radford Ruether are Christian theologians with significant influence on social ethical reflection and ecclesiological praxis in the contemporary church in the United States, especially among mainline Protestants. Official Catholic social teaching as developed in the Papal social encyclicals and the pastoral letters of the U. S. Conference of Catholic Bishops have defined social ethical responsibility for the Catholic Church. Each has provided a fully developed interpretation of the Christian faith and an interpretation of the challenge to that faith which life in a modern liberal political culture represents. Each provides a compelling argument for the posture that the Christian community ought to adopt toward that culture. Each offers a distinct conception of what it means to be a faithful Christian and a faithful Christian community in the United States in the late twentieth century.

In many respects those conceptions are incompatible. Niebuhr, of course, provided sophisticated theological rationale for an aggressive participation by individual Christians and the Church in the domestic and international controversies that dominated politics in the United States from World War I and the great depression to the civil rights movement and the war in Vietnam. His work reflected and influenced the widespread belief among Christians in the United States that utilizing the opportunities for direct political participation provided by liberal democratic institutions and participating in the controversies under the terms in which they were cast in our liberal political culture was a requirement of a faithful and responsible Christian life. That sense of the basic compatibility between responsible Christian life and the institutions of a liberal government included an acceptance of the prominent international role which the United States came to play in World War II and thereafter. For Niebuhr, influencing public policy at both the domestic and foreign level was the primary way in which Christians were to exercise their moral responsibility in the world.

Niebuhr's voice was not the only one shaping Protestant Christian praxis in the middle of this century. Yet it does seem fair to say that he provided the dominant theological framework that expressed the way most mainline Christians in the United States understood the relationship between the church and the political world in which they lived. His thought articulated the rationale for and the terms of the political involvement of many, if not most, Christians and the mainline Protestant churches with which they were associated. While Niebuhr's influence remains strong in the mainline churches, several alternatives to his political realism and his theological defense of liberal political institutions[1] are competing for influence in the contemporary Christian community in the United States.

As the culture has grown increasingly secular and the strength and influence of the churches has waned, many have looked for an understanding of Christian political ethics that pays greater attention to the distinctive responsibilities and contributions of the Church. In addition, a yearning for "community" was created by the break–up of familial and communal associations caused by the geographic and social mobility and the rapidity of change which are characteristic of the modern industrial society of the United States. The Church came to be seen as one of several intentional communities which could satisfy the yearning which many felt. Moreover, disillusionment with political institutions and governmental policy resulted in greater attention to the Church itself as an instrument of Christian political responsibility. For example, the inability of U. S. policy in Southeast Asia, Latin America, and Africa to effect change toward more peaceful, democratic, and prosperous societies, indeed a growing sense that U. S. policy had often been a part of the problem in those regions rather than an instrument of positive social change, led to a profound doubt about the wisdom of regarding U. S. governmental institutions and policy as the primary vehicle of Christian political and social responsibility. Domestically, the realization that civil rights laws and governmental social programs had not resulted in ideal relations between races or the elimination of poverty had the same impact.[2] These factors, it seems to me, account in large measure for the growing influence of Stanley Hauerwas. Hauerwas has argued that the primary political responsibility of Christians and of the Church is to be a faithful Christian community. He has expressed an unwillingness to address issues of public policy and has challenged the appropriateness for Christians of the terms in which public policy debates are cast. He refuses to endorse the view that national political institutions and policies can be an instrument of Christian responsibility.

Hauerwas' perspective is not the only, nor even the first, alternative to the Niebuhrian perspective which has risen to a position of influence among mainline Christians in the United States. Disillusionment with U. S. policy at both the domestic and foreign levels has led many Christians to the conviction that liberal democratic institutions (including free market economies) have to be radically altered if they are to serve as vehicles of

Christian concern. Liberation theology, rather than questioning the appropriateness of Christian participation in national politics, has called for more aggressive participation toward a radical social, economic, and political change. Rosemary Ruether has been an important contributor to theological reflection in the liberation tradition in the United States. She has appropriated Latin American liberation theology and its Marxist social analysis and expanded it to address the concerns of women.

Catholic thinking about these matters followed a somewhat different course. From the birth of the United States until the middle of this century, deep tensions existed between the views of many Catholics in the United States and the official teachings of the Church. Many Catholics, if not most, believed that the liberal polity of the United States, with its separation of church and state and religious liberty, was a friendly environment for Catholicism and that the Church was flourishing on these shores. On the other hand, Church authorities in Rome, whose understanding of liberalism was shaped largely by the French Revolution with its anti–clericism and persecution of Catholicism, condemned liberalism and "Americanism"throughout the 19th century. This tension did not fully dissipate until the Second Vatican Council in the early 1960's. On the eve of the Council Pope John XXIII promulgated the encyclical *Pacem in Terris* which included an affirmation of the civil and political rights for which liberalism was famous. The Council itself affirmed religious liberty and separation of church and state and radically re–thought the whole question of the Catholic Church's relationship to the modern world. Since the Council a succession of Papal social encyclicals have built upon the conciliar breakthroughs, and in the 1980's the U. S. Bishops have produced their own pastoral letters on nuclear deterrence and the U. S. economy. This official teaching, drawing as it does upon what might be called a pre–liberal basis for democracy and influenced as well by liberation theology, has provided Catholics a rich body of material for coming to terms with and for critiquing the liberal polity of the United States.

This study is an attempt to understand how Niebuhr, Hauerwas, Ruether and official Catholic social teaching conceive the relation between the church and the world. A central assumption upon which this study is based is that the question of the church's relationship to the world, particularly to the political culture of which it is a part, is one that can only be resolved contextually. That is to say, borrowing the categories which H. Richard Niebuhr made so familiar in *Christ and Culture*, the church is never against, of, above, in paradoxical relation with, or transforming the world or culture *per se*. Rather, such postures are adopted or advocated in relation to some particular culture. If this hypothesis is correct, the posture that any theologian or church adopts toward the world is shaped not only by its basic understanding of the proper relationship between church and world, but as well by the particular features of the cultural world of which the theologian's or the religious community is a part and by the theologian or church's understanding and interpretation of those features.[3] It is also assumed here that the political ethos of the contemporary United States is one which liberal theory is able to describe and for which it is able to provide a compelling justification. Thus, in the contemporary context in the United States, a theologian's conception of the church/world relation is shaped by liberal political culture and his or her understanding and evaluation of it. Understanding Niebuhr's, Hauerwas', Ruether's, and Catholicism's analysis and critique of the liberal culture which dominates political life in the United States is essential to understanding their conception of the church/world relation and their arguments for the particular posture that the church should adopt toward our liberal political world.

Three Factors Shaping the Church/World Distinction

There are at least three factors which deeply influence the way theologians draw the ethical distinction between church and world, or three ways in which that distinction may be drawn. I will call these factors the epistemological factor, the moral factor, and the human possibilities factor.[4] A theologian's judgments with reference to each of these profoundly effect his or her conception of the church's relation to the world and the posture toward the world which he or she regards as appropriate for the church. The epistemological factor has to do with the theologian's conception of how valid moral knowledge is gained and whether the church is thought to have distinctive moral knowledge which is not available to the world. The moral factor refers to whether the theologian regards the same moral principles or values as valid for both church and world such that persons in each are held accountable to the same standards of conduct. The human possibilities factor has to do with whether the theologian regards the church as characterized by its greater possibilities for conforming its life to the norms or achieving the ideals which are regarded as valid.

With reference to the epistemological factor the question is: does the Church have distinctive moral knowledge, on the basis of its particular relation to Jesus or the Holy Spirit or on the basis of the revelation given to it, which the world cannot have? Or is the world capable of the same ethical insight available to people of faith? In principle, there seem to be three possibilities with reference to the epistemological factor. First, the theologian may regard the church as having no ways of knowing or no sources of moral knowledge that are not available to those outside the faith community. Those who hold such a view will tend not to draw a sharp distinction between church and world, or at least the distinction will not be drawn on epistemological grounds. A second possibility is that the theologian will recognize distinctive Christian ways of knowing or distinctive sources of Christian knowledge, such as scripture, tradition, or prayer, while not denying the validity of those sources which are available to those outside the church. Indeed those sources of knowledge available to the world may also be regarded as authoritative to the church. Such an epistemological perspective suggests a distinction between church and world, or a distinction between Christian and non–Christian ethics, but not necessarily a sharply drawn one. The United Methodist quadrilateral indicates this sort of epistemological judgment. According to that principle of theological reflection, scripture, tradition, reason, and experience are all valid sources of theological and moral knowledge or insight. Scripture and tradition may be seen as distinctive to the church: in general, only those who identify themselves with Christianity or the Christian community regard them as authoritative. Reason and experience are available to all human beings and the church regards them as valid sources for its own reflection (even though scripture is regarded as primary).

A third possibility may be called "epistemological sectarianism." This view emphasizes the absolute distinctiveness of Christian sources of knowledge or ways of knowing. Those who regard Scripture as the sole source of authority for Christian life fall into this category as would moral relativists who deny the possibility of any general or universal perspective from which valid moral knowledge is gained. Christians who adopt a relativist perspective need not deny that reason and experience are valid sources of human knowledge. Rather they need only deny that there is any universal reason or experience which is not interpreted from some particular perspective. On this view the particular perspective or commitments which Christians adopt will shape their reason and influence the way in which experience is interpreted. In the same way the different perspectives of those in the world, or those not of the Christian community, will give a different shape to worldly reason and a different interpretation of shared experiences. Such an epistemological perspective suggests a sharp distinction between church and world.

With reference to the moral factor the question becomes: Do the same moral principles apply to each or is the church held to a different standard? James Gustafson has drawn a broad distinction between those who argue that "Christian ethics and universal human ethics are convertible terms" and those who argue that to be a Christian is "to be a distinctive people with a distinctive way of life" (1975:171). For those who belong to the first camp, and Gustafson cites St. Thomas, Luther, and Calvin as exemplars, church and world are regarded as held to the same moral standards and are not distinguished on this basis. For those who take the second view—Gustafson lists the early monastic movement, Anabaptists, and radical Puritans— church and world are sharply distinguished on the basis of the principles, values, and virtues to which those in the church are to conform as distinguished from those applicable to the world. For this group, the distinctly Christian norms do not simply require a going beyond or higher than worldly norms; they are largely contradictory to them.

Gustafson's categories need to be nuanced however. Those in his first camp do not regard Christian ethics and universal human ethics as absolutely convertible terms. Rather, they are only largely so. There are distinctive Christian norms, values, and virtues which go beyond those recognized by those outside the church, even if they do not contradict those worldly terms and even if the worldly ones are regarded as authoritative for the church. Moreover, those in the second group do not necessarily hold to an absolute distinction between church and world with reference to the moral factor. There is always the possibility of some moral agreement.

There is an obvious relationship between the epistemological and the moral factor. In general those who regard the church as having no distinctive sources of moral knowledge or ways of knowing will argue that the same moral principles apply to both church and world. Those who see the church as having distinctive sources of knowledge, but who still regard the more generally shared sources as valid, will tend to see a wide measure of overlap between the moral principles that apply to the church and those that apply to the world. Moreover, they will tend to see the distinctive knowledge available to the church as going beyond rather than contradicting the principles and ideals recognized by the world. Harlan Beckley attributes such a view to Gustafson and that is also his own view (1985:217–219). Finally, those who draw a sharp epistemological distinction tend also to draw a sharp moral distinction. That is to say, certain of the uniquely Christian principles are often seen as contradictory to those which the world regards as valid.

In principle, however, the correspondence here between the epistemological and the moral judgments is not exact. This is particularly important with reference to the epistemological perspective which I have labeled sectarian. Put simply, while the sources of valid knowledge or the ways of knowing may be sharply distinguished there may be significant overlap between what is known. Those who adopt an epistemologically sectarian position may still find moral grounds for cooperation with the world. There is another way in which the epistemological and moral factors may diverge. Beckley has written that some in the contemporary Religious Right in the United States believe that "Christian moral principles should be enforced upon all persons" (1985:215). This suggests that an epistemological distinction is drawn which regards the perspective of the church as the only one from which valid ethical norms can be known. However, on this view, all are appropriately held responsible for obedience to Christian norms. Of course, all those who draw the epistemological distinction are likely to regard the norms that are only knowable from a Christian perspective as valid for all. However, many would not regard it as appropriate to hold those outside the Church or outside of Christian faith accountable to those norms.

My judgment that the ecclesiastical posture toward the world or the understanding of the relation of church and world which a theologian advocates is contextually determined means that two particular factors deeply influence that posture and that understanding: 1) the theologian's moral interpretation of those elements which are unique to the church, that is, the scriptures and particularly the life and teachings of Jesus, and 2) the moral ethos that is characteristic of the particular culture in which the church finds itself and the theologian's interpretation of it. That is to say, a theologian's judgment as to whether or not Christian people may actively participate in the roles made available to them by the world or culture in which they live and in the moral debates which that culture's ethos engenders is largely determined by the theologian's interpretation of the moral import of scripture and of Jesus' life and teaching and by the particular moral ethos in which the church finds itself and his or her interpretation and evaluation of it. In the contemporary United States that interpretation and evaluation will be couched in terms of an evaluation of liberalism.[5]

The third factor which may have an important impact on the way in which the relation between church and world is understood has to do with the possibilities that each has for conforming life to the norms and or achieving the ideals which are regarded as valid for it. Even where church and world are regarded as knowing and being accountable to the same moral principles and rules, they may be distinguished with reference to the resources available to the church which enable living in conformity with those norms. The beliefs that are unique to Christians, the character traits that are shaped only in Christian community, the power of grace poured out on Christians may be regarded as making it possible for Christians to live up to the norms to which all are accountable in a way that others are not. They may indeed be able to achieve ideals of behavior and for human relationships that others cannot achieve. Christians may be regarded as able to go up to and beyond what universally valid rules to which all are accountable require in a way that others may not.

Where the distinction and relation between church and world is drawn with reference to the moral norms which apply to both and the epistemological resources available to both, attention is focused on the relation between distinctly Christian sources of knowledge and those which are universally available. Questions of the relation between scripture and reason or natural law will be prominent. Judgments about whether or not the distinction between church and world can be drawn with reference to the church's greater possibilities for conforming life to valid moral

principles or achieving moral ideals often will be focused on the relation of
Christian eschatological hope to human history. The Christian hope for the
reign of God at the end of human history includes the idea that human sin
and discord will have been eliminated. Those who emphasize the church's
greater moral possibilities often do so by insisting that eschatological hope
is partially realized in the life of the historical church. Where the church is
not distinguished from the world on the basis of its greater moral
possibilities the absolute transcendence of the eschatological reign of God
over human history will be emphasized.

My analysis of the work of Reinhold Niebuhr, Stanley Hauerwas,
Rosemary Radford Ruether and of official Catholic social teaching will
display the relationship between their understandings and assessments of
liberalism and these possible ways for drawing the distinction between
church and world. My focus will be upon their epistemological judgments
and their evaluations of the epistemological adequacy of liberalism, their
conceptions of the relationship between Christian norms and ideals and
liberal ones, and their understandings of the human possibilities which are
available to those in the liberal world and those in the church. Their
various conceptions of the relationship between church and world will be
understood primarily with reference to these three factors.

Endnotes

1 While it is fair to say that Reinhold Niebuhr offered a theological defense of
the political values and institutions associated with liberalism, one of the things we
will be considering is the degree to which his reasons for supporting such
institutions are liberal ones.

2 As a result of the rightward shift in the political climate in the United States as
represented by the so-called "Reagan Revolution," even those governmental
accomplishments, which were seen by many as necessary but not sufficient for the
exercise of Christian responsibility, are extremely fragile.

3 I understand the view that John Howard Yoder defends in his unpublished paper
"Christ and Culture: A Critique of H. Richard Niebuhr" to be supportive of the
contextual position I am stating. Yoder, who writes of course from within a tradition
that Niebuhr would regard as having adopted an "against culture" posture, argues that
Niebuhr has misunderstood both the biblical perspective on culture and the teaching
of Jesus. As a result he has misunderstood the posture of those radical or "sectarian"
groups which base their position on the authority of scripture. According to Yoder's
analysis, Niebuhr assumes that culture is monolithic and autonomous, that is, "the
value of culture is not derived from Jesus Christ but stands somehow independently of
him and prior to his criticism of it" (Yoder, n. a.: 8). But, says Yoder, it is precisely
culture's claim to autonomy and monolithic unity which the New Testament denies in
its claim that Jesus is Lord. Moreover, Niebuhr interprets Jesus "as pointing us away
from full and genuine human and historical existence" (11). towards "something else
incomparably more important" (9).: the spiritual realm. According to Yoder, the New

Testament's denial of the unity and autonomy of culture and Jesus' concern about human existence in history and culture indicate that "the cultural position of the Christian church according to the New Testament is therefore not a matter of seeking for a strategy to be applied globally, either accepting or rejecting (paradoxing or transforming) all of 'culture' in the same way; it proceeds precisely by denying such a global character to culture and moves rather by discrimination" (9). Yoder is correct that Niebuhr seems generally to ignore such a contextual, or discriminating perspective on the question of the relation of the church and the world in favor of a global or generalized one. He does however make occasional comments suggestive of a more contextual understanding of the relation. For example, he says that the sectarian, or Christ against culture, posture is adopted "when men are in despair about their culture" (1951:68). Moreover, in noting the lack of a synthesis between Christ and culture in the modern world comparable to that provided by Thomas Aquinas in the Middle Ages, Niebuhr refused to decide "whether the synthetic answer is absent from modern Christianity on account of the nature of our culture, or because of the understanding of Christ that prevails. . ." (1951:141).

This contextual view does not deny that different Christian communities and traditions will find it more or less difficult to change its basic posture as a result of certain theological convictions. But it is to say that even those traditions which tend toward a counter-culture or iconoclastic posture, for example because its central norms are derived from a literal reading of scripture rather than from reason or experience, or, because of a strong "eschatological proviso" that prohibits it from regarding any human culture as absolutely consistent with or directly leading to the reign of God, will find themselves more at home in some cultures than others if for no other reason than that some cultures will be more hospitable than others to the particular form of community life and religious expression that a particular church tradition seeks to adopt.

4 I am not claiming that these are the only factors which effect a theologian's understanding of the distinction between church and world. These do seem to be the most important in terms of an ethical distinction between church and world. Moreover, the ones that are identified here have proven helpful for organizing the ways Niebuhr, Hauerwas, and Ruether draw the ethical distinction between church and world. These are the factors that have determined their understanding of the distinction.

5 Emphasis will be placed on natural law or human reason as a dominant source of authority for Christian ethical reflection when it is judged that the particular cultural ethos in which the church finds itself provides roles, norms, and modes of reasoning which are not inconsistent with the moral importance of scripture or the life and teaching of Jesus as interpreted by the theologian. In such a context the church will not be regarded as a distinctive moral community and tension between church and world will not be apparent. Where that ethos is regarded as inconsistent with scripture and the life and teaching of Jesus these uniquely Christian sources will be emphasized as the fundamental authorities for the church's life and the distinctiveness of the church and the tension between it and the world will be emphasized.

If scripture, tradition, reason, and experience are always regarded as sources of Christian theology, I am insisting that scripture and tradition take priority over reason and experience where the cultural ethos in which the church operates is regarded as fundamentally at odds with the more uniquely Christian sources. Moreover, the interpretation of experience itself may vary. Where the cultural world is regarded as consistent with Christian norms universal human experience will be regarded as an authoritative source; where it is not Christian experience will be emphasized.

This way of putting the matter should not be interpreted as suggesting that the theologian's interpretation of scripture and of the life and teaching of Jesus is not itself influenced by the cultural ethos in which the theologian lives. Surely it is. It is only to indicate that where significant dissonance between the interpretation of the Christian sources and cultural norms is present natural law and reason will diminish in importance in the church's ethical methodology, the church as a distinctive community will be emphasized, and the sense of tension between church and world will be heightened. Nor is this to suggest that appeal to natural law or reason is inherently conservative in that where such are regarded as the primary sources of authority the ethos, institutions, and practices of a particular culture are accepted as acceptable and just. It is to suggest that where appeal to reason or nature is prominent in the work of a Christian theologian it is because some way of arriving at a conception of basic norms and institutions is available to him or her from the culture which is not inconsistent with the understanding the uniquely Christian sources.

1

Describing the World:
The Central Features of Liberal Political Theory

A PRIMARY assumption here is that the political culture of the United States is a liberal one and that liberal theory provides the best description and defense of the our public institutions and values. My first task is to provide an account of liberal theory. That account draws upon the work of classical liberal theorists such as John Locke, Immanuel Kant, and John Stuart Mill and contemporary liberals, including Ronald Dworkin, H. L. A. Hart, and John Rawls. While I intend this account to be authentic to the actual beliefs of a representative contemporary liberal, I hope it is broad enough to describe the historical tradition of liberalism which lies behind those beliefs. Moreover, it is not my intention to tie this account to any particular set of public policies, but rather to offer a description of liberalism that shows how liberals think about political questions, those having to do with the constitution of a political order and of particular public policies within it. I will be concerned to make clear the tensions within the broad tradition of liberal political philosophy which make possible a variety of sets of public policies, sets that may even be in contention with each other in a given period, but which all may be understood as justified within the liberal tradition. I will be concerned that my account makes it possible to distinguish a liberal way of thinking about politics from non-liberal ones.[1]

Liberalism is generally associated with limited democracy. Liberal government is *democratic* in that government derives its authority or legitimacy from the consent of the governed or from its respect for the rights of those governed and that the will of the majority or the majority of their representatives generally determines governmental policy. It is *limited* in that the people or the majority may not do anything; specifically they may not violate the rights of individuals. Thus liberal democracy protects against the tyranny of the majority. Liberalism is also associated with free market economy. Broad rights of private property are recognized and resource allocation and distribution decisions are generally based upon the choices of individuals rather than the decisions of government. The account of liberalism I will provide here is meant to describe the basis of the liberal commitment to limited democracy and free economies. The account will be divided into three major parts: 1) liberal moral anthropology, 2) liberal rights language, and 3) liberal neutrality.

Autonomy and Equal Liberty:
The Moral Anthropology of Liberalism

Liberalism is characterized by a belief in the fundamental moral equality of all individuals grounded in their capacity for autonomy. Because the capacity for autonomy is the basis of the fundamental equal moral status that every individual is believed to have, liberalism insists upon a wide measure of respect for human liberty equal for all.

The fundamental claim that is made in one way or another by all liberals is that every individual is a source of moral claims on the basis of his or her capacity (or potential capacity[2]) for autonomy or liberty. It is on the basis of that capacity that human beings are regarded as equal. Thus, the characteristically liberal affirmation of the Declaration of Independence that "all men are created equal"[3] is *not* the claim that all persons are exactly the same in all respects.[4] It is, rather, with respect to their having a capacity for autonomy that human beings are equal, and it is their each having that capacity which makes individuals equal sources of moral claims upon one another.[5] The liberal affirmation of human equality claims that all are deserving of a range of equal treatment and respect because we are relevantly equal with reference to the capacity for autonomy. For liberals, our capacity for autonomy is the essential morally relevant feature of our humanity.

On the liberal view, the respect and concern that is owed equally by all to all is for their liberty or autonomy; the *prima facie* moral claim which each of us holds equally against all others is that our liberty or autonomy be respected, that each of us be allowed to exercise and express our autonomy on equal terms. As Maurice Cranston has said: "By definition, a liberal is a man who believes in liberty" (1967:458). Of course, it is not just that the liberal believes in liberty, but that he or she believes in the equal claim of every human person to liberty. Thus, the first principle in John Rawls' contemporary liberal theory of justice is the principle of equal liberty: "each person is to have an equal right to the most extensive basic liberty compatible with a similar liberty for others" (1971:60). From the perspective I am drawing here, those who share a belief in the fundamental equality of all human beings, grounded in some kind of conviction that our equal dignity as human beings is grounded in a capacity for autonomous rationality or autonomous choice,[6] stand within the liberal tradition of political and moral philosophy.

It may be important to indicate in a broad way how the liberal conception of human equality distinguishes it from other approaches to morality. The liberal conception is surely different from any approach that does not begin with a conviction that human beings are fundamentally equal in some morally relevant way, that is, in a way that is relevant to the way they are to be treated by other individuals and basic societal institutions. Any conception that begins with an acceptance of different standards of concern or respect for persons based on racial or gender differences between them[7], differences having to do with their family relationships or social role, differences having to do with their conformity to some traditional moral standard, or differences having to do with their birth into a religious caste, for example, is clearly to be distinguished from the liberal perspective. This difference may be the most obvious one, but it should be noted that the understanding of liberal equality that I am describing here would also distinguish it from conceptions which began with a fundamental belief in the equality of human persons, but on a different basis. Some might regard human beings as equal in a fundamental way, but based on a different conception of human nature from the liberal one. For example, some regard human beings as equal in that they are all fundamentally social or capable of human relation. Such a conception, while not excluded by the liberal conception of human nature, is different from it. Also, some might regard all human beings as equal in a fundamental way, but one not having to do with their nature as human beings. In a religious context some might regard all people as equal in that they are all sinners, all disobedient to God's law, and/or on the grounds that all were offered salvation in Jesus Christ and called to life under him. While such a conception might regard all human beings as sharing some equal status and due some measure of equal respect and concern on that basis, it is not a characteristically liberal understanding of the basis of human equality. Again, a religious conception of human equality such as this does not necessarily contradict the liberal conception. Indeed they may be conjoined. However, the characteristically liberal understanding of human equality has to do with its view of man as autonomous.

Autonomy as self-direction and a sense of justice

There are two aspects of the capacity for autonomy which, according to liberals, makes each of us a source of moral claims: autonomy as self-direction and as a sense of justice. Liberal anthropology or liberal conceptions of the human self stress the capacity of every individual for at least some degree of transcendence over the particular aspects of his or her existence, the capacity for self-conscious reflection on the goals, values, or ends which shape human life. The individual human person, as liberalism sees him or her, is capable of the autonomous choosing of ends and means free from the absolute determination of those choices by human desires or passions and by the historically shaped values and practices of the communities of which the individual is a part. This is autonomy as self-direction. In addition, liberals also ground the dignity of the human being in the capacity of the human individual for a sense of justice. Many liberals point to the ability of every human being to discover from an autonomous standpoint whatever moral limits there are on the exercise of that autonomy. The individual human person is thought of as capable of discovering those limits independently of the historically shaped values and practices of the communities of which he or she is a part. Other liberals, such as John Rawls and those which Thomas Spragens calls "traditionalists" (See below), point to a human capacity for justice without denying the importance for a liberal society of the way that capacity is shaped by culture.

Liberals may emphasize one or the other of the two aspects of autonomy which I have identified and they use different terms to refer to those aspects. John Locke, for example, tended to emphasize autonomy as a sense of justice in terms of the idea of rationality. For him, the defining characteristic of the human person which justifies individual liberty is his or her rationality. He writes, "The freedom then of man and liberty of acting according to his own will, is grounded on his having reason, which is able to instruct him in that law he is to govern himself by, and make him know how far he is left to the freedom of his own will" (1960:352 [Sec. II, 63]). Robert Nozick, a contemporary liberal, tends to emphasize self-direction but also notes the sense of justice aspect of autonomy. He points to the individual's "ability to regulate and guide its life in accordance with some overall conception it chooses to accept" and connects that ability with "that elusive and difficult notion: the meaning of life" (1974:50). He writes that the human person is

> a being able to formulate long-term plans for its life, able to consider and decide on the basis of abstract principles or considerations it formulates to itself and hence not merely the plaything of immediate stimuli, a being that limits its own behavior in accordance with some principles or picture it has of what an appropriate life is for itself and others, and so on (1974:49).

The moral importance of such a conception of the human person has to do with the view that "a person's shaping his life in accordance with some overall plan is his way of giving meaning to his life; only a being with the capacity to so shape his life can have or strive for meaningful life" (1974:50).

John Rawls' famous device for deriving liberal principles of justice, the "original position," has built into it the conception of the person as autonomous in precisely the two aspects to which we have referred. Rawls wrote that in his conception of liberal justice persons are regarded as free "in virtue of what we may call their moral powers, and the powers of reason, thought, and judgment connected with those powers."[8] The moral powers which the idea of persons as free requires are "a capacity for a sense of justice and a capacity for a conception of the good" (1985:233). A sense of justice refers to "the capacity to understand, to apply, and to act from the public conception of justice which characterizes the fair terms of social cooperation" (1985:233). However different the way in which Rawls derives his principles of justice may be from Locke's conception of the natural law and however different their understandings of the basis of a person's capacity for recognizing moral limits, Rawls' assumption that persons have a capacity for justice and Locke's idea of rationality are similar in that both are understood as fundamental for justifying respect for the equal liberty of human individuals.

Rawls' idea of the capacity for a conception of the good has to do with what I am referring to as autonomy as self-direction. It is "the capacity to form, to revise, and rationally to pursue a conception of one's rational advantage, or good" (1985:233). Rawls acknowledges that very often a person's conception of the good is not necessarily his or her own; it may be one the individual shares with the communities of which he or she is a part. Individuals

> may have, and normally do have at any given time, affections, devotions, and loyalties that they believe they would not, and indeed could and should not, stand apart from and objectively evaluate from the point of view of their purely rational good. They may regard it as simply unthinkable to view themselves apart from certain religious, philosophical, and moral convictions, or from certain enduring attachments and loyalties (1985:241).

However, persons are regarded as capable of standing apart from these socially constructed conceptions of the good and choosing to disassociate themselves from them. Moreover, the individual's equal moral status and identity as a moral subject is independent of his or her changing conceptions of the good. Thus, Rawls writes that persons

> are regarded as capable of revising and changing this conception [of the good] on reasonable and rational grounds, and they may do this if they so desire. Thus, as free persons, citizens claim the right to view their persons as independent from and as not identified with any particular conception of the good, or scheme of final ends. Given their moral powers to form, to revise, and rationally to pursue a conception of the good, their public identity as free persons is not affected by changes over time in their conception of the good (1985:241).

Liberalism and Foundationalism

A recent treatise on liberalism has commented that the early liberal theorists were engaged in a "search for foundations."

As a movement set to challenge many of the traditions of the societies in which it came to birth, liberalism could not rest content with a self-image in which it was only an episode in the adventure of modernity. All the great liberal theorists sought a foundation for their commitment to individual liberty which was not merely local in scope, but potentially universal. Liberal demands were seen by liberals themselves as the demand, not of any sectional interest or cultural circle, but of all humanity. The justification of liberalism, for this reason, must be compelling to all [persons], and not only for the few who live already in individualist societies (Gray 1986:45).

That insight is correct with reference to the founders of liberal theory and many of its contemporary followers. Having said this is not to indicate that all liberals have understood the foundation for their commitment to protect individual liberty the same way. For example, John Locke, Immanuel Kant, and John Stuart Mill, each of whom may be regarded as a liberal theorist, displayed distinct and sometimes incompatible patterns of justification for that commitment. John Locke justified his commitment to liberty in a conception of natural law whose authority was derived from its origin in the will of God and its accessibility to autonomous human reason. Kant justified autonomy as a condition of the possibility of morality itself in a formalistic deontological moral theory. Mill regarded autonomy as justified because it was necessary for the maximization of utility or happiness. Even though he regarded some enjoyments as higher than others, their being a source of happiness at all depends upon their being freely chosen and experienced by the individual.

Not only is there no single foundation upon which the liberal commitment to individual autonomy is based, certain contemporary defenders of individual autonomy do not regard their justification as foundational in the way suggested by the above quotation. Michael Walzer says that the argument of his *Spheres of Justice*, which many regard as a liberal treatise on justice, "is radically particularist." The defense of equality and liberty which he makes "is relevant to the social world in which it was developed; it is not relevant, or not necessarily, to all social worlds" (1983:xiv). John Rawls also denies that he regards his theory of justice as universally valid, though his work has been interpreted that way. In his later works he has argued that his conception of justice as fairness

is a political conception in part because it starts from within a certain political tradition. We hope that this political conception of justice may at least be supported by what we may call an "overlapping consensus," that is, by a consensus that includes all the opposing philosophical and religious doctrines likely to persist and to gain adherents in a more or less just constitutional democratic society (1985:225–226).

He now contends that his effort is aimed at enabling agreement among many conflicting philosophical and religious conceptions of morality. Such agreement is possible despite the divergence of these particular moral views, so long as those who hold these various conceptions of morality share certain fundamental convictions. That which Rawls' theory presupposes, and that which he hopes all the philosophical and religious conceptions of morality in our society have their own reasons to accept, is the view that persons are to be regarded as free and equal. It is that shared conviction which is meant, on Rawls' account, to shape our particular conceptions of justice so that we can agree on the general principles of justice which are to guide the basic institutions under which we all must live.

My claim here is that whether liberal theorists regard their convictions as universally valid and accessible or potentially compelling to every human being or as reflecting only the commitments which are necessary for the justification of a particular sort of society, liberals share the conviction that every individual is equal in a morally relevant way on the basis of his or her capacity for autonomy or liberty. Moreover, basic institutions have, according to liberal theory, as their fundamental task respecting and protecting that shared capacity for autonomy and the fundamental equality that is ours because of it.

Liberal Rights: The Defense of Liberty and the Justification of Coercion and Government

Liberalism defends a wide measure of equal liberty in the language of rights. Rights are understood as valid independent of and prior to institutional efforts to define or recognize them. They justify coercion or restrictions of individual liberty. The primary purpose of government is the securing, protection, and enforcement of rights.

Rights: Justifying Coercion in the Interest of Liberty

Ronald Terchek has said that liberalism is a theory that seeks "to expand the range of choices for individuals in ways that do not interfere with the legitimate choices of others" (1986:15). It also seeks "to justify and ensure the moral autonomy of men and women." It seeks these goals *"through the language of rights"* (1986:16). Clearly liberalism seeks to guard a wide range of individual liberty and ensure the ability of individuals to think and act for themselves. But there are limits to the range of freedom[9] justified and protected by the liberal defense of individual autonomy, primarily because the freedom of one individual can conflict with the freedom of another. That is why I have been careful in the previous section to say that liberalism requires "some measure" or "a wide measure" of respect for human liberty. Any comprehensive liberal moral and political theory will have to specify the measure of that respect for liberty. Or, in terms of Rawls' first principle of justice, it will have to specify the content of "the most extensive basic liberty compatible with a similar liberty for others" (1971:60).

That task is carried out, as Terchek indicates, in the language of rights, particularly the language of universal rights. Universal rights have to do with those things to which (1) all persons (2) equally (3) may lay moral claim (4) against all others (5) without regard to "special" conditions which may be unique to particular individuals or particular relationships between and among them.[10] Special rights claims may arise on the basis of some particular relation between individuals. These may come to be valid in a variety of ways. For liberals, the most important is through some explicit, voluntary creation of a moral obligation by an individual. Promises, agreements, or contracts are the standard examples of situations which create or generate valid rights-claims of one or more individuals against another or others. Liberals may also recognize the natural relationship between parents and children, as entailing special rights. Special merit, effort, or achievement by an individual may also be the basis of such rights claims in certain settings.

An important formal feature of rights is that rights are always correlated to duties; a right is always held against someone or binds someone to certain forbearances of performances. Everyone is bound to respect universal rights; the freedom of everyone is bound or limited by them; no one's freedom allows the violation of the rights of others. In addition, those universal rights which are regarded by liberals as necessary to protect the individual capacity for autonomy are generally regarded as justifying the sanctions and use of force necessary to enforce compliance with the duties correlative to them. To say, "such and such is a universal right necessary for the protection of individual autonomy" is to say "there ought to be a law" which protects that right. It is to argue that there ought to be enforcement of the right or protection of individuals' ability to exercise or enjoy the right.[11] David Little has said that Locke's concept of a right can be formulated as "a title for or being entitled to a justifiable and sanctionable demand by one party upon an appropriately situated other party for a certain performance or forbearance."[12] The demand justified by a right is a sanctionable one, according to Little's formulation of a Lockean right. In other words, the right justifies some sort of punishment or threat of punishment which serves to compel or coerce respect for the liberty protected by the right. Mill[13] and Kant[14] made similar points.

Liberty as independence not license

The liberal tradition employs the language of rights as the mechanism for protecting individual liberty.Moreover, rights are matters of such moral priority and stringency that the duties they imply may be enforced by the use of coercion. The protection of such rights or the prevention of their violation is the primary purpose for which governments exist. But what universal or human rights do individuals actually have? And is there a single basic right in which all other rights are grounded? My account thus far has stressed the protection of individual liberty as the basic commitment of liberalism. Does it make sense to speak of a basic right to liberty? H.L.A. Hart has argued that that if there are any basic moral rights at all there is surely one: the "equal right of all [persons] to be free" (1970:61). On the other hand, Ronald Dworkin denies that there is any such thing as a general right to liberty. For Dworkin, a right to "treatment as an equal" rather than a right to liberty is the basic liberal right (1977:266–278).

While Dworkin's critique of a general right to liberty is persuasive, liberalism can still be made sense of in terms of a belief that liberty is the single foundational right of individuals. The debates among liberals has primarily to do with what is meant by liberty. That debate can be made sense of in terms of a distinction, which Dworkin himself draws, between liberty as license and liberty as independence. Put simply, liberty as license means the freedom to do whatever one wants. Liberty as independence refers to one's ability to choose one's own values and act upon them consistent with a life plan in which such values are thought by the individual to be realizable. Of course, liberalism insists upon equal respect for the liberty of all persons. Whether understood as license or independence, liberty is restricted by the proviso that its exercise must not limit the equal liberty of another. Dworkin's own idea of "treatment as an equal" is a version of the concept of liberty as independence.[15]

To regard liberty as independence as central to the liberal project is to suggest that the universal rights generally associated with liberalism— rights of physical security, rights of conscience, speech, press, rights to participate politically, etc.—can be understood in terms of a desire to protect an individual's capacity to develop his or her own autonomous life plan and to exercise autonomous self-direction. The freedom to do as one pleases, liberty as license, may be restricted in the interest of protecting the independence of another.

Of course, to affirm human liberty in this sense as a fundamental value does not mean that one is unconcerned about liberty as license. Dworkin notes that there is a close relation between the two ideas of liberty. "If a person is much cramped by legal and social constraints, then that is strong evidence, at least, that he is in a politically inferior position to some group that uses its power over him to impose those constraints" (1977:262). We might put it another way. Independence is of little value apart from a wide measure of liberty to act according to our independently or autonomously chosen values. Moreover, that the only justification for restraints on one's liberty as license are those made necessary by our desire to protect another's liberty as independence, means that all will enjoy a wide range of liberty as license. Where there is no such wide range of liberty as license it is reasonable to suspect that other reasons besides those justified by our desire to protect liberty as independence are being appealed to to justify limits to liberty as license, reasons which liberals regard as illegitimate or invalid. When the liberty of one individual to act upon his or her self-chosen values conflicts with the liberty of another so to act the resolution of the conflict will be in terms of which action is a greater threat to the independence of the other.

To summarize this portion of our discussion: because the liberty of one individual may conflict with another, the liberal commitment to a wide range of equal liberty entails the necessity of restricting certain exercises of individual liberty. The language of rights is employed to designate the liberties that are to be protected by the use of sanctions or coercion. That the liberal language of rights entails restrictions on individual liberty does not require that liberty is not the foundational value of liberalism. It does mean that the understanding of liberty which is fundamental in liberalism is one that has to do with the individual's ability to form his or her own values and plans of life and act upon them. Restrictions on the exercise of individual liberty are justified in terms of what is regarded as necessary to protect such liberty as independence. Moreover, restrictions of individual liberty of action (liberty as license) are primarily, if not exclusively, justified by liberals in terms of this more profound concept of liberty as independence.

The Question of Positive Rights: Liberalism and Economic Rights

Hart contends that the equal right of all persons to be free requires certain "forbearance on the part of all others from the use of coercion or restraint against him save to hinder coercion or restraint on the part of all" (1970:62). This comment captures the correlation of rights and duties to which I pointed above. Rights are held or are assertable *against* others; if I have a right someone else as a duty to respect or honor that right and my exercise of it. In the case of general or human rights all have the right and all have the correlative duty. Hart's contention is that those duties require only forbearance on our part and not positive actions to assist others in the exercise or enjoyment of their liberty; the fundamental right of all to be free is a negative and not a positive right.[16] Hart is not alone in this view. The idea that rights require forbearance only, that rights are genuinely honored when individuals are left alone to pursue their own interests within the constraints imposed by the rights of others, is often associated with the classical liberal tradition represented by Locke, Kant, and Mill which has been re-appropriated in the contemporary setting by Milton Friedman and Robert Nozick, among others.

The Argument Against Positive Rights. There are a variety of arguments that have been presented to defend the view that rights entail only negative duties. I will mention only three. First, Hugo Adam Bedau has based such a view on what he calls the "analogy to crime."[17] "[I]n general, causing someone a personal injury is much worse than failing to confer on someone a personal benefit" (1980:38). Since rights are regarded as defining primary or fundamental moral claims, establishing moral priorities, and negative duties have more weight than positive ones and seem to have moral priority over them, the prior claims based on rights correlate with the prior negative duties. A second argument has been advanced by Maurice Cranston. On his view, one of the "tests" of a claim based on a universal or human right is its "practicability," that is, for there to be such a right it must be the case that it is always possible for it to be respected. "It is not my duty to do what it is physically impossible for me to do. . . . What is true of duties is equally true of rights. If it is impossible for a thing to be done, it is absurd to claim it as a right." Clearly, it is always possible for me to forbear, to not do something, it is not always possible to provide assistance. "You cannot say it was my duty to jump into the Charles River in Cambridge to rescue a drowning child if I was nowhere near Cambridge at the time the child was drowning" (Cranston 1983:13). Only negative rights or rights interpreted as entailing only negative duties can meet the test of practicability. It is always possible not to interfere; it is not always possible to provide positive assistance. Finally, and maybe most fundamental of all, many liberals would contend that to enforce positive duties on individuals itself represents a fundamental violation of their rights. Recall that a right entails the justification of coercion. If rights are interpreted positively then coercion may be used to compel me to do something I would not otherwise do. Understood this way, rights serve to increase intrusion into the lives of individuals rather than to minimize it. Such an interpretation tends to justify a large and activist government rather than one which is limited and allows a wide range for individuals to act freely. Such intrusion clearly limits the range of individual activity or individual liberty as license.

The Lockean Argument for Positive Rights. Interestingly, however, there is not universal agreement with regard to this rejection of a positive interpretation of rights in the liberal tradition. John Locke, for example, clearly posited the validity of positive rights. In his *Essays on the Law of Nature* Locke points to "the consoling of a distressed neighbor, the relief of one in trouble, the feeding of the hungry" as obligations laid on human beings by the natural law (1954:195). Moreover, in the first of his *Two Treatises of Government*, Locke writes:

> But we know God hath not left one Man so to the Mercy of another, that he may starve him if he please: God the Lord and Father of all, has given no one of his Children such a Property, in his peculiar Portion of the things of this World, but that he has given his needy Brother a Right to the surplusage of his Goods; so that it cannot justly be denied him, when his pressing Wants call for it. . . . As justice gives every Man a Title to the

product of his honest Industry. . . ; so Charity gives every Man a Title to so much out of another's Plenty, as will keep him from extreme want, where he has no means to subsist otherwise; and a Man can no more justly make use of another's necessity, to force him to become his Vassal, by with-holding that Relief, God requires him to afford to the wants of his Brother, than he that has more strength can seize upon a weaker, master him to his Obedience, and with a Dagger at his Throat offer him Death or Slavery (1960:205–206 (Sec. I, ¶ 42)).

John Stuart Mill, who like Locke is often interpreted as a champion of exclusively negative rights, also made statements which suggested that positive actions may be justifiably compelled as a matter of right. He wrote that "acts which are injurious to others" are not to be left unrestrained, and explains injury as including not only "[e]ncroachment of their rights; infliction on them of any loss or damage not justified by his own rights; falsehood or duplicity in dealing with them; unfair or ungenerous use of advantages over them," but also "selfish abstinence from defending them against injury—these are fit objects of moral reprobation, and in grave cases, of moral retribution and punishment" (Mill 1939a:1010). Elsewhere in *On Liberty* he wrote: "There are also many positive acts for the benefit of others, which he may rightfully be compelled to perform." Mill mentioned providing testimony in court, participating in the defense of the community, but also "certain acts of individual beneficence" (1939a:957). Of course, the thesis that positive assistance to others can be required as a matter of right has been controversial in the United States. While it is not incorporated in the Bill of Rights and it is denied by Ronald Reagan, Presidents Franklin Roosevelt and Jimmy Carter have affirmed it.[18]

We can make sense of Locke's (and Mill's) claim that there are valid positive rights in terms of the two arguments against positive rights cited above. First, Locke's view challenges the relevance of Bedau's distinction between "causing someone a personal injury" and "failing to confer on someone a personal benefit." For Bedau the first is clearly worse. Locke's view presupposes that a further distinction can be made between "failing to confer a personal benefit" and what I will call "failing to prevent a serious fundamental harm." While it may be much worse to do evil, or cause some personal injury or harm, than to fail to confer some benefit, Locke's view entails that to fail to provide aid when it is necessary for the avoidance of a serious fundamental harm, and when one can easily do so, is as wrong as to cause another harm. The words *serious* and *fundamental* are important here. By "serious" I have in mind, with reference to the degree of harm, a profound and catastrophic evil, and by "fundamental" I am referring to threats to something of "paramount importance"[19] such as life or liberty.[20]

Moreover, Locke's view depends upon distinguishing the existence of rights and corollary duties from the specific circumstances under which

those rights and duties become effective.[21] We have said that human or
natural rights are universal rights in that they are held by all persons
against all others. Cranston's test of "practicability" requires that for a right
to be a human right it must be capable of being met under any and all
circumstances. He notes that there are circumstances under which it would
be impossible to say that someone had a duty to assist someone else.
Locke's view presupposes that there can be positive duties which all
persons have toward all others, but which only become effective under
certain circumstances, that is, when one is in need of assistance (in the face
of a serious fundamental harm) and another is in a position to render that
assistance (faces no serious fundamental harm in so doing). Thus, Locke
says, "in these matters we are not under obligation continuously, but only
at a particular time and in a particular manner. For we are not obliged to
provide with shelter and to refresh with food any and every man, or at any
time whatever, but only when a poor man's misfortune calls for our alms
and our property supplies means for charity" (1954:195).[22]

The Terms of the Debate within Liberalism

Historically, the move toward the recognition of positive or economic
rights in the liberal tradition represents a response to the great disparities of
wealth and poverty that were generated by the economic development
made possible by the combination of liberal policies and the technological
innovations of the industrial revolution. It may well be the case that the
recognition of such rights both in philosophical analysis and in public
policy represented a reaction to the more radical proposals of socialists and
Marxists and an effort to ameliorate the conditions which made their
revolutionary message attractive to many. A case could also be made,
however, that if the idea of individual independence is the meaning of the
liberal concept of liberty then a recognition of a right to the material
resources necessary to exercise that independence is inherent in the liberal
tradition. I am not suggesting that the idea of liberty as independence
requires a positive interpretation of rights. Indeed, I believe that the
classical liberal view which rejects the idea of positive rights must also be
understood as working with the idea of liberty as independence; it too
recognizes that liberty of action must be restricted and individual
independence seems to provide the principle of restriction.[23]

Any argument for positive rights within the liberal framework as I am
defining it will have to make a connection between such rights and the
fundamental liberal affirmation of equal liberty. One possible approach that
might be taken would build upon the embodied quality of human liberty. A
positive responsibility on the part of others to assist one who faces a
serious fundamental harm and on the part of government to protect
individuals from such harms through the recognition of, and measures to
ensure the enjoyment of, what have been called economic or subsistence

rights (or rights to decent minimums of some essential goods, such as food, housing, or health care) would be justified on the grounds that without such positive measures to protect bodily well-being the enjoyment or exercise of individual independence is impossible. Henry Shue's argument for rights to "subsistence, or minimum economic security" can be understood in this way (see 1980:13–35), as can Norman Daniels' attempts to provide an argument from within a Rawlsian framework for a guaranteed minimum of health care (see 1979 and 1981).

Specifying the precise content of positive economic rights to which individuals may be entitled is a difficult and inexact endeavor on any account. The important point for our purposes, however, is that liberal supporters of economic rights regard some minimal measure of physical well-being as a necessary condition for the expression of the capacity for autonomous self-direction and argue that societies that seek to protect and enhance that human capacity must guarantee certain economic rights. Moreover, that the content of such positive rights is relatively loose and may vary according to the level of economic and technological development that is available in a particular nation should not obscure the basic moral point of those who defend economic rights from within a liberal perspective. They are insisting that it is an affront to the equal worth and dignity of human persons which liberalism has sought to defend for a person to suffer deprivation to such an extent that devising and acting upon autonomous life plans is impossible, even though the resources to avoid such deprivation are readily available. Also, the point that even universal rights may not be effectively binding except under certain circumstances should not be forgotten.

The controversial nature of the argument for economic rights within liberalism should not be minimized, nor should the political difficulty of achieving the recognition and protection of economic rights in liberal societies. The fact that those resources which make the avoidance of deprivation possible do not just "exist" independent of human activity, but are the product of human choices, has led many liberals to argue that they cannot be made subject to coercive redistribution under the authority of the language of rights. Indeed, such redistribution is itself a fundamental violation of human liberty. Liberal arguments for positive economic rights are highly controversial and they are not generally recognized in the United States.

Liberal Neutrality:
Basic Institutions and Plural Conceptions of a Good Life

The liberal commitment to the protection of individual autonomy entails that basic institutions, including government and the economy, be neutral with regard to the various conceptions of a good human life. This neutrality is justified because it enables individuals to devise and put into practice their own life plans, because it is impossible rationally to resolve the conflicts between various conceptions of the good, and because such neutrality is an effective means of avoiding conflict based on different conceptions of the good. This principle of neutrality also applies to theological or religious beliefs. This liberal commitment to neutrality may not be absolute however, as the various philosophical and religious conceptions of the moral life in a liberal society must have their own reasons for accepting the terms of a liberal system of justice. Those which do not may be beyond the range of liberal tolerance.

Liberalism is characterized by some version of the claim that it is wrong to legislate morality. The belief that some behavior is morally right or wrong, or that some kind of life is a good one, is not *by itself* adequate justification for the use of coercive measures to require or prohibit that behavior or to encourage that form of life or to design basic institutions such that such behavior is encouraged and such good lives are formed; to do so would be to fail to respect adequately the individual capacity to form and pursue an autonomous life-plan. To justify legal enforcement of a moral dictate or to design public institutions so as to encourage obedience to it requires further that the legal enforcement and institutional encouragment of that dictate is necessary for the protection of that capacity.

Mill's Argument for Neutrality in *On Liberty*

It is not clear precisely what John Stuart Mill meant by "harm" when he formulated his "very simple principle" that the only justification for coercive interference with the liberty of an individual was "to prevent harm to others." He says that the sort of conduct which may be restricted is that which consists in "injuring the interests" of others, but he adds "or rather certain interests, which, either by express legal provision or by tacit understanding, ought to be considered as rights" (1939:955–956). He might be interpreted as having in mind both those physical injuries and harms which personal security rights are meant to prevent and those harms which are regarded as illegitimate according to the rules which regulate conflicts of interest by a set of mutual restrictions which are necessary for a joint enterprise.

While Mill is not clear about the harms which do justify coercion, he is clear about what *does not* justify it. And that is restricting an individual's freedom of action on the grounds that "it will be better *for him* to do so, because it will make *him* happier, because, in the opinions of others, to do so would be wise, or even *right*" (1939:956, italics added). The sense of this is clear: an individual may not have his liberty of action restricted because someone else regards it as *better for that individual* to be so restricted either in the sense that such restriction will make him or her happier (maximizes utility) or because the restricted behavior is inherently wrong independent of consequences, thus contributing to a loss of moral integrity. Such laws disregard the equal respect for liberty which is owed to all persons as autonomous. Such laws violate the individual's liberty as independence.

Mill's argument about law and morality, about the justification for coercion, is an argument for governmental neutrality with regard to conceptions of what constitutes a good human life. It assumes a realm of action which is strictly personal because actions within that realm make no impact on the objective well-being of others. This is the realm of private or personal morality. The liberal concept of governmental neutrality with regard to those aspects of morality not captured in the language of rights and not justified in terms of the equal liberty of all human beings has implications for all the basic institutions that regulate the distribution of coercive power and rights in a liberal society, and not just the criminal law. For example, part of the liberal argument for free economic institutions is that the economy is to be structured so that it is neutral with regard to possible life plans in the same respect as the law or government is.

Liberalism and Religious Toleration

The liberal idea of governmental neutrality has to do not only with the full conceptions of morality or of a good life which citizens in a liberal state might adopt, but also with religious beliefs. Indeed, it seems fair to suggest that liberalism's concern about governmental neutrality first emerged with reference to religious questions. Only later was the connection made with what I have been calling full conceptions of morality or of a good life. Locke's *Letter Concerning Toleration* is a classic formulation of the liberal idea that government must be neutral with regard to questions of religion and the corollary ideas of the separation of church and state and religious liberty. William Galston has presented an accurate summary of Locke's argument in the *Letter*. He contends that Locke actually makes five separate arguments for governmental neutrality with regard to religion. We will concern ourselves with four of them.[24] The point I want to make with reference to each is that it applies not only to questions of religion, but also to questions having to do with the broadest question which morality and ethics addresses: the question of what constitutes a good human life or what makes human life good.

The first Lockean argument for neutrality identified by Galston is epistemological. It is derived from the nature of religious truth. For Locke, the speculative or metaphysical beliefs of religion are simply beyond reason's ability to provide a definite and dependable confirmation. Of the controversies between the various religious sects about doctrine and appropriate forms of worship he says all are equal in the strength of their belief and there is not to be found "any judge . . . upon earth, by whose sentences it can be determined" (Locke 1955:25).

Locke's second argument, according to Galston, has to do with the nature of coercion, but it could more accurately be said to have to do with the nature of religious faith. This argument, says Locke, is his main one. It says that "even if religious truth could be intersubjectively established the coercive weapons at the disposal of civil society could not possibly achieve their purported end—the inculcation of true belief" (Galston 1984:132). Locke's point here is similar to his contention that it is only the fact that the reason of everyone is capable of discovering the principles of morality that makes them binding. If there is a sense in which it is true for Locke that "you can't legislate morality," it is even more true that "you can't legislate religion," for while morality involves both outward conduct and inward disposition, religion for Locke is purely an inward matter.[25]

A third major argument in the *Letter* has to do with the purpose for which civil government is formed. Galston calls this "rights-based neutrality." Locke saw it as a matter of first importance "to distinguish exactly the business of civil government from that of religion" (1955:17). For Locke the sole purpose for which persons form government is the effective protection of the rights which are theirs under the law of nature, rights to life, liberty, and property. The authority of government over these external matters is as far as its legitimate power goes. But, of course, even if contracting individuals had chosen to give government such authority they could not have legitimately done so. Since "one man does not violate the right of another by his erroneous opinions and undue manner of worship, nor is his perdition any prejudice to another man's affairs, therefore, the care of each man's salvation belongs only to himself" (1955:46).[26] As Mill would have said, since one person's religious beliefs cause no harm to the religious prospects of another, there is no justification for preventing him from holding those beliefs.

Fourth and finally, Locke contends that "even if it were proper for the magistrate to intervene in religious practices of the citizenry, it would not be wise to do so. . . . [T]he suppression of diversity is in no way necessary to the peace and good order of civil society" (Galston 1984:132). This is religious neutrality based on prudential considerations, according to Galston.[27] This argument suggests that an effort on the part of government to enforce religious matters will cause such turmoil that the government will be distracted from matters more central to its task.

Each one of these arguments with reference to the relationship between government and questions of religious truth can be applied to questions having to do with what constitutes a good human life. Just as Locke regarded religious truth as ultimately inaccessible to or beyond reason, it seems fair to say that for liberals none of the various conceptions of the good life and the moral principles and rules which may be regarded as consistent with such conceptions can be regarded as superior to others on rational grounds accessible to all. According to liberals, we cannot know or come to rational agreement about what kind of life is best beyond saying that that life is best which tolerates the freedom of others to pursue their own particular conceptions of a good human life. Secondly, just as Locke insisted that the nature of religious faith is such that it cannot be coerced, it can also be said that one's enjoyment of or participation in whatever makes life good cannot be coerced. Just as one's muttering a religious creed under threat of punishment can hardly be called religious faith, partaking of something regarded as good and respecting the moral limits regarded as necessary for its enjoyment under the threat of punishment can hardly be regarded as enjoying or participating in that good. Religious faith and moral goods must be one's own in a way that precludes external compulsion.[28] Thirdly, just as no one's wrong opinions about religion jeopardize the religious prospects of another, likewise the fact that one may have a low or morally reprehensible conception of what makes life good does not, on the liberal view, prevent another's pursuit of a higher or better life. Notice, with reference to both religious and moral matters having to do with a good human life, liberals need not deny that there is such a thing as truth. What they are denying is that such truth is accessible to human reason such that agreement with reference to such questions is possible and that coming to such agreement is necessary in order to allow the expression of that aspect of human nature which they regard as essential, our capacity for autonomy. Finally, just as Locke regarded the enforcement of religious doctrine as imprudent in the face of diversity about such matters, so also liberals can regard governmental preference for particular ways of life as imprudent in the face of the moral pluralism which characterizes the world.

Prominent contemporary defenders of liberalism illustrate the centrality of the idea of governmental neutrality to the liberal project. John Rawls' distinction between primary and secondary goods and his insistence that liberalism offers only a "thin theory of the good" reflects the characteristically liberal concern that the basic institutions of society remain neutral with regard to various conceptions of what a human life ought to be or how it ought to be lived.[29] Bruce Ackerman proposes that liberalism be understood in terms of the idea of "constrained conversation" about power. Liberal conversations about power are *constrained* in that only neutral reasons are good reasons.[30] Ronald Dworkin has also argued that liberalism is characterized by the view that the equal concern and respect which a government owes to those in its charge entails that it "must be neutral on what might be called the question of the good life." Conservatives, by contrast, maintain that "good government consists in fostering or at least recognizing good lives" (1978:127).

It should be noted that the precise nature of the responsibilities of government that are entailed by the idea of neutrality is not uncontroversial in the same way that the responsibility of government to respect individual rights is not uncontroversial. Some will contend that governmental neutrality with regard to whatever conceptions of the good life its citizens happen to devise and act upon entails only that the government not interfere with the choices that individuals make. Others will argue that government has a responsibility to promote the ability of its citizens to devise and put into action as wide a range of life plans as possible.[31] The important point is that the debate about such matters within liberalism will be centered around the capacity of each individual to autonomously choose his or her values and the life-plan which he or she believes best reflects those values, or is most likely to realize them, and the idea that the use of coercive governmental power cannot be justified on the grounds that some set of values or some conception of a good life is preferable to another.

The Limits of Liberal Neutrality: The Problem of a Sense of Justice

It should be noted that a liberal polity cannot be absolutely neutral. Its health and survival depends upon fostering an appropriate sense of justice in the body politic. Thomas Spragens has written of this limited neutrality in terms of several possible ways of relating a liberal state to a liberal society. It can also be formulated as a question of the relationship between the liberal theory of justice and the various philosophical and religious conceptions of the good according to which people in a liberal society live. According to Spragens, even if the state can be distinguished and separated in some respects from society the question remains as to "what type of social underpinnings are most conducive to a successful liberal regime and what social norms and practices are logically entailed by liberal values" (1986:36)? To put the matter differently, even if a liberal theory of justice is to be neutral with reference to the full theories of the good human life which are justified and pursued in a liberal society the question remains as to whether any and all such conceptions are consistent with and supportive of liberal justice.

Spragens identifies four approaches to the issue: neutralist, contractualist, traditionalist, and radical. His distinction between neutralist and contractualist approaches is not extremely clear. Both insist on a strict neutrality and neither seems to be concerned that a liberal state might be vulnerable apart from certain shared moral convictions. Both are skeptical about arriving at dependable moral knowledge or achieving moral consensus. This much is clear, but it is not clear what Spragens means when he says that the neutralist approach says there is "no such thing as 'liberal culture'" while in the contractualist view "the distinction between liberal society and the liberal state is eroded" (1986:39). The distinction that divides both the neutralist and contractualist views from the others *is* clear. From the perspective of the traditionalist and the radical "it would be unreasonable to expect a liberal state to remain viable and coherent in the context of any sort of culture whatsoever" (1986:40). This implies that the liberal state cannot be absolutely neutral with regard to the various moral conceptions operative in the state, for there are conceptions possible which, if dominant in culture, could undermine the liberal state itself. These views believe "that only a certain range of cultural norms and social practices are really consistent with the requisites of a healthy liberal polity" (1986:40). Traditionalists see a need for restraining human selfishness in the interest of society. Liberal traditionalists are hopeful "that liberal culture can find within itself the resources to accomplish the restraint on selfish passions that they agree is necessary for a viable polity" (1986:41). Spragens lists Locke, Mill, James Madison, Walter Lippman, and Reinhold Niebuhr as examples of this traditionalist liberalism. The radicals share the traditionalist's view that the liberal state cannot be absolutely neutral with regard to the moral conceptions operative in society. They part with the traditionalists, and join with the neutralists and contractualists, in that they are not concerned about controlling selfish human passions. They see the appropriate liberal culture as a "liberated" one: "the appropriate social setting for the liberal state is a society that produces liberated individuals" (1986:42). Spragens seems to mean by the radical liberal perspective what John Rawls calls liberalism as "a comprehensive moral theory" (Rawls 1985:245). This view sees individual autonomy not just as a human capacity which merits respect and protection, but as a moral ideal. Rawls' version of liberal neutrality requires that the liberal state show no preference for this version of liberalism. This version, he argues, is but another form of sectarianism that is ultimately a threat to political liberalism (1985:246).

Spragens regards the radical view as one that "seems to lapse at times into romantic illusions and infantile dreams about a world in which everyone can be perfectly free and happy pursuing his or her own pleasures in the absence of any obligations or constraints." For him, the traditionalist view is more accurate in its appraisal of human potential and it recognizes a dilemma that the other views ignore.

> This dilemma arises from the fact that some of the most essential limitations and imperatives of the liberal state prevent it from undertaking a comprehensive effort to shore up some of its enabling conditions. Specifically, it is imperative upon the liberal state to be 'neutral' to its

surrounding and sustaining culture in significant ways: a legitimate liberal state may not establish a religion or impose a particular set of values on its citizens. . . . Yet a liberal society cannot really be totally 'neutral'—in the sense of being utterly indifferent—to the character of its citizenry. . . A citizenry without public spirit, without self-restraint, and without intelligence accords ill with the demands of effective self-governance (1986:43).

Spragens' solution to the liberal dilemma is in terms of a what he calls "the community of discourse and the discipline of reason" (1986:45–53). He argues that "liberalism has become a philosophy of will rather than of reason" and proposes a renewal of "belief in the moral competency of reason" (1986:46). He holds up a vision of liberal democratic polity as an opportunity for participation in a practical dialogue in which "all individual desires must be set into a framework of evaluation that focuses upon general interests and concern" (1986:51).

The Rawlsian conception of neutrality is also less than absolute in certain interesting ways. There are several ways to see how this is so. The first concentrates on Rawls' assumption that persons in the original position have a sense of justice. Built into Rawls' original position is an assumption that persons are free and equal. Rawls writes that "in virtue of what we may call their moral powers, and the powers of reason, thought, and judgment connected with those powers, we say that persons are free. And in virtue of having those powers to the requisite degree to be fully cooperating members of society, we say that persons are equal." The moral powers which the idea of persons as free and equal requires are "a capacity for a sense of justice and a capacity for a conception of the good" (1985:233). Stephen De Lue has pointed to the fact that Rawls' theory presupposes the importance of a sense of justice as indicating "the centrality to liberal societies of a moral culture, especially one that facilitates (and necessitates) the capacity to make judgment of the moral worth of society" (1986:95). Thus, on De Lue's reading, the Rawlsian conception requires a concern that society inculcate a concern for justice and thus cannot be absolutely neutral with regard to that culture. With reference to our claim that the basis of the liberal commitment to equal liberty is the capacity for autonomous self-direction and a sense of justice, a perspective like Rawls' and that which Spragens calls "traditionalist" includes the recognition that the human sense of justice is not absolutely autonomous. While individuals are regarded as having a sense of justice, this sense is formed in different ways in different cultures. Moreover, not every culture, and every possible way in which the sense of justice is formed, is regarded as consistent with the liberal enterprise. In other words, there are limits to liberal toleration. Political liberalism is incompatible with views that cannot find their own particular reasons for regarding the capacity for autonomy as the essential aspect of human selfhood which must be respected by basic institutions. The neutrality of liberalism must be limited in some respect to those who have their own reasons for accepting the neutrality of basic institutions.

Liberalism, Democracy, and Free Markets

Liberalism's commitment to limited democracy and free market economic institutions is grounded in the fundamental moral relevance it attaches to the individual capacity for transcending in some measure the influence of culture, community, and history which, on its view, makes possible autonomous self-direction. This capacity is the source of our moral dignity and respect for its development and expression is owed to every human person. In this respect we are equal. Liberalism attempts to guarantee and institutionalize respect for human dignity through the recognition of individual rights. The possession of a right justifies coercive measures to ensure its protection. Generally, on the liberal view, one's rights are respected and protected when other individuals, communities, and institutions are prevented from interfering with an individual's legitimate exercise of his or her rights. Some liberals also argue that respect for individual rights requires more than non-interference, but some measure of positive assistance in the development and implementation of one's autonomous life plan. Respect for human dignity requires, however, that basic institutions be neutral with regard to such life plans, showing equal respect for the various conceptions of a good human life that individuals autonomously create and pursue.

The measures generally associated with liberal democracies, the separation of the powers of government, wide suffrage, election (and recall) of public officials, recognition and protection of broad liberties of speech, press, and association, are justified by liberals in a variety of ways. First, democratic measures are instrumentally justified as the most effective means for keeping government limited in the ways required by liberal justice. A government with separation of powers between its various branches, powers which check and balance each other, a government which is regularly and effectively held accountable to the people by means of elections and by mechanisms such as free speech, press, and association which enable public pressure to be applied to government, is regarded as less likely to violate the individual rights which justify governmental authority in the first place.

Such an understanding of the grounds for democratic institutions tends to regard the political rights, that is, rights to vote and to seek office, to freedom of speech, press, and assembly, as secondary to more basic personal rights (for example, rights to be free of torture and detention without cause, rights to hold private property, to marry, to worship as one chooses, to think and believe what one chooses) and as justified in terms of their being necessary to secure respect for those more basic personal rights.[32] On the other hand, democratic procedures and practices may be regarded as more than merely instrumentally valuable. They may be regarded as intrinsically valuable forms of the expression of individual autonomy. On this view, freedoms of speech, press, and assembly and the rights to seek office and vote are not justified simply because they are mechanisms which keep government in check and thus prohibit its violation of individual rights, but because they are themselves rights belonging to autonomous persons.[33] Finally, democratic institutions and wide popular participation in the political process may be regarded as valuable because they contribute to the development of individuality and of individual moral capacities.[34]

A comparison may be drawn here between liberal arguments for democratic political institutions and for a free market economy. Just as rights of free speech, press, and assocation, wide suffrage, and frequent elections are justified primarily because they are fundamental expressions of individual independence, so also the free exercise of one's productive efforts and the free exchange of the products and value produced by that effort is also so regarded. Property rights have often been employed by liberals as a metaphor for the whole range of rights which are regarded as necessary for the protection of individual independence.[35] But, it is also the case that the protection of rights of private property are an essential aspect of the liberal strategy for protecting individual independence. Private property and free markets are justifed by liberals because they are seen as "uniquely consistent with individual liberty." For most liberals, especially the classical liberals, private property and free markets are "the institutional embodiment of natural liberty" (Gaus 1983:236).

Gerald Gaus has noted that a protective argument which parallels the protective argument for democracy is also made for free economic institutions, but it is secondary to the argument that they are necessary for the expression of a fundamental aspect of individual independence. On the protective view, "a 'competitive economy based on private property is the institutional guarantee of freedom.' Here the idea is that the dispersion of power that results from a private property market economy protects civil and political liberty against encroachment by government" (1983:236).[36] Utilitarian liberals have also suggested two additional justifications for free economic markets. They have seen freedom in the economic sphere as important for the development of individuality and of individual moral capacities just as democratic political institutions promote such development. They have also suggested that the free markets are justified because they are the most effective way to increase the aggregate wealth and the welfare or utility of a society.[37]

The relationship between free markets and liberal neutrality is also fundamental. The market, according to liberal theory, determines the value of various goods and services and allocates limited resources in response to the autonomous choices of individuals as they pursue their particular conceptions of what constitutes a good life. No preference is shown for particular conceptions of the good life. Government intervention in the pricing and resource allocation process represents a violation of that neutrality. To lower prices for certain goods (and therefore to raise the relative price of others) or to direct resources into their production (and away from other goods) is to show a preference for those conceptions of the good life for which such goods are particularly important. It is to violate the respect owed to those individuals who prefer other goods. Of course, where certain economic rights are recognized or where certain material goods are regarded as primary goods (that is, as goods necessary for whatever full conception of a good life one pursues), liberals may justify fairly extensive governmental intervention in the pricing and resource allocation functions of the market.[38]

My tasks in this introductory chapter are now complete. I have outlined three important factors in terms of which Christian theologians draw their general understanding of the relationship between church and world. I have also provided an account of the liberal philosophical commitments which provide the most important description of and justification for the primary features of the public culture of the United States. With this background I am now prepared to examine in detail the work of three important theologians who have shaped the faith and practice of the mainline Protestant churches in the United States and official Roman Catholic social teaching. My purpose is to understand and evaluate the posture that they advocate for the church toward the liberal political culture of the United States.

Endnotes

[1] In an essay entitled "Liberalism," Ronald Dworkin cited four "conditions for a satisfactory description of the constitutive morality of liberalism:" authenticity, completeness, distinction, and frugality and comprehensiveness. By "authenticity" Dworkin means that the description must conform to positions or beliefs that people in our national culture actually hold. "Completeness" refers to his effort to offer a definition of liberalism that is "sufficiently well-tied to a particular liberal settlement," that is, to the particular set of policy goals that contemporary liberals espouse. In addition, Dworkin intended for the definition of liberalism which he was providing to distinguish liberal political morality from other available options. Finally, he argued that a good account of liberalism should be frugal, but not so sparse as to fail to comprehensively describe the essential elements of liberal morality (Dworkin 1978:20). The goals of my account are somewhat different. For example, while I believe that it is authentic, I do not intend for it to be "complete" as he describes it. Also, from my perspective the frugality of Dworkin's description of

liberalism has prevented it from being comprehensive enough to capture the constitutive morality of the broad liberal tradition. My account will aim at simplicity if not frugality, but it will not do so, I hope, at the expense of comprehensiveness.

2 Children, or minors, are not afforded the same liberties nor regarded as having the same responsibility for their actions within the liberal framework because the capacity for autonomous choice is not fully developed in them. Likewise, the mentally ill, the retarded, and senile elderly persons are not afforded the same rights and responsibilities as normal adults, because they lack the capacity for autonomous choice. Still neither children, the mentally ill or retarded, nor senile adults are treated as beings who lack the capacity for autonomy entirely, that is, like animals for example. Their previous autonomy or potential autonomy is sufficient to secure their moral status as human beings, though some would argue that that status is maintained only very precariously within liberal thought. John Stuart Mill apparently regarded the capacity for autonomy as something that also developed over time in history and within particular societies. "Those who are still in a state to require being taken care of by others, must be protected against their own actions as well as against external injury." In such a state they are not to enjoy the same liberties as those who could take care of themselves. For Mill, this not only applies to children but also to all people in some societies. He continued, "For the same reason, we may leave out of consideration those backward states of society in which the race itself may be considered as in its nonage. . . . Despotism is a legitimate mode of government in dealing with barbarians, provided the end be their improvement, and the means justified by actually effecting that end" (1956). As is clear, he did not regard the stage of societal immaturity as a permanent one and the object of non-liberal governance of such persons must be to bring them to a state of maturity where their liberty must be respected.

3 The Declaration's claim that persons are created obviously presupposes a belief in a Creator. The claim that human beings are equal because of shared features or capacities is the distinctively liberal claim. They may have them because they were created that way by God, as the Declaration says, or they may just have them. In either case, human beings share the essential liberal feature. Which is to say that secular liberalism is still liberalism. The question as to whether such a belief in the equality of human beings can be sustained without the theological beliefs, however thin, affirmed in the Declaration is an interesting one, but one that I am not addressing.

4 To hold that they are identical is clearly false, but that is not what liberals have meant to affirm and to point to the fact that human beings are not all identical (with reference to intelligence or physical strength or moral virtue) is no challenge to the liberal claim.

5 Human beings are equal, from the liberal perspective, in that they *have* or *potentially have* a capacity for autonomy, not in that they have that capacity *equally*. Thus, that some are more autonomous than others does not entail that they are deserving of more respect than others within the range of equality justified by their capacity for autonomy.

[6] I say a particular *kind* of conception because I am not claiming that all liberals have the same understanding of the human person. It is characteristic of liberalism to share certain anthropological conceptions however. Thomas Spragens is right when he says that there is no single liberal theory, but only a "family resemblance" (1986:36).

[7] The liberal conception that the essential feature of human nature is the capacity for rationality or autonomy is present in earlier philosophical thought. However, that capacity was often associated with particular races and with males and regarded as deficient in other races and females. All persons were not regarded as sharing this capacity to such an extent that they were to be treated equally. Rosemary Ruether will show that some early liberals were themselves ambiguous as to the universality of the capacity for autonomy. Despite this ambiguity my argument is that the preponderant tendency within liberalism and the direction which liberal thought has taken is toward regarding all persons as deserving a wide measure of equal respect on the basis of their having this capacity to a relevantly equal degree.

[8] It should also be noticed that Rawls regards persons as *equal* "in virtue of having those [moral] powers to the requisite degree to be fully cooperating members of society" (1985:233). Which is to say, people are not regarded as equal because they have these moral powers equally but simply because they all are thought to have some measure of them. Rawls has also used the phrase "the capacity for moral personality" to refer to the two aspects of autonomy to which I am pointing. With regard to the moral equality of persons he says the requirement for being included "is not at all stringent."

When someone lacks the requisite potentiality either from birth or accident, this is regarded as a defect or deprivation. There is no race or recognized group of human beings that lacks this attribute. Only scattered individuals are without this capacity, or this realization to the minimum degree, and the failure to realize it is the consequence of unjust and impoverished social circumstances, or fortuitous contingencies. Furthermore, while individuals presumably have varying capacities for a sense of justice, this fact is not a reason for depriving those with a lesser capacity of the full protection of justice. Once a certain minimum is met, a person is entitled to equal liberty on a par with everyone else (1971:506).

[9] I am using liberty and freedom interchangeably.

[10] Richard Wasserstram has identified four characteristics which characterize universal rights and distinguish them from what are called special rights.

First, [a universal right] must be possessed by all human beings, as well as only by human beings. Second, because it is the same right that all human beings possess, it must be possessed equally by all human beings. Third, because human rights are possessed by all human beings, we can rule out as possible candidates any of those rights which one might have in virtue of occupying any particular status or relationship, such as that of parent, president, or promisee. And fourth, if there are any human rights, they have the additional characteristic of being assertable, in a manner of speaking, 'against the world'(1970:100).

Gregory Vlastos says that "the value which persons have simply because they are persons: the 'infinite value' or 'sacredness' of their individuality as it is often been called" is necessary and sufficient to justify such universal or human rights (1970:91). The argument I have made here is, of course, that it is the individual capacity for autonomy which is the basis for the liberal sense of the equal worth or "sacredness" of human beings. And it is that capacity which universal rights are aimed to protect.

[11] Henry Shue emphasizes the enjoyment of a right as opposed to its mere recognition. He says: "A moral right provides (1) the rational basis for a justified demand (2) that the actual enjoyment of a substance be (3) socially guaranteed against standard threats" (1980:13). Thus, according to Shue, a moral right provides a rational argument for *legal* measures (social guarantees against standard threats) to secure its actual enjoyment

> That a right provides the rational basis for a justified demand for actual enjoyment is the most neglected element of many rights. A right does not yield a demand that it should be said that people are entitled to enjoy something, or that people should be promised that they will enjoy something. A proclamation of a right is not the fulfillment of a right, any more than an airplane schedule is a flight. . . .

> The substance of a right is whatever the right is a right to. A right is not a right to enjoy a right -it is a right to enjoy something else, like food or liberty. . . . Enjoying a right to, for example, liberty normally means enjoying liberty. It may also mean enjoying liberty in the consciousness that liberty is a right. Being a right is a status that various subjects of enjoyment have. . . .

> Being socially guaranteed is probably the single most important aspect of a standard right, because it is the aspect that necessitates correlative duties. A right is ordinarily a justified demand that some other people make some arrangements so that one will still be able to enjoy the substance of the right even if—actually, *especially* if—it is not within one's own power to arrange on one's own to enjoy the substance of the right (1980:15–16).

With reference to special right-claims the relation to coercion and the claim that legal sanctions are justified is less clear. Not all special right-claims are subject to legal protection. For example, if two persons agree to meet somewhere for lunch, it may be said that each has a right to the other's presence at the agreed upon place and time, but such a right would not be subject to governmental protection of enforcement. It is simply too trivial. Similarly, while parents may be regarded as having a right to their children's obedience, it would be unlikely for one to argue that a child would be subject to legal sanctions for refusing to obey his parents command that he eat his green beans. On the other hand, liberals are committed to the view that government exists for the purpose of enforcing contracts made between individuals. Thus, with reference to special rights it is necessary to qualify the relation between rights and legal sanctions or coercion. Special relationships or interactions may create rights which are too trivial to be subject to legal enforcement or which are more appropriately left to other forms of enforcement.

12 This quotation is from class notes.

13 Mill regarded "justice" as implying "something which is not only right to do, and wrong not to do, but which some individual person can claim from us as his moral right" (1939b:935). Moreover, having a right is "to have something which society ought to defend me in the possession of" (1939b:939). The moral necessity of such claims are "analogous to physical [necessity], and often not inferior to it in binding force," which suggests the connection between rights and coercion. Kant made the connection explicit. His "universal principle of justice" was that "every action is just that in itself or in its maxim is such that the freedom of the will of each can coexist together with the freedom of everyone in accordance with a universal law" (1965:35 (230)). He noted that this principle called for "a general reciprocal use of coercion that is consistent with the freedom of everyone" (1965:36(232)). Thus, those rights which spell out the equal liberty which all are to enjoy entail a justification for coercion.

14 Kant accurately described the grammar of liberal rights, whether justified by natural law, the formal dictates of morality, or the principle of utility, when he said that "right" or "justice" implies "the principle of the possibility of external coercion." "'Right,'" he said, "and 'authorization to use coercion' means the same thing" (1965:37(132)).

15 A part of the problem with Dworkin's discussion of liberty and equality in both "What Rights Do We Have?" (1977:265–278) and "Liberalism" (1978) is that he fails to keep separate two distinct goals: providing a descriptive account of liberalism and argument for his own particular version of liberalism. My goal is to provide a broad account of liberalism. "Liberty," I believe, does a better job than "equality" at providing a unifying value for the entire liberal enterprise. Of course, I have tried to capture the liberal commitment to equality by reference to "equal liberty." At the level of universal rights, every individual's claim to liberty is equal. In general, the liberal commitment to equality is given up once we move beyond the level of universal rights because the exercise of equal liberty generates inequality that is justifiable, according to liberals, because it is a product of the exercise of individual liberty.

16 Joel Feinberg drew the distinction between negative and positive rights in the following way: "A positive right is a right to other persons' positive actions; a negative right is a right to other persons' omissions or forbearances. For every positive right I have, someone else has a duty to do something; for every negative right I have, someone else has a duty to refrain from doing something" (Feinberg 1973:59).

17 Actually, Bedau did not argue that there were no positive rights, but that negative ones are more basic or have priority. His argument, however, is one that could be used to support the view that there are only negative rights.

18 Roosevelt connected his affirmation of what he called "economic rights" to the liberal defense of freedom. "Necessitous men are not freemen," he said. "In our day these economic truths have become accepted as self-evident. We have accepted, so to speak, a second Bill of Rights under which a new basis of security and prosperity can be established for all—regardless of station, race, or creed." He went on to list such rights as "the right to a useful and remunerative job," "the right of every family to a decent home," "the right to adequate medical care and the opportunity to achieve and enjoy good health" (Lacquer and Rubin 1979: 269–270).

Carter's Secretary of State, Cyrus Vance, stated that human rights were understood as "the right to be free from governmental violation of the integrity of the person, . . . the right to the fulfillment of such vital needs as food, shelter, health care, and education," and "the right to enjoy civil and political liberties" (Lacquer and Rubin 1979:199–300).

19 The phrase "paramount importance" is borrowed from Cranston (1983:14). It is the third of his tests for a universal right. In my interpretation of the Lockean view, the question of "paramount importance" tends to favor a recognition of positive rights.

20The distinction I am trying to make between conferring a benefit and aiding in the prevention of a serious fundamental harm might be made more clear in this way: One confers a benefit whenever one provides aid that is relevant to the particular life plan of an individual. For example, when I help a man get his car out of the ditch, or provide financial assistance to a medical student for her education, or when I help a child learn to tie a shoe, I am conferring a benefit. Assuming no rights created by promises or special relationships, neither the man in the ditch, the medical student, nor the child has a right to my aid. There is no justified *demand* for it. The matter is different when one aids in the avoidance of a serious and fundamental harm, that is, when one acts to protect the life or liberty of a person or community against an immediate threat. I aid in the avoidance of a serious fundamental harm when I save a person from drowning, provide food for someone who is starving, or health care to someone whose life is threatened by illness. Indeed he or she may have something more nearly like a justified claim to my emergency aid, assuming that it is necessary for survival and that I am able to provide it. By being able to provide it I mean, respectively, that I can swim, I have enough food to save the other person, I know how to perform an appendectomy, *and,* that so doing will not represent a serious fundamental harm to myself.

21 This distinction is sometimes expressed as a distinction between general and specific duties. I have avoided that language to avoid confusion with the distinction between general and special rights. I am not talking about duties that are corollary to general rights as opposed to those which are corollary to special rights, but rather the question of when any duty becomes effective for a particular person.

22 My analysis of Locke here is similar to the discussion by Beauchamp and Childress of the duty of beneficence, which is a variation of an argument developed by Eric D'Arcy. According to Beauchamp and Childress:

X has a duty of beneficence toward Y only if each of the following
conditions is satisfied:

> (1) Y is at risk of significant loss or damage,
>
> (2) X's action is needed to prevent this loss,
>
> (3) X's action would probably prevent it.
>
> (4) X's action would not present significant risk to X, and
>
> (5) the benefit that Y will probably gain outweighs any harms
>   that X is likely to suffer. (Beauchamp and Childress
>   1983:153).

Locke's claim is somewhat narrower in that what I have called "serious fundamental
harm" is more constricting than "significant loss." The loss of some valuable
property or of the opportunity to get a medical education might represent a
significant loss, and the Childress and Beauchamp analysis might regard it is a duty
to prevent such significant loss if one could do so without any "significant risk."
Such a loss would not be a "serious fundamental harm" and would not, according to my
argument, provide occasion for a justified claim upon my assistance based on a basic
human right (unless of course the loss of property was so serious as to threaten my
survival).

23 John Gray's recent account of liberalism associates the concept of
independence with Kant and argues that it holds a crucial liberal insight. However, he
rejects the idea that rights imply a claim to the necessary material resources for
exercising one's moral independence (see 1986:57–61).

24 Galston calls Locke's third argument the "character-based" argument for
neutrality. It refers to Locke's contention that people who claim that a desire to save
souls and love of truth motivates their use of government coercion to force
conformity to religion are really motivated by "cruelty and a lust for power"
(Galston,1984:132). That "argument" is a minor one in the *Letter* and depends, it
seems to me, on the first two arguments which Galston identifies.

25 Locke writes:

> But, after all, the principal consideration which absolutely determines this
> controversy is this: Although the magistrate's opinion in religion be
> sound, and the way that he appoints be truly evangelical, yet, if I be not
> thoroughly persuaded thereof in my own mind, there will be no safety for me
> in following it. No way whatsoever that I shall walk in against the dictates
> of my conscience will ever bring me to the mansions of the blessed. I may
> grow rich by an art that I take not delight in, I may be cured of some disease
> by remedies that I have no faith in; but I cannot be saved by a religion that I
> distrust and by a worship that I abhor. It is in vain for an unbeliever to take
> up the outward show of another man's profession. Faith only and inward
> sincerity are the things that procure acceptance with God (1955:34).

26 Locke quickly adds that he does not mean "to condemn all charitable admonitions and affectionate endeavors to reduce men from errors, which are indeed the greatest duty of a Christian" (1955:46). The point is, of course, that one person may surely make another person's salvation his concern in that he may try to persuade him with argument and exhortation, but he has no right to force him with the threat of sanctions and it is, of course, futile to try. Locke grants that even the magistrate may use persuasion "but this is common to him with other men." The point seems to be that the magistrate may do this as a private person. "Magistracy does not oblige him to put off either humanity or Christianity; but it is one thing to persuade, another to command; one thing to press with arguments, another with penalties" (1955:18–19).

27 I do not see this argument having a prominent place in the *Letter*. I think Galston is correct that it is surely behind Locke's and liberalism's insistence on the separation of church and state.

28 It might be argued that Mill held the second view, but not the first. He believed that there were true goods or higher goods and superficial or lower ones and that every human being was capable of discovering which were which. This discovery was a matter of experience rather than reason, however. Moreover, his argument in *On Liberty* by no means suggests that because the higher goods are discoverable by all they can legitimately be forced on those who haven't made the discovery. They are only good when experienced freely.

29 Primary goods are, according to Rawls, "things which it is supposed a rational man wants whatever else he wants." Secondary goods are those additional things that men and women want in order to complete the life they have chosen or to fulfill the conception of the good life which they value. The idea of primary goods depends upon the assumption that

> regardless of what an individual's rational plans are in detail, it is assumed that there are various things which he would prefer more of rather than less. With more of these goods men can generally be assured of greater success in carrying out their intentions and in advancing their ends, whatever these ends may be. . . . Now the assumption is that though men's rational plans do have different final ends, they nevertheless all require for their execution certain primary goods, natural and social. Plans differ since individual abilities, circumstances, and wants differ; rational plans are adjusted to these contingencies. But whatever one's system of ends, primary goods are necessary means (1971:92–93).

Primary goods, then, are those things necessary for autonomous choice and action. For Rawls, the basic structures of society determine the distribution of those primary goods and a theory of justice which established the distributive principles of those basic structures is not to concern itself with secondary goods. The theory of the good upon which a liberal conception of justice is based is a "thin theory of the good" and is to be distinguished from a "full theory of the good" which has to do with the ends which individuals seek as they live out their life-plans in accordance with autonomously chosen values or conceptions of the good. (1971:396ff). For Rawls, an adequate theory of justice "must allow for a diversity of doctrines and the plurality of conflicting, and indeed incommensurable, conceptions of the the good" which individual human beings affirm (1985:225).

30 "No reason is a good reason," he says, "if it requires the power holder to assert: (a) that his conception of the good is better than that asserted by any of his ·fellow citizens, *or* (b) that, regardless of his conception of the good, he is intrinsically superior to one or more of his fellow citizens" (1980:11). Part (a) of Ackerman's account of neutrality is similar to Rawls' argument that principles of justice do not have to do with secondary goods or the full conception of good that individuals attempt to fulfill. The second aspect reflects liberalism's basic affirmation of the measure of equal respect owed to all persons as capable of autonomous choice and the formation of plans of life according to their own values.

31 One of the results of Dworkin's contention that equality rather than liberty is the fundamental liberal value is that he overestimates the extent to which liberalism requires equality in the distribution of goods, resources, and opportunities. Of course, one could respond that Dworkin wasn't just trying to provide an account of liberalism to distinguish it from non-liberal political options, but also to provide an argument for a particular version of liberalism. I think this is probably correct, but Dworkin ought to have distinguished his two aims. My argument is that to the degree that he intended his account as a definition of liberalism he has overstated liberalism's commitment to equality in the distribution of goods, resources, and opportunities. His account does not provide a way to make sense of the disagreement over just these matters within liberalism.

32 The versions of liberalism which regard democracy as an instrumental value or as a defensive mechanism for the protection of individual liberties correspond roughly with what C. B. Macpherson has called the "protective" and "equilibrium" models of liberal democracy (1977), and with what Benjamin Barber has called "thin democracy" (1984). According to Macpherson, the earliest liberal democratic theory of government, which he attributes to the utilitarians Jeremy Bentham and James Mill, was essentially protective; it was protective of individual rights against encroachments by other individuals and by government upon those rights, particularly their rights to property. These early classic utilitarians regarded human beings as aggressively self-interested maximizers of their own utility and society as a collection of conflicting individuals. The foundation of government, according to James Mill, was "that one human being will desire to render the person and property of another subservient to his pleasures, notwithstanding the pain or loss of pleasure which it may occasion to that other individual" (quoted by Macpherson 1977:26). Democracy, according to Bentham, is justified because it "has for its characteristic object and effect, the securing its members against oppression and depredation at the hands of those functionaries which it employs for its defence." Every other form of government leaves people "in a perfectly defenceless state" (quoted by Macpherson 1977:36). To fulfill its defensive function does not require anything approaching universal suffrage for Bentham and Mill. Indeed, Macpherson's account of Mill's reflections on the question of suffrage suggest that Mill sought the least extensive suffrage necessary to secure democratic protection; a wider range, and particularly universal suffrage, might actually be dangerous for individual rights, particularly private property rights. The liberal democratic fear of the "tyranny of the majority" is characteristic of the protective model of democracy. Macpherson concludes that under

the protective model "there is no enthusiasm for democracy, no idea that it could be a morally transformative force" (1977:43).

[33] Both Macpherson and Barber have paid too little attention, in my view, to tensions within the versions of liberal democracy they describe as "protective" and "thin" which indicate a more positive justification in liberalism for certain democratic institutions. The tension is that while all governments are viewed suspiciously because of their potential for violating individual rights, those very rights are generally thought to include protection of the individual's participation in the social and public realms of life. In other words, some of the rights generally associated with democratic government, rights of speech, press, assembly and association, for example, may be regarded as valid not just because of their value for protecting more basic personal rights that are exercised in the private sphere, but as themselves basic individual rights which protect fundamental elements of the exercise of individual autonomy. The liberal concept of autonomy can be understood in terms of the idea of self-governance. Surely, participation in the public exercise of power that is necessary for the protection of individual autonomy is a fundamental form that such self-governance will take. The tension is further illustrated when it is recognized that certain of the liberals cited by Barber had a greater sense of the social nature of human persons than Barber suggests. His descriptions of the liberal conception of the human person as radically self-interested and competitive fits Hobbes, and possibly Bentham and James Mill, more than it does Locke, for example.

Recognizing that a tension exists between liberalism's mistrust of all forms of government (including and maybe even *especially* democratic ones), and its conviction that among the basic rights of individuals are rights to participate in the political processes of self-government, suggests that the tendency toward wider suffrage in liberal democracies is not *just* a response by liberals to restlessness on the part of the propertyless working class (or women), as Macpherson suggests, but is a tendency justified in terms of their own basic convictions. Or, to put it another way, as the propertyless classes and women struggled to secure their status as voting citizens they could find within liberalism resources to justify that appeal in terms of individual rights. Macpherson's account seems to minimize the relevance of this. In his defense it should be noted that he does recognize other models of liberal democracy that do place greater value on democratic institutions and political participation. Barber's account of liberal democracy is overdrawn, though it may be applicable to some of the radically individualist and libertarian versions of liberal theory, and it ignores the liberal justifications for democracy cited by Macpherson which are more positive than those he described and criticized. My point, however, is that liberalism may provide a more positive justification for democratic institutions and political participation apart from the developmental model which Macpherson does recognize.

[34] Macpherson and, more recently, Gerald Gaus have pointed to a utilitarian model of liberal democracy which builds upon and develops the thought of John Stuart Mill rather than that of his father James and his utilitarian mentor Jeremy Bentham. Macpherson calls this utilitarian model a developmental account of democracy which corresponds to a very different understanding of human possibilities than those held by the defenders of protective democracy and a very different understanding of the justification of human autonomy. We have already seen

that for Mill autonomy is justified as being a necessary condition for the development of human individuality which is itself justified in terms of the principle of utility. Human happiness is maximized, according to Mill, where the person is free to develop his or her own character and personality. Political participation, for Mill, is an important means for the development of human individuality. This does not mean that the protective function of democracy is ignored by Mill. Both Macpherson and Gaus emphasize that Mill regarded democracy as justified on the grounds that it was necessary for the protection of individual rights and liberties. "But he saw something even more important to be protected," writes Macpherson, "namely, the chances of the improvement of mankind. . . . Mill's mode of democracy is a moral model. What distinguishes it most sharply from [the protective model] is that it has a moral vision of the possibility of the improvement of mankind, and of a free and equal society not yet achieved" (1977:47).

Gaus has pointed to three benefits of individual participation in political life on the developmental model of democracy as defended by Mill and others. First, it has intellectual and moral benefits in that it introduces persons to a wide range of ideas and perspectives and engages them in the resolution of dilemmas and the solving of problems that they would otherwise not experience. Gaus notes that "this sort of expansion can take even if one's aim when participating in politics is to advance self-interest. By taking the pursuit of self-interest into the political realm the citizen will face new problems and gain a wider perspective of his own welfare than if, say, he restricts himself to commercial activities." But the benefits of democratic participation are more than intellectual; they are also moral as "one undergoes an expansion in aims and thus gains new perspectives on problems and, in general, the nature of the social order" (Gaus 1983:207). Even Rawls, surely no utilitarian, can argue that the expansion of the range of one's intellectual reflection which occurs through political participation can have moral benefits; such participation and reflection "leads to a larger conception of society and to the development of his intellectual and moral faculties" (Rawls 1971:234, quoted by Gaus 1983:207). Recalling our previous discussion of the limits to Rawls' conception of liberal neutrality, it can be seen that democratic participation has for Rawls the benefit of encouraging the development of the sense of justice which his principles of justice presuppose.

In addition to the development of one's intellectual and moral capacities, Gaus argues that those who have supported a developmental model of democracy have identified two additional benefits: the development of a "consciousness of community" and of "communal sentiments." The two are not easily distinguishable, but by "consciousness of community" Gaus seems to have in mind a rational awareness of shared interests and values, while "communal sentiments" refers to an affective or emotional feeling of attachment to those with whom one shares these interests and values. The idea of the utilitarians cited by Gaus is that democratic participation enables individuals to be aware that shared values and interests exist and to develop feelings of patriotic loyalty to their community. Moreover, both of these are regarded as good on utilitarian grounds.

Gaus is aware that the emphasis of utilitarians on the development of a sense of shared values or of a common good can result in a despotic conception of democracy, that is, one that is antithetical to the liberal conception of government as limited by individual rights and the principle of neutrality. He notes that a conclusion drawn by

Hobhouse and Bosanquet was "that democratic institutions are not sufficient to avoid oligarchy, or even despotism," and that "government is apt to be simply the vehicle of one group's will ruling over that of another" (Gaus 1983:214). Yet he notes that many of the modern utilitarian followers of Mill's developmental justification did not share his concern about the tyranny of the majority over individual rights and freedom. Such a concern is an indispensable element of a liberal version of democracy as I have been outlining it here. To the degree that a developmental justification for democracy leads to the elimination of that concern in the interest of developing a conception of the common good it can no longer be termed liberal. However, as Gaus' discussion of Rawls suggests, and as our own discussion of the limits of his liberal conception of neutrality indicated, even a liberal conception of justice requires some sense of community in terms of a shared commitment to justice. As Gaus says with reference to Rawls: "some 'spirit of community' seems essential" if the commitment of individuals to liberal principles of justice is to be maintained.

Thus, the developmental justification of democracy may indicate an important psychological element that those who tend to a protective version of democracy with limited participation have overlooked, an element which can contribute to less offensive, less overtly coercive government. Liberalism's conception and defense of individual rights entails a moral obligation on the part of individuals to limit the exercise of their wills as is necessary for respecting the just rights of others. Democracy may be essential to liberalism in terms of contributing to the individual's moral awareness of the importance of those limits and to the development of the fellow-feeling and respect which makes respect for those limits more likely. Democracy and wide democratic participation in political life may be justified in terms of developing the virtue of justice in people which makes the exercise of justifiable governmental coercion less necessary. To the degree that coercion is always suspicious and to be minimized, the development of such virtue is a positive good from a liberal perspective.

35 John Locke, for example, used the term "property" to refer to the whole package of rights which a person was thought to have under the natural law. Thus, he can say that a person has the authority "to preserve his property, that is, his life, liberty, and estate, against the attempts of other men" (1960:367 [Sec. II, 87]). Peter Laslett has written that, to Locke, property "seems to symbolize rights in their concrete form, or perhaps rather to provide the tangible subject of an individual's powers and attitudes" (Laslett 1960:116). Understood in this broad way it made sense for Locke to say that the "great and chief end of men's uniting into Commonwealths, and putting of themselves under Government, is the Preservation of their Property" (Locke 1960:395 (II,124)).

A recent contemporary defense of liberalism demonstrates the continued influence of the concept of private property on the liberal understanding of individual liberty. D. A. Lloyd-Thomas has argued that the fundamental liberal commitment is to "rights of self-ownership" and has commented on the analogy between such rights and private-property rights.

Rights of self-ownership share a feature with private-property rights: they are both 'rights of control'. Rights of control held by one person exclude others from making choices regarding the things over which the rights are held without the permission of that person. There is a clear analogy between the rights of control people have over their own persons and the rights of control owners of property have over what they own. In both cases the recognition of a right of control by P over O implies the exclusion of others from the right to control O. And in both cases, if we believe that a right of control exists we believe that legitimacy is conferred upon the situation arising from the exercise of the rights (1988:8–9).

Lloyd-Thomas goes on to suggest that there is no simple path from the argument for rights of self-ownership to a specific set of property rights. In fact, he himself argues for very restricted private property rights. For Lloyd-Thomas, the relationship between private property and liberal rights is, more than anything else, a relationship of analogy based on the shared feature of control.

36   The parallel with the protective argument for democracy is only partial. Liberals sometimes showed no particular enthusiasm for democracy, regarding it as instrumentally valuable as a means of assuring that a government respects individual liberties and remains limited in terms of those liberties. Gaus suggests a similar justification for private property and free markets; they are justified because they create diffused centers of power that serve as a check upon the power of government. However, the early liberals were certainly not unenthusiastic in their defense of free markets as they may have been in their arguments for democracy.

37 The utilitarian liberal argument Gaus cites may also be regarded as secondary, though surely important. That argument suggests that "a market economy premised on private property and the pursuit of private interest promotes the commonweal by increasing the aggregate wealth of society" (1983:235). Gaus calls this "the first dimension" of the classical liberal defense of free markets. I do not doubt that it has been extremely important, particularly for utilitarian liberals, but for those of a deontological bent it would have to be more of an "added attraction." It is surely not an insignificant one and continues to appear in terms of the debate as to how best to eliminate massive poverty.

38   Ronald Dworkin provides a good account of the relationship between neutrality and the market. Given the fact of pluralism, that is, the existence of various conceptions of good human life, there is for the liberal "no better mechanism" than the market "for decisions about what goods shall be produced and how they shall be distributed."

The market, if it can be made to function efficiently, will determine for each product a price that reflects the cost in resources of material, labor and capital that might have been applied to produce something different that someone else wants. That cost determines, for anyone who consumes that product, how much his account should be charged in computing the egalitarian division of social resources. It provides a measure of how much more his account should be charged for a house than a book, and for one book rather than another. The market will also provide, for the laborer, a measure of how much should be credited to his account for his choice of productive activity over leisure, and for one activity rather than another. It will tell us, through the price it puts on his labor, how much he should gain or lose by his decision to pursue one career rather than another. These measurements make a citizen's own distribution a function of the personal preferences of others as well as of his own, and it is the sum of these personal preferences that fixes the true cost to the community of meeting his own preferences for goods and activities. The egalitarian distribution, which requires that the cost of satisfying one person's preferences should as far as is possible be equal to the cost of satisfying another's, cannot be enforced unless those measurements are made (1978:130–131).

The liberal argument for the market, according to Dworkin, has to do with the fact that it sets the costs and advantages of various human choices with regard to consumption and productive activity without reference to any particular conception of the good. For the government to set prices and make investment decision on the basis of behaviors it wanted to encourage and consumption patterns it regarded as preferable would violate neutrality.

Dworkin notes that the market certainly allows and produces inequality in the distribution of material resources. Those inequalities are justified, however, to the degree that they are produced only by the fact that persons have different conception of the good life. Some place greater value on leisure as opposed to productive activity than others. Each person prefers to consume a different package of consumer goods based on his or her own conception of the good life. There are different preferences with regard to present consumption as opposed to saving to secure the prospect of future consumption. These different preferences produce inequality, but it is an inequality made necessary by and in no way offensive to the liberal conception of equality as Dworkin understands it. Of course, he notes, inequality is also produced by other factors: people are born with different abilities, some have handicaps that create special needs, and different individuals will start life with different prospects due to the fact that they are children of parents who were more or less successful economically. All of the inequalities produced by these realities are offensive to the liberal concept of equality, says Dworkin, so the liberal will favor a scheme of redistribution "that leaves the pricing system relatively intact" but sharply limits inequalities that are due to something other than different preferences (1978:133).

2

Reinhold Niebuhr:
The United States as Church

AN APPRAISAL of the thought of Reinhold Niebuhr on any particular issue or from any particular point of reference is always difficult because Niebuhr's perspective was constantly developing as he responded to political events and their interpretation in the United States and Europe. He was not a systematic theologian or ethicist whose judgment on some matter of political controversy could be logically extrapolated from the central premises of his thought. Rather, whatever consistency there was in Niebuhr has more to do with the particular tenor with which he approached the political controversies about which he endlessly cogitated, wrote, and spoke.

The label most consistently applied to Niebuhr is "Christian realism" and Niebuhr himself referred to realism as nothing more than a "disposition," specifically, "the disposition to take into account all factors in a social and political situation which offer resistance to established norms, particularly the factors of self-interest and power" (1953:119). His realism was *Christian* because he always sought the closest approximation of the transcendent moral norms of Christian faith which was possible given the fact of inevitable resistance to them. Thus, his realism was not outright cynicism.[1] Richard Fox, who has written the most satisfactory biography of Niebuhr to date, has commented that the character of Niebuhr's Christian realism accounts for the changes in his thought. "The living of Christian realism promoted changes of opinion as the Christian constantly renegotiated the balance between taking the world as it was and demanding that it embody higher standards of justice" (Fox 1986:10).

The changing character of Niebuhr's thought as the historical factors that hindered or promoted the embodiment of those higher standards changed is nowhere more evident than in his appraisal of liberalism. In 1932, after theological training and more than a decade of personal political activism (largely motivated by the liberalism of the Social Gospel movement), he published *Moral Man and Immoral Society*. It presented a resounding attack on liberal culture which borrowed heavily from Marxism. Liberalism, according to Niebuhr's argument in that book, is far too naive and sentimental to face the challenge of constructing and protecting a just order in a context of contending class interests. By the end of his career, however, Niebuhr was a staunch defender of liberal political and economic institutions and looked much more favorably on the ability of liberal culture to face the facts of individual self-interest and of power.

Ronald Stone identified four periods in Niebuhr's thought: liberal, socialist, Christian realist, and pragmatic liberal. He argued that "the organizing principle" of his typology is "Niebuhr's definition of and judgment about liberalism in each period' (1972:11). My focus here is not primarily historical but analytical, and my attention will be on Niebuhr's mature thought as represented by *The Nature and Destiny of Man* and works produced thereafter rather than trying to trace the development of his thought over the course of his adult life. Despite my analytical approach and the focus on what may be regarded as the fully developed stage of Niebuhr's thought, my conclusion disagrees somewhat with Stone's. I will argue that the ambiguity of Niebuhr's relationship to liberalism never entirely disappears even as Niebuhr comes to a greater appreciation of liberal institutions and culture in the later stages of his career. It does not disappear because, in certain respects, Niebuhr's justification for the institutions generally associated with liberalism— political democracy and a free economy—are not typically liberal ones; the "pragmatic" considerations which led Niebuhr to defend liberal institutions are not all of the sort that liberals typically appeal to in justifying democracy and capitalism.

But the judgment that Niebuhr's defense of liberal institutions is on non-liberal grounds cannot be made without qualification. In the previous chapter I showed how certain anthropological convictions are fundamental to liberalism. Similarly, Niebuhr's thought is built upon his conception of human nature. There are certain parallels between the anthropological convictions which Niebuhr defends and the typically liberal anthropology: Niebuhr also emphasizes the human capacity for autonomy as a justification for a wide range of individual liberty. I will argue, however, that despite the parallels between liberal anthropology and Niebuhr's there are sharp contrasts which are never resolved. As a result there is consistency to his critique of liberalism that is evident from the period of his initial disillusionment until the end of his life, including his so-called pragmatic liberal period.[2]

A Dialectical Understanding of Human Nature

According to Niebuhr's account, which he regarded as the biblical or Christian view, human nature is dual. On the one hand, the human person is a "creature" or "child of nature." As such we are "subject to [nature's] vicissitudes, compelled by its necessities, driven by its impulses, and confined within the brevity of the years which nature permits its varied organic forms, allowing them some, but not too much latitude" (1941:3). As a child of nature, the human person or self is characterized by "weakness, dependence, and finiteness"; as such, we are "involved in the necessities and contingencies of the natural world" (1941:150). Niebuhr associates the creaturely aspect of the human person with the physical qualities we share with other animals, including bodily existence, dependence on nature for the sustenance of that existence, and vulnerability. The creaturely aspect of human nature is also the source of human sociality and supplies us with "both selfish and unselfish impulses."

> The individual is a nucleus of energy which is organically related from the very beginning with other energy, but which maintains, nevertheless, its own discreet existence. Every type of energy in nature seeks to preserve and perpetuate itself and to gain fulfillment within terms of its unique genius. The energy of human life does not differ in this from the whole world of nature (1932:25).

Thus, it is fair to say that for Niebuhr the human person is naturally social and naturally endowed with instinctive, but limited, regard for others.[3] The human self is always "organically" related to other selves in community and this is a part of the natural or creaturely side of human being.

Yet, we are not *just* creatures or children of nature, the human person is also a spiritual being "who stands outside of nature, life, himself, his reason, and the world" (1941:3). As spirit, the individual human person is capable of a measure of transcendence over nature "in such a way as to be able to choose between various alternatives presented to him by the processes of nature" (1941:163). Moreover, we are also able to transcend the communities of which we are a part as evidenced by "the peculiar phenomenon of the moral life, usually called conscience." Niebuhr had no doubt about "the social character of most moral judgments and the pressure of society upon an individual" (1932:36). However, he saw in the experience of conscience the capacity of individuals to view their communities and their socially given morality from a transcendent perspective.[4] While the individual is organically related to a human community by virtue of the creaturely aspect of human nature, the spiritual quality of human nature means that the individual transcends the community. Thus, the individual both "looks up at" the community and "down upon" it.

> He looks up at the community as the fulfillment of his life and the sustainer of his existence. By its organization his physical and moral needs are met. . . . The individual looks down upon the community because he is, as it were, higher than it. It is bound to nature more inexorably than he. It knows nothing of a dimension of the eternal beyond its own existence. It therefore clings to its life desperately and may sacrifice every dignity to preserve its mere existence. The highest moral ideal to which it can aspire is a wise self-interest, which includes others in its ambition for security. Looking down at the community from his individual height the individual is embarrassed by the difference between the moral standards of the community and his own (1955:35).

Self-transcendence: The Highest Expression of the Human Spirit

The spiritual quality of human existence accounts not only for a measure of transcendence over nature and over the communities to which individuals are naturally or organically related, but also for a self-transcendence or self-consciousness. "Consciousness is a capacity for surveying the world and determining action from a governing centre. Self-consciousness represents a further degree of transcendence in which the self makes itself its own object in such a way that the ego is finally always subject and not object" (1941:13–14). Whereas human transcendence over nature means that the human person is able to choose between the various alternatives made possible by natural processes, self-transcendence means that the human person "must choose his total end." This, says Niebuhr, is a task of "self-determination" (1941:162).

The capacity for self-transcendence or self-consciousness means that the human self is always in dialogue with itself and this dialogue is the most distinctive mark of human personhood. "We may say that the human animal is the only creature which talks to itself" (1955:6). Niebuhr understands "will" and "conscience" as two aspects of this internal dialogue. The will "is the result of the self's transcendence over the complex of its impulses and desires. The will is in fact the self organized for the attainment of either a short-range or a long-range purpose" (1955:12). We have already seen that conscience represents an experience of individual transcendence over the community. Niebuhr also sees it as an experience of self-transcendence. Conscience may be defined "as any aspect of the self's judging its actions and attitudes in which a sense of obligation in contrast to inclination is expressed. . . . This sense of obligation is powerful enough to allow the self freedom to achieve what it desires only when it is able to persuade itself that what it desires is consonant with this more general system of values" (1955:13–14).

Self-transcendence represents the highest pinnacle of the spiritual aspect of human nature, according to Niebuhr. It is the aspect of human nature which is the basis of Niebuhr's conclusion that the "essence of man is his freedom" (1941:17). This freedom is "radical" because the human person transcends both the order of nature in which he or she is enmeshed (by virtue of the creaturely dimension of human existence) and his or her own reason and the rational coherence which the human person is able to give to life (1984:10). Another way of putting the matter is to say that, for Niebuhr, reason does not represent the highest pinnacle of human transcendence; reason is not to be equated with self-transcendence. Thus, reason does not provide a universal order to which human nature is to conform itself. "No pattern of human reason but only the will of God can be the principle of the form and order to which human life must be conformed. . . . The forms, unities and patterns of human reason are themselves involved in historical relativity according to Christianity" (1941:28). Because the self transcends its own reason, reason is not capable of providing full restraint on selfish impulses. Indeed, reason can be made their servant. Rational forces, says Niebuhr, "always remain bound to the forces they are intended to discipline. The will-to-power uses reason, as kings use courtiers and chaplains to add grace to their enterprise" (1932:44). This conception of radical freedom is the basis of Niebuhr's critique of natural law theories (1941:278–298; 1953:157; 1960:167–172). [5]

Christian thought has the self-transcendence of the human person in mind in its idea that the human person is in the image of God (1941:150). Moreover, it is this aspect of human nature which provides both the "ground of all religion" (1941:14) and the "internal precondition of sin" (1941:182). Self-transcendence is the ground of all religion because the human capacity to transcend itself and the world means that the human spirit is characterized by an "essential homelessness . . . which prompts great cultures and philosophies to . . . seek for the meaning of life in an unconditioned ground of existence" (1941:14). As the ground of religion, self-transcendence is also that which enables human being to imagine and strive for fulfillment beyond history. While the human person is always limited within history, he or she can "transcend the given circumstances to imagine a more ultimate possibility" (Niebuhr, 1943:2). However, while self-transcendence will give to every action an end as *telos,* it also makes possible the realization that history allows no ultimate *telos* but only an end as *finis.* [6]

Sometimes, the recognition that human being strains toward an ultimate meaning and fulfillment of life lying beyond history results in a religious view that denies meaning to history altogether. In such instances the human person is regarded as trapped in the finitude and contingency of history, and salvation entails emancipation from that evil in an eternity in which history is negated. Niebuhr regarded Christianity in its orthodox expressions as a religion which regards history as "contributing to the meaning of life." From such a religious perspective, the problem is to understand

> how the transcendent meaning of history is to be disclosed and fulfilled, since man can discern only partial meanings and can only partially realize the meanings he discerns. In modern corruptions of historical religions this problem is solved very simply by the belief that the cumulative effects of history will endow weak man with both the wisdom and the power to discern and to fulfill life's meaning (1943:4).

Niebuhr's view was that "history provides a disclosure but not a fulfillment of meaning" (Fitch 1980:370). The historical revelation in Jesus Christ represented that disclosure of meaning.

Self-transcendence is the internal precondition of sin because it is by virtue of this capacity that the human person is aware of its dual nature as both creature and spirit, aware that human transcendence of nature and history is incomplete, aware that there is no ultimate fulfillment in history, and aware that he or she will die. This awareness results in anxiety. The human person is anxious "because his life is limited and dependent and yet not so limited that he does not know of his limitations. He is also anxious because he does not know the limits of his possibilities. He can do nothing and regard it perfectly done, because higher possibilities are revealed in each achievement"(1941:183).

This inescapable anxiety and temptation, while only the precondition of sin, still makes sin inevitable for human beings. In every action, the human self manifests either sensuality or pride. Through sinful sensuality the self "seeks to escape from his unlimited possibilities of freedom, from the perils and responsibilities of self determination." Through pride the self "seeks to raise his contingent existence to unconditioned significance" (1941:186). Pride represents an effort to deny or escape the creaturely aspect of human nature. It manifests itself as pride of power, pride of knowledge, and pride of virtue, that is, in a "lust for power" over nature and over other human beings, in the pretension of possessing unconditioned knowledge, and in a self-righteousness with reference to moral knowledge and achievement (1941:186–203).[7]

Indeterminate, But Limited Human Possibilities.

Niebuhr always tried to hold the dual nature of the human person in dialectical relation in his thought. That is to say, as he reflected on and described one side of human nature he was always quick to remind himself and his reader of the way in which the other side qualified what he was saying at that moment. Therefore, even as he spoke of the finite and creaturely qualities which were an integral aspect of human selfhood, he would remind himself of the transcendent qualities of the human person which prevent us from being absolutely bound by the limits of our creaturely nature. Moreover, as he spoke of our capacity for transcendence, which he did in almost reverent tones, he would quickly qualify his remarks by reference to the limits within which that transcendence operated by virtue of our creaturely nature.

The result of this dialectical method is that there is a constant tension in Niebuhr's thought between the two aspects of human nature, a tension which may be expressed by the phrase "human possibilities as indeterminate, but limited." Because of human transcendence the manifestations of human vitality and self-expression are indeterminate, but because of human creatureliness those indeterminate manifestations of creativity, conscience, and self-determination always find a limit beyond which they may not pass. Thus, Niebuhr can write that in the task of self-determination the human person "is confronted with endless potentialities and he can set no limit to what he ought to be, short of the character of ultimate reality. Yet this same man is a creature whose life is definitely limited by nature and he is unable to choose anything beyond the bounds set by the creation in which he stands" (1941:163). Similarly, he can write that the individual "may reach a height of uniqueness which seems to transcend his social history completely," and that "the highest forms of art," while using insights and styles of expression which "betray the time and place of the artist," may "if they rise to very great heights of individual insights . . . achieve a corresponding height of universal validity." Yet, immediately he suggests that the achievement is not literally universal, but only one which is able to "illumine the life of a more timeless and wider community" (1944:50–1).

Similarly, Niebuhr can say that because of human transcendence the human person is a "creator" of history, but because that transcendence is limited we are also "creatures" of history (1955:51). Thus, while the human person is free in history, free to make history rather than be determined by it, that freedom is not absolute.

> There is freedom in history; otherwise tribal communities, held together by consanguinity and gregariousness, would not have developed into wider communities of empires and nations, in which human intelligence has added various artifacts to nature's original minimal force of social cohesion. But there is no absolute freedom in history; for every choice is limited by the stuff which nature and previous history present to the hour of decision. Even today when statesmen deal with global politics they must consider ethnic and geographic facts which represent nature's limitations upon man's decisions; and they must take account of affinities and animosities which ages of previous history have created (1944:54).

Love and Justice

Love as the Law of Life. While Niebuhr regarded natural law theories as deficient because of their failure to take account of the radical freedom which was the unique feature of *human* nature, he himself recognized one natural moral norm as corresponding to that radical freedom: love.[8] Love represents for Niebuhr a "perfect relation of the soul to God," "perfect internal harmony of the soul," and "the perfect harmony of life with life," that is, harmony between persons (1941:288–289). "Love is the final requirement of human relations, if the freedom of the persons who are involved in mutual relation be considered" (1941:294). According to Niebuhr, love is "the law of life. It is a basic requirement of existence which men transgress at their peril" (1960:133–134).

It should be noted that Niebuhr refers to love as "law" because he regarded it as a requirement of human nature in both its dimensions. Yet, because "law is distinguished by some form of restraint or coercion" (either inner or outer), it is impossible for love to be "law" (1953:147). The enforcement of love "negates it" because such enforcement is necessitated by a "conflict between the self and society, or between the self and its higher self, which real love would overcome. For it is the very character of love that it desires the good freely and without compulsion" (1960:134). Thus, love is the "law and not law" (1960:134) and the "law that transcends law" (1953:148).

Given the inevitability and universality of human sin, love requires self-sacrifice; it requires "sacrificial abandonment of the claims of the self for the needs of the other" (1953:169). Every experience or achievement of the perfect harmony which love seeks depends upon self-sacrifice. Even the most intimate relations which are possible and in which the self finds itself both lover and loved depend upon sacrificial acts of self-forgetfulness. They could not be maintained by love as mutuality, that is, a love which seeks a return on its love. Thus, the love which is the law of life requires self-sacrifice, an act of complete self-transcendence.

The perfect harmony which sacrificial love seeks is a requirement of human freedom. Yet, because the spiritual aspect of the human person is dialectically related to its finite dimension and because human sin is universal, love is no simple possibility in human history.

> Love is the law of freedom; but man is not completely free; and such freedom as he has is corrupted by sin. The idea is an impossibility because both the contingencies of nature and the sin in the human heart prevent men from ever living in that perfect freedom and equality which the whole logic of the moral life demands (1960:135–136).

Moreover, self-sacrifice cannot be "justified historically." It violates "standards of coherence and consistency" whereby "all claims . . . must be proportionately satisfied and related to each other harmoniously" (1943:69). Just as our radical freedom requires that we conceive of our ultimate fulfillment as beyond history, self-sacrifice "transcends history" and requires religious justification. Not only can self-sacrificial love not be justified historically, it "is not able to maintain itself in historical society"

(1943:72). A self which seeks not its own is annihilated in human history. Jesus' life represents the highest expression of human nature and the highest moral achievement. His fate reveals that love is not triumphant in human history; rather, it suffers.

Niebuhr did not regard love as unequivocally transcendent and, therefore, irrelevant for human conduct and the struggle to achieve a just social order. Love is not a simple possibility; but neither is it a simple impossibility. Rather, according to Niebuhr, it is an impossible possibility.

> This means that, while love is never fully embodied in any human motive or human action, it remains relevant as a standard for both motive and action. It is relevant because we are judged by it and because, if in humility before God we avoid the pretensions which most seriously distort our life, we are able to approximate such love. The chief warning must always be that whenever we do approximate it, at that moment even the best that we do is in greatest danger of corruption (Bennett, 1984:107).

Justice: Love's Approximation Within the Limitations of History. Love is made relevant to social and political life through its mediation by justice. Niebuhr regarded the effort to realize a satisfactory life in community with our neighbor as a requirement of our social nature, and, therefore, as more than a negative task forced upon us by the proximity of others with whom we have competing interests. "Community is an individual necessity; for the individual can realize himself only in intimate and organic relation with his fellowmen" (1943:244). Justice represents the accommodation of the indeterminate possibilities of human fellowship (which our social nature and radical freedom make obligatory upon us through the law of love) to the limits imposed by the inevitability of our sin. Love, according to Niebuhr, cannot be compelled; it must be freely given. But human sinfulness makes restraint and coercion necessary. Justice represents love in a form that does not transcend law.

> Love is an ideal which transcends all law; but the sinfulness of the human heart threatens the common life of man with anarchy if it is not restrained; if natural impulses are not brought under the discipline of accepted standards; if standards are not enforced by some kind of social will, stronger than the potentially recalcitrant will of the individual; and if methods of arbitration are not found for the inevitable conflicts of social will and interest between various members of the human community (1960:134).

Justice represents the effort to approximate the requirements of love, to create a social order in which the intimacy between persons which our nature requires for its fulfillment is made possible, given the fact that human sin requires coercion and restraint if chaos is to be avoided and some measure of community is to be achieved.

Thus, justice approximates love (and Niebuhr can say that "anything short of love cannot be perfect justice" (1960:177–178)); yet every such achievement of justice in history is contradicted by love. ". . . [T}he achievements of justice in history may rise in indeterminate degrees to find their fulfillment in a more perfect love and brotherhood; but each new level of fulfillment also contains elements which stand in contradiction to perfect love" (1943:246).

Niebuhr distinguishes between principles of justice and the structures of justice "in which these principles and rules are imperfectly embodied and made historically concrete" (1943:257). Love is more nearly approximated in the principles than in the structures of justice; yet both "are servants and instruments of the spirit of brotherhood in so far as they extend the sense of obligation towards the other" that is prompted by love (1943:248).

Principles of justice. Despite Niebuhr's view that natural law theories failed to account for the radical freedom of the human person, Niebuhr not only regarded love as a requirement of human nature, but also thought that liberty and equality are "essentially universal principles of justice" (1943:254).[9] Niebuhr does not make clear either the precise way in which love and liberty are related, or, particularly, how liberty represents an approximation of love. They are obviously related in that both are grounded in the spiritual dimension of human nature and the indeterminate possibilities for creative human action and interaction that it entails. The relationship of equality and love is more clear. Equality is rational consideration of what love requires under the conditions of finitude and sin. It

> stands in a medial position between love and justice. If the obligation to love the neighbor as the self is to be reduced to rational calculation, the only guarantee of the obligation is a grant to the neighbor which equals what the self claims for itself. Thus equality is love in terms of logic. But it is no longer love in the ecstatic dimension (1960:175).

Because equality allows a consideration of the self's own interests and claims it falls short of sacrificial love. Moreover, because as a principle of justice and as incorporated into law equality entails coercion and obligation, it establishes a structure of relationship between persons which would be made unnecessary if the full intimacy which their social nature and the law of love "requires" were realized.

Love under the condition of human finitude and sin, that is, love as justice, entails equality between the self and others, as suggested in the previous quotation, but also equality among others. "A higher justice," that is, one which more nearly approximates the love which is the law of our being, always means a more equal justice. Since all human morality rests upon the presupposition of the value of all human life and since there are no *a priori* principles by which the value of one life may be preferred to that of another, the problem of dividing the privileges of common human enterprises can only be solved by implicit or explicit standards of equality (1960:175).

At its highest, where justice meets love and all the contradictions between them are resolved, it implies "anarchism" and "communism." Speaking of the social consequences of the ethic of Jesus,which is the ethic of sacrificial love, Niebuhr wrote, "In practical terms it means a combination of anarchism and communism dominated by the spirit of love." Love in its perfection makes coercion unnecessary. Perfected love "would mean communism because the privileges of each would be potentially the privileges of all. Where love is perfect the distinctions between mine and thine disappear" (1960:133). Thus, it is fair to say that at the level of principle Niebuhr's conception of justice is radically egalitarian. Ideally and in principle relations between persons should be characterized by a perfect equality.

The radical egalitarianism of Niebuhr's conception of justice, at least at the level of principle, distinguishes it from a typically liberal perspective. As we have seen, liberalism regards human beings as equal on the basis of the capacity for autonomy which they share as human persons. The equality that is ours has to do with our capacity to form our own particular conception of a good human life and to discover from an autonomous perspective the necessary restrictions on our pursuit of that good. Egalitarian tendencies within liberalism are always in terms of and limited by its commitment to protect our capacity for an autonomous conception of the good. Thus, even where redistributional schemes are regarded as required by justice or equality they are so regarded in terms of the need to protect or make possible the exercise of that capacity. However, such schemes are also limited with reference to that same capacity for autonomy since the effort to protect its exercise by some entails restricting its exercise by others. Liberty is set against liberty and no telos or good regarded as applicable to all may be appealed to to settle the conflict.

Niebuhr's conception of equality is also tied in no small measure to a sense that our capacity for transcending the limits placed upon us by our historical particularity is a defining characteristic of our personhood and a source of moral status. However, the basis of Niebuhr's conception of human equality has two elements which distinguish it from typically liberal approaches and which render his conception more egalitarian in practice. First, Niebuhr posits a general and overriding telos—a perfect mutuality between persons—while liberal neutrality requires that no such telos is relevant to considerations of justice. While Niebuhr's telos cannot be realized perfectly unless it is freely or autonomously chosen, because his conception of equality is meant to serve that end or enable its realization it allows the overriding of individual liberty to an extent that liberal schemes do not. Secondly, Niebuhr's more dialectical sense of the human person, that is, his sense that our material or creaturely dimension is also an essential aspect of our selfhood, gives weight to the material needs and desires that is missing in liberalism. As I have argued with reference to liberalism's commitment to private property, liberals are aware of the embodied quality of human autonomy and therefore are not insensitive to the physical needs of human beings. However, attention to the physical aspect of human being is limited to those minimal levels which may be regarded as necessary for the autonomy of individuals. Niebuhr's attention to human physical needs and desires has no such built-in limits. His view that mutuality is our telos and his sense that our creaturely aspect is also a fundamental aspect of our human selfhood means that the equal attention and respect which justice requires me to give to the claims of the other is not limited to that which is necessary for the protection of my capacity for autonomy.

These basic differences between Niebuhr and liberalism at the level of theory are mitigated at the practical level because Niebuhr's conception of the human good in terms of the law of love is rather formal and thin: he does not work out the implications of our striving toward mutuality nor does he relate that ultimate telos to any lower but equally fundamental goods. Furthermore, his "realistic" sense of the limitedness and provisionality of any historical approximation of our ultimate telos gives a high level of tentativeness to whatever practical egalitarian conclusions might be derived from his principles of justice, and allows a toleration of great inequality. Of course, his sense of the indeterminate possibilities of human creativity gives great weight to individual liberty even if there are counteracting tendencies in his thought which are lacking in liberalism.

Both liberty and equality are transcendent norms, according to Niebuhr, in that they are not perfectly attainable under the conditions of human history; like love they are impossible possibilities. Perfect liberty is impossible because human sin requires restraint. Niebuhr cites several reasons why perfect equality is impossible. He notes that nature "arbitrarily benefits some men more than others." This is not particularly illuminating with regard to the impossibility of perfect equality in history because the question which a principle of equality raises is what moral relevance the inequalities of nature are to have. Why is it impossible for those natural advantages to be disregarded when weighing the merits of the claims that various persons make upon us or upon a system of justice? More instructive is Niebuhr's comment that "social prudence will qualify the ideal" of equality. "The most equalitarian society will probably not be able to dispense with special rewards as inducements to diligence" (1960:175). Considering human sin, the prospect of earning some disproportion of wealth or privilege is necessary to encourage human productivity and the assumption of burdensome social tasks.[10]

Liberty and equality are also impossible possibilities in history because they themselves are in conflict within the limitation of history. They are "mutually limiting. . . . A society may destroy liberty in its search for equality; it can annul the spirit of equal justice by a too consistent devotion to liberty" (1960:176).

Structures of Justice: Order and the Balancing of Organic Vitalities. Strategies for achieving justice in society are served by the recognition of liberty and equality as transcendent, regulative principles of justice, but such stategies must also attend to what Niebuhr called the structures of justice. These structures include the legal system which sets the terms of human interaction and determines the basis and limitations of political authority in a particular community. However, Niebuhr meant more than that; the structures of justice also have to do with relations of conflict and cooperation among the various centers of power in a community and between these and the organizing power represented by government. The structure of justice in a particular society, Niebuhr says,

> is never merely the order of a legal system. The harmony of communities is not simply attained by the authority of law. *Nomos* does not coerce the vitalities of life into order. The social harmony of living communities is achieved by an interaction between the normative conceptions of morality and law and the existing and developing forces and vitalities of the community. Usually the norms of law are compromises between the rational-moral ideals of what ought to be, and the possibilities of the situation as determined by given equilibria of vital forces. The specific legal enactments are, on the one hand, the instruments of the conscience of the community, seeking to subdue the potential anarchy of forces and interests into a tolerable harmony. They are, on the other hand, merely explicit formulations of given tensions and equilibria of life and power, as worked out by the unconscious interactions of social life (1943:257).

Niebuhr wants to insist that the dynamic interplay of forces or vitalities in society, operating and influencing us without our always being aware of them and independent in some measure of our intentional manipulation of them, is as relevant to the actual realization of justice in a particular society as are our more conscious and intentional moral commitments and rational judgments. Given that human transcendence over the contingent factors in our lives is never complete, though its possibilities are indeterminate, our conscious rational and moral judgments are more influenced by these factors than we often realize. Indeed, because conscience and reason are never absolutely transcendent—and because of sin, they are among the types of power or force which are a part of the balance of power in a society and not simply ordering mechanisms over and above the balance of power. Niebuhr refers to conscience and reason as spiritual or soul powers.

The balance of power between the competing centers of vitality and the organizing power of government are permanent features of the structure of justice in a particular society. They both serve the cause of love and justice and threaten it. The balance of power in society is a means of avoiding the complete "domination of one life by another." Without such a balance "no moral or social restraints ever succeed completely in preventing injustice and enslavement. In this sense an equilibrium of vitality is an approximation of brotherhood within the limits of the conditions imposed by human selfishness" (1943:265). It is not a perfect realization of the human potential for intimate relation, just as the social restraints of custom and law are not, because it is a state of "covert or potential conflict." It is a situation in which power is pitted against power in such a way that the tyrannical potential of any particular center of power is suppressed without directly[11] serving to mitigate the selfish or inordinate expressions of human vitality through moral means. To the degree that those expressions are not mitigated by moral and rational considerations, the balance of power threatens to become anarchy, or, to use the term of Hobbes and Locke, a "state of war."

The anarchy of contending forces may also be prevented if the other dimension of power, the organizing power of government, is able to "arbitrate conflicts from a more impartial perspective than is available to any party of a given conflict" (1943:260). Of course, government is an ambiguous servant of justice. The impartial perspective it is able to provide is only relative to the more interested perspective of particular factions. It never represents a universal mind, as Hegel had claimed. As itself a center of concentrated power, primarily because of its virtual monopoly on political power, government can threaten tyranny even as it prevents a state of war in society. It can be tyrannical either when it is a means of the "dominance which one portion of the community exercises over the other," that is, when the power of government is captured by a particular faction of society rather than representing all such factions, or when it is tempted to destroy the vitality and freedom of component elements in the community in the name of "order" (1943:267). In this instance, government becomes an independent source of tyranny.

Niebuhr warns that governments are prone to regard the order which they are able to achieve as an ultimately valid order, that is, to identify it "with the principle of order itself." This is idolatry because no order based on social restraints and a balance of power conforms to the ultimate "order" of the law of love. This religious pretension is a perennial temptation because the stable rule of any government depends upon an "uncoerced submission" to its authority by the vast majority of its citizens. Citizens give such submission on the basis of a sense of "religious reverence for 'majesty'" which a government is thought to represent and not simply because they have given their rational consent. The necessity of this reverence for government for the maintenance of a stable order leads to exaggerated claims by government in which it presents itself not simply as representing or approximating an ultimate principle of order but as having achieved it (1943:267–268).

Order in society represents a limitation on liberty and can threaten to destroy liberty altogether. Moreover, it also requires falling short of the ideal of perfect equality. Order requires that some have authority over others and with that authority go certain privileges which reflect and justify the sense of "majesty" which makes voluntary compliance with authority possible. This, it seems, is the sense of Niebuhr's comment that the "necessities of social cohesion and organic social life" provide a reason why perfect equality is impossible in human history (1935:90). While order is in conflict with the transcendent principles of justice, Niebuhr apparently regarded order as a prerequisite to whatever measure of justice can be achieved in society. "If the central problem of politics is the problem of justice, the prior question is how to coerce the anarchy of conflicting human interests into some kind of order, offering human beings the greatest opportunity for mutual support" (1960:174). Without order, without some relatively stable balancing of the conflicting forces in society and some mitigation of the level of competition at least below the level of outright violence, there is no possibility for the interpersonal intimacy which our nature requires for its fulfillment. While order is somehow "prior" to justice and represents a compromise with both regulative principles of justice, "only an order which implicates justice can achieve a stable peace. An unjust order quickly invites the resentment and rebellion which lead to its undoing" (1960:177).

Niebuhr believed that it was impossible to adjudicate between order and justice, or equality and liberty, in abstraction. "Historical contingencies must determine whether order must be given preference over justice and whether equality or liberty must be given preference." Because these judgments can only be made contingently, "every strategy of social peace and every system of justice should be regarded as tentative and fragmentary, as embodying some, but not all our responsibilities to our fellow man; as adequate for a given historical occasion, but not necessarily adequate for all occasions." Order, justice, equality, and liberty are "fixed principles and norms in the political realm, but there is no fixed principle for relating the norms to each other" (1960:177).[12]

Summary: Niebuhr's Dialectical Understanding of the Moral Relevance of the Two Dimensions of Human Nature

The key for interpreting Niebuhr's understanding of human nature and his critique of liberalism (to which we will turn presently) is to see the way in which his conception is dialectical with reference to the moral relevance of the two dimensions of human nature he described. The interpretive point which I am contending is key is something other than the familiar dialectical relation between the two dimensions of human nature which I described above, although it is surely related to it. Here I am referring to Niebuhr's dialectical understanding of the *moral relevance* of the two dimensions of human nature. Both dimensions are morally relevant because attention must be paid to both if a successful theory of justice in society is to be discovered and each makes important *moral contributions* to such a theory. Moreover, the moral relevance of the spiritual nature is understood dialectically in that it is the source of other indeterminate possibilities for both good and for evil.

First, Niebuhr sees a dialectical relation between the creaturely and the spiritual dimensions, in that both must be attended to in an effort to construct a livable and just social order in which the (limited) possibilities for the fulfillment of human nature in history are realized. The attention that is owed to the spiritual dimension is obvious. It is the dimension in terms of which the human person's essential nature is defined; it is the dimension in which the fulfillment of the norm which is the law of human life is possible. The creaturely dimension must also be attended to because human transcendence is never complete in history. The way in which the human person is determined by the contingent factors of his or her existence can never be overlooked. A human community is always partly a contrivance of human consciousness and self-direction, but there are also always "organic" elements which are influential apart from human consciousness and contrivance.[13] Attention to these organic elements is part of the balancing of power which is essential for a strategy for justice.

Moreover, both dimensions have positive contributions to make to the moral life. Again, the contribution of the spiritual dimension is obvious. What is less obvious, but what must also be kept in mind, is that the creaturely dimension also has a positive function for Niebuhr. He insists that Christian thought does not regard this aspect of human nature as evil, or as something from which to escape. Rather it looks for the manifestations of the highest human possibilities in its creaturely or finite dimension. For Niebuhr, our creaturely nature supplies social impulses which draw us out of ourselves toward our fellows. Moreover, our organic ties to communities supply us with broader moral perspectives than we are able to achieve on our own, even though the highest reaches of individual conscience transcend even those broader prospectives which our communities provide. It is from the heights to which our communities lift us that our transcendent spirits finally take their flight.

Secondly, of course, Niebuhr's understanding of the moral relevance of the spiritual dimension of human nature is dialectical in that, while the ultimate moral norm of human existence is derived from that spiritual dimension, it is also the source of human evil. The human capacity for transcending the particular and contingent aspects of his or her existence accounts for the experience of individual moral conscience, an experience which enables the individual to achieve critical perspective over against the activities of the communities of which he or she is a part and over against his or her own activities. It is that capacity which enables the individual to imagine more perfect moral achievements in and beyond human history. Moreover, it is that aspect of human nature which, for Niebuhr, makes the fulfillment of the highest human possibilities a possibility, though only a possibility beyond history.

On the other hand, it is that same capacity which provides the condition of the possibility of human evil and sin and which makes for the indeterminate possibilities of human evil. Self-transcendence is that which makes human evil sink to depths which cannot be accounted for on the basis of the natural instinct to preserve itself. Niebuhr says that there is "a pathetic quality in human self-consciousness."

> Self-consciousness means the recognition of finiteness within infinity. The mind recognizes the ego as an insignificant point amidst the immensities of the world. In all vital self-consciousness there is a note of protest against this finiteness. It may express itself in religion by the desire to be absorbed in infinitude. On the secular level it expresses itself in man's effort to universalize himself and give his life a significance beyond himself. This root of imperialism is therefore in all self-consciousness (1932:41–42).

As a result of the anxiety produced in human self-consciousness or self-transcendence, while "the beast of prey ceases from its conquests when its maw is crammed, man's lusts are fed by his imagination, and he will not be satisfied until the universal objectives which the imagination envisages are attained" (1932:44).

Because of this dialectical understanding of the moral relevance of human autonomy in its highest form, Niebuhr speaks of both the creative and the destructive potential of the human person, both our potential for good and for evil, as indeterminate. "[B]oth desires and qualms of conscience about the desires are indeterminate" because "both are the fruit of the self's capacity to transcend every situation, historical or natural, which offers either preliminary restraints upon its ambitions, limits for its desires, or justifications for its undue selfishness" (1955:20).

Thus, the radical freedom of the human person is a source of our "dignity" and is the justification for a wide measure of liberty in human society. "A free society," he says

> is justified by the fact that the indeterminate possibilities of human vitality may be creative. Every definition of the restraints must be tentative; because all such definitions, which are themselves the products of specific historical insights, may prematurely arrest or suppress a legitimate vitality, if they are made absolute and fixed. The community must constantly re-examine the

presuppositions upon which it orders its life, because no age can fully anticipate or predict the legitimate and creative vitalities which may arise in subsequent ages (1944:63–64).

Yet he can immediately add that "The limitations on freedom in a society are justified, on the other hand, by the fact that the vitalities may be destructive" (1944:64).

Niebuhr saw the "crux of the issue" in the area of the study of human nature as

whether the distinctive marks of man as a unique creature shall be so defined that the proofs of his "dignity" are also the proofs of his virtue; or whether his dignity shall be defined in terms of the radical character of human freedom. In the latter case his dignity would have the same ground as his destructiveness or his sin (1984:10).

There can be no doubt that for Niebuhr the matter is most accurately described by the second option. Human dignity and human sin have the same source.

The consequence of this dialectical understanding of the moral relevance of human nature in its spiritual dimension is that any increase in the ability to transcend nature through scientific and technological knowledge, any expansion of the human capacity to transcend communities and to consciously manipulate or contrive communal arrangements according to rationally devised goals and values, and any progressive escape from the way in which human persons are products of history such that they may become creators of that history, promises greater evil as well as greater good.

Niebuhr's Critique of Liberal Anthropology

In Chapter 1, I described two related but distinguishable ways in which liberal anthropologies stress human autonomy or transcendence. I referred to these as autonomy as self-direction and autonomy as a sense of justice. Autonomy as self-direction refers to the capacity of the individual to transcend the particular aspects of his or her own existence through self-conscious reflection on the goals, values, or ends which shape life, and by acting on those goals, values, or ends as redefined or reformulated by the individual. Autonomy as a sense of justice refers to the alleged ability of every human being to discover the valid moral limits on the exercise of his or her autonomous action from a standpoint independent of the historically shaped values and practices of the communities of which he or she is a part. Moreover, the argument was made that it is on the basis of these aspects of the human capacity for autonomy that individuals are regarded by liberals as sources of moral claims upon one another and that, on this same basis, the fundamental content of the moral claim that every individual has against every other (and against communities and institutions) is a claim to liberty or freedom. The validity and weight of this claim is equal for every human being because everyone has the capacity for autonomy to the relevant degree. Therefore, it can be said that liberalism not only notes the fact of the human capacity for autonomy but regards it as morally relevant and fundamental in three ways: 1) it is by virtue of this capacity that human beings are individuated sources of moral claims; 2) it is by virtue of this capacity that the fundamental moral claim of the individual is for liberty; and 3) it is by virtue of this capacity and from the standpoint it provides that individuals are able to discover the valid moral limits to the exercise of their liberty. Because of this third way in which individual transcendence is morally relevant, individuals may be regarded as morally responsible.

There are some fairly obvious similarities between Niebuhr's anthropology and that which we have said is characteristic of liberalism. Niebuhr's understanding of the transcendent or spiritual dimension of human nature includes the liberal understanding of autonomy as self-direction. He understands that spiritual dimension as being a source of individual worth (or dignity) and as justifying a wide range of liberty. Moreover, Niebuhr believed that it is possible to identify basic, universally valid moral principles of justice from an autonomous standpoint and that individuals have natural moral sentiments which direct them to the observance of those principles. Thus, he had a conception of autonomy as a sense of justice.

Yet, Niebuhr regarded his moral anthropology as profoundly different from liberal perspectives because of his dialectical understanding of both the autonomous or transcendent dimension of human nature and of the relationship between that dimension and human nature's creaturely aspect. Liberals generally see the human capacity for autonomy as either unambiguously positive or as a condition of the possibility of moral action or responsibility; the goal of liberalism is to maximize the range of autonomous choice, and such a maximization is seen either as a positive moral good or as simply a condition of the possibility of the realization of any moral good. For Niebuhr, on the other hand, the transcendent dimension of human nature is a source of both good and evil. A society in which individual autonomy is given such respect must be prepared for both indeterminate creative or positive possibilities and, on the contrary, indeterminate prospects for destruction and evil. Furthermore, while he recognized the positive moral relevance of the autonomous individual conscience and of individual liberty over against the contingent historical and social factors that influenced human existence, he thought that liberalism overestimates the degree to which individuals are capable of achieving such an autonomous perspective, and he assigned positive relevance to aspects of the creaturely dimension as he believed liberals do not. Community, the historical factors which shape human selfhood, and natural moral impulses have a positive importance for Niebuhr. He believed liberals tend either to deny these or to ignore them as irrelevant to political ethics (except insofar as they present a problem to be resolved by a liberal political ethic).

Thus, Niebuhr regarded himself as a critic of liberalism. His most consistent criticism was that it has an unjustifiably optimistic view of human nature, a sentimental belief in the possibility of moral progress in human history, and a naive understanding of the difficulty of achieving a just social order. Niebuhr regarded this as particularly true of those interpretations of Christianity, such as the Social Gospel movement represented in the United States by Walter Rauschenbusch, which had imbibed the spirit of liberalism. While praising liberal Christianity for insisting on the relevance of love or *agape* to the historical task of constructing just societies and governments, he heartily criticized liberal Christians for believing that applying love to human life and history was a "simple possibility." It regarded the Christian hope of the perfection of the human individual and the human community in the Kingdom of God as a progressive human achievement in history. It regarded the uniqueness of Jesus as having to do with his moral perfection, a perfection which was possible for all human beings. Because liberal Christianity, on Niebuhr's view, regarded human perfection as a possibility in history it did not recognize coercion as a necessary element of strategies to achieve justice and thus regarded pacifism as an effective means for its realization.[14]

Because of its unjustified optimism, its sentimentality, and its naiveté, liberalism, in either its secular or Christian forms, was incapable of providing an understanding of how a relatively just social order is established and maintained, according to Niebuhr. In the pages that follow I will attempt to make sense of Niebuhr's judgment that liberalism was politically dangerous by focusing on his critique of the liberal understanding of the human capacity for autonomy and its moral relevance. I will always attempt to connect the relationship between each aspect of Niebuhr's critique and the charge that liberalism is optimistic, sentimental, and naive.

Liberalism's Overestimation of the Human Capacity For Autonomy.

Niebuhr criticized the liberal understanding of autonomy because he felt that liberals tended to overestimate the degree to which individuals were capable of transcending the social and historical dimensions of existence in order both to direct their lives according to self-chosen values and norms (autonomy as self-direction) and to discover the moral limits to their self-direction (autonomy as a sense of justice). As a result, liberals, fail to pay adequate attention to the organic and historical factors that shape human life and to appreciate their positive contribution to the struggle for a just society.

The liberal overestimation of the capacity of the individual to transcend the unconscious organic and historical factors which influence human life meant that its conception of individuality was mistaken. "No one can be as completely and discreetly individual as bourgeois individualism supposes" (1941:22). Moreover, this overestimation meant that the ability of human persons to give conscious direction to history is limited in ways that the liberal spirit ignored. The Renaissance, which Niebuhr regarded as an important component of the liberal heritage, had overestimated "the freedom and power of man in history." In fact, the "actions and decisions" which the human being makes "are less unique than he imagines them to be." Consciously made actions and decisions "are less potent in determining historical direction than the Renaissance had assumed" (1941:68). Moreover, Niebuhr contended that liberals overestimate the autonomy or independence of the individual conscience. "Consistently 'liberal' or 'bourgeois' notions of conscience as purely individual do not do justice to the fact that the individual is best able to defy a community when his conscience is informed and reinforced by another community, whether religious or political" (1955:15).

Similarly, even though he himself derived principles of justice from his analysis of features of human nature which he regarded as universal and independent of the influences of historical and social contingency, he consistently denied that individuals were capable of achieving a disinterested, transcendent rational perspective from which such principles could be interpreted and applied to the conflicts and dilemmas of human political life. "Rational forces" in human nature are inadequate for limiting the expressions of self-interest because they have "no impartial perspective from which to view, and no transcendent fulcrum, from which to affect human action. They always remain bound to the forces they are intended to discipline" (1932:44).[15]

Of course, Niebuhr himself recognized the human capacity for self-direction and the role of autonomous human reason in discovering principles of justice. His criticism of liberalism for overemphasizing this dimension of human nature does not mean that it should be ignored. What it means is that both dimensions must be attended to and appreciated in any strategy for achieving a just society. Niebuhr believed that liberalism failed to attend to the factors of the human creaturely dimension in that its strategy for justice focused on the discovery of autonomous principles of justice and their application to concrete historical situations and ignored what he called the structures of justice, that is, the balancing of the various organic vitalities in a particular society. Moreover, it failed to appreciate the contribution of the human creaturely dimensions to the degree that it denigrated natural social impulses and the moral inclinations which contribute to the achievement of justice and ignored the way in which principles of justice are illuminated by their interpretation and application within a particular historical situation with its interplay of contending vitalities.

The importance of Niebuhr's argument that liberalism tended to overestimate the human capacity for autonomy (taken independently of his argument that liberalism fails to appreciate the full depth of that autonomy) can easily be misunderstood. The primary point, it seems to me, is *not* the degree to which human individuals are able to rise above the factors of time, place, and social setting, or the ease with which such an autonomous center of self-direction and moral reason is achieved. There is surely room for disagreement within the liberal perspective in this regard and Niebuhr tends to overemphasize the way in which his dialectical understanding of human nature represents a critique of liberalism in this respect.

More important than the degree to which individuals are able to achieve such an independent perspective is the way in which this capacity, however extensive, is regarded as morally relevant. As I have already noted, Niebuhr shares the liberal sense that this capacity for autonomy is a source of the moral status or "dignity"of the human person (See 1984:10). It justifies a wide measure of liberty, and provides a perspective from which universal principles of justice can be derived. Niebuhr regarded his view that liberalism overestimated the human capacity for autonomy as a significant critique because that overestimation contributed to the liberal failure to attend adequately to the sub-conscious, uncontrived organic influences on human life and to appreciate their contribution to achieving a livable social justice. Both in terms of attention and appreciation there is a measure of accuracy in Niebuhr's critique of liberalism in this respect, although it would seem that liberalism can absorb the Niebuhrian critique without abandoning its basic viewpoint.

Liberalism's Failure to Recognize the Moral Relevance of Natural Organic or Communal Factors.

Liberalism does *attend to* the influence of organic factors on the struggle to achieve justice. It could be argued that such factors have been the primary concern of liberalism. Historically, liberalism emerged as a response to the bloody and divisive conflicts between various traditional religious communities, and, in the contemporary world, it continues to serve as a framework for dealing with pluralism in modern societies. Yet, if Niebuhr is correct *both* with regard to his estimation of the degree to which such an autonomous center of self-direction and moral reason is achievable *and* with respect to his view that liberals have overestimated that capacity for autonomy, then he is also correct that liberals have failed to attend adequately to the importance of organic factors in devising a strategy for justice.

Niebuhr also seemed to regard his insistence that the natural social impulses of the human person were an important moral resource as a critique of liberalism and its emphasis on autonomous moral reason. It is not just that liberalism has not attended adequately to what Niebuhr called the creaturely dimension of human nature; it has also failed to appreciate its contribution to the struggle for justice. "Reason," he wrote, "is not the sole basis of moral virtue in man. His social impulses are more deeply rooted than his rational life. Reason may extend and stabilize, but it does not create, the capacity to affirm other life than his own." He pointed specifically to Kant's scorn for human sympathy "if it did not flow from a sense of duty" (1932:26). Kant's perspective on the question of natural moral sentiments is not essential to the liberal perspective, however.

Many liberals, it would seem, could agree with Niebuhr's contention that "the function of reason . . . is to support those impulses which carry life beyond itself, and to extend the measure and degree of their sociality" (1932:26). Contemporary liberals are aware that the neutrality and tolerance of basic institutions must be limited. Many agree that attention must be paid to the cultural factors that support and develop the sense of justice which they assume. Rawls suggests that a liberal society will survive only if the dominant groups in it have their own reasons for supporting the limitations implied by his concept of the original position. All of this indicates an appreciation of the relevance of factors which Niebuhr saw rooted in the creaturely aspect of human nature. Niebuhr did not attribute such appreciation to liberals. Thus, it is with good reason that Thomas Spragens included Niebuhr among those whom he called "traditionalist liberals." Still, as I hope to show below, Niebuhr's understanding and defense of both democratic political institutions and free economic ones shows greater attention to and appreciation for the organic, communal, or traditional factors in his conception of a just society than liberalism has generally shown. Niebuhr's critique here is slightly overdrawn, but it is valid none the less.

Liberalism's Failure to Appreciate the Negative Moral Relevance of Autonomy

Niebuhr complained that modern conceptions of human nature, including liberal[16] ones, do not "do justice to the height of human self-transcendence" (1941:123). In my view this aspect of Niebuhr's critique of liberalism represents a more fundamental attack upon essential liberal tenets than does his view that it overestimates the capacity for autonomy. Even here, however, a distinction must be drawn between an aspect of Niebuhr's critique that is significantly overdrawn and another that is an accurate portrayal of the essential liberal spirit.

Because of liberalism's failure to do justice to the height of human self transcendence, Niebuhr says it fails to recognize that the capacity for autonomy entails a radical freedom which invalidates any order which is discoverable in nature or by reason and it fails to recognize that the very autonomy which it seeks to protect and enhance promises universal and indeterminate manifestations of human evil. But, I will argue below, liberal conceptions of universal order are less comprehensive and more flexible, and therefore more like his own conception, than Niebuhr suggests. His view that liberals fail to appreciate either the source or the depth of human evil seems to be more on target, however. Indeed, this is the most important aspect of his liberal critique. Niebuhr's sense that human evil is rooted in the transcendent or autonomous aspect of human nature means that Niebuhr is more willing than liberals tend to be to appeal to traditional structures of order and authority as a check upon that evil. In the previous section we argued that Niebuhr regarded organic communal factors as morally relevant, both because of the limitations on the human capacity to transcend such factors and because of their positive moral contribution. Here we see an even more compelling reason for Niebuhr's attention to them: they are an absolutely essential element of control over the evil potential in human freedom.

Radical Freedom and the Absence of Natural or Rational Order. Human freedom "must be defined as 'radical,'" says Niebuhr, "to indicate that, when man rises above the necessities and limits of nature, he is not inevitably bound in his actions to the norms and universalities of 'reason'" (1984:10). Niebuhr regarded as mistaken any view which sought fixed moral norms in the regularities of nature or in the coherence that human reason is able to give to human existence. Thus he rejected Stoic and Roman Catholic theories of natural law as well as modern perspectives which tried to discover some fixed moral order in human nature or reason. "Stoic natural law," he wrote, "assumes a determinate human freedom and falsely equates the fixed structures of nature and the less fixed structures of human nature." Roman Catholic natural law theories also assumed such fixed structures. For Niebuhr, the human person is essentially free and "the indeterminate character of human freedom and the variety and uniqueness of historic occasions produce fewer things than supposed in Catholic natural law theory, about which one may be sure that they must be done or not done" (1953:157). "No law," wrote Niebuhr "can do justice to the freedom of man in history. It cannot state the final good for him, since in his transcendence and self-transcendence no order of nature and no rule of history can finally determine the norm of his life" (1943:40).

This criticism is less relevant to liberal theories of natural law than it is to Stoic or Catholic theories, however. Liberal theories do not delineate the requirements of human nature as comprehensively as traditional Roman

Catholic natural law; traditional Roman Catholic natural law theories are teleological in a way that is contrary to liberal neutrality or the thin theories of the good with which liberalism is associated. Yet, Niebuhr apparently regarded the critique he applied to Roman Catholic natural law as applying also to liberal theories. The "naturalistic" and "rationalistic" conceptions of human nature which Niebuhr critiques in the opening chapters of *The Nature and Destiny of Man* conform roughly to the Lockean and Kantian accounts of liberalism which I have described. Thus, even liberal natural law theories conflict with Niebuhr's conviction, as described by Paul Ramsey,

> that there is no explaining things by reference to a fixed and given human nature. Man is largely what he becomes; he isn't ready made at first. . . . The thread running through Niebuhr's criticisms of naturalism, rationalism, and romanticism in *The Nature and Destiny of Man* is his contention that man's self-transcending freedom rises above the limits or even the vitalities of physical nature and above the patterns of reason or the uniquely individual organic structures discovered by romantic idealism (Ramsey 1962:113).[17]

Thus the "norms and universalities of reason" must not be prematurely or irrevocably imposed; the limits to human freedom which reason regards as necessary are always provisional and contingent. Liberal views, according to Niebuhr, see human vitality as ultimately conforming to a structure of order found either in nature or in the self's own autonomous reason. The liberal conception of autonomy recognized the possibility of human transcendence over the limitations of time, place, and community, but saw the human person in terms of its place in the order of nature or in terms of the structures which human reason was able to discover and impose on chaotic nature.[18]

On Niebuhr's view, because liberalism fails to understand the significance of self-transcendence, it does not appreciate the way that the norms which it identifies as required by human nature or reason violate or prematurely restrict the radical freedom of the human person. Liberalism fails to recognize that the human person is always capable of transcending the order it discovers in its own nature or the coherence its rationality is able to create. Thus, liberalism is too confident about the validity of the particular order or norms it believes it has discovered and about the "fit" between that order and human nature; it underestimates the "strain" of radical human freedom "against the bit" of its order and norms. Niebuhr seems to regard the indictment of rationalists in the following passage as including liberal rationalists[19]:

> Men seek a universal standard of human good. After painful effort they define it. The painfulness of their effort convinces them that they have discovered a genuinely universal value. To their sorrow, some of their fellow men refuse to accept the standard. Since they know the standard to be universal the

recalcitrance of their fellows is proof, in their minds, of some defect in the humanity of the non-conformists. Thus a rationalistic age creates a new fanaticism. The non-conformists are figuratively expelled from the human community (1960:18).

But to regard liberalism as seeking a "universal standard of human good" is surely mistaken. Owing to the fact that the "thinness" of liberal theories leaves a great deal to be determined by individual human beings in their freedom, Niebuhr's position seems clearly to have more affinities with liberal than traditional Roman Catholic natural law. However, it should not be forgotten that Niebuhr believed that liberal theorists were more confident about the ability of the average person to discover and apply the dictates of the natural law.

Radical Freedom and the Indeterminacy of Human Evil. We have already seen that Niebuhr regarded the self-transcendent aspect of human nature as the source of the anxiety which is the precondition of human sin and which makes human sin inevitable. We have also seen that because human sinfulness is rooted in the spiritual dimension of human nature, that dimension which gives human possibilities their indeterminate character, he also regarded the expressions of human evil as indeterminate. Niebuhr regarded the liberal ignorance of this aspect of human autonomy as the most fundamental source of its optimism and sentimentality. It meant that liberalism built its understanding of politics on the idea of "an essentially harmless individual" (1944:18). If individuals were set free from the traditional authorities, and if their pursuit of happiness as they conceive it were controlled only by the principles of right which they can discover independently of those traditional authorities, then their capacity for evil is greatly diminished.

Niebuhr's point is not that liberals were unaware of the persistence of an inordinate individual self-interest which threatened the well-being of others and the possibility of a just human community. Liberals surely were aware of human evil; their concern to determine the basis of justified coercion and legitimate governmental authority (what Benjamin Barber has called liberalism's "realistic" disposition (1984)) reflects such an awareness. But Niebuhr's point was that liberals tended to be unaware of the source of sin or evil in the essential nature of the human person and therefore to underestimate both its irradicability and its indeterminate potential for expression in human life. Thus, liberals have tended to be overly optimistic about the degree to which human self-interest can be mitigated and brought into harmony with the interests of others.

On Niebuhr's view, liberals have tended to view the sources of human evil in the natural survival impulses of living beings. That is to say, liberals see human evil as associated with the aspect of human nature which we share with other animals, or, with what Niebuhr has referred to as the creaturely dimension of human nature. Because evil is in fact rooted in the spiritual dimension of the human person, "the conflicts between men are never simple conflicts between competing survival impulses." Rather, "they are conflicts in which each man or group seeks to guard its power and prestige against the peril of competing expressions of pride and power" (1944:20; see also 1955:157). Liberal political theory, he says, saw the possibility of harmonizing the self-interest of competing individuals not just in terms of "natural limits of egoism" but also in "the capacity of reason to transmute egotism into a concern for the general welfare, or upon the ability of government to overcome the potential conflict of wills in society" (1944:26). The height of liberal optimism with regard to the ability to overcome the conflicts arising from individual self-interest, according to Niebuhr, is represented "by the utilitarians of the 18th and 19th centuries" who had "faith in an identity between the individual and the general interest." Interestingly, the utilitarian liberals emphasized the social nature of the human person, or that the fulfillment of human personality required intimate interaction with others, as did Niebuhr. Unlike Niebuhr, they tended to believe that in a context of equal opportunity to participate with others in the social and political affairs the social nature of human persons could be developed to such a degree that conflicts and competition could be virtually eliminated.

The optimism which Niebuhr regards as an essential characteristic of liberalism is surely an important element for certain utilitarian, developmental versions of liberalism. Furthermore, this was the dominant version of liberalism with which Niebuhr had contact during part of his life. Still it may be argued that other versions may incorporate a profound sense of human evil into the liberal framework without necessarily abandoning its basic commitments and strategies. For example, it seems not to be the case that liberals have disregarded the human will-to-power and other manifestations of human pride.

Still, Niebuhr's view calls into question the liberal confidence in autonomous reason as a source of valid moral restraints on human evil, what I have called autonomy as a sense of justice. The transcendence of the human person over his or her own reason by virtue of our radical freedom implied that there is no absolute order discoverable by reason to which human nature ought universally to conform itself. That our radical freedom is also the source of our capacity for evil meant for Niebuhr that our reason is as likely to be the servant of human evil as the source of its restraint. Thus, for Niebuhr there was an "ideological taint" in all the "discoveries" of human reason, an ideological taint which undercuts the pretension in all versions of rationalism or naturalism which think itself to have discovered universally valid moral norms. This awareness of the ideological taint of all human reasoning was always, for Niebuhr, a virtue of both the "Romantic protest against rationalism" and of Marxism (1941:33–37; 1953:80).[20,21] Again, it would seem that liberalism is able to absorb this criticism given that its conception of natural or rational order is more limited and flexible than older traditional natural law theories and that a certain skepticism is built into its moral epistemology; it is certainly skeptical of reason's ability to discover any full theory of human good.

There is a difference between liberalism's response both to human evil and the tainted character of human reason which it may recognize and Niebuhr's response to these factors. Niebuhr is much more ready to appeal to traditional, organic structures of authority as a solution to human evil and to the frailties of autonomous reason than even the most realistic liberals. Previously I have shown that the liberal account of human nature is inadequate from the Niebuhrian perspective because its overestimation of the capacity for human transcendence over contingent historical and organic factors meant that it did not pay due attention to those organic factors in its theories of justice. Niebuhr's emphasis on structures of justice reflects his appreciation for the ongoing moral relevance of those factors. Earlier, I suggested both that there is room for disagreement within liberalism as to how far individual transcendence extends and that Niebuhr's critique suggests an addenda to liberal theories of justice but no fundamental challenge to the liberal approach. Here the Niebuhrian criticism represents a more significant strike at the heart of the liberal enterprise. For here Niebuhr's claim is not simply that organic factors and traditional patterns of authority must be attended to because of the inability of the human individual to absolutely transcend them in history, but that those factors and patterns of authority make a significant moral contribution in terms of the restraint they place upon the destructive expressions of human evil and the inability of human reason to find a disinterested perspective from which to devise or discover a universally valid order in which the expressions of human evil may be restrained. I have already suggested that the awareness by many liberals of the limits to liberal neutrality reflects an appreciation of the contribution that traditional communities and authorities can make to the establishment of a liberal society. Yet the importance that Niebuhr gives to organic factors and traditional sources of authority goes significantly beyond the attention and appreciation which liberal theories may extend to them.

Community and Tradition in Niebuhr's Thought

Because liberalism overestimates human autonomy, both as self-direction and as a sense of justice, and because it fails to appreciate the radical quality of human evil, it neither pays adequate attention to the organic, communal factors that affect any achievement of justice nor appreciates their vital contribution to such an achievement through the restrictions they place on the evil potential in human freedom. This basic critique of liberalism is at the heart of Niebuhr's criticism of the liberal justification of democratic political institutions and capitalist economic institutions. His claim to have provided an alternative understanding and justification for these institutions has to do with the role he assigns to organic factors. This is evident in both *The Children of Light and the Children of Darkness* and in *The Self and the Dramas of History,* which are the works on which our attention here will focus.

The Niebuhrian Justification of Democracy.

Niebuhr contends in the preface of *The Children of Light* that liberal optimism keeps it "from gauging the perils of freedom accurately and from appreciating democracy fully as the only alternative to injustice and oppression" (1944:xiv). Despite its association with democracy, liberalism, according to Niebuhr, does not really understand why democracy is necessary if a just society is to exist.

Niebuhr seems to regard the liberal account and justification of democracy as having two fundamental points beyond the obvious relationship between liberty and democracy, which Niebuhr shared with liberalism. (I am referring to the view that democracy, as wide or universal suffrage and the right to present oneself for election to positions of authority, is justified as an expression of individual liberty.) First, liberalism believes, says Niebuhr correctly, that if individuals are set free from the prejudices of traditional outlooks they can discover universal principles of justice by which "an easy resolution of the tension and conflicts between self interest and the general interest" can be achieved (1944:7). Liberals may or may not be optimistic about the inclination of individuals to conform to those principles, although those who provided a developmental argument for democracy believed that both knowledge of principles and inclination to obey them were what Niebuhr would call "simple possibilities." Liberals like Locke, Kant, and Rawls may have had a less complimentary sense of human inclinations, but their confidence in the possibility of deriving valid principles of right, principles which legitimate the coercive measures which may be necessary to force compliance with the requirements of justice, supports Niebuhr's claim that liberalism regards the accommodation or harmonization of conflicts as a relatively simple matter, or at least, more simple than Niebuhr regarded it. Liberalism believes democracy is justified, according to Niebuhr, because it makes possible this harmonization of individual interests according to principles of justice.

Secondly, Niebuhr believed that the idea that all legitimate public authority was derived from the explicit consent of autonomous individuals was an essential component of the liberal concept of democracy. As we have shown above, liberals have long recognized the failure of consent theory to provide a credible account of political obligation or governmental legitimacy, and alternative approaches which ground legitimacy in natural justice have emerged. Because of Niebuhr's apparent failure to recognize this, his account of legitimate authority represents no profound critique of the more sophisticated liberal arguments based on fairness or natural justice.

Democracy and justice. The fundamental principle of justice which liberals regard as grounded in the individual capacity for autonomy and which they believe the autonomous individual is capable of discovering, is the principle of equal liberty. This principle justifies the rights of all autonomous persons to participate in the political process by voting and presenting themselves for election to positions of authority. Moreover, as we have seen, that same basic principle of liberty requires that a *liberal* democratic government be limited by the obligation to respect basic individual rights; while governmental authority is necessary for the protection of liberty and is justified in terms of the rights which protect individual liberty, it is also a potential threat to that liberty. Thus, liberal democratic institutions, (that is, wide or universal suffrage, government limited by individual rights, divisions of powers and checks and balances within government, etc.) have what we have called both an expressive and protective justification in liberalism. Democracy is justified as an expression of individual rights and as a necessary means to protect those rights from governmental intrusion.

Niebuhr shares with liberals a sense that the principle of liberty plays a role in the justification of democracy. However, his understanding of the role of democracy in the creation of a just social order is different from a typically liberal approach in several respects. First, because the capacity for autonomy as self-direction is limited, that is, because individuals are always organically related to particular communities, the question of a just social order involves structures as well as principles of justice; it involves maintaining a relative balance of power between the various organic vitalities present in a particular society. This is a part of the reason for Niebuhr's denial that the coordination and harmonization of various interests is the relatively easy achievement liberals believe it to be. It means that liberalism fails to account for the perennial impact of such irrational factors as class, race, national, and religious loyalties. For Niebuhr, these organic ties are insuperable factors in human life related to the creaturely dimension of our nature. Those ties also provide an experience of intimate interpersonal relationship which hints at the ultimate fulfillment of the human person.

The achievement of justice is also more difficult than liberals imagine because they are ignorant of the radical source of human evil and the infinite possibilities for its manifestation in human life. That radical evil means, as we have seen, that setting individuals free from the traditional restrictions imposed by their ties to tradition allows for the elaboration of new and potentially more destructive mechanisms of evil, both individually and corporately expressed. "If we survey any period of history, and not merely the present tragic era of world catastrophe," Niebuhr wrote during World War II,

> it becomes quite apparent that human ambitions, lusts and desires are more inevitably inordinate, that both human creativity and human evil reach greater heights, and that conflicts in the community between varying conceptions of the good and between competing expressions of vitality are of more tragic proportions than was anticipated in the basic philosophy which underlies democratic civilization (1944:22).

Niebuhr believed, of course, that human beings do have some capacity for justice. His pessimism does not result in the view that democracy is impossible.[22] Yet, because liberalism is ignorant of the difficulty of achieving a just and stable order, it does not understand why democracy is "the only alternative to injustice and oppression." Democracy is the only alternative to injustice because its dispersion of political power among all autonomous persons helps prevent the development of disproportionate centers of power in a society or to break down those which may already exist. The broad dispersion of power is an effective mechanism for preventing an imbalance in the structures of justice.

There is a certain similarity between Niebuhr's view that democracy is justified as a mechanism which prevents the development of disproportionate centers of power and the liberal defense which regards democracy as instrumentally valuable as a means to protect individual liberty. Niebuhr's argument also sees democracy as an instrumental value. There are major differences, however, between the liberal defenders of protective democracy described by C.B. Macpherson, and Niebuhr. First, we saw that these early liberals lacked a sense of the social nature of the human person. Moreover, they had no particular enthusiasm for democracy and were satisfied with the most limited suffrage necessary to enable democratic control of governmental abuse of individual liberty. Neither of these views can be attributed to Niebuhr. Most fundamental of all, the "protective" model of democracy of early liberals saw the government as the center of power from which the individual needed protection, but their attention was not directed toward the various sub-governmental vitalities which Niebuhr has primarily in mind. The "equilibrium" model of certain 20th century liberals to which Macpherson refers is more similar to Niebuhr, but even here the concern is to achieve balance among the various interest groups with which autonomous individuals associate themselves and not the various ethnic, class, and religious communities which Niebuhr had in mind.

The problem of legitimate authority and political obligation. Although Niebuhr was extremely critical of liberal consent theory, his problem with it was not the traditional Humean one. Hume regarded consent as the best way to establish legitimate authority, and believed that individuals originally left their natural liberty and formed corporate structures of authority by consent. However, he contended that if explicit consent is the basis of legitimacy, then few if any present governments are legitimate and few if any of us are obligated since we have never explicitly consented to our government's authority over us. Moreover, implied consent will not work because it lacks the voluntary quality which gives explicit consent its force. For Hume, the account of political authority that will establish the legitimacy of most governments[23] is one based on principles of justice and fidelity which themselves are justified upon consideration of "the necessities of human society, and the imposssibility of supporting it, if these duties were neglected" (Hume 1962:160). We have already seen how the Humean argument has been developed by John Rawls in terms of the idea of natural justice. Rawls' argument shows that it is possible to develop a liberal account of political obligation that does not depend upon consent theory but which is faithful to the fundamental liberal commitment to equal liberty of every individual upon which that earlier theory of political obligation was based.

Niebuhr did not anticipate the development within liberalism of an account like Rawls', and his own conception of legitimate authority represents no significant challenge to the Rawlsian perspective. This is not to suggest that there are no differences between the Niebuhrian and Rawlsian alternatives to consent theory. Those differences have to do, however, with their alternative conceptions of justice.

For Niebuhr, the liberal perspective is characterized by the view that community and government are creations of the human will. As we have seen, Niebuhr insists on the social nature of the human person and that individual fulfillment occurs in intimate relation with others. For Niebuhr, there is no such thing as an individual apart from community and the community is not a creation of the autonomous individual. On Niebuhr's view, "the community is as primordial as the individual" (1955:165), and social contract theory completely obscures this fact in its view that community and government are a creation of the individual will.

For Niebuhr, the organic patterns of relationship which exist apart from their conscious creation by the individual will include patterns of authority. These are necessary because of the human capacity for evil. The community must exert authority over the individual and restrict individual freedom in order to protect itself and, ultimately, the individuals within it, since they depend upon communal bonds for their own fulfillment. Government, social hierarchy, and property all exist as "organs of communal integration" (1955:166) which provide the order which is made necessary by human sin.

We have already seen that while Niebuhr regarded order with its unequal relationships of authority as in conflict with the transcendent principle of equality, he regarded the achievement of order as "prior" to the question of justice in society. That is to say, there must be some coerced order within and among the various vitalities in a society for any measure of justice to be achieved. This is not to deny that authority can either be maintained or regarded as legitimate apart from its ratification or acceptance by those among whom authority is exercised. Even those organic patterns of authority depend upon what Niebuhr calls a sense of "majesty," which engenders "uncoerced submission," for that authority to be legitimate. Majesty has three "ingredients" according to Niebuhr: "historic prestige," which any particular order comes to enjoy as a result of its duration over time; "religious aura," which arises from the belief that the authority has divine sanction,[24] and "moral prestige," which is gained only if authority is exercised justly (1955:169). It would seem to be primarily in terms of its "moral prestige" that Niebuhr can say that the majesty a government enjoys "is legitimate in so far as it embodies and expresses both the authority and power of the total community over all its members, and the principle of order and justice as such against the peril of anarchy" (1943:267).

Niebuhr denies that this majesty is based on "'rational' consent" (1943:267). The moral prestige which gives majesty legitimacy does not require that everyone has explicitly granted the government's right of authority over them and surely not that every individual participates in establishing the specific terms of that authority. Yet, Niebuhr does eventually employ the language of consent in his effort to provide an account of legitimate government. Niebuhr draws a distinction between "an established government" or "the fact of government" and "a particular government" (1955:169, 175). What he calls an establishment of government or the fact of government depends upon majesty and this majesty entails "implicit consent." "[T]he possession of majesty spells the difference between legitimate and illegitimate government, that is, between the government which rules by implicit consent or that which rules by 'force and fraud'"(1955:169). While the legitimacy of the fact of government depends upon implied consent, particular governments, he says, are "made and unmade by explicit consent" (1955:169).

Niebuhr's distinctions between the fact or establishment of government and a particular government, and between implied and expressed consent are never made clear. Moreover, his choice of the terminology of consent is, in some respects, an unfortunate and unhelpful one. Apparently what Niebuhr has in mind by the distinction between the fact of government and a particular government is simply a distinction between the need for order and authority and a particular set of authorities and terms of authority. Moreover, consistent with his theme that every community has both organic and artificial elements, the distinction is meant to supplement Niebuhr's argument that some structure of authority is legitimately a part of every organic community though the particular structure of authority is subject to conscious contrivance and manipulation. Thus he can write with reference to "the fact of government" that it "is not in the competence of any generation to create [government] out of hand." Yet he can insist that a particular government "rests upon explicit consent" (1955:175).

We have already seen that the early liberal concept of consent as the basis for political obligation could not stand up to scrutiny. But for Niebuhr to resort to the terminology of consent is all the more unfortunate because he never meant to contend that authority and its terms are justified primarily by an intentional and voluntary adjustment of the structure of rights by each individual under authority. Surely by associating implicit consent with the fact of government Niebuhr in no way means to suggest that the legitimacy of order depends upon a recognition of the need for order on the part of all those among whom order exists, as the language of consent implies. The point Niebuhr was primarily concerned to make at this level of the argument, it seems to me, was simply that the coercive element of authority, that element which means that whatever moral achievement it secures falls short of the ideal of free recognition and response to the claims of others upon us, is reduced and rendered less objectionable where its necessity is generally recognized.

Even at the level of particular governments the language of consent, especially explicit consent, is unhelpful. Again, the language of consent is somewhat misleading as a means for making Niebuhr's conception of legitimacy clear. What Niebuhr wants to argue is that the power of any government ought to be limited, that it ought to respect individual liberty, that it ought to be subject to the scrutiny and criticism of the people, and that government ought not to be the instrument of particular groups or factions within the community. But Niebuhr does not mean to suggest that no government is legitimate and no individual is obligated to obedience apart from an explicit grant of authority according to specific terms.

The focus of Niebuhr's entire discussion is on the relationship between the organic, unconscious elements of order that shape a community and the consciously contrived efforts by which a particular generation attempts to adjust that order such that greater justice is achieved. Niebuhr's primary concern is to argue that the achievement of a just order is never a new creation. Niebuhr's sense that the liberation of persons from the restraints of traditional authority promises new and indeterminate expressions of human evil and injustice requires that he oppose any view which disparages the contribution that the traditional authority rendered and must continue to render.

None of this is to deny that the dignity of the individual and individual liberty are irrelevant with reference to the question of political legitimacy. Niebuhr insists that older traditional societies paid too high a price in injustice in order to secure order. His understanding of human dignity and justice, and his sense that the terms of cooperation in society must always remain open to criticism and adjustment in the light of the inability of human beings to achieve a transcendent perspective from which comprehensive universal principles of justice can be discovered, both require that government be subject to the scrutiny and criticism of the governed and that all be allowed broad opportunities for participation in the process of governance. It is this to which Niebuhr meant to point by his unfortunate choice of the language of consent (despite his fierce criticism of that language).[25]

Ultimately then, for Niebuhr, the goal to which good government must strive is a balance between order and justice, between organism and artifact in human community. Speaking of a political theory which understood both the need for order and the threat to justice which all power and authority represents, Niebuhr wrote:

> Thus a balance was reached between proper reverence for the ordinance of government and affirmation of the principle of consent by which particular governments are made and unmade; between the conception of the community as an organism and as an artifact; between the factors which are beyond the power, and those with the power of a given generation. This balance is also creative of a government with a maximum of stability and a maximum of justice. The former created by traditional forces and the latter by the workings of a democratic order in which the people measure out "in ounce by ounce weights" the power which they wish to entrust to a particular ruler (1955:175–176).[26]

The question which finally must be raised is whether Niebuhr's account of political obligation and legitimacy differs significantly from that provided by liberals like Rawls who have not depended upon an exclusively voluntarist conception for their own attempts to deal with these problems. It would seem that by grounding his account of obligation in "natural justice" Rawls was recognizing the prima facie claim of traditional patterns of authority while at the same time requiring that those claims be subject to the scrutiny of a liberal conception of justice. The most relevant differences between the Niebuhrian and Rawlsian accounts of political obligation have to do with their divergent accounts of justice. As we have already suggested, Niebuhr is not confident about the prospect of arriving at principles of justice through a method such as that proposed by Rawls. For Niebuhr the terms of cooperation in society are more fluid and reflect both the balance of power in society and its accumulated wisdom and experience in ways that Rawls does not recognize. Furthermore, Niebuhr's conception of justice is significantly more egalitarian than Rawls'. Whereas Rawls' theory only requires that everyone have equal liberty and that any inequalities in the distribution of primary goods raise the share of the worst off, on Niebuhr's account there is no limit in principle to the degree of equality which justice might require. Indeed, perfect justice, he insists, is perfect equality. It is fair to say, then, that to the extent that both the Rawlsian and Niebuhrian accounts of political obligation and legitimacy depend upon their conceptions of justice and represent a recognition of the prima facie legitimacy of traditional authority, they are similar, and Niebuhr's position represents no fundamental critique of a non-consent based liberal conception. To the degree that Niebuhr's conception of justice is different from Rawls', and I have argued that it is significantly different both because Niebuhr pays greater attention to the organic and historical factors and because it is more egalitarian, his understanding of political obligation is different. Niebuhr's conception of justice and political obligation is much more pragmatic and less theoretical, more a matter of prudence and wisdom and less a matter of appeal to principles. At the same time, for Niebuhr, inequalities are much more likely to undermine the legitimacy of a particular order.

Niebuhr and Free Economic Institutions

That Niebuhr gradually came to accept private property and free market mechanisms (as tempered by the welfare state) after having been a socialist for many years is well-known. However, commentators have been so quick either to lament or hail this change in his thought that few have grasped the full complexity of his mature views with reference to economic institutions.[27] The primary reasons for Niebuhr's rejection of socialism have to do with his distrust of any view which promises a simple solution to the problem of injustice and his own emphasis on the balancing of various centers of power as essential to the achievement of justice. To the degree that socialists and Marxists were prone to regard the dissolution of private property and social control of the means of production as a final solution to the problem of injustice Niebuhr could only regard them as victims of the same optimistic illusions which characterized their liberal adversaries. Moreover, Niebuhr came to view the concentration of power in the hands of governmental managers of business enterprise as a threat to justice as serious as its concentration in the hands of private capitalists. Concentrated power in either form prevented both the wide dispersion of power in many centers and a balance of power among those multiple centers which human evil made necessary if justice were to be achieved. Moreover, control of property was but one of several types of power to be considered. Modern democratic government had attempted to separate political and economic power, and the achievements of Franklin Roosevelt's New Deal demonstrated that liberal governments were not simply the tools of economic power. The socialist solution, on the other hand, guaranteed that political and economic power would be joined together in the hands of a state bureaucracy.

Despite this well-known rejection of socialism, Niebuhr's position on economic matters as reflected in both *The Children of Light* and *The Self and the Dramas of History* represents a much more tentative and pragmatic acceptance of private property and free market institutions and a much less enthusiastic and fundamental defense of them than has been typical of liberal thought.

Two aspects of Niebuhr's views on economics are important for highlighting the differences between his conception of justice as it relates to economic institutions and typically liberal conceptions. First, Niebuhr associated property primarily with the organic or creaturely dimension of human existence rather than with the dimension of human freedom. For Niebuhr, property is seen as one of the mechanisms of communal integration and order made necessary by the fact of human evil. It is not regarded as a fundamental necessity of individual liberty. According to Niebuhr, the liberal conception of property recognizes it as "one of the 'inalienable' rights, guaranteed by natural law" (1944:90). He argued that such a view tends "to emancipate property relations from all political control or moral restraint" (1944:98). He explicitly contrasts the liberal conception of property with the Christian conception with which he identified himself.

> According to the Christian theory . . . property, as well as government, is a necessary evil, required by the Fall of man. . . . Such a theory has the advantage of viewing the "right" of property with circumspection and of justifying it only relatively and not absolutely. It was justified as an expedient tool of justice. The right of possession was not regarded in early Christian thought as a natural extension of the power of the person but rather as a right of defense against the inordinate claims of others (1944:90–91).

That property is seen as a necessary mechanism of communal integration and traditional authority[28] does not mean that it is an unambiguous servant of justice, of course. Just as Niebuhr distinguished between the justification of government as such and the legitimacy of any particular government, he also recognized that any particular distribution of property rights and their regulation is subject to moral evaluation. The problem in a modern society as in any other is "to come to terms with the necessities which have created [the phenomenon of property], for these necessities are indeed perennial." Recognizing property as one of the mechanisms of authority in any community, a mechanism justified in principle on the same grounds as any other mechanism of authority, the further task is "to apply the regulative principles of liberty and equality so

that they will be more effective than in the older organic societies"
(1955:184).

Thus, Niebuhr seems to regard private property as legitimate on the
basis of its necessity as a defensive mechanism for the individual in the
face of the perennial desires of others for dominance and control.
Apparently property, like government, would be unnecessary were it not
for the fact of human sin. Thus, while the anarchist and socialist
tendencies of certain groups within the early Church and among the
Radical Reformers of the 16th century are comprehensible, those
tendencies are ill-advised because they indicate a failure to take into
account the persistent relevance of human sinfulness. An interesting
parallel can be seen between the protective argument for democracy
among some early liberals and Niebuhr's argument for private property.
We have seen that some liberals saw the wide dispersion of political
power as necessary in order to protect individual liberty against its
violations by government. This "protective" justification for democracy
was often associated with a lack of enthusiasm for government by the
people and with the most limited extension of suffrage necessary to gain
the protective advantage. There was little sense, among some liberals, that
democracy was justified as an expression of individual liberty. Niebuhr
seems to regard private property as a protective or defensive necessity.
Moreover, his defense lacks enthusiasm to the extent that the control of
property is not seen as a valuable expression of individual liberty.

Secondly, based on this conception of property as a necessary
mechanism of order, and the recognition that property relations are subject
to evaluation and adjustment in terms of the principles of liberty and
equality, Niebuhr sees the question of the distribution and limitation of
property rights as an ongoing one which is subject to pragmatic
manipulation in terms of the problem of maintaining a balance of power.
Whereas liberal limitations on rights of property typically must be justified
in terms of the requirements of individual liberty, and are also severely
restricted on those same terms, there is no such built-in basis for and
limitation upon the way questions of property are to be handled in
Niebuhr's conception of the problem of justice and economic institutions.

In *The Children of Light,* Niebuhr was still maintaining that
ownership of large productive enterprises ought to be socialized, despite
his rejection of the view that all private property should be done away
with.[29] "There is a serious gulf," Niebuhr wrote, "between [the] social
function of modern property and the emphasis upon its private character in
legal tradition and social thought" (1944:99). This gulf widened in a
technically advanced industrial society in which "collective production
became the primary source of wealth. The modern factory is a great
collective process. . . . The 'private' ownership of such a process is
anachronistic and incongruous; and the individual control of such

centralized power is an invitation to injustice" (1944:103). Niebuhr immediately recognized, however, that "this is the kind of question which cannot be solved once for all," and he called for "the property issue" to be "continually solved within the framework of the democratic process" (1944:115). The important point for our purposes is that Niebuhr's emphasis upon the importance of maintaining a wide dispersal of power and a balance among various centers of power suggests a much more flexible approach to the question of property rights than typically liberal perspectives tend to allow. While liberals may recognize limitations on rights or property and call for redistributional schemes those limitations are primarily understood in terms of the relationship of property to human liberty. Thus, those who argue for positive economic rights which entail the justification of the redistribution of wealth and property do so in terms of the necessity of minimal levels of control over reason for the exercise of liberty.

Of course, Niebuhr also eventually gave up his call for the social ownership of large productive enterprises. He did so in response to the various welfare programs of Roosevelt's New Deal and the rise of labor unions as a countervailing power over against the power of capitalist owners of the means of production. Niebuhr's judgment in this regard represents no fundamental shift in his perspective with regard to property, however. It merely represents an adjustment of his judgment about what the conception of justice which he had developed called for given the particular facts of the situation of the United States at mid-century. It is certain that Niebuhr had not anticipated that democracy could have achieved what he believed it had under Roosevelt and Truman. Moreover, it is this achievement which accounts in no small measure for the increasingly respectful tone he employed with reference to traditionally liberal institutions. Still, his judgment was that the achievements of liberal institutions were in spite of and not a result of the insights of liberal theory. What made a society in which private property and free market economic institutions reigned livably just was the unconscious adjustment of social forces which democratic freedom or "an open society" allowed. Speaking of what had happened to change the grim picture of capitalist destiny which Marx had forecast, Niebuhr wrote

> What happened was an analogy of the organic adaptations of traditional societies within the new conditions of a technical society. Social forces not too conscious of themselves, or at least not armed with explicit philosophies, took immediate actions to fend off particular forms of injustice. The workers were individually weak in bargaining with the employer. They could redress some of the balance by collective action. Thus the trade unions were born. . . . A theory was never developed which would determine just how much privilege would be justified by special social function or power or for the purpose of providing incentives for the performance of function. But the steps which were taken to prevent inordinate inequalities of privilege from arising—chiefly by preventing

inordinate disbalances of power from developing—proved adequate to save
modern society from revolution and disintegration.   It saved at least the
healthiest members of modern civilization (1955:195–196).[30]

Niebuhr's confidence that the United States had made the adjustments
necessary for achieving and maintaining a healthy balance of power not
only led to a greater appreciation on Niebuhr's part for the institutions of
liberal society, but also to a reduced attention to the great injustices that
remained in the life of the United States: great poverty continued to exist
despite the emergence of the welfare state, and racism persisted. Yet,
Niebuhr's voice grew increasingly mellow over the years. Paul Merkley
has lamented that mellowing and perceives an irony in it that Niebuhr,
who became increasingly attentive to ironic elements in U. S. history,
apparently did not.

> Niebuhr's reputation as a political commentator will always remained colored by
> the fact that he became a fixture of the liberal establishment in days when men
> of a reformist bent were, for the most part, genuinely persuaded that problems of
> social policy were settled in principle in America.   Retrospectively, their
> complacency is difficult to credit, and impossible to excuse. In Niebuhr's case,
> this lapse is doubly problematical, for it implicated him in the propounding of a
> variant on that heresy of American exceptionalism which he so vigorously
> condemned in old-line liberal-idealists (1975:178).

Merkley attributes Niebuhr's complacency in part to his attention to
world affairs. Whether or not one regards Niebuhr's belief that the
problem of justice had been solved in the United States as a mistake, and
however one attempts to explain that mistake, it is important to recognize
that Niebuhr's judgment represented no fundamental change in his basic
understanding of the justification of private property and free economic
institutions and the way those institutions are to be regulated in terms of
the principles of justice. Moreover, it should not be forgotten that Niebuhr
regarded such adjustments as ongoing matters given the dynamic character
of society and the provisional quality of human judgment. His confidence
that a relatively just equilibrium had been achieved in the late forties and
early fifties suggests no reason for confidence about these matters thirty
years later.

The Liberal Political World and the Church

Despite the critique he leveled at the liberal theory which has provided
the rationale for the basic institutions of the United States, Reinhold
Niebuhr came to believe that the practice of those institutions was superior
to their justification in liberal theory. For Niebuhr, the political culture of
the United States reflected the best insights Christian thinking had to offer.

He saw no need to develop a unique account of the church's responsibility in that culture, for there is no irreconcilable conflict between being a faithful Christian and being a full participant in the political institutions of the United States, according to Niebuhr. Indeed, Stanley Hauerwas may not go too far when he says that "America was his church" and that for Niebuhr "the subject of Christian ethics was America" (1985:31).

In the introduction, I distinguished three factors which deeply influence the way theologians draw the distinction between church and world, or three ways in which the distinction between church and world may be drawn. Each of those factors have implications for the church's distinctiveness in the world and for the posture toward the world which is regarded as appropriate for the church. The first factor is whether or not the same moral principles or values are regarded as valid for both church and world such that persons and institutions associated with each are held accountable to the same standards of conduct. The second has to do with whether or not the church represents a unique epistemological perspective which enables it to have moral knowledge which is unavailable to the world. The third has to do with the possibilities for the achievement of the norms and ideals which are regarded as valid. Even where church and world are regarded as knowing and being accountable to the same moral principles and rules, they may be distinguished with reference to the resources available to the church which enable living in conformity with those norms. In a general way, it is fair to say that Niebuhr draws no sharp distinction between church and world in any of these three ways. He regards the same norms as applying to both church and world. Moreover, both church and world are able to recognize those norms. Specifically, the norms which are regarded as relevant in the liberal framework and which liberals have derived from their understanding of human nature are not inconsistent with the ones which Niebuhr regards as applicable to Christians. Finally, Niebuhr does not regard the church as significantly more capable of the embodiment of what our nature requires than is the liberal world. This judgment that Niebuhr did not distinguish church from world in any of these three ways must be nuanced a bit if it is to be understood. Moreover, our appraisal of his judgment must consider whether or not there is such overlap between the Christian and liberal perspectives that the lack of a sharp distinction between church and world is justified.

My claim that Niebuhr saw no distinction between the norms that apply to the church and the world and no epistemological privilege or advantage for the church seems mistaken given the place that love had in his thought. As the law of life, love was, for Niebuhr, the single basic moral principle relevant to all human life. Surely the assignment of love to such a central place can only be derived from distinctly Christian convictions and cannot be regarded as valid universally. Recall, however, that Niebuhr regarded love as required by our human nature. "Love," he wrote, "is the final requirement of human relations, if the freedom of the persons who are involved in mutual relation be considered" (1941:294). It is "a basic requirement of existence" (1960:134). Thus, he regarded the identification of love as the fundamental moral principle to which all are held accountable to depend on no particular Christian convictions. Our nature requires that love be our fundamental moral guide. Thus Niebuhr draws no epistemological distinction between church and world—the basic norms of social ethics as derivable from human nature and accessible to all.

Surely Niebuhr overemphasized the degree to which the liberal reading of human nature and the norms which that nature required overlapped and was consistent with his own reading. Love plays no role in liberal political theory as I have described it. Moreover, as I have already suggested, Niebuhr's conception of love has a teleological character—it sees human life as directed toward a perfect relation of the self to God, to others, and to itself—that violates liberal neutrality. Even if liberal neutrality is limited, even if liberalism defends a thin theory of the good or has its own partial telos or its own conception of the minimal requirements of a good society, that limitation on liberal neutrality is in terms of a commitment to individual autonomy or liberty and not to a situation where interpersonal relations are ones in which "one individual penetrates imaginatively and sympathetically into the life of another" (1953:156). Surely it is not one in which an individual's proper relation to God is thought of as a fundamental aspect of human flourishing which liberal institutions must promote.

Even if we keep in mind Niebuhr's view that love was not immediately applicable to social and political life, but required the mediation of the principles of justice, we must still raise the question as to whether Niebuhr understood those principles the way liberals typically do. Niebuhr, like liberal theorists, understands liberty as justified because of the essential role that our capacity for autonomy plays in human selfhood. Niebuhr also shared with the liberal perspective the view that liberty justifies the political institutions associated with liberal democracy. Still, there were also important differences in his understanding of liberty having to do with Niebuhr's sense that not only individuals but also communities require liberty, and his sense that our freedom is the source of our universal sinfulness and therefore must be constrained in the name of order. And while Niebuhr's understanding of equality suggests that he shared with liberals the view that human beings all have a basic moral worth or dignity and are equal sources of basic moral claims upon each other, we must recall that equality is not understood by Niebuhr with reference to liberty—as for liberals, but rather with reference to that ultimate telos to which love directs us. Thus, the relationship of equality and liberty is fundamentally different in Niebuhr. For Niebuhr, the commitment to equality is limited by liberty in the sense that the recognition of the equal claims of all required by love is only in conformity with love when it is freely given. There are no limits to the equal claims another may make upon me, however. By way of contrast, in liberal thought, because equality is understood with reference to liberty—the equal claim that we make upon one another is respect for liberty—the positive assistance to others which justice may require is limited to that which is necessary for the exercise of their autonomy. There is no such built in limit to what equality requires for Niebuhr since the ultimate object is a perfect intimacy between the self and others.

Niebuhr does seem to have believed that the understanding of love as self-sacrifice depended upon uniquely Christian convictions. Recall that for Niebuhr, the inevitability and universality of human sin means that love requires "sacrificial abandonment of the claims of the self for the needs of the other" (1953:169). Every experience or achievement of the perfect harmony which love seeks depends upon self-sacrifice. He insists that such self-sacrifice cannot be "justified historically." It violates "standards of coherence and consistency" whereby "all claims . . . must be proportionately satisfied and related to each other harmoniously" (1943:69). Not only can self-sacrificial love not be justified historically, it "is not able to maintain itself in historical society" (1943:72). Jesus' life represents the highest expression of human nature and the highest moral achievement. His fate reveals that love is not triumphant in human history; rather it suffers. All of this suggests that Niebuhr does draw a tentative distinction between church and world at the level of moral principles and their discovery. Surely the identification and justification of self-sacrifice as a moral principle requires specifically Christian commitments. The world cannot be expected to know or be held accountable to this principle.

Yet, this possibility for a sharp distinction between church and world in Niebuhr's thought is mitigated by several factors. First, Niebuhr seems to have understood love as self-sacrifice as going beyond rather than contradicting the demands of justice which were identifiable by the world and which were in fact identified and institutionalized in liberal society. Secondly, Niebuhr regarded self-sacrifice as a critical principle which stood in judgment over all our efforts to achieve the ideal relation of self to others and to God and not as a principle which was to guide the conduct even of Christians in all aspects of life. Thirdly, Niebuhr did not regard a life of self-sacrifice, the style of life taught and modeled by Jesus, as possible even for Christians. Niebuhr wrote:

> The teachings of Christ have a rigor which points beyond simple historical possibilities. The ethical demands made by Jesus are incapable of fulfillment in the present existence of man. They proceed from a transcendent and divine unity

of essential reality, and their final fulfillment is possible only when God
transmutes the present chaos of this world into its final unity (1960:135).

Finally, not only is a life of love in conformity with the teachings of
Jesus seen as impossible, but to live according to that teaching would
render Christians ineffective and irresponsible in the realm of politics.
Those teachings may have fairly broad applicability to private personal
relations but in public or political life they are nearly useless. This can be
seen in Niebuhr's critique of pacifism. He regarded Christian pacifism
justified as a witness to the partiality of all historical embodiments of love
as orthodox. However, he refused to see pacifists as having a political
ethic. For Niebuhr, politics has to do with power and its exercise by
individuals and groups, and that power necessarily takes physical form (as
violence or coercion) from time to time. Politics is the art of organizing
power in such a way that a tolerable balance of power between competing
individuals and groups in a society is achieved and maintained (See
1943:256–259). Power is a perennial aspect of politics, according to
Niebuhr, because of two basic anthropological considerations:

> The one is the unity of vitality and reason, of body and soul. The other is the
> force of human sin, the persistent tendency to regard ourselves as more
> important than any one else and to view a common problem from the standpoint
> of our own interests (1943:258–259).

These "facts" of nature entail that power and its physical manifestations
are inescapable aspects of political life. The rejection of their use by an
individual or group implies, then, a withdrawal from politics and a
disavowal of responsibility for one's neighbor. In a sense, it is fair to say
that pacifism represents a refusal to do what love demands, given the fact
of human sinfulness.[31]
      In summary, Niebuhr draws no sharp distinction between the church
and the liberal world because he regards the fundamental principle which
is to guide our life in the world as rooted in a universal human nature
which is accessible to all. Identification of that principle and the mediating
principles of justice which make its embodiment possible under historical
conditions requires no uniquely Christian perspective or convictions. Self-
sacrificial love which enables the movement beyond the particular
historical accomplishments of justice and which leavens all such
accomplishments does depend upon such particular convictions, but it
does not serve as the basis for a sharp distinction between church and
world because:1) its requirements are seen as going beyond or above the
requirements of justice and not as contradicting them, 2) it serves more as
a critical rather than as a guiding principle for human life, 3) its fulfillment
is considered impossible even for the church, and 4) to live according to it

would render Christians ineffective and irresponsible in the public or political realms of life.

The third way that the distinction between church and world might be drawn is with reference to the church's greater potential for conforming its life to the principles, or achieving the ideals, which are regarded as valid for human life. It is possible to argue that the church is distinguished from the world in this way without committing oneself to a perfectionist conception of life in Christ or giving up a sense of the perennial influence of human sin even in the church. I suggested in the introduction that the question of the church's moral potential is often addressed in terms of the question of the relationship between Christian eschatological hope and the church's historical existence. Niebuhr's understanding of that relationship is consistent with his failure to draw a sharp distinction between church and world.

For Niebuhr, New Testament eschatology can only be seen as a symbolic expression of the tension between time and eternity, between human finitude and transcendence, and between the moral achievements that are possible for human beings in history and the hope for the perfection of our transcendent nature. Jesus separated "two facets of history's culmination" which had been united in the prophetic and apocalyptic traditions of Judaism, namely, the disclosure of "the hidden sovereignty of God" and its actual establishment. Thus, according to Jesus' understanding, history becomes an interim between the disclosure of that sovereignty which has already taken place in the life, death, and resurrection of Jesus and its establishment with his second coming. Niebuhr rejects both this literal or chronological understanding of the relationship between time and eternity and a "realized eschatology" which insists that the sovereignty of God is already established. This rejection is tied to his insistence that "sin is overcome in principle but not in fact. Love must continue to be suffering love rather than triumphant love." Jesus' erroneous belief, shared by Paul, that the establishment of the kingdom would come quickly derives from a failure to understand the relation of time and eternity.

> The *eschata* which represent the fulfillment and end of time in eternity are conceived literally and thereby made a point in time. The sense that the final fulfillment impinges on the present moment, the feeling of urgency in regard to anticipating this fulfillment, expresses itself in chronological terms and thereby becomes transmuted into a "proximate futurism," into the feeling that the fulfillment of history is chronologically imminent (1943:52).

The absolute demand of Jesus' ethic, according to Niebuhr, does not finally derive from his belief in the imminent establishment of the Kingdom of God, as Albert Schweitzer had argued. Rather, Jesus uncompromising ethic of sacrificial love conforms to the actual constitution of man and history, that is, to the transcendent freedom of man over the contingencies of nature and the necessities of time, so that only a final harmony of life with life in love can be the ultimate norm of his existence. Yet man's actual history is subject to contingency and necessity and is corrupted by his sinful efforts to escape and to deny his dependence and his involvement in finiteness. The idea that the time is short expresses Christianity's understanding that these limitations and corruptions of history are not finally normative for man (1943:51–52).

Niebuhr's understanding of Christian eschatology surely does not mean that Jesus' ethic and the Kingdom of God have no historical relevance—they always stand in judgment over human activity and exert an influence upon it. It does mean, however, that history is seen as having no particular direction, no story line. There is little or no sense of divine providence, no need for the discernment of how God might be acting in human history, and no sense that the church represents a community distinguished by its further progress along the path that God has in mind for human history.

Endnotes

[1] Daniel Williams probably goes too far when he says that "Niebuhr is never more blunt than he becomes when he criticizes theological ethics which try to keep the realm of law and social order sharply separated from the imperatives of the Gospel." He goes too far simply because Niebuhr is so often vitriolic that it is hard to say that he is more blunt in one circumstance rather than another. Nevertheless, he indicates correctly that Niebuhr must be declared "not guilty" to the charge of cynicism (1984:279–280).

[2] Niebuhr's own reflection on the development of his thought justifies both my focus on his work after *Nature and Destiny* and my judgement that his defense and appreciation of liberal institutions was on non-liberal grounds. In writing a brief "intellectual autobiography" and commenting on *Nature and Destiny* and the volumes which immediately followed, Niebuhr says: "The intellectual pilgrimage which [the works succeeding *Nature and Destiny*] reveal shows that I began to criticize liberal viewpoints from a Marxist perspective in the first instance, and that I learned gradually to subject both viewpoints to a Christian criticism" (1984:9–10). This statement suggests both that his thought reached its final stage with *Nature and Destiny* and that he did not regard himself as other than a critic of liberalism. This, of course, represents a denial of the appropriateness of Stone's fourth period: the period of pragmatic liberalism. I am not denying that Niebuhr came to regard the institutions generally associated with liberalism as important achievements. I am denying that his justification for these institutions were unambiguously liberal ones. Arthur Schlesinger seems also to have arrived at a conclusion similar to my own when he writes that "Niebuhr's method was to use 'conservative' arguments to make a stronger case for 'liberal' policies" (1984:221).

[3] There is a certain terminological ambiguity involved in Niebuhr's explanation of human nature which need not cause difficulties so long as one is aware of it. I refer to the fact that Niebuhr describes human nature as having two aspects, one creaturely,

the other spiritual. The creaturely aspect he associates with "nature" but *human* nature includes both aspects, that is to say, the human person has both a natural nature and a spiritual nature. I hope it is clear despite this confusion of terms that when I say that Niebuhr regards human beings as naturally social I mean to say that sociality is a part of or given with our creaturely aspect.

4 Conscience is, according to Niebuhr, a relatively indefinite or contentless "sense of obligation" (1932:37, and 1955:14). In *Moral Man and Immoral Society* Niebuhr said that conscience "does not give content to moral judgments" (1932:37). In *The Self and the Dramas of History*, he says that while "the content of conscience is obviously very relative to time and place . . . the minimal terms of our obligations to our neighbors . . . are fairly universal" (1955:14). We may defer for the moment the important question as to the degree to which Niebuhr regarded it as possible to derive universal moral norms from the universal aspects of human nature.

5 Paul Ramsey has written:

Readers of any of Niebuhr's books need not be reminded that he too believes that there is no explaining things by reference to a fixed and given human nature. Man is largely what he becomes; he isn't ready made at the first. There are no fixed structures of nature or reason or history which man does not transcend by virtue of his spiritual freedom. What Niebuhr actually objects to when he rejects the idea of natural law is the view ordinarily associated with it, that human nature conforms wholly to stable structures and nicely reposes within discoverable limits (1962:113).

6 See *The Nature and Destiny of Man*, Vol. 2, p. 287 for Niebuhr's discussion of *telos* and *finis* in history.

7 It is evident and has been commented upon extensively that Niebuhr focused almost exclusively on the sin of pride to the exclusion of sensuality. Feminist and liberationist critics have particularly noted this imbalance in Niebuhr's thought.

8 Ramsey has commented that Niebuhr's method for establishing this norm is a negative one, that is, it is by way of showing what is left as a norm for human nature after all the inappropriate understandings of the norms appropriate to human nature have been dismantled:

. . . [L]ove is the moral law for man, whose nature is what is indicated in Niebuhr's writings; and his way of pointing us to this conclusion is by showing that the natural moral law elaborated in the philosophies of naturalism, rationalism, and so on, fails and must fail to captivate and fulfill the special dimension of freedom in man's essential nature. Among the ruins of these systems love still stands as the relationship in life which was meant for man and for which man was intended (1962:114).

9 Davis and Good suggest that Niebuhr had a "scale of moral relativity" which descended from the universal and absolute "love ideal" through "absolute natural law, relative natural law, 'political principles,' positive or civil law, basic social structures and institutions, and finally the level of naked power conflicts"

(1960:166). Paul Ramsey has suggested that such distinctions are characteristic of traditional theories of natural law and that Niebuhr's own view is not as different from them as Niebuhr himself imagines (1962:122–131).

[10] Niebuhr also points to the "necessities of social cohesion and organic social life" as a reason why perfect equality is impossible in human history (1935:90). Our discussion of what this means will be deferred until we discuss his understanding of the role of structures of justice.

[11] Given the relationship which Niebuhr suggests between the interplay of various centers of vitality and power in society and human reason and conscience, one can say that where the power of one faction is met by the countervailing power of another such that a relative stalemate is achieved we are likely to see both groups coming to the rational or moral deduction that the claims of the other are valid. On the other hand, in the absence of such a balance of power, the dominant group is more likely to be satisfied with the rational and moral basis of its ignoring of the claims of the minority or powerless group. The oppressed group is more likely to see its oppressors as purely evil. Thus, the civil rights movement of the 1950's and 1960's organized black people in such a way that they were able to form a measure of countervailing force over against the dominant white community. They combined their physical power with spiritual or soul force, that is, moral and rational arguments against segregation. The result of bringing both types of force to bear against the dominant white power was that whites were able, rationally and morally, to come to the conclusion that the black claims were valid. Niebuhr's analysis suggests that the rational and moral conclusion of whites was influenced by the organized force of the minority group.

Of course, the recognition that the claims of black people were valid does not represent the highest moral possibility. To the degree that white relinquishment of power is motivated by a rational conclusion or a sense of moral obligation it is still not free. There is still an absence of the internal harmony of the soul which Niebuhr included in his concept of love.

[12] Niebuhr's discussion of the considerations which are required for an understanding of the possibilities of justice in human history and for the development of strategies for achieving a measure of justice make the complaint that Emil Brunner raised against him comprehensible. Brunner wrote:

> Brilliant as Reinhold Niebuhr is in his analysis of existing social conditions or of historical movements and cultural trends, this critical analysis seldom give rise to definite, concrete ethical postulates for social action. We who, in various ecumenical study groups, often marveled at the brilliance of his analyses, nevertheless noted time and again this deficiency between criticism and construction. And the reason for this is evident: the lack of an adequate concept of justice (1984:84–85).

Brunner's frustration is all the more comprehensible given the setting out of which it emerges. Niebuhr's understanding of justice does not provide a standard by which anyone may determine the relative justice of a particular situation and the necessary steps to take toward achieving a greater justice. Moreover, it suggests different obligations and responsibilities for those in different roles. For private actors it entails an obligation to be aware of the legitimacy of the claims of others and to diminish the sense of the moral weight of one's own claims. For the statesman or politician it suggests both a responsibility to manipulate the various vitalities in a society, such that a measure of order and balance is achieved, and a self-critical awareness that one may be a tool of particular interests or an independent instrument of tyranny.

[13] Niebuhr says that "every human community is both organism and artifact" (1955:163), meaning that there are elements that are outside the bounds of human consciousness and contrivance (the organic aspect) and those which are the product of human self-direction (the artificial aspect) We will consider Niebuhr's discussion of human community as organism and artifact in more detail when we look at his conception of government below.

[14] Daniel D. Williams contends that the liberal Christianity which Niebuhr described and criticized "is not to be found in this 'pure form' in the more adequate expressions of liberal theology." He does admit that it was accurate with regard to "much popular Christianity, and in the extreme views of a few theologians." He noted that Niebuhr was prone to exaggerate "what he regards as the essential tendency and outcome of all liberal faith." Yet Williams agrees that Niebuhr "exposes the heart of the issue about moral progress in history which is the central difficulty of liberalism" (1984:196–197).

[15] Niebuhr's criticism of the idea of a scientific politics also depends upon his view that the achievement of an disinterested, transcendent perspective is impossible (See 1960:43–63).

[16] In his interpretation and critique of modern theories of human nature in *The Nature and Destiny of Man* Niebuhr seldom refers to "liberalism." When he uses the term it is with reference to liberal Christianity. However, he does refer to both naturalistic and idealistic rationalism. Naturalistic rationalism attempts to understand human nature in terms of its place in the order of nature; human reason is capable of discovering that order. Idealistic rationalism emphasizes the order-creating capacity of human reason. These correspond roughly to the Lockean and Kantian versions of liberalism in my account.

[17] Of course, romanticism is regarded by Niebuhr as a protest against both naturalistic and rationalistic versions of liberalism. Romanticism is subject to the same criticism, however, to the degree that it too identifies fixed structures which determine and limit the possible expressions of human freedom.

[18] Niebuhr's justification of human freedom with reference to the transcendent aspect of human nature and his judgment that his conception of transcendence points to a radical freedom which liberalism did not recognize seems at first glance to give a wider place to individual liberty than even the most libertarian versions of liberalism. This only *seems* to be the case, of course. Niebuhr was especially critical of libertarian versions of liberalism. The apparently limitless range that Niebuhr allows to individual liberty in this paragraph is immediately taken away in the next where he begins to speak of the destructive possibilities of human vitality.

Moreover, Niebuhr regarded both liberty and equality as regulative principles of justice. Equality, as Niebuhr understands it, implies valid limits to the range of individual liberty which libertarian liberals would surely not accept.

[19] Niebuhr identifies rationalism with the Enlightenment in the previous paragraph and the Enlightenment, like the Renaissance, is regarded by Niebuhr as a part of the liberal heritage. Davis and Good seem to be correct in including the passage, which is taken from *Beyond Tragedy,* in the chapter on liberalism.

[20] Niebuhr regarded it as ironic that Marxism applied its awareness of the ideological taint of all human knowledge to every ideology but its own.

[21] Niebuhr's critique of natural law is twofold, it seems to me. First, human reason is unable to achieve an absolutely transcendent, disinterested perspective from which it is able to discover the universal principles of natural law. Secondly, because human self-transcendence includes transcendence over reason, and that self-transcendence is the source of the indeterminate human capacity for sin, the self is able to make reason the servant of its evil endeavors. Thus, Niebuhr criticized "both the Catholic and the liberal confidence in the dictates of the natural law" because "both fail to appreciate the perennial corruptions of interest and passion which are introduced into any historical definition of even the most ideal and abstract moral principles." He does note that the Enlightenment or liberal confidence in the reason of "common men" was greater than that of Catholic natural law theorists (1944:70).

[22]Despite Niebuhr's "realism" or "pessimism" about human nature he did not reach the authoritarian conclusions of such thoroughgoing pessimists as Luther and Hobbes. Although justice is no simple possibility, although human beings are capable of achieving no impartial perspective from which they can survey the whole field of claims and counterclaims and dispassionately apply universal principles of justice, we are able, because of our natural sociality and because love is the law of our essential being, to hear and respond to the claims of our fellows. We are able to recognize that they are owed a measure of liberty and worthy equal regard. It is this capacity for justice which, according to Niebuhr's well-known aphorism, makes democracy possible.

[23] Hume believed that most governments were in fact legitimate because they were regarded as such by their citizens. "[T]hough an appeal to general opinion may justly, in the speculative sciences of metaphysics, natural philosophy, or astronomy, be deemed unfair and inconclusive, yet in all questions with regard to morals, as well as criticism, there is really no other standard, by which any controversy can ever be decided" (1962:165).

[24] Niebuhr associates majesty with religious reverence for authority. It is justified on biblical grounds in terms of the idea that government is a divine ordinance made necessary by human sin (1944:267).

[25] One way to put the matter is to say that Niebuhr saw authority, both at the level of government and below it, as justified or legitimated as much or more by the destructive potential of individual liberty as by the need to protect its expression. If one were to base judgement entirely on what Niebuhr actually says in *The Children of*

Light and in *The Self and The Dramas of History,* one could say without reservation, it seems to me, that Niebuhr regarded authority as justified *more* by the destructive potential of individual liberty than by the need to protect it. Such a judgement might be misleading however, owing to the polemic nature of Niebuhr's writing. His concern to provide an alternative justification for democracy leads him to emphasize the differences between his account and liberalism. This should not obscure the fact that he too has a fundamental principle of liberty and regards it as a part of the justification of authority. To put the matter another way: the radical human potential for evil justifies authority, the radical human potential for good justifies the participation of all in the exercise and control of that authority.

[26] Niebuhr is speaking here about the insights of "later Calvinism" and, specifically, of Samuel Rutherford. He also praises Richard Hooker and Edmund Burke for understanding this balance between order and freedom.

[27] Among those who are guilty of missing this full complexity because of their disappointment at his rejection of socialism is John Cort (1988: 266–279). Michael Novak and John Cooper have misinterpreted Niebuhr in their haste to recruit him as a theorist of "democratic capitalism" (Novak, 1982:313–332; and Cooper, 1985:131–135). I find Merkley's discussion of Niebuhr's views on economics most accurate and helpful (1975:169–180). Merkley seems to recognize as others do not that Niebuhr's mature view represented a highly critical perspective on capitalism, even if socialism had been abandoned. Interestingly, Merkley regards Niebuhr's abandonment of the socialist label as a strategic move. In this he seems to be going too far, at least if socialism is defined as the social or governmental ownership of productive property. Niebuhr clearly abandoned that view.

[28] Niebuhr says it is "the primary mechanism for transmitting authority and privilege from generation to generation" (1955:183–184).

[29] Niebuhr recognized and utilized the distinction between personal and productive property. His view that large productive enterprises should be socially owned is not based solely upon that distinction, however. It seems that his flexible, pragmatic approach allows distinguishing between productive enterprises that are small enough that their ownership represents no significant accumulation of power and larger enterprise that threaten a balance of power because of the great power concentrated in them.

[30] This view that a just balance of power occurred in the U. S. "unconsciously" suggests Adam Smith's argument about the "invisible hand" working out a perfect economic equilibrium where individual economic relations are left free of government intervention. Niebuhr consistently denied the validity of Smith's "invisible hand." But what he denied within the confines of purely economic relations, he saw working at the level of the total equilibrium of all the forces, economic and otherwise, at work in a particular society. It should also be pointed out that just as he came to see democracy as conducive to the "accidental" achievement of a balance of power independent of the virtue of those persons who inhabited such a society, he also saw the value of having economic productivity depend upon self-interest.

3

Stanley Hauerwas:
Resident Aliens in the United States

FOR STANLEY HAUERWAS, the fundamental responsibility of the Church is to be the kind of community which makes possible a faithful telling of the story of Jesus through the developing of persons with the virtues necessary for that faithful telling. In a way unparalleled by almost any other contemporary Christian ethicist, he has consistently argued that the United States with its predominantly liberal political culture is a strange and inhospitable land for the Church; the United States provides a context which makes fulfilling the Church's fundamental responsibility a most difficult challenge.[1] Much of Hauerwas' work is dedicated to the task of convincing his theological colleagues and fellow Christians that the land in which we dwell is a foreign one, and that the story we have to tell will sound strange here. Not knowing that the land in which we dwell is inhospitable, that is, being seduced by its facade of tolerance, makes the danger of telling our story untruthfully all the more likely. Indeed, that we do not recognize the strangeness and inhospitality of our liberal world indicates that we have forgotten the true story we have to tell and made other stories normative for our lives as Christians.

The best of the church's teachers and interpreters in the United States have not regarded its liberal culture as an alien or inhospitable context for the church. As we have already seen, despite the critique he leveled at the liberal theory which has provided the rationale for the basic institutions of the United States, Reinhold Niebuhr believed that the practice of those institutions was superior to their justification in liberal theory. For Niebuhr, the political culture of the United States reflected the best insights Christian thinking had to offer. He saw no need to develop a unique account of the church's responsibility in that culture; there is no irreconcilable conflict between being a faithful Christian and being a full participant in the political institutions of the United States.[2]

In this Niebuhr was no different from the liberal Christians he criticized so vehemently. According to Hauerwas, this basic commitment continues to be shared by most North American theologians and church people, including such apparently disparate figures as the bureaucrats of the National Council of Churches and Jerry Falwell's Moral Majority.

All, he contends, share the conviction that the liberal democratic political culture of the United States represents, if not a "best possible" political expression of Christian convictions, at the very least a cordial framework within which Christians may faithfully express the social and political responsibilities that are theirs.   Almost all Christian ethicists and theologians in the United States "especially since the nineteenth century, have assumed that Christianity and democracy are integrally related" (1988:175).[3] The contemporary left and right on the Christian political spectrum, according to Hauerwas, have the "common goal of making American democracy as close as possible to a manifestation of God's kingdom" (1988:180).[4] Hauerwas' theological convictions compel him to stand outside this consensus.

There is an important sense in which it can be said that Hauerwas' insistence that the United States is a foreign land for the church is predicated on his view that the church is not at home anywhere this side of God's eschatological kingdom. Yet, it is also apparent that he regards a liberal political culture as particularly inhospitable to the church.[5] I hope to make evident why this is so. In so doing I believe it can also be shown why those who criticize Hauerwas for his reticence to speak on important matters of public policy, usually by employing the charge that he is a sectarian, have misunderstood his argument in important ways. Yet, as I will also demonstrate, there is an important sense in which the sectarian label is applicable. Hauerwas does call for the church to see itself as required to set itself over against the liberal culture of the United States.

The Narrative-Dependence of Ethics

Hauerwas' sharp critique of liberalism is grounded in his conviction that ethics is "narrative-dependent." This conviction includes three claims which entail that the liberal effort to provide an account of and justification for basic political and economic institutions is profoundly mistaken. The first is that there is no universal, non-contextual, epistemological and moral standpoint "above" the historical particularities in which all communities exist and from which all such communities develop the convictions that enable them to make sense (more or less) of their existence. In other words, to comprehend the moral convictions of a particular community, it is necessary to understand the life experiences in which those convictions emerged and the stories or narratives which that community uses to shape, remember, and pass on those experiences. The second claim related to the insistence that ethics is narrative-dependent is that moral agency and responsibility must be understood in terms of the concept of character. Hauerwas' understanding of character entails a dialectical relation between individual autonomy as self-direction and the way in which human beings are determined by the communities and histories of which they are a part. Finally, the narrative-dependence of ethics means for Hauerwas that moral notions are intelligible only with reference to the *telos* or end which a moral community envisions as worthy of its pursuit and worthy of pursuit by individuals within it. That is to say, all morality is dependent upon some conception of the good for human beings and the community.

Each of these claims contradicts fundamental elements of the liberal political enterprise. The first challenges those liberal theorists who attempt to offer a foundational account of justice or one which is universally valid. Even with reference to a somewhat more humble effort such as that of John Rawls (as it has been developed since the publication of *A Theory of Justice*—whether the later works represent a change in position or only the clarification of certain ambiguities in the book), Hauerwas' claim that all ethics is narrative-dependent, together with his interpretation of the ethical import of the Christian narrative, represents a challenge to the view that Christians have their own particular reasons for supporting a liberal conception of justice. The second claim challenges the moral relevance which liberalism attaches to the human capacity for autonomous self-direction. On Hauerwas' view, not only is it impossible to derive universally valid moral norms from that capacity, it is also a mistake to understand moral agency and responsibility with exclusive reference to it. The liberal emphasis on autonomy means that it fails to account for the importance of the development of virtue or the development of the self as virtuous.[6] The third claim represents a critique of liberal neutrality. On Hauerwas' view, all conceptions of justice depend upon some particular conception of the good. The liberal claim to discover valid principles of justice apart from some such conception is self-deceptive in that it obscures the conception of the good upon which even liberal justice is based. Each claim and the challenge it represents to liberalism will be considered in turn.

The Epistemological Question:
Hauerwas' Historicism vs. Liberal Foundationalism

According to Hauerwas, all moral knowledge is contextual; morality, he says, "is the ongoing experience and conversation of a people that enables them to have a history sufficient for community identity" (1981:100). There is no universal perspective from which to know ourselves or our world, no independent language in which convictions about ourselves and our world could be expressed, no such thing as a universal human nature to which human knowledge has access, no natural, universal moral norms upon which ethics can be founded. The beliefs, virtues, norms, and conceptions of the good which shape the moral life of a particular community are discovered in the process of living and are expressed in narratives which are the primary vehicle of their passage across time.[7] Moreover, as Harlan Beckley has described Hauerwas' view,

> Attempts to justify principles independent of particular histories mask, but cannot avoid, this narrative dependence. Moral philosophy which ignores this dependence cannot adequately see the moral significance of institutions and is deceived by believing that its principles are above history, controlling its direction and determining the character of a people. Ironically, such philosophy and the polity it supports produce people whose individualistic and ahistorical character binds them to their unacknowledged particular history (1981:298).

In Chapter I, we noted that the patriarchs of liberal theory attempted to discover a foundation for their commitment to the equal liberty of individuals and to the institutions which are regarded as necessary to the protection or expression of that liberty. That search for foundations has been an important feature of liberal theory from Locke, through Kant and Mill, and even in the work of some contemporary liberal theorists. Hauerwas recognizes liberalism's commitment to protect the individual capacity for self-direction. Moreover, he regards the liberal enterprise as a foundational one. He writes:

> In the most general terms I understand liberalism to be that impulse deriving from the Enlightenment project to free all people from the chains of their historical particularity in the name of freedom. As an epistemological position liberalism is the attempt to defend a foundationalism in order to free reason from being determined by any particularistic tradition (1985:18).

Thus, for Hauerwas, liberalism represents a paradigmatic example of foundationalism and, as such, a paradigmatic example of a moral theory which misunderstands the nature of the moral notions which shape human communities and by which human beings live their lives.

Gene Outka and Paul Nelson have noted a certain ambiguity in Hauerwas' early writing as to whether he intended to claim that all social ethics is narrative-dependent or only that Christian convictions require narrative display. Hauerwas has unambiguously made the more narrow claim. "The nature of Christian ethics is determined by the fact that Christian convictions take the form of a story, or perhaps better, a set of stories that constitutes a tradition, which in turn creates and forms a community" (1983:24). Even the traditional doctrines of the faith, such as the doctrines of creation, justification or the Trinity, for example, cannot be understood apart from the biblical and ecclesial stories. Doctrines, says Hauerwas, are "the outline of the story" or "tools to help us tell the story better" (1983:26). Outka notes that Hauerwas sometimes defends the claim about the narrative-dependence of Christian convictions apart from any appeal to the broader claim.

More importantly, he and Nelson point to Hauerwas' development of a "list of working criteria" for judging among stories, his acknowledgement that there are certain virtues common to every society or community, and his affirmation of the universalizability requirement in moral justification as expressing "the fundamental commitment to regard all [persons] as constituting a basic moral community" (1974:85, quoted by Outka 1980:118) as each calling into question his claim that all moral knowledge or all moral convictions are narrative-dependent. With reference to the list of criteria for judging the truthfulness of a narrative, Outka says that if the thesis about sheer narrative-dependence is valid, then the effort to devise a list of criteria for evaluation is "wasted." If all moral convictions are narrative-dependent, then the key terms in Hauerwas' list of criteria "find their context of intelligibility within particular and often irreducibly different narratives. Their meaning cannot, *ex hypothesi*, be univocal. How then can they ever serve as criteria for distinguishing good and bad stories" (1980:117)?[8] Moreover, says Outka, if universalizability is a requirement of moral justification, then "a 'natural' requirement is then binding even though it is independent of status, biography, commitments, beliefs, and so on, i. e., fundamental features of narrative" (1980:118).

While there may be some ambiguity in the execution of his argument, it seems to me beyond question that Hauerwas has intended to claim that "every social ethic involves a narrative" (1981:9). Moreover, he specifically rejects the view that Christian ethics is distinctive because of its dependence on narrative.[9] He consistently criticizes foundationalist moral theories as self-deceptive and as lacking an adequate moral psychology, that is, on grounds independent of the appropriateness of foundationalist accounts for making sense of Christian convictions (See 1981:94–101; 1983:11). While he has said that the belief "that we have a common creator provides a basis for some common experience and appeals" (1981:106), and that "Christian theology has a stake in a qualified epistemological realism" (1988:10), he does not regard these as undermining his fundamental critique of foundationalism. There may have been an element of ambiguity in Hauerwas' early thought which Outka and Nelson have correctly identified.[10] Even there, however, it is important to note that Hauerwas' recognition of certain common features in all morality does not undermine the view that he has intended to claim that all ethics, and not just Christian ethics, is narrative-dependent.

Consider for example his discussion of lying in *Vision and Virtue*. "[A] rule against lying," he wrote

might be institutionalized in a society to include all behavior except that
involving exchange of goods. The rule might be perfectly universalizable
carrying the content of its particular social setting but yet in terms of the
characterization of the practice of truth telling there would be no thought of
its application to the economic sphere. In other words, in such a society
the story associated with the rule not to lie is limited to specific personal
relations between men. The example suggests that a higher morality may
influence the form basic moral rules apply that are unspecified in the rule
itself. If that is the case, then clearly the basic morality is not independent
in either its form or its substance. One could change the story and thereby
change the rule (1974:87–88).

Hauerwas' comments suggest that he would not deny that there are
certain common features shared by all persons and societies, nor that the
morality of every society is concerned with "resolving the problem of
cooperation" which arises due to "limited human knowledge and
intelligence, limited resources for satisfying human needs and wants,
limited rationality, and limited sympathy for others" (Little and Twiss
1978:28, 27). Nor would he deny that every culture must deal with such
questions as truthful communication, the infliction of pain, killing, sexual
relations, reproduction, and the nurture of children. But to acknowledge
this is in no way to deny the narrative-dependence of ethics. For even if it
is the case that there are certain problems and concerns with which the
morality of every society must deal, and even it there are certain formal
features, such as universalizability, which all moralities share, attention
must still be directed to the particular history of that society, and to the
stories which that society tells about itself to make sense of its life in the
world, to understand how those concerns are dealt with.

Therefore, on Hauerwas' view, to claim that there are certain human
commonalities or that the cooperation and trust which makes society or
community possible requires a handling of certain common problems in
no way entails that those problems will be handled in similar ways or that
there is any universal rational perspective from which to determine *the*
right way such problems are to be handled. Moreover, it surely does not
entail that the problems of cultural conflict and pluralism within a society
can be resolved by appeal to universal human features embedded in
"nature" or "reason." For Hauerwas, solving such problems requires
attending to the narratives or stories which shape the particular moral
convictions of each group and discovering the resources that are present in
each culture or moral community for resolving conflict.

Paul Nelson's discussion initially acknowledges that there is a
circularity in Hauerwas' argument, a circularity which Hauerwas would
not deny. He notes that "Hauerwas himself seems to acknowledge the
narrative-dependent relativity of his criteria" for evaluating various stories
(1987:128). He properly cites Hauerwas' comment that "[t]he criteria for
judging among stories . . . will most probably not pass impartial

inspection. For the powers of recognition cannot be divorced from one's own capacity to recognize the good for humankind" (Hauerwas 1977:35; cited by Nelson 1987:128). Yet, he points to the phrase *the good for humankind* to suggest that some natural or universalist conception is indicated and "that there is in Hauerwas's position a submerged theory of something like natural law" (1987:128). I see no reason to interpret the reference to the good for humankind in this way. It seems perfectly logical to believe that Hauerwas intends for the substantive content of the good for humankind to be regarded as narrative-dependent in precisely the same way as other moral notions. Nelson provides no reason why this particular notion should be singled out as indicating a natural or universal norm with substantive content apart from a particular societal narrative.

Nelson's and Outka's comments suggest two ways of understanding the claim that all ethics is narrative dependent. It may mean that every complete system of morality, every moral system that shapes a particular culture, has narrative-dependent features which are essential for a proper understanding of that system. It may mean, more broadly, that every moral notion within each system of morality requires narrative display for its comprehension. Nelson seems willing to grant that Hauerwas makes the first claim unambiguously, but questions whether he has actually carried out a defense of the second one. If Hauerwas is interpreted as not defending the later claim, then, on his view "[t]here is no reason in principle why philosophers may not articulate universal features of morality such as universalizability or the requisites of social existence" (1987:129). But, if this is the way Nelson (and Outka) are suggesting that Hauerwas is to be read, they confuse the matter by distinguishing a claim that all ethics is narrative-dependent from one that says only that Christian convictions require narrative display. What their comments suggest is the distinction drawn at the beginning of this paragraph which indicates the possibility that every system of ethics requires narrative display for its comprehension, and that every system, including a Christian one, has elements which can be abstracted from the narrative and which are common to every system.[11]

While Hauerwas' early comments on universalizability suggest this possibility, the important point is that he regards liberalism's effort to establish principles and procedures of justice based on such abstracted common elements as a failure. It fails both for doing too much and too little. It does too much by giving a substantive content to those formal elements which different societies and communities may have in common, but which can only be fully understood by attending to the meaning attached to them by a society or community with reference to the particular historical project of that society or community (and of particular interests within it). It does too little by believing that a truly just society can be built on elements which are regarded as independent of the society's own historical narrative. The second and third basic elements of Hauerwas' claim that all ethics is narrative-dependent have to do with this way in which liberalism provides too sparse a conception of a just society. Even if Rawls' may be regarded as a non-foundational account, it is subject to the Hauerwasian critique. For the anthropological convictions built into his original position may not be shared by Christians, and they are not enough, according to Hauerwas, upon which to base a satisfactory theory of justice.

Of course, even if the acknowledgement of certain commonalities does not represent a denial of the claim that all social ethics is narrative-dependent, Hauerwas' position still faces profound challenges. If one acknowledges, as Hauerwas does, a stake in some version of "epistemological realism," which I take to be the recognition of the possibility of adjudicating between conflicting truth-claims, one must provide an account of the way in which such adjudication is possible. Outka and Nelson probably overestimate the significance of Hauerwas' development of lists of criteria for adjudicating between stories. Hauerwas would not deny, it seems to me, the element of circularity in those criteria. But the burden upon him is to show how to make the escape from that circularity which even a "qualified epistemological realism" seems to require. His denial of a foundational approach to adjudicating between conflicting moral claims entails the recognition "that there are often tragic and unbridgeable divisions between people." But such a recognition, he says, does not amount to a denial that "rational discourse and argument" are possible (1981:101). It must be admitted, however, that Hauerwas has not made it clear how he understands that possibility.[12]

While it is not clear how Hauerwas understands the process of rational discourse and argument which keeps the unbridgeable divisions between communities from becoming a Hobbesian war of all against all (at an intercommunal rather than interpersonal level, of course), it is clear that he regards a commitment to "peaceableness" as the crucial contribution that the Christian community has to make to the problem created by those divisions. Or, to put the matter another way, for Hauerwas, peaceableness—understood as the refusal to defend one's truth claims with violence, and as hospitality to the stranger and his strange stories and truth claims—represents an alternative to a foundationalist or even a Rawlsian strategy for maintaining peace and enabling cooperation among various communities. Our discussion of the role of Christian peaceableness in resolving the problem of moral relativism will be discussed more fully in the following section.

Narrative and Character:
the question of moral agency and responsibility

Hauerwas' attention was drawn to narrative as a way of making sense of human agency or intentional action. He says in the introduction to *The Peaceable Kingdom* that "the more I thought through the problem of describing intentional action, the more I was convinced that narrative was a crucial concept for displaying agency" (1983:xxv). What Hauerwas apparently believes narrative has enabled him to do is to provide an account of human agency that avoids reliance on the liberal idea of an autonomous or transcendental self which is able to choose his or her ends in independence from the histories and communities of which one is a part.

Hauerwas' early attempts to provide an account of agency in terms of character but without reference to narrative failed to avoid that reliance on a liberal conception of the self. Gene Outka has pointed out certain inconsistencies in Hauerwas' early work on the relation of character and agency. Those inconsistencies have to do with his reliance on the liberal language of autonomy in his effort to describe character. Outka notes that Hauerwas has claimed that persons "are in essence self-determining beings" and that to be a person "is to be an autonomous center of activity and the source of one's own determinations" (1975:18). Moreover, the concept of character is directly tied to this concept of personhood. "What lies 'at the center of the idea of character' is the fact that each person has the capacity to be an agent; and to believe that character is important is 'to be normatively committed to the idea that it is better . . . to shape than to be shaped'" (Outka 1980:111; quoting Hauerwas, 1975:17–18). Character is "that which we are and are responsible for, rather than just the product of social forces upon us" (Hauerwas 1975:103).

At the same time Hauerwas was claiming "the essential sociality of man's nature" and that "we are selves only because another self was first present with us" (1975:102). He also appealed to Iris Murdoch's conception of vision as an important corrective "to modern man's one-sided understanding of himself as actor and self-creator" (1974:30). Outka notes that Murdoch regarded her emphasis on vision as an attempt to correct modern Anglo-American moral philosophy's understanding of the person as "essentially and inescapably an *agent.*" Moreover, she recognized that the emphasis on vision results in "a different and lesser place to human freedom" (1980:114). Outka correctly notes that Hauerwas cannot have it both ways: he cannot define the concept of character or of human personhood in terms of "an autonomous center of activity," while at the same time affirming the sociality of human nature and an ethics of vision like Murdoch's.

Hauerwas quickly turned to narrative as a part of the solution to this problem, yet, on Outka's reading, his earliest appeals to the concept of narrative showed the same ambiguity.[13] While the appeal to narrative helped Hauerwas express his conviction that the self is a social or communal construction over time and not an autonomous entity characterized primarily by rationality, he still wanted to say that our having a character meant the capacity to assume responsibility for our actions and the stories which make those actions intelligible. Outka complains,

> We are never told how the second set of assertions is to be reconciled with the first. The account of the "I" is accordingly blurred, an "I" who is formed but yet adopts a given narrative, who requires some narrative and yet can ask "which narrative." Sometimes Hauerwas seems allied with those who grant that at any rate certain narratives for certain people can be oppressive. When oppression occurs, it is difficult to see what efficacy the question of "which narrative" can have. . . . At other times he appears to agree with those who insist that the agent *qua* agent possesses some *inherent* autonomy over against any narrative, inherited or not, that a "self" cannot survive as a self without some ability to reflect critically about particular narratively articulated traditions, that we cannot assume responsibility for owning our own actions apart from this ability (1980:116).

On Outka's reading, the appeal to narrative has failed to resolve the ambiguity of Hauerwas' earlier account of character, agency, and selfhood.

Hauerwas' later efforts tried to resolve that ambiguity by holding on to his conviction that we are essentially social and historical selves and by redefining agency, responsibility, and character in such a way that they do not depend exclusively upon an autonomous center of action. Rather, they are understood in terms of a dialectical relation between our capacity for autonomy and the way in which our selfhood is determined by the history and communities which shape us. In Hauerwas' mature view, agency, responsibility, and character are reconstructed in terms of a capacity to accept our actions as our own, to accept responsibility for them, even as they are determined by our pasts and our communities. Character does not mean being autonomously self-determining or being able to choose the stories that shape our lives from a perspective independent of a narrative. Rather, to have character is to have "a coherent sense of self" that enables the acceptance of our actions as our own even when we have not chosen them in perfectly autonomous fashion.

Having character means that the fact of our being socially and historically formed persons is "our destiny rather than our fate" (1981:123). I understand this somewhat ambiguous phrase (which Hauerwas gives several formulations) as indicating the following: Being persons who are socially and historically formed is an unbearable fate unless the narrative which shapes us enables the formation of a character which binds our past, present and future as persons such that our lives are given a meaning and direction which we can accept as our own. When we can accept that narrative as our own then the meaning and direction it gives is our destiny and we can claim responsibility for our actions.

Hauerwas is aware that his account of character makes freedom, agency, and responsibility problematic, particularly from a liberal perspective. He notes that what he calls the classical view has understood "being human" as "standing between nature and spirit, between finite limits and infinite possibilities." Moreover, that view has emphasized that it is the spiritual aspect which has been associated with our capacity to be "actors capable of forming a history," that is, to be free agents with moral responsibility (1983:35). It is evident that Hauerwas has in mind here a view like that of Reinhold Niebuhr. Hauerwas notes that his view, by way of contrast with the classical or Niebuhrian view, entails that our being historic beings means being shaped by a narrative and notes that

> this emphasis on the historic character of our existence seems to qualify in a decisive way what many assume is essential to our status as free beings. In their view our ability to be historic depends on our first having a freedom that always, at least in principle, guarantees our ability to step back from our engagements and thus is prior to our history. My insistence that our historic nature is prior to our being free seems to rule out the freedom necessary to claim our history as our own (1983:36).

Hauerwas is aware that his account of human selfhood entails a new conception of freedom, a freedom that does not depend upon our ability to make autonomous choices. Rather, Hauerwas argues that having character "is the source of our freedom" (1983:37).

But how can this be possible, Hauerwas asks? ". . . [I]f freedom is dependent on our character, then how did I acquire the freedom to acquire character in the first place? Surely I must first be free to develop my character as my own, hence the assumption that my freedom is a correlate of my character seems wildly mistaken" (1983:38). Hauerwas attempts to solve the problem by turning again to the question of agency. He insists that it is necessary "to understand the self fundamentally as agent" (1983:38), but argues that "it does not seem necessary to posit a self free from all determination. Agency encapsulates our sense that we are responsible for what we are" (1983:38–39). Or, "agency but names our ability to inhabit our character" (1983:40).

Again, Hauerwas insists that inhabiting our character does not require positing an autonomous or transcendental self. Such a view suggests that "our real identity is not our history, but the 'fundamental stance' or 'option'—that is, a stance by which we exercise that transcending kind of freedom in order to define ourselves as persons" (1983:41). My freedom and agency is not in the exercise of my capacity for autonomy because there is no self to exercise that capacity apart from the self as historically and communally shaped. Therefore, the freedom and agency which

makes me a responsible actor in history comes not by the making of
autonomous choices. Rather, I am free and responsible by the attention I
give to all that shapes me and the intention with which I act in that context
of circumstances beyond my control. Moreover, the primary exercise of
my agency is in describing what is going on and what I am doing.

> I am not an agent because I can "cause" certain things to happen, but
> because certain things that happen, whether through the result of my
> decision or not, can be made mine through my power of attention and
> intention. The "causation" proper to agents and their actions is not
> rendered by cause and effect, but by the agent's power of description. My
> act is not something I cause, as though it were external to me, but it is mine
> because I am able to "fit" it into my ongoing story. My power as an agent
> is therefore relative to the power of my descriptive ability. Yet that very
> ability is fundamentally a social skill, for we learn to describe through
> appropriating the narratives of the communities in which we find ourselves
> (1983:42).

Hauerwas' effort to redefine freedom and agency within the context of his
conception of ourselves as social and historic beings has come full circle.
For here our ability to act as agents, the way in which we inhabit our
character, is an act of description made possible by the narrative which is
given to me by the history and the community of which I am a part. Thus,
he can finally say, "we are not the creators of our character; rather, our
character is a gift from others which we learn to claim as our own by
recognizing it as a gift" (1983:45).

It cannot be said that Hauerwas' account of freedom and agency in
terms of the concept of character and the historic and social character of
human selfhood is totally satisfying. It is not clear that he has solved the
problem of freedom and agency which he recognizes his account of
human selfhood entails. Even if his account is not easily comprehended,
some comparative comments can be made about it, comments which
indicate the way in which it represents a critique of liberal efforts to make
sense of the conviction that we are free and responsible beings.

In the previous chapter, I distinguished between disagreements about
the degree to which we have a capacity to stand apart from the history and
the community which shapes us, and disagreements having to do with the
moral relevance of that capacity, to whatever degree it may be ours. I
argued that there is room within the liberal framework for disagreements
about the degree to which we are capable of autonomous self-direction.
To argue that that capacity is limited, as do both Reinhold Niebuhr and
Stanley Hauerwas, is not necessarily to challenge the liberal perspective.
What is fundamental to liberalism is not the fact that it believes that we
have such a capacity and a large measure of it. Rather what is fundamental
is the moral relevance that it assigns to that capacity. It is that capacity
which is the source of our moral worth as individuals and which makes us

a source of moral claims; it is what makes us free and responsible moral agents. The rights and the political institutions which liberalism defends and sees as morally justified are defended and justified because they protect and allow the expression of that capacity for self-direction. I showed that Reinhold Niebuhr regarded our capacity for autonomous self-direction as more limited than liberalism has generally thought. More importantly, Niebuhr saw that protecting and promoting individual autonomy was not an unambiguous good, for it promised to unleash indeterminate evil as well as good. As a result, he devoted greater attention to those historical and communal aspects which shape our lives and our moral beliefs and insisted that such factors make an important moral contribution by limiting the destructive expressions of our autonomy.

Similarly, the fundamental challenge that Hauerwas makes to liberalism has not to do with his sense that our capacity for autonomous self-direction is more limited than liberals have tended to think (though he surely believes that it is more limited) but with the fact that he does not see that capacity as determinative of our identity as human beings, nor as the source of our moral worth and dignity. In contradistinction to both liberalism and Niebuhr, he does not associate freedom with that capacity. Moreover, on his reading, protecting and allowing the widest possible expression of that capacity is no positive moral good, as it is for liberalism, nor does he seem to associate it with the highest human accomplishments, as even Niebuhr does. Hauerwas does not deny that we have any such capacity. If we were not capable of some degree of transcendence, it would make no sense to talk of freedom and responsibility at all. Nor would it make sense to speak of inhabiting our character or making it truly our own. The role that our capacity for autonomy plays for Hauerwas has to do with the fact that it makes possible our participation in a narrative and in the history of a community such that it is truly our history and our community. The ability to stand outside ourselves and our communities, to gain a momentary perspective outside our stories, does not make truly autonomous choice and action possible, but only makes possible our intentional participation in that process of keeping the community and its story going and in the process of describing what it is we are doing and where we are going. This last point could be put another way. Even if it were possible to act or to choose autonomously, such action and choice would not be worthy of the protection and enjoyment that liberalism gives it because it would only discourage the development of character which is necessary for the freedom and responsibility which is possible for us. To the degree that liberalism is successful in protecting and giving expression to our autonomy it has only made the freedom and agency that is possible for us more difficult to realize.

It is important to emphasize the term "participation" in the preceding paragraph. While it is not a term that I find prominent in Hauerwas' work, he does use it occasionally. It seems to me that he ought to use it more frequently and with greater intentionality in order to make clear that the perspective he is developing can avoid the totalitarian implications which could be drawn from his work. Hauerwas' view does not represent a denial of the dignity of the individual. Rather, it describes individual dignity in a way that is profoundly different from the way in which liberalism has understood it. For Hauerwas, our dignity comes not from our ability to autonomously direct our lives in absolute independence from the communities and histories which shape us. Indeed, we do not have such a degree of autonomy. A polity which respects our dignity is not one which acts as if we do and which sets up moral principles and institutions to protect it. In so doing, liberalism forgets

> that the most basic task of any polity is to offer its people a sense of participation in an adventure. For finally what we seek is not power, or security, or equality or even dignity, but a sense of worth gained from participation and contribution to a common adventure. Indeed, our "dignity" derives exactly from our sense of having played a part in such a story (1981:13).

What our transcendence allows us is the possibility of participation in an adventure, of playing a role or inhabiting a character which enables us to reshape the narrative which shapes us in our own retelling of it. A polity that respects us and gives us worth is one that enables our participation in this adventure; it is one that enables individual participation in the social process of self-creation or character formation, rather than one that allows a wide range of freedom for the expression of a self that is given apart from the social process in which self and community are formed and related.

The Teleological Character of Ethics

The conviction that all morality is narrative-dependent represents a critique both of liberalism's attempt to construct basic institutions on a foundation of universal moral principles (or upon a shared commitment to the autonomous self as the exclusive subject of justice) and of its normative account of the human capacity for autonomous self-direction. It is also a critique of the liberal argument that the basic principles of justice can be neutral with reference to particular conceptions of a good human life or a good community. For Hauerwas, when moral notions are provided the narrative display which is necessary if they are to be adequately understood, they are shown to be embedded in particular ways of life or particular manners of pursuing the goods of life. Thus, all moral notions have a teleological character. Just as Hauerwas regards liberal convictions as being a product of a particular historical enterprise, that is, as having and requiring a narrative (despite the pretension of some liberal theorists to the contrary), so also the liberal enterprise entails its own *telos* or its own conception of the good human life despite its claims to neutrality.

Moral notions, reason-giving, and vision. In a new introduction to *Character and the Christian Life,* Hauerwas wrote that "the underlying contention of this book is that the moral life, and in particular the Christian moral life, requires a teleological conception of human existence" (1985b:xxvii).[14] While that contention was not well-articulated in the book, it is suggested in an earlier collection of essays called *Vision and Virtue.* His conception of "moral notions" which is discussed there, as well as his arguments about the relation between thought and action and on the role of vision in the moral life all suggest the view that morality is a teleological enterprise.

In explaining what he means by moral notions, Hauerwas begins by noting the similarity between such concepts and strictly descriptive terms. Using the example of the descriptive concept "table," he points out "that it is impossible to simply perceive an object that is a table, for what we see are qualities given to our sense as hardness, smoothness, and the color of the object." But these have nothing to do with what we mean by table. "Rather the reason we have our notion of table is the need we have for tables that is embedded in our social conventions to sit, to eat on, or to place objects off the floor. . . . It is therefore our need for tables that determines what counts for some things to be tables while others are excluded" (1974:15). Even descriptive notions may be said to be teleological in the sense that what makes the objects that are described by such notions correspond to their description is the purposes for which we need such objects. Or, as Hauerwas says, "The formal element of our notions is but the recognition that we never simply know facts, but that we know them for some reason" (1974:16).

Moral notions share this formal feature with descriptive ones. The difference between them has to do with the "reason or the object" for grouping together "some of the significant and recurring configurations of relevant facts in our lives" as a single notion. Whereas descriptive notions have to do with our need to "identify" objects, moral notions have to do with "our need to avoid or promote, to excuse, blame, praise, or to judge and command" (1974:16). Obviously, such a need or purpose is an extremely thin or formal one which no liberal would deny. Hauerwas can even say that "our moral notions are in principle capable of being learned and understood by anyone, as their very meaningfulness is dependent on their 'grouping' aspects of our experience that we have in common" (1974:18). Once again this *suggests* the possibility of universal moral norms which are not narrative-dependent, but it is only a suggestion and

Hauerwas quickly denies this implication of his claim that moral notions depend upon common experiences. Immediately he adds that "it is only as our notions are needed in a way of life that they acquire meaning" (1974:18). So it is not just some universal need to avoid, blame, or judge certain behaviors and promote, praise, or command others in order to secure the basic cooperation that is necessary for a society to exist that gives meaning to our moral notions. It is only through their connection with a particular way of life that such notions come to have "meaning." He contends that theological ethics involves giving common moral notions a particular meaning in terms of "ideas about the world, man, and God" to which a religious community adheres (1974:28). Hauerwas' argument that meaningful moral notions are connected to particular ways of life suggests the teleological character of morality, for, by a way of life he seems to have in mind institutions and organized patterns of behavior that gain their coherence in terms of the goods towards which they are directed.

The same point is also suggested by Hauerwas' discussion of the relation between thought and action, or the relation between action and the reasons that we give in order to explain or justify our action. Hauerwas argues that "the relation between thought and action is not causal but necessary" (1974:80).

Our reasons for our actions are not the "cause" of our behavior; the cause and effect are separable events. From the agent's perspective, what I have done is not separable from the intention of my action including my motive. If I am asked what I am doing at this moment, I will respond that I am writing an essay and such description will not nor cannot be contingently related to my reason for acting since it is logically dependent on an accurate description of what I am doing. Put differently, the very condition of my being an agent is that the knowledge (reasons for) that I have of what I am doing is in fact what I am doing. My "reasons" do not "cause" me to act, but by embodying them I act to form the corresponding action.

This refusal to separate reason or motive from action, as cause is separated from effect, means for Hauerwas that religious or other convictions that entail certain ways of life as good or better than others cannot be meaningfully distinguished from moral notions. He denies that religion, for example, simply provides the motive for acting in ways that can be known to be morally appropriate independent of particular convictions, or that it provides a higher morality which goes beyond the minimal requirements that are necessary for a society.

Drawing upon a distinction between morality and ethics, or between lower and higher morality (the former term in each dyad referring to minimal, universalizable rules or modes of behavior necessary for society, and the latter having to do with a higher standard drawn from religious ideals, visions of the good, and various possible construals of the nature and meaning of existence), Hauerwas writes,

> understanding of religion and morality in terms of the separation between higher and lower morality is deficient, for religion can and does influence the form and substance of basic morality. . . . [N]o morality is sufficient for society life that merely aims at preventing evil. For every society must necessarily try to provide ways of encouraging men to do the good, to create institutions of basic trust, if that society is to survive. . . . For every society's basic morality (rather than minimal, for these are not the same thing) involves much that in principle must be considered essential to and part of the realm of the ethical (1974:89).

Again, what is suggested is that it is impossible to distinguish some basic level of morality from a fuller conception which includes a conception of the good. Even bare survival, Hauerwas claims here, depends upon structuring basic moral institutions in terms of a conception of the good.

Hauerwas' emphasis on "the significance of vision" also reflects his conviction that all ethics is teleological in character, for precisely what moral vision attempts to bring into focus, he insists, is the human good. We have already seen that Hauerwas regards the emphasis on vision in the moral life as providing "an important corrective" to what he calls the image of "man the maker" and the emphasis on human will and action in liberal moral theory. That emphasis has lead liberalism to regard whatever is valuable or good as being so by virtue of its having been chosen by autonomous individuals. Or, in Hauerwas' words, "value is no longer given reality apart from man's willing of it. Man is thus conceived to be as free as he chooses, creating his values in relation to an empirical world he can easily comprehend" (1974:33).

By contrast, Hauerwas insists that "morality is made up not only of [man's] choices but of his vision" (1974:35). While it is clear that the metaphor of vision is meant to undermine the liberal emphasis on choice and its sense, based on liberalism's neutrality or its skepticism with reference to the good, that value or the good is subjective, the status of the good in the reality on which our attention is focused is not evident. Hauerwas insists that emphasis on vision reflects a conviction that "the moral life cannot be divorced from the substance of the world." "The ethics of vision" he says "is therefore the ethics of realism." Yet, reality does not present itself to us with a prior order or coherence "which can give meaning to our lives." Therefore, "the Good is undefinable" and learning "to see the world as it is" is a "strenuous moral task" that "can never be finished" (1974:36–7).

Love, in the framework of this emphasis on vision and the indeterminacy (but not subjectivity) of the good, is understood as a constant attention to the reality of the world, including the reality of other selves. Love is a form of "unselfing"; it is "any relationship through which we are called from our own self-involvement to appreciate the self-reality that transcends us" (1974:39). Freedom is also understood in this context in terms of our attention to reality. Freedom is "not the ability to have our way or to assert our will in an efficacious way. Rather, it is the disciplined overcoming of the self that allows for the clarification of our vision; to be free is to exist sanely without fear, to perceive what is real" (1974:40). Thus, love and freedom are intimately related, for it is love which enables us to "recognize and respect" reality, particularly the reality of other selves.

For Hauerwas, then, the moral life is primarily a matter of vision, a matter of learning to see reality as it is, to find value outside ourselves. But, because this value or this objective Good does not present itself to us in a coherent order but as "unrepeatable particularity" (1974:38), the envisioning of the good, or the discovery of the good, seems also to be partly a matter of human creativity, though it is not a matter of the creativity of an autonomous self. Through language reality is provided coherence, but language is clearly a public or corporate enterprise. Moreover, that reality presents itself in its particularity and without prior order means that the moral life is always an "adventure."[15] This metaphor suggests that the moral life is subject to false starts and grave risks and that its goal is not the realization of some final good which is known *a priori*. Rather, the moral life requires becoming the kind of person who is ever open to the possibilities of discovery and of fulfillment that reality in all its particularity and contingency presents to us.

Hauerwas' argument that the reality on which our attention must be focused does not present us with the good as some *a priori* value is surely consistent with his assault upon foundational ethics. It reminds us that a teleological conception can be as "guilty" of foundationalism as can liberalism, given the latter's skepticism about the possibility of common discovery of a common telos for our lives together. Hauerwas' perspective represents a denial of the view often associated with Roman Catholic theories of natural law that the human telos is written into human nature. This means that Hauerwas' conception cannot result in the authoritarianism which is often associated with ethical theories that are both foundational and teleological. In Hauerwas' conception there is no room for the view that authority can be legitimately exercised over persons on the basis of some *a priori* conception of the good for human persons. For, on Hauerwas' view, the attention to the reality of other persons which the emphasis on vision entails means that every person must be a part of the envisioning process or the conversation by which the good is discovered.

Teleology, the Common Good, and Justice. As I have already suggested, for Hauerwas, the discovery of the good is not an endeavor of the autonomous individual; rather, it is a corporate or communal endeavor.

Moreover, the good that is discovered communally is a good held in common by that community of discovery. That is to say, for Hauerwas, both the process of discovery and the good so discovered are common. Hauerwas' conception of the common good is related to his view that the human selfhood is "socially constituted." He writes:

> The common good represents that good of society beyond the individual or group interests that may happen to comprise it in fact. The common good is not simply the sum of individual or group interests, but it is genuinely a good that is common. Implied in this idea is a view of man that sees man as essentially social—not just descriptively, but normatively. We are not individuals who come to the social order to get what we can from it, but rather in being fully individuals we must be socially constituted (1974:236).

On the basis of his belief that we are socially constituted beings and his appeal to the common good, Hauerwas can say our liberal society "lacks the means to generate an intelligible account of justice." It is an "illusion" to believe "that the larger social order knows what it is talking about when it calls for justice" (1986a:15). He explicitly connects our society's ignorance about justice to its belief that justice can be a neutral concept. He says,

> We live in a society that assumes that there are not, nor can there be, any agreed upon accounts of what goods we ought to hold in common. Nor can we agree about the kind of people we ought to be. . . . In such a society justice necessarily becomes the overriding norm of social practice. For justice seems to suggest what is minimally necessary to hold such societies together in a reasonable harmony. In short, justice is the name for the procedural rules necessary to secure enough fair play so that everyone will be able to pursue their private goods. Which may explain why the primary good most theories of justice are now said to distribute is liberty, and in particular, liberty of the individual (1986a:14).

While the general framework of Hauerwas' disagreement with liberal justice is evident, he has not articulated a full critique of it, nor has he provided an alternative conception that can generate guidance on what policies and programs are worthy of support. I regard Hauerwas' contention that the idea of the common good implies the essentially sociality of man, or that individuals are socially constituted, as being in fundamental agreement with the much more developed critique of liberal justice presented by Michael Sandel. It seems to me that the implications of Sandel's arguments are also applicable to Hauerwas.

Sandel's critique of liberal justice is focused on the liberal conception of human selfhood which he believes is entailed by John Rawls' theory of justice. He argues that Rawls' description of the original position, with its veil of ignorance, reflects a particular conception of the self or of the human person. Sandel points to two features of the Rawlsian conception of the self as fundamental: the idea that the self is plural, and the idea of the self as a subject of possession. The plurality of the self means that individual persons are distinct from one another; they can be differentiated. Moreover, there is a particular way of differentiating them or telling them apart, a "principle of individuation." "For Rawls, our individuating characteristics are given empirically, by the distinctive concatenation of wants and desires, aims and attributes, purposes and ends that come to characterize human beings in their particularity" (1982:51). This way of conceiving how selves are distinguished or individuated means that the self is "a subject whose identity is given independently of the things I have, independently, that is, of my interests and ends and my relations with others" (1982:55). But, according to Sandel, Rawls not only wants to distinguish human selves from their ends and traits, but also show how they are related, and the key to understanding that relationship is the idea of "the self as a subject of possession." As subject of possession, the self continues to be distinguished from the ends and traits it possesses; they are "*mine* rather than *me*" (1982:55). The self is related to those ends in that it *chooses* them; they belong to the self by an act of will. Therefore, in Rawls' complete view of the self, "the self is distinguished from its ends—it stands beyond them, at a distance, with a certain priority—but also related to its ends, as willing subject to the objects of choice" (1982:59).

Sandel contends that Rawls' view is individualistic in a fundamental way that goes beyond psychology or moral motivation. The idea that a person is "a subject of possession, individuated in advance and given prior to its ends" (1982:59), in no way implies that persons are motivated only by self-interest, nor does it "bias the choice of principles in favor of individualistic at the expense of communitarian ones" (1982:61). The Rawlsian self might have such values and this is not what his conception of the self makes impossible. Possible values or conceptions of the good are not what is determined in advance by Rawl's notion of the original position; it would not be a neutral conception if they were. Rather, "the bounds of the self are fixed in advance." What Rawls' view precludes is the possibility that the self might be understood in terms of its ends or as constituted by those ends. If I am as Rawls conceives me, says Sandel,

> No commitment could grip me so deeply that I could not understand myself without it. No transformation of life purposes and plans could be so unsettling as to disrupt the contours of my identity. No project could be so essential that turning away from it would call into question the person I am (1982:62).

What is ruled out, says Sandel, is that my identity might be inseparable from the communities of which I am a part and the socially discovered conceptions of the good shared by those communities. It precludes what Sandel calls a "constitutive conception of community," in which

> community describes not just what [I] have [with my] fellow citizens but also what [I am], not a relationship [I] choose (as a voluntary association) but an attachment [I] discover, not merely an attribute but a constituent of [my] identity   (1982:150).

Sandel's claim is that Rawls' conception of the self is inadequate, that in fact our loyalties and allegiances to a particular family, a community, a nation, and a people are constitutive of our identity. There is no self that can be understood apart from the ends it seeks and the traits it possesses, no self that autonomously chooses certain values. Rather, we find ourselves as parts of various communities in which certain ends are valued and pursued; our identity, our sense of self, is inseparable from those communities and those ends. This is not to suggest that we are incapable of achieving some critical distance from our communities and their conceptions of the good. That capacity is limited, however. Moreover, to see ourselves as Rawls does is to deprive ourselves of the capacity for freedom and rationality which is actually ours. It is to imagine ourselves "wholly without character, without moral depth."

> For to have character is to know that I move in a history I neither summon nor command, which carries consequences none the less for my choices and conduct. It draws me closer to some and more distant from others; it makes some aims more appropriate, others less so. As a self-interpreting being, I am able to reflect on my history and in this sense to distance myself from it, but the distance is always precarious and provisional, the point of reflection never finally secure outside the history itself. A person with character thus knows that he is implicated in various ways even as he reflects, and feels the moral weight of what he knows   (1982:179).

For Sandel, then, a conception of justice such as the liberal one, which regards the individual capacity for autonomy as the essential or defining characteristic of the human self, or as that aspect which merits nearly exclusive respect, is deficient. Because the individual capacity for autonomy over against the communities and the history which constitute it as a self is limited, there there can be no Archimedean point of view from which to derive universally valid principles of justice. Even if Rawls' theory is interpreted as merely reflecting the convictions about the freedom and equality of the self shared by the various full moral theories in a modern liberal society, Sandel's attack is significant. For it questions the validity of those shared convictions.[16] If the human self is constituted in part by the goods it pursues and by the communities in which such goods are identified and realized, then there can be no conception of justice which seeks to respect human persons which is not teleological in character; a conception of justice which takes into account the nature of human selfhood and respects that selfhood cannot be neutral.

From the perspective of those, like Sandel and Hauerwas, who regard the self as socially constituted, the liberal conception of justice is profoundly inadequate. If we are in fact in large measure situated selves or selves whose character is the gift of a narrative we share with others, if we are persons whose ends and loyalties are constitutive of our identities (though not absolutely determinative), then justice as liberalism conceives it cannot be the only nor even the primary standard by which basic political institutions are to be judged. This is so for two primary reasons. First, making such a conception of justice primary, depending as it does on viewing ourselves as given prior to and independent of our ends and loyalties, threatens the capacity for autonomous agency which *is* possible for us.[17]   Moreover, seeing ourselves as unencumbered and making justice primary on that basis prevents conceiving of the possibility of the discovery of some shared or common good. If our conceptions of the good are largely constitutive of our identity, and such conceptions are socially constructed and discovered, then allowing political institutions to be guided by the goods we discover in common represents no violation of the self, no oppression, no injustice. Sandel recognizes the limits of the idea of the common good and the importance of liberal justice. "Justice finds its occasion because we cannot know each other, or our ends, well enough to govern by the common good alone. This condition is not likely to fade altogether, and so long as it does not, justice will be necessary." But to have political institutions determined entirely by liberal justice is to leave them impoverished. It overlooks "the possibility that when politics goes well, we can know a good in common that we cannot know alone" (1982:183). Another way of putting the matter is that if we are socially constituted selves, the alternative is not liberal neutrality or the autocratic use of government authority to impose the good of the few on reluctant others, as Rawls suggests. There exists a third possibility: politics understood as a process whereby the goods we hold in common are discovered. Politics as a discovery of who we are.

Of course, Hauerwas does not accept the liberal claim that it is neutral. It is self-deceived in this respect.[18] In fact, liberal justice, like any other conception of justice, depends upon a conception of the good. Hauerwas' definition of liberalism reveals what he regards this operative teleology of liberalism to be. He regards liberalism as

> that impulse deriving from the Enlightenment project to free all people from the chains of their historical particularity in the name of freedom. As an epistemological position liberalism is the attempt to defend a foundationalism in order to free reason from being determined by any particularistic tradition. Politically liberalism makes the individual the

supreme unit of society, thus making the political task the securing of cooperation between arbitrary units of desire (1985a:18).

On this view, the telos of liberalism is the autonomous individual with which it begins. The goal of liberalism is to allow the widest possible expression to the individual capacity for autonomy as self-direction. It is to set individual persons free from any restraints upon them which are unnecessary for the protection of the equal liberty of other persons. For communitarian critics of liberalism, like Sandel and Hauerwas, such a conception of the human telos results in a society which destroys the bonds of community, and by so doing is unsatisfying to individuals because it destroys those bonds which make the discovery and realization of our good possible. It also results in an ungovernable society in which a public policy response to important crises is impossible.[19] For Hauerwas, it means that liberals fail to comprehend the moral significance of such important human activities as getting married and having children.[20] Moreover, "in the absence of an [adequate] account of the good, individuals are led to believe all their needs are legitimate. Justice thus construed leads to efforts to create societies which are free of constraints upon the needs of its members" (1986a:14).

Another theme in Hauerwas' critique of liberal justice merits brief attention: the alternative conception of authority which a teleological conception of justice implies. For Hauerwas, liberals fail to understand the basis of authority within certain ordinary human practices and in society as a whole. Authority, he says, is justified not because the one under authority has consented but because the one having authority has particular skills which are necessary for realizing the goods which both share. Moreover, in contrast to either an Augustinian or liberal realism which regards authority as necessary because of human sin, a tradition within which Reinhold Niebuhr clearly stands, Hauerwas follows Yves Simon in regarding authority as necessary because of the plurality of goods and the plurality of means for achieving those goods.

Simon contends that authority originates in the plenitude of human purposes, rather than in the deficiency of human nature. . . . Simon contends human nature is social exactly because community provides the means whereby the many goods people rightly desire can be actualized. Consequently, there should be a plurality of means in the pursuit of a community's common good. Indeed, the pursuit, or the conversation necessary for that pursuit, is in many ways the common good. For any conversation to occur a plurality is required, as well as a sufficient method of steadily procuring union of action. Authority, therefore, is exactly that power which allows unified common action for the achievement of the common good (1985a:44).

Christian Peaceableness

Hauerwas' insistence that all ethics is narrative-dependent means that Christian ethical convictions, and the convictions of every community, are distinctive. Those convictions can only be understood with reference to the historical experience of that community and the narratives or stories which it tells as a way of giving its life a coherence which stretches from the past and into the future. Moreover, despite certain common types of human experience and certain formal elements which all ethical systems may share, it is impossible to discover basic moral principles the content of which is independent of the particular historical narrative of some community and which, as a result of their universal validity, are valid for adjudicating between the conflicting claims of various communities and for establishing valid terms of cooperation between them. Such an effort is particularly invalid if the terms of cooperation are understood as neutral with reference to the question of a good human life or a good human community. Since all moral notions reflect both the historical experience of the community in which they are held to be valid, and its own conception of what constitutes a worthy end for human beings and human societies, the terms of cooperation in a liberal society lack both the universal validity and the neutrality which liberal theorists claim for them. A society living on such terms will tend to undermine the ethical system and forms of life of the smaller communities which make it up and it will do so because of its preference for a human telos that emphasizes autonomous individual choice.

As was indicated above, Hauerwas does claim to have a stake in some version of "epistemological realism." I interpreted that stake to entail a recognition of the possibility of adjudicating between conflicting truth claims. Or, to put the matter another way, while Hauerwas' view certainly entails an element of ethical relativism, he does not regard that relativism as vicious. On the epistemological level, he believes that it is possible to make truth claims that one regards as universally valid and it is possible for such claims to be evaluated, though not with absolute certainty, but only provisionally. On the practical level, Hauerwas does not believe that his rejection of the liberal approach to dealing with moral disagreement and moral relativism[21] means that social cooperation between communities is impossible, or, that in the absence of a foundation for determining valid terms of cooperation, relations between communities can only be competitive or even violent. The alternative to foundationalism is not chaos and civil war.

Because there is no universally valid set of moral principles accessible from the perspective of an autonomous self (that is, there is no autonomous sense of justice), the particular narrative which shapes the Christian community and provides its identity and character is the unique source of moral authority for that community. It is to Hauerwas' reading of that narrative, and the moral guidance it provides for the Christian community, to which we now turn. Our particular concern will be to show the way in which Hauerwas' understanding of the Christian moral life represents it as alternative to the liberal strategy for dealing with the plurality of human communities and conceptions of the good. A key for understanding Hauerwas' critique of liberalism, and the ardor with which he has waged that critique, is to recognize that he sees both liberal and Christian ethics as entailing methods for dealing with the relativism of moral convictions which both recognize. Those methods are, on his reading, contradictory (in part because they define the problem of relativism differently). Thus, Christian use of liberal arguments and methods represents a profound loss of integrity. It means accepting norms of conduct or terms of cooperation which are derived from a story other than the Christian story, and which are valid in terms of a particular conception of the good which is different from the Christian conception.

Peaceableness as the hallmark of the Christian life

For Hauerwas, "peaceableness" is "the hallmark of the Christian life" (1983:xvii), and "peacemaking" or "peace keeping" is a virtue "intrinsic to the nature of the church" (1988:95). Hauerwas identifies himself as a pacifist but seems to prefer the alternative terms used above in order to guard against interpreting his view as legalistic, and because of his recognition that not all Christian ethics has rejected violence as he does.[22] What Hauerwas endeavors to show is how living peacefully with others is related to central Christian convictions about the Lordship of Jesus, the presence and reality of the Kingdom of God, and the forgiveness and reconciliation which has been accomplished in the life of the one who made that Kingdom present and real. Moreover, having a narrative which enables a people to live together peaceably as forgiven and forgiving people means that developing character is possible. Peaceableness and character are central to Hauerwas' solution to the problem of relativism. A narrative is regarded as true to the degree that it can give the gift of character and to the degree that it regards violence as inappropriate in order to protect itself and its truth-claims.

Peaceableness and the Authority of Jesus. Living peaceably is not justified primarily because it makes character possible and solves the problem of relativism, however. Living peacefully is justified for Christians because it is the way Jesus lived and the way he taught. That matters because Christians believe that through Jesus and their own incorporation into his story they have come to know the truth about themselves, the world, and God. On Hauerwas' account of the Christian faith, Jesus is the sole authoritative norm for the church, and Christian ethical reflection must begin with Jesus as we meet him in the scriptural narrative. Indeed, the church for Hauerwas is the community formed by that narrative and the man to which the narrative (and the church) bears witness.   The story of Jesus forms a canon within the canon of the Christian narrative. The rest of the narrative, both the biblical narrative of Israel and the early Church and the narrative of the Church over the intervening centuries, is interpreted as a story of faithfulness or deviation from the norm of Jesus' own life. Because there is no transcendent universal or natural foundation which stands alongside Jesus as authoritative or in terms of which Jesus must be understood, Hauerwas can say that, "[i]f we have a 'foundation,' it is the story of Christ. 'For no other foundation can anyone lay than that which is laid, which is Jesus Christ' (I Cor. 3:11)" (1983:67).

Hauerwas rejects any distinction between the "Jesus of history" and the "Christ of faith," and the conclusion of modern biblical scholarship that it is impossible to know anything about Jesus from the scriptural narrative that is not already shaped by faith in him does not bother Hauerwas or undermine his insistence that Jesus of Nazareth is uniquely and solely authoritative for the church.

> The historical fact that we only learn who Jesus is as he is reflected through the eyes of his followers, a fact that has driven many to despair because it seems they cannot know the real Jesus, in fact is a theological necessity. For the "real Jesus" did not come to leave us unchanged, but rather to transform us to be worthy members of the community of the new age (1983:73).

Moreover, Hauerwas rejects a Christology that begins with claims about Jesus' ontological status or a Christological ethics that is rooted in anything other than the story of his life. He writes: "It is a startling fact, so obvious that its significance is missed time and time again, that when the early Christians began to witness to the significance of Jesus for their lives they necessarily resorted to a telling of his life" (1983:73).[23]

Peaceableness and the Eschatological Kingdom. For Hauerwas, then, the story of Jesus in scripture can be the church's unique authority because there is no universal perspective from which Jesus can or must be interpreted.   Hauerwas seems to assume that there is no great hermeneutical problem that makes understanding the Jesus story difficult. Moreover, the Jesus story has direct "ethical significance" for Hauerwas because the forgiving, peaceable, and "out of control" way of life he lived and taught is a "present possibility" for the church. Hauerwas is perfectly willing to acknowledge that the kingdom which Jesus proclaimed was an eschatological one, and that his ethic is eschatological. This does not mean, however, that the example of Jesus or his teachings are an unrealizable ideal impossible to fulfill and not meant for perfect embodiment in the world which is not the kingdom.[24] The ethic of Jesus is not an ideal in this sense because "the very announcement of the reality of the kingdom, its presence here and now, is embodied in his life."

> In him we see that living a life of forgiveness and peace is not an impossible ideal but an opportunity now present. Thus Jesus' life is integral to the meaning, content, and possibility of the kingdom. For the announcement of the reality of this kingdom, of the possibility of living a life of forgiveness and peace with one's enemies, is based on our confidence that that kingdom has become a reality through the life and work of this man, Jesus of Nazareth. His life is the life of the end—this is the way the world is meant to be—and thus those who follow him become a people of the last times, the people of the new age (1983:85).

The world's rejection of Jesus and its continuing violence make it evident that the kingdom's reality has not yet negated the world's reality. Thus, one would expect to find a temporally expressed tension between the kingdom's present reality in and through the life of Jesus and the community he formed and its future fulfillment at the end of time.[25] But Hauerwas does not speak of a tension between the kingdom's already and its not yet or of the tension between church and world in temporal terms. The "not yet" aspect of Christian hope is swallowed up by the "already" of the kingdom's establishment in Christ's resurrection. It is striking that Hauerwas seems consciously to have avoided the future tense in speaking of the kingdom of God. His constant theme is that Jesus, through his life, death, and resurrection, has made the life of peace a "present possibility." Though the resurrection of Jesus is "a decisive eschatological act," it does not simply establish some future possibility. Rather, through it "we see God's peace as a present reality."

> Though we continue to live in a time when the world does not dwell in peace, when the wolf cannot dwell with the lamb and a child cannot play over the hole of the asp, we believe nonetheless that peace has been made possible by the resurrection. Through this crucified but resurrected savior we see that God offers to all the possibility of living in peace by the power of forgiveness (1983:88–89).[26]

Hauerwas can go so far as to say "the kingdom has been established" (1985a:165),[27] and that Christians believe "that history has already come out right" (1985a:166). Thus, for Hauerwas, the tension is not between present and future, but between the church, the people for whom the kingdom of God is a present reality in Jesus, and the world which knows neither Jesus nor his kingdom.

Finally then, being a follower of Jesus means learning to be *like* him, as he is shown to be in the gospel narratives of his life, particularly the story of his cross.[28]

[T]hat likeness is of a very specific nature. It involves seeing in his cross the summary of his whole life. Thus to be like Jesus is to join him in the journey through which we are trained to be a people capable of claiming citizenship in God's kingdom of nonviolent love—a love that would overcome the power of this world, not through coercion and force, but though the power of this one man's death (1985a:76).

The responsibility to be like Jesus is not mitigated by the fact that the world is not the kingdom. The church is to be "a transformed people capable of living peaceably in a violent world" (1985a:83). Of course, it is our eschatological perspective, the belief that we have seen the end, that the kingdom is already established, that makes such a way of life possible. "We believe that history has already come out right and just because it has we can take the time in a world threatened by its own pretensions of control to seek patiently a truthful peace" (1985a:166).

Hauerwas cannot completely escape anticipatory language even as he talks of the kingdom's already being established as the basis for the possibility of living like Jesus.[29] Yet, what is most noteworthy is that he applies the language of anticipation and transformation to the self rather than to society as liberal theology had done. For Hauerwas, it is the church/world split as it is displayed in the life of the Christian believer which must be eliminated as the self comes gradually to develop the virtues necessary for faithful witness to the Jesus story. Thus, Hauerwas does not anticipate the gradual transformation of the world, but the sanctification of the individual Christian as she develops the virtues necessary for an ever more faithful witness to the reality of the kingdom which is always over against the world. The final triumph of the kingdom always remains for Hauerwas an eschatological reality which is a work of God and not the product of the human effort to transform the world.

Peaceableness as Patience, Hope, Forgiveness and Hospitality to the Stranger. Living peaceably for Hauerwas means a great deal more than simply refusing to use violence or using violence only as a last resort, although it surely means that there is a strong presumption against violence and coercion if not an absolute refusal to resort to such measures. The peaceableness which Hauerwas believes is the fundamental characteristic of the Christian life is not a requirement of conformity to an absolute moral principle of respect for life or non-maleficence laid on individual Christians. Rather, it is a communal pattern of behavior which bears witness to the fact of God's benevolent providence in human history, God's forgiveness of human sin, and the reconciliation between God and human persons that has been accomplished in the life, death, and resurrection of Jesus. The peaceableness which characterizes the life of the Christian community entails that it be a community in which forgiveness and reconciliation overcome the tragic divisions occasioned by the evil that human beings perpetrate on one another.[30]

The association of peaceableness with witness to divine providence means that patience and hope are virtues inseparable from Christian peaceableness. Christians are free "to live out of control," by which Hauerwas means

> that we are an eschatological people who base our lives on the knowledge that God has redeemed his creation through the work of Jesus of Nazareth. We thus live out of control in the sense that we must assume God will use our faithfulness to make his kingdom a reality in the world (1983:105).[31]

Hauerwas follows John Howard Yoder in arguing that Christians are under no obligation "to make history come out right" (1983:106). The Kingdom that Jesus proclaimed and made present is totally a work of God. Therefore, Christians do not build the kingdom, but bear witness to it, trusting that the future is in God's hands. To live out of control requires patience, and to sustain the witness to the Kingdom which our patience entails requires hope.

> The virtues of hope and patience are central for the story that forms the church. For the adventure in which the church plays a part is sustained only through hope, a hope disciplined by patience, since we recognize that our hope is eschatological—that is, that we live in a time when that for which we hope is not soon to become a full reality (1981:5).[32]

The peaceableness which is necessary if the life of the church is to bear witness to the reality of the Kingdom which Jesus made present, and is yet to come, is made possible by receiving forgiveness and entails a commitment to forgiveness and reconciliation. "Through this crucified but resurrected savior we see that God offers to all the possibility of living in peace by the power of forgiveness." To bear witness to this reality and to build a community in which the power of forgiveness holds sway requires learning "to be forgiven" (1983:89). That peaceableness requires a commitment to being a community of forgiveness and reconciliation means that it often creates conflict. Commenting on Matthew 18:15–22, which commands a confrontation with the Christian brother who offends, Hauerwas suggests that "we will understand peacemaking as a virtue only if we see that such confrontation is at the heart of what it means to be a peacemaker" (1988:90). Peace, he says,

> is not the name of the absence of conflict, but rather peacemaking is that quality of life and practices engendered by a community that knows it lives as a forgiven people. Such a community cannot afford to "overlook" one another's sins because they have learned that such sins are a threat to being a community of peace. . . (1988:91).

A community established as peaceful cannot afford to let us relish our sense of being wronged without exposing that wrong in the hopes of reconciliation (1988:91–92).

Finally, peaceableness requires openness to the stranger. The stranger, for Hauerwas, is the paradigmatic neighbor for whom the Christian believer is responsible, in the way that the enemy often was in Jesus' sayings about love. Hauerwas also speaks of our responsibility for the neighbor and the enemy,[33] but it is the stranger to whom Hauerwas characteristically refers as the test case of Christian peaceableness.

The kingdom of peace initiated by Jesus is also the kingdom of love which is most clearly embodied in the Christian obligation to be hospitable. We are community on principle standing ready to share our meal with the stranger. Moreover we must be people who have hospitable selves—we must be ready to be stretched by what we know not. Friendship becomes our way of life as we learn to rejoice in the presence of others (1983:91).

Hauerwas says that the stranger "often comes in the form of our own children" (1981:1), and the hospitality that is owed to the stranger is interpreted to mean that Christians must be willing to receive children. Abortion, on Hauerwas' account, is a highly dubious practice for Christians because it represents an unwillingness to receive the strange gift of a child.[34]

Peaceableness, Character, and the Problem of Relativism

We have seen that on Hauerwas' understanding of the self as a social and narrative construct, human moral agency and responsibility cannot be understood in terms of our capacity for autonomous choice. Rather, we are responsible moral agents to the degree that we have a character which enables us to claim our actions as our own despite the way and degree to which they are limited by the communities and narratives which shape us. What can be added at this point is that Hauerwas regards character as made possible by the Christian narrative, and the peaceableness it enables and requires. Or, to put the matter another way, to have a character defined by the virtues associated with peaceableness is to have a character which makes possible moral agency and responsibility, as Hauerwas defines them. He writes:

When we exist as a forgiven people we are able to be at peace with our histories, so that now God's life determines our whole way of being—our character. We no longer need to deny our past, or tell ourselves false stories as now we can accept what we have been without the knowledge of our sin destroying us (1983:89).

Forgiveness enables claiming the communities and narratives which shape us as our own. It means we can tell our community's story and our own story truthfully. Moreover, Hauerwas makes clear that this means "[t]hat we are only able to have a history, a self, through the forgiveness wrought by God" (1983:90).

This theme is raised again in a later essay which addresses the question of the relationship between the Christian story and the other stories that shape our lives. Hauerwas treats the matter autobiographically in terms of the relationship between his being a Texan and being a Christian. Moreover, that essay suggests the way in which the matter of character is related to the epistemological problem entailed by Hauerwas' insistence that all ethics is narrative-dependent. It becomes clear that, for Hauerwas, character itself is a criterion of truthfulness. A truthful narrative is one that offers the gift of character by enabling us to accept the community and the stories which shape us.

In that essay, Hauerwas again rejects the liberal notion of the self which indicates that "what it means to be a person, to be free and/or autonomous, is to be capable of creating or 'choosing' our 'identity.'" He notes the conflict between that notion and the idea that we are socially-formed selves. On the liberal view, "we do not think of ourselves as inheriting a family tradition or a group identity with which we must learn to live. Rather, our particular story is that we have no history and thus we can pick and choose among the many options offered by our culture" (1988:27). By contrast, he argues

> that there is something very misleading and self-deceiving about the description many have accepted that they are or should try to become free from all stories except those they have "freely" chosen. For I will try to suggest that freedom comes not by choosing our stories, but by being formed by a truthful narrative that helps us appreciate the limits and possibilities of those stories we have not chosen but are part and parcel of who we are. Moreover, we will have some hint as to the truthfulness or falsity of the stories that grasp us just to the extent that they provide us appropriate skills to accomplish that task (1988:29).

It is not important here to recount all of what the story of being a Texan means for Hauerwas. What is important for our purposes here is that, on Hauerwas' reading of the story of Texas, it does not allow Texans to "acknowledge the injustices we have perpetrated or benefited from unless we think we can make it a right. As a result we cannot face the fact that there are some things that cannot be made up for, cannot be made right" (1988:38). Moreover, this inability of the story to account for its "own limits and tragedies" is a characteristic of the other stories which bind Texans; Hauerwas names stories of being a husband, a teacher, or a liberal. The inability to deal with limits and tragedies means that Texans are tempted to tell their story untruthfully, denying the injustices and cruelties which are a part of it. Such an untruthful account makes character and agency impossible. "Thus, to the extent 'being a Texan' functions as our primary story it determines us more than it makes us capable of action, in that it inextricably functions as an ideology that denies that injustice is part and parcel of our history" (1988:37). Moreover, such an untruthful story "must ultimately rely on violence to secure itself against other competing stories in the world. For people do not fight for selfish gain so much as they fight to preserve the good bound up in their limited stories" (1988:38). Thus, Hauerwas suggests "that one has an indication of one of the ways a story might be false exactly at the point where it must appeal to violence in order to protect itself" (1988:38).

The story that shapes the Christian community and to which it bears witness is "about a God who is capable of forgiveness—indeed, whose very nature is forgiveness" (1988:41). Because that is who the story portrays God to be, those for whom that story is the central story of their lives "have no reason to seek to hide from others and ourselves in the sinfulness of our fathers' and our own history. Unlike the story of Texas, therefore, the story of Jesus provides the skill for us to make our lives our own—in short to be free from our self-imposed fears" (1988:41). What Hauerwas might have said is in fact that the story of Jesus, by providing the skill for us to make our lives our own, provides the gift of character.

Hauerwas does not believe, that if the Christian story is our central story, we must abandon the other stories that have shaped us, if that were possible, or deny their influence in our lives. Precisely what the story of Jesus does is to give "the skill to make the story of being a Texan our own."

> By teaching us what it means to be forgiven, the Christian story gives us the freedom to understand our particular stories as Texans. As Augustine shows in the *Confessions*, our own particular history seems like a chicken yard full of patternless tracks until, in Jesus' redemption, we come to see that the maze is in fact a story of grace which we can affirm despite its suffering and sin (1988:41).

To return to the language that Hauerwas uses elsewhere, the Christian story allows turning the fate of being a Texan into a destiny. Of course, while the Christian story's authority does not entail abandoning or denying the influence of other stories, it does entail—as its "most decisive difference and challenge. . . for 'being a Texan'"—a "prohibition on the use of coercion to sustain its truth. The followers of Jesus can attract others to the way of Jesus only by living faithful lives" (1988:41).

There is a great deal that is not fully worked out in Hauerwas' tale of two stories. For example, the question arises as to how the Christian story comes to be one's own. This is an autobiographical tale, and Hauerwas indicates that he regards himself as fated both to be a Texan and a

Christian. What does Hauerwas' account of the relationship between the
Christian story and our other stories have to do with those who were not
born into a family that is already Christian in a culture in which the Church
is prominent? What are the implications of his view for evangelism?
Another set of questions would have to do with whether or not Hauerwas
regards all the stories which shape us, other than the Christian story, as
being characterized by an inability to deal with sin and injustice, such that
the forgiveness which the Christian story proclaims becomes essential for
a truthful telling of it. Those writing from a liberation perspective might
argue that the problem for oppressed people is that they are shaped by
stories which justify their oppression with reference to a history of
sinfulness on their part. The problem for oppressed people is not that their
stories are untruthful about their sinfulness, but that they untruthfully
regard sin and inferiority as ultimately determinative of their identity.

Despite the questions that remain, the important point for our
purposes here is that Hauerwas regards his account of Christian
peaceableness as providing a solution to the epistemological "problem"
entailed by his view that all ethics is narrative-dependent. Or, as he has
said, "Christian peaceableness as the hallmark of the Christian life helps
illumine other issues, such as the nature of moral argument, the meaning
and status of freedom, as well as how religious convictions can be claimed
to be true or false" (1983:xvii). Their truth has to do with the way in
which the narrative in which they are displayed is capable of giving the gift
of character and with the fact that violence is not regarded as necessary in
order to protect their truth.

We are also now in a position to see the way in which Hauerwas'
understanding of peaceableness is intended to keep the relativism entailed
by a view that insists upon the narrative-dependence of ethics from being
vicious in the practical sense. That is to say, we are in a position to see
how peaceableness for Hauerwas is a solution to the practical or political
problem of his moral relativism as it is to the epistemological problem.

It is evident, first, that the alternative to a foundationalist approach,
which seeks to adjudicate between the plural conceptions of the good
which prevail because of the fact that human beings are shaped by various
communities and commitments, is not a war of all against all. Hauerwas
posits as a resolution to the problem a community which refuses to protect
the truth by violence. Nor does Hauerwas' view entail that individuals are
vulnerable to injustice as their own wills are made subject to the
conception of the good and the practices and patterns of authority that
prevail in their community. The peaceableness which is a requirement of
truthfulness entails hospitality to the stranger. Moral truth as it is known is
never so firmly established that it is not open to challenge. As Hauerwas
loves to remind us, quoting Aristotle, a certainty cannot be assigned to our

moral convictions which is inappropriate to their nature. Moral matters are about things that could be otherwise.

It is safe to assume that Hauerwas' concern about hospitality to the stranger includes hospitality to the member of the community who makes himself a stranger by his or her dissent. He is clear that the value placed on forgiveness and reconciliation in the Christian community means that the one who "refuses to listen must be treated as a tax collector or Gentile," that is, barred from the community (1988:94). Thus there is a limit to Christian hospitality. Of course, liberal tolerance also has its limits. And, the limits to Christian hospitality do not justify coercion or violence in the way that liberal limits do.

Paul Nelson has complained that if one refuses to engage in a process of "abstraction and distanciation from particular stories" in order to develop universal rules and principles by which conflicting moral judgments can be adjudicated, "it would seem that the prospect of moral evaluation is bleak" (1987:42). There are two responses available from a perspective like that of Hauerwas. The first would be to raise the question as to why such evaluation is necessary. On what account of the good is such evaluation and adjudication between various communities necessary? I suspect that Hauerwas would contend that only where one assumes that the development of a nation-state as a super-community sovereign over the various communities of which human beings are a part is a moral good is such evaluation necessary. But Hauerwas sees no obvious reason to be committed to such a sovereign community. Or, to put the matter another way, even if one were to argue that wider and wider communities of cooperation are both possible and desirable in terms of realizing the goods that are available to human persons, on Hauerwas' view the building of such a community requires the slow process of dialogue and cannot be built on coercion. A second response would claim that while the evaluation which Nelson seeks is not immediately available with any degree of certainty (once again an appeal to Aristotle is in order), there is a way to test the truthfulness of various moral claims over time, and that is in terms of the degree to which they are able to maintain themselves without resort to violence and their capacity to provide the gift of a coherent socially-constituted self, the gift of character.

Foundationalism's Threat to Christian Integrity

Since there are no universal and transcendent norms grounded in human nature and discoverable from an autonomous perspective available to everyone, the church may not accept norms derived from such foundationalist accounts of ethics as authoritative over against or beside the sole authoritative norm of its existence, Jesus. All foundational approaches to ethics, including natural law approaches, are illusory because they represent an effort to find a universal and objective foundation for the moral life. They are a threat to the integrity of the Christian life because they result in the accepting of an authority other than Jesus in the Christian life. As well, to the degree that the effort to express Christian convictions in a so-called universal idiom is successful, it seems that the original theological warrants for those convictions become expendable.[35]

Hauerwas notes that the historical forms foundational theories have taken have tended to regard as absolute and universal what is only relative to a particular community or to particular groups. The development of such an approach within Christian ethics is sometimes regarded as essential for discovering the terms for dialogue and cooperation with persons from different particular traditions, that is, it attempts to identify norms accessible to everyone and not dependent on specifically Christian convictions. Therefore, it may be argued that natural law is particularly important for Christians as a means of enabling their dialogue with non-Christians and their effective participation in settings that are not clearly Christian, such as the pluralistic society of the modern United States. Hauerwas contends, however, that historically the natural law tradition has merely codified a particular consensus rather than identifying universal norms. For example, the natural law tradition in Roman Catholicism "reflects more the consensus within the church than the universality of the natural law itself. . . [N]atural law became the means of codifying a particular moral tradition" (1983:51).

Moreover, Hauerwas contends that, while liberalism is defended as a mechanism for preventing violence and engendering cooperation between various communities,[36] since such convictions are falsely regarded as universal the justification of coercion and violence against those who do not accept the specific terms of cooperation becomes easier.

> Indeed, when Christians assume that their particular moral convictions are independent of narrative, that they are justified by some universal standpoint free from history, they are tempted to imagine that those who do not share such an ethic must be particularly perverse and should be coerced to do what we know on universal grounds they really should want to do (1983:61).[37]

Hauerwas hastens to add that he does not mean that those who defend foundationalist accounts "are inherently more violent, but rather that violence and coercion become conceptually intelligible" from such a standpoint. He argues that the language of universal rights "in spite of its potential for good, contains with its logic a powerful justification for violence" (1983:61). His insight is correct. In the liberal framework, rights, particularly those which are regarded as natural or human rights, function to justify coercion; human rights delineate that aspect of morality that is legitimately subject to legal enforcement through sanctions.

Moreover, at the level of popular political discourse, the view that a particular country refuses to respect democratic rights is regarded as legitimating sanctions such as the withholding of foreign aid, or in extreme cases, military intervention on our part. Such a view of a particular government seems to be the easiest way apart from an appeal to self-defense to justify the use of military force.

I assume that what Hauerwas says here about how Christians are tempted to use violence by the illusion that their convictions have universal validity also applies to non-Christians. However, he apparently regards Christians as particularly susceptible. "When Christians rule," he says, "they tend to create international and national disorder because they have such a calling to make things right" (1988:183). Rights regarded as universal become the criteria by which Christians try to make things right. The point is particularly troubling from the perspective of the Christian community because its convictions surely carry a heavy presumption against coercion and violence. Hauerwas' remarks here suggest that when Christians accept foundationalist approaches to ethics the result is not simply the acceptance of another norm alongside the norm of Jesus, but in fact a rejection of the authority of Jesus and his kingdom upon the church and the world.

It is important at this point to remind ourselves that Hauerwas' anti-foundationalist epistemology means that he regards all norms as narrative dependent or as historically derived and relative. Natural law, or any ethic based on an anthropology regarded as universally valid, represents an effort to deny the historically relative character of some particular perspective; it is guilty of a false universalism. Thus, the acceptance of natural law as a norm for ethics by the church represents, for Hauerwas, the acceptance of some story or some historical experience as normative alongside or above the story of Jesus. Since there is no universal perspective from which Jesus may be interpreted or understood, to accept natural law, and to allow it and its anthropological considerations to determine our understanding of Jesus, is in effect to accept some other story as more truthful, more authoritative for our lives than Jesus himself. Moreover, it is to pose a false solution to the problem of moral relativism.

The Church and the World: Hauerwas' "Sectarianism"

On the basis of his anti-foundationalist assumptions, Hauerwas denies that there is any autonomous universal and normative culture or world over against which the church (or any other particular community) can and must define itself. We cannot assume "we know what we are talking about when we talk about 'culture'" (1987:88). Thus, speaking of the "world" at all, or of the general "culture" within which some particular community exists, can only be done from the perspective of that community. For the church, "the body of people formed by the story of Jesus' life, death, and resurrection," this means that it does not "know what the world is apart from that story" (1987:88). And, from the perspective of the church's story the world is simply "all of that in creation that has taken the freedom not yet to believe." Hauerwas is quoting John Howard Yoder here, and it may be helpful to set the quotation in context.

> We must remember the "world" as that opposed to God is not an ontological designation. . . . The only difference between church and world is the difference between agents. As Yoder suggests, the distinction between church and world is not between realms of reality, between orders of creation and redemption, between nature and supernature, but "rather between the basic personal postures of men, some of whom confess and others of whom do not confess that Jesus is Lord. The distinction between church and the world is not something that God has imposed upon the world by a prior metaphysical definition, nor is it only something which timid or pharisaical Christians have built up around themselves. It is all of that in creation that has taken the freedom not yet to believe."
>
> In this respect, moreover, it is particularly important to remember that the world consists of those, including ourselves, who have chosen not to make the story of God their story. The world in us refuses to affirm that this is God's world and that, as loving Lord, God's care for creation is greater than our illusion of control. The world is those aspects of our individual and social lives where we live untruthfully by continuing to rely on violence to bring order (1983:100–101).[38]

It is important to notice the nature of the absolute distinction that Hauerwas draws between the church and the world. Since it is one having to do with the "personal postures" of agents, and because Hauerwas recognizes that relevantly different personal postures can exist in the same person ("The world in us refuses to affirm. . ."), it seems that the distinction between church and world is not absolute at an institutional or sociological level. No discrete boundary between institutions or communities marks the chasm between church and world. Something of the worldly posture or orientation remains even in those people who are formed into the community called church. In a manner of speaking, then, Christians carry the chasm between church and world around in their own persons. Hauerwas does not suggest that there is also something of church in the personal postures of those who have not become a part of that community either because such contending postures are written into human nature or are a universal aspect of human experience. The chasm between church and world is created by the personal response to one's encounter with Jesus of Nazareth in the narrative of his life which is borne by the community which is formed around it. It is the human response to Jesus that divides church from world, and that some affirm and some deny him cannot be attributed to some contrary or dialectical element in human nature.

Hauerwas' understanding of the church/world relationship is complex, and it is not without ambiguity. For example, in an early essay he criticized Yoder for having drawn the distinction between church and world too sharply, indicating that it is "more dynamic" than Yoder had suggested (1974:220). For example, "Christian ethical reflection cannot completely divorce itself from the world's categories of justice," though it is "not limited by them" (1974:220) and has as its task "to transform the language of justice" (1974:219) in terms of the ultimate Christian norm which is Jesus himself. It is interesting that Yoder has since addressed the positive aspects of worldly conceptions of justice.[39] Meanwhile, Hauerwas has come to ask whether Christians should "talk so much about justice" (1986a), suggesting that many Christians show a much too positive appreciation for secular conceptions. Still, as Hauerwas has made clear, his conception of the distinction between church and world does not entail Christian withdrawal or non-participation in all societal institutions. He has written extensively, for example, on Christian contributions to the practice of medicine and in the university.[40]

Sectarianism of Some Kind

On the basis of his sharp and sharply pejorative distinction between church and world, his insistence that Jesus' nonviolent ethic is the sole authoritative norm for the church, and his rejection of a foundationalist epistemology and theories of natural law (which seem to promise a universal moral language for dialogue with those outside the Christian community), Hauerwas has often been "accused" of sectarianism. His position, those who label him a sectarian contend, is both intellectually and morally irresponsible. According to these critics, Hauerwas' view entails both a refusal to submit Christian claims to public scrutiny and a withdrawal of the church from the world. James Gustafson has said that Hauerwas' view has the effect of "isolating Christianity from taking seriously the wider world of science and culture and limits the participation of Christians in the ambiguities of moral and social life in the patterns of interdependence in the world" (1985a:84).[41] Wilson Miscamble has written that Hauerwas shows a willingness for the Church to let weak and vulnerable people in the world suffer rather than dirtying its hands in the tragic but necessary business of coercion and violence. "Hauerwas effectively removes the church from the life and death policy issues of the human community" (1987:73). Referring to his insistence that the Church must serve the widow, the poor, and the orphan while eschewing responsibility to make the nation-state system work, Miscamble adds:

> The difficulty in Hauerwas' position is that in our world, where the widow's husband may have been murdered by Chilean police, where the poor include the starving millions of Africa, and where the orphan may be seeking sanctuary in the United States, what this nation-state does and how it works are directly relevant to a Christian's concerns (1987:75–76).

Paul Nelson also adopts the sectarian label (1987:133), and criticizes Hauerwas on the grounds that his insistence on conformity to the authority of Jesus is "a harsh legalism" (1987:135) and because his approach has not yielded "determinate conclusions" about the roles which Christians may play in a society (1987:137). Finally, he has written that Hauerwas

> is largely indifferent or, at best, insufficiently committed to dialogue beyond the parameters of Christian narrative and the community it shapes. His disposition in this regard is not only a consequence of his sectarian understanding of the church's social task and ethics but of his nearly exclusive focus on virtue and character as well (1987:138).

Hauerwas' writing is often passionate, but nowhere is it more so than when he denies the charge that he is a sectarian, "if by that is meant a retreat or withdrawal from the world" (1981:253, n. 37). Noting that Miscamble levels the sectarian charge "because I have argued that the church ought to stand apart in order to witness to society," Hauerwas says: "For the life of me, I do not understand why that position ought to be understood as sectarian" (1987:90). Hauerwas regards the term as hopelessly pejorative.[42] Its use represents an effort to dismiss his argument without a serious effort to understand it. Thus he pleads for its abandonment. "It simply does not help us get with the business of discerning the particular challenge before us as Christians" (1987:94).

The particular challenge that Hauerwas seems to have in mind is precisely that of discovering the way in which the church is to relate to and serve the world without losing its separate and unique identity as the people formed by the story of Jesus. For Hauerwas, the question of the church's relationship to the world or culture is not one of choosing between "either *complete* involvement in culture or *complete* withdrawal." Rather, "[t]he issue is how the church can provide the interpretative categories to help Christians better understand the positive and negative aspects of their societies and guide their subsequent selective participation" (1988:11).

Because of his historicist epistemology, Hauerwas denies that the criteria for the church's selective participation in society can be "developed in the abstract." "The gospel," he says, "does not simply contain a theory of society or government."

> That does not mean that Christians, along with others, will not try, through the study of history and social and political thought, to gain wisdom about

how societies, the law, and government best work. Such knowledge, however, lacks the status of "gospel truth," as we are too much the product of accidents of geography, climate, and history to speak with certainty about what society ought to look like. Every society has its strengths and weaknesses which change through time. How Christians relate to those strengths and weaknesses will and should also change through time (1988:11–12).

Thus, Hauerwas' position does not preclude Christian participation in society or politics *a priori*, unless such participation includes violence. Christians must withdraw from participation only when governments and societies use violence

in order to maintain internal order and external security. At that point alone Christians must withhold their involvement with the state. Such an admission, however, hardly commits me to a sectarian stance, unless one assumes, as some do, that every function of the state depends on its penchant for violence (1988:25).

There is a certain ambiguity to Hauerwas' position here that requires some clarification on his part. Does he mean to say that if governments and societies use violence to maintain order or defend themselves from external aggression that Christians must disavow all participation in that society or government? Or does he mean only that Christians must not participate in those roles that require the use of violence? If he means to maintain the first, it would seem that Christian participation in very few societies or states, if any at all, would be allowed. Is any civil society able to maintain internal order without some measure of violence? I suspect that Hauerwas means to defend some version of the second position, that is, that Christians may participate in societies that use violence while selectively withdrawing cooperation from those aspects of order that depend upon its use. It would seem as well that he would want to call for minimal cooperation with societies where violence is the primary basis of order, even if Christians were allowed conscientious withdrawal from the roles that required the use of violence.

Hauerwas has consistently refused to define political life in terms of violence and coercion. It is precisely this refusal that enables him to maintain that his pacifist position implies no "sectarian" withdrawal of the church from the political dimensions of life in the world. For Hauerwas, an adequate conception of political life must recognize the shared effort to identify and experience the common good. "To insist on the importance of the common good is to argue that if the political is to have significance, it must deal with those things that are general for the society in a general way (not just as a problem of harmonizing interests)" (1974:237). As I understand Hauerwas, he is arguing that our conception of politics is impoverished when we see it primarily as a matter of balancing the claims of various individuals and groups (and balancing the power that is behind those claims), and ignore the effort to deal with those "goods" of our life together that all individuals and groups share. When the concept of common good is at the center of our understanding of politics, the physical dimensions of power become less important. "Violence," says Hauerwas,

> is necessary not as the essence of community, but when community is no longer sustained by the common wills of those that make it up. True authority does not need violence as it is the recognition and obedience given by the citizen to the governors who legitimately lead in accordance with the common good of that society.
>
> This does not mean that power is excluded from the state, but it is a power that is nonviolent in the sense that the individual is directed to the good of the society in the context of his own wider loyalty to the society. For power is the essence of the state, not simply because some refuse to obey from evil intention, but because of the richness of the various visions of the good that must be directed toward the whole of the common good (1974:218–219).

From this perspective, Hauerwas can claim that "politics only begins" with the disavowal of the use of violence,

> for only then are we forced genuinely to listen to the other, thus beginning conversations necessary for discovering goods in common. From my perspective, far from requiring a withdrawal from the political arena, pacifism demands strenuous political engagement, because such a commitment forces us to expand our social and political imaginations (1988:15).

While it is evident that Hauerwas' position entails no *a priori* withdrawal from the world and political involvement, Michael Quirk has appropriately raised the question as to whether it does involve "sectarianism of *some* sort" (1987:78). Quirk suggests that Hauerwas does in fact argue for a sectarian stance over against liberal culture. Quirk approaches the question in terms of Hauerwas' historicist epistemology. This historicist perspective can lead to an epistemological sectarianism. This form of sectarianism

> entails the impossibility of any rational dialogue with those outside the "sect," on the grounds that their epistemically and morally central convictions are corrupt and diametrically opposed to those of "insiders." Attempts at forging a consensus would, then, be not merely futile but dangerous, since arguing the point on "their" terms would only serve to undermine "ours." Sectarians are then faced with the options of either proclaiming their confession to "the world" and having it fall upon deaf ears, or articulating only among themselves the truth to which they bear witness (1987:78).

Quirk shares Hauerwas' historicist epistemological perspective and credits him with having recognized and avoided the sectarian pitfall toward which such a perspective tends. Hauerwas has avoided it because, while he denies any universal, foundationalist framework in terms of which all particular, historically rooted claims can be adjudicated, he does not deny the possibility of communication across communities or traditions. "Religious and theological claims are thus not immune to challenge, though they may be, like many other activities, not susceptible to definitive refutation or confirmation; they can nevertheless be tested and argued about" (Hauerwas 1985a:6). Indeed, despite his insistence that all knowledge is historically derived and narrative-dependent, he does not deny the possibility of "common experience and appeals" among various communities and traditions—though this has not to do with sharing a common nature, but with the belief that human beings have "a common creator" (1981:106). Moreover, as we have seen, character and non-violence are also tests of truthfulness.

On this basis, Quirk contends that Hauerwas' position need not result in the epistemological sectarianism he has identified. "As long as church and world share at least *some* beliefs in common, a dialogue between them can take place. . . . A quantum of incommensurability between the Christian and the secular paradigms does not preclude the possibility of their rational comparison and practical judgment about their comparative worth" (1987:85). Thus, at least in principle, it is possible for there to be dialogue and understanding between church and world. But the matter cannot be left there.

> Even if *rapprochemant* between those "inside" and those "outside" the Christian story cannot be ruled out *in principle*, it may be true that *in fact* such reconciliation is impossible. It might be the case that the degree of dissensus between church and secular polity is too great to secure any substantial moral community. This can not be known *a priori*, but it can be discovered in the practical efforts to reach some sort of consensus. And if this is the case, then perhaps "sectarianism" is not a bad idea. If modern politics *in fact* is as pervasive and corrupting as Hauerwas maintains, "sectarianism" may even be an idea whose time has come (1987:85).

Thus, according to Quirk, the question of the church's separateness from the world is not a question that can be resolved once and for all, but depends in large measure on the world in which the church finds itself. Hauerwas' emphasis on the the church as a separated community and his concern for the maintenance of its integrity must be evaluated in terms of his critique of the particular world or culture in which it finds itself. In terms of the church in the United States, this finally hinges on the validity of Hauerwas' critique of liberal culture.[43] Quirk contends that the chasm between church and the liberal world may not be as great as Hauerwas suggests because of the historical relationship between Christianity and liberalism in the west. Hauerwas' argument can be improved, he says, by being "supplemented by an understanding of the ways in which the history of Christianity has affected the fortunes of the secular world" (1987:83).

Quirk's analysis forces a return to the question of sociological sectarianism and moral irresponsibility which Miscamble, Gustafson, and Nelson raise. Do the inadequacies of liberal culture as it exists in the United States merit the measure of non-cooperation and the attention to its own separate integrity to which Hauerwas calls the church? Of course, if one rejects Hauerwas' anti-foundationalist epistemology, as Miscamble, Gustafson, and Nelson do, if in fact it is possible to discover a set of universally valid moral principles which can be discovered independent of the particular histories and communities of which we are a part (or which can be abstracted from the common aspects of those histories and the experiences of those communities), then the ethic which Hauerwas reads out of the story of Jesus cannot be regarded as the sole authoritative norm for Christian faith and practice.

Even this suggestion only establishes the possibility of deep Christian interaction with the particular culture in which it finds itself. The question would still need to be raised as to whether liberal theory has correctly identified those universally valid moral principles. This perspective does clearly establish grounds for full participation in the dialogue about such principles, however.

But Quirk's analysis suggests another approach. His acceptance of Hauerwas' epistemology, and his valid indication that there is a relationship between Christianity and our secular culture which Hauerwas has not addressed, suggest a different way of posing the question of Christian separation from our culture. If Hauerwas' epistemological perspective is correct, then, despite the denial of some liberal theorists, liberal moral notions have their own history and require narrative display for their comprehension. Moreover, those notions are teleological in character, that is to say, they gain their meaning in the context of a particular conception of what constitutes a good human life and good human community. Seen in this light the debate between liberal and Christian ethics is one between different conceptions of the good. This suggests the possibility of the Hauerwasian Christian community as playing a fundamental role in society in terms of its participation in a conversation about the nature of the good. Such conversation is possible if there are any points of commonality, any shared sense of what constitutes a good human life. Given the intimate historical relation between Christianity and liberalism, one suspects that the possibility of conversation is great.

Interestingly, Hauerwas' earliest work actively addressed this question and suggested that democracy might be justified in terms of its ability to facilitate the discovery of the common good. Liberal theory, he wrote, "does not encompass the richness of possibilities in the democratic experience." "[T]he crucial question for us today," he added, "is how to make efficacious a substantive notion of the common good within a democratic framework" (1974:229). Now, Hauerwas apparently regards that possibility as extremely remote and has followed the lead of Alasdair MacIntyre in suggesting that the only hope for our polity is for small particular communities (whose practices are based on a common conception of the good) to attend to their own internal life.

Is that judgement justified? Or, to put the matter as has Bernard Yack, "Does liberal practice 'live down' to liberal theory?" (1988:147–169). Yack suggests that communitarian critics of liberalism fail to distinguish between the theory that has been developed to justify liberal institutions and the actual practice of liberal societies. We have seen that Reinhold Niebuhr made such a distinction. Niebuhr was also highly critical of liberal theory but came to the conclusion that the practice of democracy in America was better than its theoretical justification. Hauerwas certainly has criteria different from Niebuhr's by which to judge political life in our culture if he were to accept a distinction between liberal practice and liberal theory. Hauerwas would seem to have a stake in increasing the impact of what Robert Bellah and his colleagues identified in *Habits of the Heart* as the biblical and civic republican traditions in American life. Hauerwas has denied that civic republicanism has ever had the influence which Bellah attributes to it. But there are reasons to believe that many of the moral fragments which continue to influence us in the United States could be made sense of if they were provided a context in a teleological conception of the good.

Of course, Hauerwas might resist the suggestion that the church has a role to play in our polity in terms of a restoration of a teleological approach to political ethics, and the conversation about the common good which such an approach requires, on grounds apart from his judgement that liberal theory is so dominant that such an approach and such a conversation is currently impossible. He might argue that such a tack represents merely another way to delude the church into thinking that it has a stake in the continued existence of democratic nation-states. Such a delusion is particularly dangerous given the history of the assumption that the church does have such a stake and its failure to adopt a prophetic stance over against the ambitions of the United States. Moreover, a teleological political ethic may be as able to justify violence to protect its conversation and scheme of cooperation as a liberal ethic. Yet there is no reason in principle why a Christian commitment to non-violence need be compromised simply because Christians are willing to participate in our society by addressing questions of public policy and practice in the idiom of the common good. Indeed, the Roman Catholic Bishops of the United

States have effectively addressed issues of public policy from a framework that is teleological in character. Moreover, their advice, while not necessarily popular, seems to be comprehensible.

Finally, if I am correct in the view that Hauerwas' communitarian critique of liberalism and its implications are the same as those of the argument raised by Michael Sandel in *Liberalism and the Limits of Justice*, then there is a basis for cooperation and participation in liberal society that Hauerwas seems to ignore. Recall that Sandel's conclusion (suggested by the title of his book) is not that the liberal framework is invalid, but that it is limited in its applicability and is not the sole measure of the virtue of basic institutions. "Justice finds its occasion," he wrote, "because we cannot know each other, or our ends, well enough to govern by the common good alone. This condition is not likely to fade altogether, and so long as it does not, justice will be necessary" (1982:183). Liberal justice as the exclusive standard for basic institutions leaves our social and political lives impoverished because it makes impossible the discovery and pursuit of goods we have in common. Yet, liberal justice remains relevant because we are not without a capacity for individual independence from those communities and ends which constitute us, and that capacity merits respect and protection. It is not the exclusive source of our humanity, not that alone which gives us dignity and makes us sources of moral claims, but it is a part of who we are that our basic institutions ought to respect.

The challenge for communitarian politics[44] is to identify political principles and institutions that enable both our discovery of a broad common good (and which enhance our realization of that good) and our recognition of the degree to which we always remain separate persons, always strangers to each other, with disagreements about what is good for us and true conflicts of interest. Oppression results when the differences between us are ignored and the good as a few envision it determines the worth and status of all. That is the liberal insight which must not be forgotten even as we come to recognize that oppression and the impoverishment of life also results when we are prevented from discovering and pursuing the good which may be ours together. If we are in large measure selves constituted by our social attachments and relations, with conceptions of the good given to us by our communities, then liberal neutrality is in large measure an unnecessary protection of our autonomy and, indeed, a violation of it. Discovering how large that measure is remains problematic. My essential point here is that the communitarian perspective recognizes grounds for some aspects of the liberal enterprise. This suggests that there is a basis for cooperation and participation in the public dialogue about policy, even in the terms set by the liberal framework, which Hauerwas does not seem to acknowledge.

Endnotes

[1] As will become evident, it is not that Hauerwas believes that there is some nation or culture, either actual or potential, in which the Church is or will be at home. Rather, he insists that Christianity "must always be a Diaspora religion" (1985a:77).

[2] Indeed, Hauerwas may not go too far when he says that "America was his church" and that for Niebuhr, as for American Christian social ethics in general, "the subject of Christian ethics was America" (1985a:31).

[3] The most notable exception is, of course, John Howard Yoder.

[4] One might note that there is a not unimportant difference between believing that Christianity and "democracy are integrally related" and having the goal of "making American democracy as close as possible to a manifestation of God's kingdom." The church might, some would say, appropriately have the goal of making whatever society it found itself in "as close as possible to a manifestation of God's kingdom." Hauerwas' point is that Christian writers in the United States have assumed that the liberal democratic aspect of our culture is consistent with any such manifestation.

[5] My own sense that a general disillusionment with our culture (resulting from the failure of the civil rights movement and the war on poverty to eliminate an underclass, the Vietnam experience, Watergate, and a general moral malaise whose symptoms include high levels of violence, divorce, and dishonesty in economic life) has led many in the church to a more critical analysis of liberalism and greater attention to the internal life of the church itself led me at the beginning of my study of Hauerwas to suspect that his apparent sectarianism was driven more by a critique of liberalism than by theological convictions. That suspicion is not entirely dispelled by an analysis of his work. I have chosen here to begin by analyzing the philosophical and theological convictions that determine his overall framework before turning to the specifics of his critique of liberalism. I am not at all certain that this is necessarily the proper way to proceed, for though it seems to make sense analytically, I am not at all certain it is the best way to understand the development of his thought. It seems obvious that the shaping of his philosophical and theological convictions took place in the context of a growing disillusionment with liberal democratic polity.

It is interesting in this regard that Hauerwas describes his discovery of the inadequacy of the Niebuhrian position in terms of its failure "to provide the resources to critically understand Vietnam" (1983:xiii). I am convinced that Hauerwas' work is best understood by setting it in contrast with that of Reinhold Niebuhr. (Hauerwas himself has recently written that he is sure that his sense of "the significance of the church as a social ethic would lack critical edge if I did not always have Reinhold Niebuhr in mind" (1988:2)). Moreover, it was soon after his discovery of Niebuhr's inadequacy that Hauerwas became acquainted with John Howard Yoder. It is interesting to speculate the degree to which disillusionment with liberal culture made him open to Yoder's theological defense of a separated Christian community.

Nevertheless, I believe that Hauerwas' work is best set out analytically in the way that I am proceeding here. The symbiotic relationship between Hauerwas' philosophic convictions and his critique of liberalism will be evident by the end.

[6] The way in which I have chosen to organize this material reflects my agreement with Thomas Ogletree's argument that "the conceptual center of [Hauerwas'] thought is not character or virtue as such, but rather the notion of vision, and more particularly narrative and story; character and virtue are in Hauerwas' thought correlated with these more basic notions" (1980:28). Paul Nelson also shares this conclusion (1987:111). This approach is somewhat controversial. His earliest work tended to emphasize character and the virtues; narrative or story emerged as a central theme only later in his efforts to make sense of the former. Moreover, it seems to run counter to Hauerwas' own understanding of his work. In the introduction to *The Peaceable Kingdom,* Hauerwas claims not to know where the emphasis on narrative has come from. He says, "the more I thought through the problem of describing intentional action, the more I was convinced that narrative was a crucial concept for displaying agency" (1983:xxv). Intentional action and agency are issues related to the question of character, so this seems to suggest that the narrative theme is a derivative of that concern.

Whether or not my emphasis on narrative rather than character is correct, shaping the study this way seems to me to be a fruitful way to get a grasp on Hauerwas' critique of liberalism. Of course, the two themes are interrelated in Hauerwas, and the way in which I am organizing the discussion does account for the way the emphasis on character represents a challenge to liberal moral theory.

[7] Paul Nelson is correct to raise the question as to what Hauerwas means by narrative (1987:112) and to suggest that one can be "a critic of Kant, a relativist, a historicist, an antifoundationalist, . . . or just a lover of stories" without appealing to narrative as a basic epistemological category (1987:141). Hauerwas seems to include a variety of types of communication in his concept of narrative. The aspect of his claim that all ethics is narrative-dependent that is most important with respect to his critique of liberalism is the one I am trying to capture here: that moral convictions are formed in history and cannot be derived from an autonomous universal perspective which is independent of historical contingencies.

[8] Hauerwas says that "any story we adopt, or allow to adopt us, will have to display" these characteristics:
   (1) power to release us from destructive alternatives;
   (2) ways of seeing through current distortions;
   (3) room to keep us from having to resort to violence;
   (4) a sense for the tragic: how meaning transcends power (1977:35).

The key words to which Outka points are "destructive," "distortion," "violence," "tragic," and "meaning" (1980:117).

[9] He writes that the first part of *A Community of Character* "introduces the basic methodological claim that every community and polity involves and requires a narrative. The distinctive character of the church's social ethics does not follow from

the fact that it is a narrative-formed community, but rather from the *kind* of narrative that determines its life" (1981:4).

10 It is hard to imagine Hauerwas saying now that "[t]he principle [of universalizability] is sufficient to establish the independence of morality from religion." And, he would certainly more carefully nuance his early judgment that "the whole natural law tradition is a sufficient indication that theologically it has always been supposed that rational men can know and do good on grounds independent of his knowledge of God" (1974:86).

11 Nelson seems compelled to contend that Hauerwas wants to argue that Christian ethics is narrative-dependent but cannot really mean that all ethics is because Nelson believes that the former view allows for the possibility of rational discourse and evaluation between Christian ethics and ethics which goes by some other qualifier while the latter claim entails an unmitigated relativism. This conviction is particularly odd because the case he makes for it depends upon an important misinterpretation of categories developed by George Lindbeck which both he and Hauerwas appropriate for their own purposes. He argues that the broader claim would require Hauerwas' association with what Lindbeck calls experiential-expressive models of religion, a model which Lindbeck has shown makes the status of religious truth-claims ambiguous. Hauerwas clearly has identified himself with Lindbeck's cultural-linguistic model and seems to see that as consistent with the view that all ethics is narrative dependent. Interestingly, Lindbeck himself associates the cultural-linguistic model with narrative (1984:34ff). I do not deny that narrative can be used in the experiential-expressive model, but I am not convinced by Nelson's argument that Hauerwas must be interpreted as belonging to that type if he holds on to the claim that all ethics is narrative-dependent.

12 Alasdair MacIntyre has considered the problem in some detail. See his chapter entitled "The Rationality of Traditions" in *Whose Justice? Which Rationality?* (1988). Hauerwas' debt to MacIntyre is obvious. It is noteworthy with reference to the particular problem we are discussing here that Hauerwas has written that MacIntyre has helped him see "that to abandon the search for a 'foundation' does not necessarily entail the loss of rationality in ethics (or anything else)."

13 See the new introduction to *Character and The Christian Life* in which he presents his own account of the way his thought has developed in response to the inadequacy of his early understanding of character and agency (1985b:xviii–xxi).

14 Hauerwas indicates that this "underlying contention" was not always evident in the book and that "my account of character at times appears like that of Kant— namely, the attempt to secure a unity to our lives not because we know where we are going but because we do not" (1985b:xxi). His later work (the book was originally published in 1975) makes evident that he regards the moral life as an adventure of discovery through which we come to know, more or less, where we are going. That is to say, the moral life has a telos toward which it aims.

15 I don't find this metaphor in the particular essay which I am discussing, but it is prominent in other of his works. See *A Community of Character*, particularly the essay "A Story-Formed Community: Reflections on *Watership Down*," where he says

that "the most basic task of any polity is to offer its people a sense of participation in an adventure" (1981:13).

16 Thus, I do not believe that Sandel's critique is valid only if Rawls is interpreted as providing a foundational account of justice or a view that sets the right as absolutely prior to the good. L. Gregory Jones argues that "Sandel's argument is persuasive if, and insofar as, Rawls' theory presupposes the priority of the right over the good," and suggests that, since Rawls has indicated that he means his conception of justice to be a political one based upon an "overlapping consensus" on the part of the various full moral theories in a liberal society, his theory must now be interpreted as one in which the good is understood as prior to the right. Thus, Sandel's critique is no longer persuasive. I don't see why this is the case. What Rawls' later view suggests is that his view presupposes or rests on the hope that all the philosophical and religious theories (all the complete theories of the good) operative in a liberal society will have their own particular reasons for supporting liberal justice. In this sense the good is prior to the right or to the theory of justice, but the good is still extremely thin in that what must be shared by all is a sense that individual autonomy (as understood by liberalism) is a part of a full theory of the good. Moreover, that shared sense is based upon shared convictions about the nature of the human self as free and equal. Since even this version of Rawls' theory depends upon a belief that human freedom (or autonomy) is the essential characteristic of human selfhood which merits respect and protection by the basic institutions of society, it is challenged by Sandel's critique.

17 Rawls regards the talents and character that a person has as not being constitutive of who the person is. Moreover, he regards the goods produced through the exercise of those talents as community assets. For Sandel, this is the central illustration of the way in which liberalism is capable of violating individual agency and autonomy. On Hauerwas' terms, by treating us as autonomous selves liberalism discourages the development or reception of the character which makes it possible for us to take responsibility for our actions, that is, to act as agents.

18 Hauerwas and Sandel, it seems to me, would be in agreement with the view of William Galston that "in practice liberal theorists covertly employ theories of the good" (1982:621). Of course, whereas Galston is willing to defend a substantive liberal conception of the good, from Hauerwas' perspective such a conception is woefully impoverished. The pursuit of such a life represents a falling short of the possibilities that are ours as human beings; a liberal life turns the adventure which is possible for us into a boring affair unworthy of our efforts.

19 Hauerwas' critique of interest-group liberalism as being unable to deal with issues of a genuinely public nature follows the analysis and arguments of Theodore Lowi and Robert Paul Wolff. See Hauerwas' essay, "Politics, Vision, and the Common Good" in *Vision and Virtue* (1974).

20 See Hauerwas' essays on the family, sexual ethics, and abortion in *A Community of Character* (1981).

21 Both liberal theory and the historicist approach defended by Hauerwas recognize moral relativism as a problem. Liberal theory is relativist or skeptical

with reference to questions of the good. In the face of widespread disagreement on religious and moral matters, and despairing of any possibility for achieving agreement on full moral conceptions of the good, it has attempted to determine valid principles of adjudication independent of those full conceptions of the good. It attempts to be neutral with reference to them. Thus, the charge that is often made in a liberal society such as ours that moral matters are regarded as relative or subjective is half true. It is true in that liberal theory is relativistic with reference to what is good. It is only half-true because liberal theory attempts to determine universally valid principles of right. So, an individual may pursue whatever wants or desires he or she regards as good, so long as the rights of others are not violated.

The historicist understanding of the problem of relativism is different because of its sense that no such universal principles of right are available.

[22] He does insist, correctly, that even where violence has been accepted as possible for Christians, as in just war theories, there has been a strong presumption against the use of violence.

[23] Hauerwas notes that many interpretations of "the ways in which Jesus is claimed to be morally significant often bear little likeness to the Jesus we find portrayed in the gospels."

> Indeed Christian ethics has tended to make "Christology" rather than Jesus its starting point. His relevance is seen as resting in more substantive claims about the incarnation. Christian ethics then often begins with some broadly drawn theological claims about the significance of God becoming man, but the life of the man whom God made his representative is ignored or used selectively. Some have placed such great emphasis on Jesus' death and resurrection as the source of salvation that there is almost no recognition of him as the teacher of righteousness. Or even Jesus' death and resurrection are secondary to claims concerning Jesus as very God and very man—for it is God taking on himself our nature that saves, rather than the life of this man Jesus (1983:72).

[24] I am not perfectly comfortable with this way of putting the matter. It may be more accurate to say that the kingdom's norms are absolutely binding despite their eschatological character and whether or not complete observance of them is possible. Whether Hauerwas means to claim that "perfection" is possible in this life is not clear. While his thought clearly tends in that direction it must also be remembered that he insists that "the world" remains in the Christian. Is complete conversion to the kingdom possible before the kingdom comes? Again, this may not be the most important consideration: the point is that Jesus' kingdom ethic remains absolutely binding for Hauerwas whether or not it may be perfectly fulfilled. The "ought" may not necessarily imply the "can."

[25] For example, one might expect some expression of the tension between the kingdom as present in Jesus and as it will be ultimately fulfilled similar to that found in Wolfhart Pannenberg. Pannenberg speaks of "the End of all occurrence" taking place "proleptically" or by way of anticipation in the resurrection of Jesus. The End or the kingdom which will be present for all and in all in the eschatological future is

proleptically present in Christ's Resurrection, but only for and in him.   (See Panneberg, 1967.)

26 It might be suggested that the language of possibility has the temporal element that I am denying is present in Hauerwas' discussion of the Kingdom of God. In the language of Aristotle, possibility implies potentiality but not actuality and the movement from potentiality to actuality, like all movement, is movement in time. This is true; however, the point would rather seem to be that just as Aristotle would insist that what is only potential is still real, likewise for Hauerwas that peace is present possibility means that it is real, at least for the Church, in such a way that its ethical significance is immediately and directly relevant.

27 The full quotation is worth repeating:

> . . . Christians are a people who believe that we have seen the end; that the world has for all time experienced its decisive crisis in the life and death of Jesus of Nazareth.   For in his death we believe that the history of the universe reached its turning point.   At that moment in history, when the decisive conflict between God and the powers took place, our end was resolved in favor of God's lordship over this existence.   Through Jesus' cross and resurrection the end has come; the kingdom has been established. Indeed it has come in such a fashion for it is a kingdom that only God could bring about (1985a:165).

28 Hauerwas writes:

> I will try to show how the very following the way of God's kingdom involves nothing less than learning to be like God. We learn to be like God by following the teachings of Jesus and thus learning to be his disciples. . .

> We are called to be like God: perfect as God is perfect. It is a perfection that comes by learning to follow and be like this man whom God has sent to be our forerunner in the kingdom. That is why Christian ethics is not first of all an ethics of principles, laws, or values, but an ethic that demands we attend to the life of a particular individual—Jesus of Nazareth. It is only from him that we can learn perfection—which is at the very least nothing less than forgiving our enemies (1985a:75–6).

29 Hauerwas uses a quotation from A. E. Harvey which reflects the inescapable tension between present and future.

> Jesus' message has power, not in spite of, but because of its promise of a future which is not ideal or utopian, nor a mere variation for the better on what we already know, but is both radically new and able to be envisaged on a human time scale, "in our generation." Faithful and eager attention to such a future introduces a new dimension into the present; for the present becomes, not a mere working out of consequences of the past, but a transition to an altogether different future. The present is transformed by the discovery of possibilities which were not apparent until it was seen in the light of the future (Harvey 1982:71–72).

[30] Hauerwas notes that, in *An Interpretation of Christian Ethics*, Reinhold Niebuhr had regarded forgiveness "as the hallmark of Christian ethics," but that over time self-sacrificial love replaced forgiveness as the central norm of Christian life in Niebuhr's work. He contends "that Niebuhr was much closer to being right by focusing on forgiveness than love as more important for the systematic display of Christian ethics" (1985a:46–47, n. 20). For Niebuhr, the natural sinfulness of man makes *agape* an "impossible possibility" and not directly applicable in history. Forgiveness, of course, presupposes sin. Sin does not make forgiveness impossible. Rather, it is sin that makes forgiveness necessary. Thus, Hauerwas' preference for forgiveness over self-sacrificial love is consistent with his sense that the characteristics of a Christian life which were displayed in the life of Jesus are directly applicable in a way Niebuhr would not allow.

[31] Hauerwas also associates living out of control with living at rest or living with Sabbath "as the form of life."

> Jesus proclaims peace as a real alternative, because he has made it possible to rest—to have the confidence that our lives are in God's hands. No longer is the Sabbath one day, but the form of life of a people on the move. God's kingdom, God's peace, is a movement of those who have found the confidence through the life of Jesus to make their lives a constant worship of God. We can rest in God because we are no longer driven by the assumption that we must be in control of history, that it is up to us to make things come out right (1983:87).

[32] Hauerwas' understanding of the importance of the virtue of hope indicates again that he is not able to completely avoid the language of anticipation. Even here, however, his judgement that living according to the norms of the kingdom is a present possibility because it has been made present and real in Jesus is not changed. Hope is necessary because the presence and reality is not "full."

[33] When Hauerwas does refer to our obligations to neighbor and enemy it is usually to make the point that those obligations are not grounded in a universal norm of respect for life, but in the example of Jesus. This is a point he draws from John Howard Yoder (See 1983:88).

[34] While I cannot find a reference to children as strangers in his essays on abortion in the same volume from which the above quotation comes, what he does say in those essays is certainly consistent with the view that the stranger often comes in the form of children. For example, he writes:

> In particular, a community's willingness to encourage children is a sign of its confidence in itself and its people. For children are a community's sign to the future that life, in spite of its hardship and tedium, is worthwhile. . . .
>
> More profoundly, children signal a community's confidence because they are bound to change our society and their existence foretells inevitable challenge. Our stories and traditions are never inherited unchanged. Indeed, the very power and truth of a tradition depends on its adaptation by each new

generation. Thus, children represent a community's confidence that its tradition is not without merit and is strong enough to meet the challenge of a new generation (1981:209).

We will see why this comment is consistent with his view that the strangers whom we must welcome often come in the form of our own children when we see the role that the stranger plays for Hauerwas in terms of the epistemological problem entailed by his understanding of the narrative-dependence of our moral concepts.

Hauerwas does refer to the fetus as a stranger in this same essay, but he uses the language there to criticize the Roman Catholic approach to abortion which stresses the fetus' "right to life." Such a view, he says, suggests that "the relationship between fetus and parent were that of a stranger to a stranger" (1981.207).

[35] See "On Keeping Theological Ethics Theological," in *Against the Nations* (1985a).

[36] Hauerwas is able to praise the accomplishments of liberal moral theory in this regard. For example, he says, "Rather than condemn contemporary moral theory for being trivial and/or abstractly irrelevant, it must be seen as an extraordinary moral project that seeks to secure societal cooperation between moral strangers short of reliance on violence" (1981:120).

[37] Reinhold Niebuhr made a similar point in the context of his own critique of the illusion of universally valid moral norms (although he himself regarded love and justice as universally valid in a very general way, at least):

Men seek a universal standard of human good. After painful effort they define it. The painfulness of their effort convinces them that they have discovered a genuinely universal value. To their sorrow, some of their fellow men refuse to accept the standard. Since they know the standard to be universal the recalcitrance of their fellows is a proof, in their minds, of some defect in the humanity of the non-conformists. Thus a rationalistic age creates a new fanaticism. The non-conformists are figuratively expelled from the human community (1960:18).

Interestingly, Hauerwas has acknowledged the Niebuhrian pedigree of his insight (See 1985a:84, n. 26).

[38] The Yoder quotation is from *The Original Revolution* (1971:116).

[39] See "The Christian Case for Democracy" in *The Priestly Kingdom*, (1984).

[40] See especially "Authority and the Profession of Medicine" and "Salvation and Health: Why Medicine Needs the Church" in *Suffering Presence*, and "Truth and Honor: The University and the Church in a Democratic Age" and "How Christian Universities Contribute to the Corruption of Youth" in *Christian Existence Today*.

[41] Quoted by Hauerwas in the "Introduction" to *Christian Existence Today* (1988:4).

[42] Ernst Troeltsch apparently regarded church and sect as descriptive categories and thought that the different ecclesiologies they designated represented inherent features of the New Testament kerygma (See Troeltsch 1981:331–342). Moreover, H. Richard Niebuhr's elaboration and development of the distinction in *Christ and Culture* is presented as describing "a series of typical answers" to the problem of how the Christian community relates to the world, answers which "represent phases of the strategy of the militant church in the world." The purpose of the study, says Niebuhr, is "to set forth typical Christian answers to the problem of Christ and culture and so to contribute to the mutual understanding of variant and often conflicting Christian groups" (Niebuhr, H. R. 1951:2). Hauerwas contends, however, that "Troeltsch assumed the superior character of a church-type ethic," and that, for Niebuhr, "Christ transforming culture is normative given the deficiencies of the other types" (1987:87). See also the "Introduction" to *Christian Existence Today* (1988) and John Howard Yoder's unpublished article "How Richard Niebuhr Reasons: A Critique of *Christ and Culture*:" upon which Hauerwas' argument depends.

[43] Hauerwas interprets Quirk's challenge this way:

> In short, he asks whether the argument I have made for the social importance of the integrity of the church is determined primarily by my criticisms of liberal social orders or is in principle a critique of any polity. As he puts it, the issue is not whether I am a sectarian but rather what kind of sectarian one should be. Is my sectarianism dependent upon the kind of challenge living in a liberal society presents, or is it in principle a sectarianism that regards every society and its correlative political form finally a form of atheism (1987:88)?

[44] The challenge is also for liberals like Amy Gutman and Emily Gill who seem to have accepted Sandel's understanding of the human self. (See Gutman 1985; and Gill 1986.) (The same might also be said for Rawls.) I would argue that neither have understood the implications of their own admission that we are partially encumbered and partially autonomous selves. Sandel himself recognized this.

Both Gutman and Gill go so far in the acceptance of communitarian convictions that they overlook the way in which the concept of the common good violates the liberal concept of neutrality. The communitarian critique of liberalism represents a fundamental challenge to the liberal idea of strict governmental neutrality, because liberal neutrality severely limits the degree to which conceptions of the good, even commonly discovered or chosen ones, can be backed by the authority of government. But, if our conceptions of the good are largely discovered together, and those conceptions are constitutive of who we are, then liberalism has misunderstood human choice and agency and its principle of neutrality has in fact undermined its exercise by preventing its broadest and most self-expressive form: in political union with others in the pursuit of a good that defines us.

4

Rosemary Ruether:
The United States and Women's Liberation

FOR BOTH Reinhold Niebuhr and Stanley Hauerwas, liberalism provides the foil against which their own positions are developed. Liberalism figures prominently in their work because each understood his own position as a corrective to the versions of liberalism which he regarded as providing the dominant approach to social and political ethics in the United States. Each developed and elaborated his conception of Christian social ethics by pointing to the contrasts between it and liberalism. Liberalism serves no such function in the work of Rosemary Ruether. Her foil and foe is patriarchy.[1] Liberalism is assessed in terms of the role it plays in undermining the ideology that supports the social structures of male domination and its power to set loose the creative human activity that forms social structures that are an alternative to patriarchy.

On Ruether's view, liberalism has played a prominent role in the effort of women to overcome patriarchy. Its fundamental conviction that all human beings are equal was and is utilized by feminists to argue against views that regard women as relevantly different from and inferior to men and to combat conceptions which would limit women to particular roles and functions in society, roles and functions which are usually supplemental or auxiliary to the more important tasks of men. Contemporary feminism, on Ruether's view, has its roots in liberalism. Yet, Ruether regards liberalism as inadequate as a tool for the liberation of women for several reasons. First, while liberal feminism focuses its attention and criticism on the factors that have prevented women's full participation in the public spheres of work and politics, it has not always been aware of the economic factors which have prevented women's effective participation in those spheres. Liberal feminists, says Ruether, have often failed to incorporate class analysis in their effort to understand the structures of patriarchy. Moreover, they have often won women the formal right to participate in the public spheres of human society only to discover that women are handicapped by the "double shift" of duties that are theirs because of the primary responsibility that they bear for the necessary tasks of the private or domestic sphere. The result is that those women who succeed as a result of the efforts of liberal feminism are those whose economic status enables them to be free of domestic responsibilities through the labor of working class women. This criticism of liberalism as it relates to the liberation of women is part of a general criticism of liberal economic theory, including its defense of private property, which is implicit in Ruether's thought. Secondly, Ruether regards liberalism as committed to a particular distinction between public and private spheres which is inherently patriarchal. While liberal feminism wins women access to the public sphere, it does nothing to break down the distinction between spheres nor does it challenge the inadequate modes of functioning within the public sphere.

Those modes of functioning are grounded in liberal anthropological convictions or a liberal conception of the self which Ruether regards as mistaken. I have argued that liberalism derives its conception of a just society from a view of human nature which emphasizes the capacity of every individual to devise an autonomous conception of the good life. Liberal rights are intended to protect that capacity and allow its expression. Basic institutions are evaluated in terms of the degree to which they protect this capacity. I will show that Ruether has a social conception of human selfhood that is in fundamental contradiction to the liberal conception. As a result, while she affirms autonomy, her conception of it is different from the liberal one. Moreover, I will argue that her conception of the human person is very similar to that of Hauerwas and that her conception of autonomy is one which Hauerwas can affirm. This suggests parallels between communitarian and radical critiques of liberalism which have been ignored for the most part. I will explore some of the poles around which a fruitful conversation between Hauerwas' communitarian critique and Ruether's radical or Marxist-inspired critique might take place.

Before considering the specific terms of Ruether's liberal critique, however, it is helpful to have a grasp of Ruether's theological base points, her analysis of the ideological and social structures of human evil, and her vision of a good or liberated human consciousness and society. In the first major section of this chapter I will examine her theological base points, including her conception of women's experience of oppression as the primary source of theological and ethical insight. I will also examine her appropriation of what she calls a "prophetic-liberating principle," which she draws from Christian scripture and employs as a fundamental hermeneutical tool. This section will conclude with a detailed examination of Ruether's ecclesiological position. The second major section of this chapter will be dedicated to Ruether's use of the concept of dualism (or alienation) to understand the ideology and social structures of evil or oppression and her understanding of a reconciled or liberated consciousness and social structure. Along the way, I will point out some of the broad terms of the relationship between her theological, ideological, and sociological analyses and her critique of liberalism. The more detailed consideration of that relationship will be delayed until the third and concluding section of this chapter.

Theological   Base   Points

Women's   Experience   of   Oppression   as   Women

We have seen that Reinhold Niebuhr's theological anthropology provided the base point from which his entire political ethic sprang. His conception of the human person was the basis of both an account of the sources of religion, a philosophy of religion, one could say, and the social ethical principles which provided the criteria by which human social and political institutions were evaluated. In the previous chapter, we commented that Niebuhr had no highly developed doctrine of the church and no sense that the church had a unique social ethical task. I attributed this, in part, to the fact that he regarded the institutions of a liberal society as embodying the insights he derived from his theological anthropology. In contrast, Stanley Hauerwas' conception of Christian social ethics is cast in terms of ecclesiology. For Hauerwas, being the church, that is, being a people whose vision and posture toward the world is determined by its relation to the story of Jesus of Nazereth, is the unique social ethical task of Christian people. This was a task made difficult by liberal convictions and by a belief, like Niebuhr's, that fundamental ethical truths were embedded in liberal institutions.

If Niebuhr's starting point was a conception of human nature, and Hauerwas' is the unique posture and vision of persons for whom the story of Jesus is uniquely authoritative, Rosemary Ruether's theology begins and remains firmly rooted in the experience of female oppression. She begins her most systematic theological work affirming "women's experience as a basic source of content as well as a criterion of truth" (1983a:12). That experience is understood by Ruether as above all else an experience of oppression as women. To take that experience as one's starting point is to regard women's liberation or "the promotion of the full humanity of women" as "the critical principle" of theology (1983a:18). On this basis she writes, "Whatever denies, diminishes, or distorts the full humanity of women is, therefore, appraised as not redemptive." And, by contrast, "[W]hat does promote the full humanity of women is of the Holy" (1983a:18–19).[2]

The tension between full or authentic human potential and the actual quality of human existence, a tension which is expressed in Christian theology in terms of the contrast between the first and second Adam or between sinful humanity and Christ, serves as something of a philosophy of religion for Ruether.

Out of this tension and contradiction arise the fundamental theological
questions about man's "nature," his "origin" and his "goal"; how man can
transform himself in his personal and social history and what "power" and
from whence mediates between this transcendent "nature," "ground" and
"goal," and his "fallen" reality. These questions can be readily recognized
by traditionally trained Christian theologians as the basic credal doctrines
of God, man, creation and fall, sin and redemption, Christology and
eschatology. But these doctrines are no longer taken so much as answers
than as ways of formulating the questions. These questions no longer find
answers in once and for all events of a particular sacred history, so much as
these histories themselves provide particular paradigmatic experiences used
by different cultures for symbolizing these questions (1972:3).

The similarities and the contrasts between the perspective expressed
here by Ruether and that of Niebuhr are striking. Both see religious
experience as arising out of fundamental tensions in human experience.
As we saw in Chapter 3, for Niebuhr the human experience of self-
transcendence over the finite and limited aspect of our nature is the ground
of all religion. Human religion is, according to Niebuhr, an expression of
the "essential homelessness" of the human spirit which arises because of
the tension between the finite or creaturely dimension of our nature and
our capacity for transcendence which makes us aware of that tension.

Whereas for Niebuhr religion springs from this ontological tension,
Ruether sees the source of religion in ethical terms. It is the tension
between what we are and what we ought to be from which religion
springs. Moreover, while for Niebuhr the ontological tension which is the
source of religion is written into the makeup of the individual human
being, Ruether sees the ethical tension to which she points as both an
individual and a corporate or social phenomenon. For Ruether, both the
individuated self and human evil are fundamentally social.

Ruether's view that the wellspring of religion is the tension between
the "is" and the "ought," or between human existence and essence, and
her own consciousness of being a member of an oppressed class which is
uniquely victimized by that tension leads her to an appropriation of what
she calls "the prophetic-liberating principle" in Christian scripture and
tradition as the most fruitful resource within the Christian faith for dealing
with and imagining a resolution of the tension. Ruether identifies four
themes which characterize this principle.

(1) God's defense and vindication of the oppressed; (2) the critique of the
dominant systems of power and their powerholders; (3) the vision of a new
age to come in which the present system of injustice is overcome and God's
intended reign of peace and justice is installed in history; and (4) finally,
the critique of ideology or of religion, since ideology in this context is
primarily religious (1983a:24).[3,4]

Eschatology and Ecclesiology

The fourth aspect of the prophetic-liberating principle, the critique of religion, has been a fundamental aspect of Ruether's scholarly work from its beginning. In the early stages of her career her attention was directed primarily toward ecclesiology. Her concern was to criticize those conceptions of the church which prevented it from being a vehicle of liberation and justice and to identify those conceptions which reflected the Christian community's effort to be such a vehicle. Later, particularly after the emergence of her own feminist consciousness, her attention was directed toward religious symbolism and the ways in which it is used to sanctify oppressive social structures or to enable the imagining of alternatives.[5] It is the ecclesiological aspect of the critique of religion with which I am concerned at this point.

In her first book, *The Church Against Itself*, Ruether developed an ecclesiological argument which can be understood as an application of the prophetic-liberating principle to the Church.[6] In the first chapter of that work, she derides "the self-delusion of a triumphalist ecclesiology which confuses the church's historical existence with its divine essence" (1967:2). The distinction or "schism" between the church's existence and its essence, between what it is and what it ought to be,

> is none other than the schism that lies at the heart of man's existence, dividing man from his own creational being. The mission of the church is the overcoming of this schism. But the church is men, and thus is itself a part of the very schism that it seeks to overcome through the power of the Good News. Thus we have the terrible paradox of the very instrument for the proclamation of man's freedom from the law of death, itself most deeply entrenched in the law of death. Here then is the final intensification of the schism in human nature that manifests the full extent of the brokenness of man's heart (1967:10).

Therefore, the basic ethical tension which is an aspect of all human experience and from which religion springs is an aspect of the church's experience as well. That tension is not overcome even in the life of that community which hopes for and bears witness to its eventual resolution.

The relationship between history and eschatology. Ruether regards a proper understanding of the relationship between history and eschatology as the key to a theology of the church which maintains a sense of the church's full participation in the fundamental ethical tension which characterizes all human life. Ruether sees two ways in which the church's eschatological hope for the achievement or restoration of the full humanity of human persons must be related to the church's historical existence. First, eschatological hope must be the basis of an effort by the church to embody in its own life the first fruits of the human restoration to full humanity. Secondly, Christian hope stands in radical judgment against the manifold ways in which that full humanity is still denied in historical existence. Ruether rejects any theology of the church which regards the eschatological hope of the Christian community either as unrelated to the historical possibilities of human life or as already perfectly manifest in the church such that the ecclesiastical institution is beyond judgment. In other words, Christian eschatological hope in the full restoration of ideal or essential humanity stands in judgment over all the ways that full humanity is denied. At the same time it means that partial manifestations of such a restoration are a real possibility in history. For that eschatological hope or vision to retain its critical function "the literal eschatology of the apocalyptic community"[7] must be translated "into one which can be mediated and renewed again and again within history" (1967:10).

Ruether wants to insist that the belief in the church as an alternative community over against the world, a community in which the restoration of essential humanity is already taking place, must be maintained despite the fact that the completion of that restoration has been forestalled and history goes on and on, *and* despite the fact that the community of redemption itself never is a perfect embodiment of that restoration. She denies that such a commitment to the church as an alternative community (itself under judgment) can be maintained so long as the relationship between history and eschatology is understood literally as it was by the early church and by the Anabaptist communities of the Radical Reformation. For such communities, the sense of living a real alternative in which the schism between the "is" and the "ought" of human existence is being bridged was able to be maintained because the full restoration of essential humanity and the fulfillment of a liberated world was thought to be about to happen in a literal historical process. Such a view could not withstand the crisis caused by the delay of that fulfillment. The result of this inability to sustain a commitment to the church as an alternative community was the triumph of the "early Catholic" ecclesiology of Luke. In the Lucan alternative to the ecclesiology of the apostolic Church, says Ruether,

> primitive Christian eschatology gives way to salvation history. . . . The parousia, having been pushed off into an indefinite future, loses its power either to beckon or to threaten, and the church, settling down into "church time," absorbs the powers of salvation into herself, while postponing the pay-off for a remote time to come (1967:57).

Contemporary Catholic ecclesiology represents a version of this Lucan solution to the problem of the apostolic understanding of Christian eschatological belief. On this view, the Christian faith is de-eschatologized because the eschatological goal, the restoration of essential humanity or the achievement of the liberated community, ceases to function as either a guiding or a critical principle over against the actual life of the church and the world. Thus, on the Catholic view as Ruether interprets it, the element of radical judgment upon the church implicit in the eschatological hope of a full humanity is lost entirely rather than being understood without the historical literalism of the early church.

Ruether's own conception of the church as the community of redemption and her conception of the way in which the church translates the historical-eschatological dynamic draws heavily on the Reformation in both its mainline (Lutheran and Calvinist) and radical (Anabaptist) forms. Despite her criticism of the Anabaptist understanding of the relationship between history and eschatology, she appreciates the ethical seriousness of Anabaptist ecclesiology with its effort "to manifest the Kingdom of God here and now" (1967:21). She also seems to regard the ecclesiology of the Radical Reformation as too inconsistently applying the critical principle implied by the eschatalogical expectation of a restored humanity to the church itself.

From the Lutheran and Calvinist ecclesiastical tradition she appropriates the view that the church stands always under judgment. On this view, the church "is to be continually remade by the direct action of God" (1967:16). Yet she is critical of the Lutheran failure to regard sanctification as made manifest in history in the life of individual Christians and in the Church. Luther's theology of the cross, she says, emphasized "forensic justification," and, while not lacking any doctrine of sanctification, it "rules out any manifestation of sanctification. Our sanctification is not non-existent, but it remains hidden for our own good. For us, here and now, we are to know only Christ crucified" (1967:27).

> But then the cry goes up: "but nothing happens! The New Life never does anything! Church history doesn't go anywhere! There is no progress or development in history!" For those of us who have been firmly taught that historical progress is a Christian doctrine, this is an intolerable saying. Few are content to remain always at the cross, but insist on passing on within history from dialectic to synthesis.
>
> Thus, the experience of judgment and justification must result in moral progress, both at the individual and at the social level. The church must move "from dialectic to new synthesis" within history (1967:27).

Ruether insists that this new synthesis is itself always "dialectical," by which she means that "the New Life has come and we live in its first fruits, and these are not barren but efficacious in man's personal and communal life. Nevertheless, constant renewal is necessary to keep it alive and new fall is always possible" (1967:28).

For Ruether, this dialectical synthesis can only be sustained if eschatology is demythologized or dehistoricized such that "the drama of the turn of the aeons," which the apostolic and Radical Reformation churches experienced in their own life, is encountered "as an ever renewable dialectic which does not exclude but rather continuously reconstitutes the historical existence of the church" (1967:60). The concentrated attention which Ruether directed in her earliest works toward the Radical Reformers, the Puritan revolutionaries, and the various utopian Christian movements from the early middle ages to the twentieth century, can be understood in terms of the commitment she shares with those groups to the church as an alternative community in which the first fruits of a fully liberated humanity are being harvested. The criticism that she directs toward those groups has to do with her view that the eschatological Kingdom of God to which the Gospel points entails a perennial judgment on the achievements of that community of liberation, a continuous openness to the new possibilities of liberation which history presents, and a constant watchfulness for new forms of oppression that arise when such future possibilities are foreclosed.[8]

A Secular Theology of the Church. In *The Church Against Itself,* Ruether's argument for an ongoing ecclesiastical posture of self-criticism led to the conclusion that the church is never bound by its own past nor its own tradition. "The Church," she wrote,

> can exist in history only in a paradoxical manner. It can retain its continuity with itself only by not clinging to what it has become, but by letting itself go. Therein lies the paradox of "tradition," for tradition is really tradition—that is, true continuity with the gospel—only when tradition is free to be discontinuous with itself (1967:61).

She also argues that "those most perceptive in understanding and most active in exercising a witness to Christ are found on the fringes of the institutional church, even outside its formal boundaries." God, she insists, is "not limited" to the church "but shall raise up people to do his will wherever he pleases" (1967:64).

A willingness to work within the Christian tradition and mine its resources while feeling no sense of being bound by its limits has always characterized Ruether's work. She has always drawn upon the experience and wisdom of those on the fringe of the institutional church and even beyond it. Thus, in *The Radical Kingdom,* she studies and plumbs the insights of the Radical Reformers, Puritan Revolutionaries, Christian and Socialist utopian communities, Marxism, and the North American youth movements of the 1960's. Later, when she begins her analysis of the religious roots of patriarchy, she does not hesitate to examine ancient pagan traditions for resources which might be helpful for understanding and withstanding the forces of patriarchy which traditional Jewish and Christian religious symbols have empowered and justified.

This openness to, or even preference for, the insights of those on the fringes of the Christian community and beyond reflects and has its roots in Ruether's conviction that the dominant conceptions of ecclesiology in both the Catholic and the Protestant traditions have profoundly misconstrued the relationship between history and eschatology. Both have tended to dull the prophetic or revolutionary edge of the gospel by interpreting the relationship between the eschatological hope of a restored humanity and the historical existence of the church in such a way as to diminish the impact of that hope on the historical reality of the world. Catholic ecclesiology has done so by seeing the restoration as indefinitely delayed and by its confidence in the institutional church as the present sacramental point of contact with that indefinite future. The mainline Protestant tradition has done so by its tendency to denigrate the possibility of personal or social manifestations of restored or redeemed humanity in the church, and, especially, in the world.

Thus, on Ruether's view, the predominant conceptions of the relationship between eschatology and history which shape the self-understanding of the church dull the sharp edge of the prophetic-liberating principle of the gospel, and, as a result, undermine its ability to serve as resource for resolving the tension between human existence and human essence. As a result, the revolutionary, or liberating potential of the Christian message,

> could only be released in a post-Christian world, in a world where the monopoly of Christian society upon history had been thrown into question. . . . Therefore it should not surprise us to discover that historical expectation reenters Western history in a social revolutionary form as a movement that sets itself in opposition to the established church and Christian society. Historical expectation reemerged with the movement of the West into a post-Christendom era (1971:17).

Ruether opts then for "a secular theology of the church" (1970:158). It is not necessary for our purposes to consider in detail the theological arguments that have been made and the debates that have been waged under the rubric of "secular theology." It is only important that we grasp what Ruether has borrowed from that perspective in constructing her own ecclesiology.

The primary importance of what Ruether wants to affirm by her argument for a secular theology of the church has already been made clear in terms of her view that religion arises from the tension between the "is" and the "ought" of human life and her adoption of the conception of full humanity or the prophetic-liberating principle of the Bible as the critical principle of her Christian feminist theology. Her concern is to affirm that the church does not exist for itself but for all humanity; that its attention should be directed to the liberation of the human community and not the preservation of its own institutional structure; that when the church is faithful to its task it is about the business of making possible and exhibiting in its own life the closing of the gap between what human life is and what she has called its "aspirational horizon"; and, that the church does not represent a spiritual sphere of human existence set apart from the secular with a purpose or *telos* which is to be distinguished from the common human aspiration for fulfillment of the human essence. "The church in its biblical definition," she says,

> is "the community of the New Creation." This new creation is creation itself redeemed and made new. Therefore if the church is the community of the new creation it is not basically a special ecclesiastical world of its own raised up in a sacred social structure beyond the life and destiny of creation; it is simply creation and human society considered from the point of view of where God's activity is renewing the world. Secular society proposes a radical testing of the church that dissolves the claim of that structure that calls itself by ecclesiastical titles to any monopoly on being the place where this renewal is most likely to be happening. If the church is human society considered from the point of view of God's renewing action in history, then it is basically a secular reality. Wherever the Spirit is stirring the waters and groups of men are on the rise to overcome alienating and false modes of existence and form a more authentic life of brotherhood, that is where the church is. This view supposes that the New Creation is not somehow the captive of ecclesiastical ministries and channels, but is a free spirit abroad in the land and whose presence is recognized wherever alienation is being overcome and human community built up (1970:159).

Ruether is quick to contend that this "obliteration of the distinction between the sacred and the secular" does not entail the dissolution of "the more fundamental distinction between the church and the world." What it does entail is that the distinction between "the arena of redemption and the arena of false, fallen modes of life," that distinction which characterizes for her the distinction between church and world, is to be differentiated "from the institutional line between ecclesiastical organizations and those nonecclesiastical or so-called 'secular' organizations that encompass the greater part of our social life" (1970:159–160).

Ruether also regards her secular theology of the church as criticizing the view that separates public or political life from private or individual matters and associates religion with the private sphere. She insists that her defense of a secular ecclesiology is not to be construed as an affirmation of the modern sense that the sacred is to be "divorced from what we call secular processes" or from political and economic life. Ruether's secular theology of the church is not an affirmation of this "secularism" which sees the secular sphere as self-sufficient and independent of the sacred, which is itself delimited to a private sphere where the individual is related to God. Rather what she means to do is "to dissolve the delimiting boundaries of church and religion that relegate these to an insignificant corner of man's life and to recover the biblical sense of the gospel as a message about the whole of life" (1970:162).[9]

At the same time Ruether's insistence that all spheres of life are to be related to the sacred is not meant to be an affirmation of "sacralism" or "an emanational view of the universe." Secular theology "wants to avoid the past mistake of relating social structures to God by making them sacred, holy, and immutable" (1970:162) as if they came to be by "flowing out of the divine and imitating it as an image founded on a divine likeness" (1970:163). The desacralization of the world which secular theology sees as necessary for restoring a sense of the world as God's creation, means that the world

> is truly finite and historical. It is not finished or predetermined in its movement, but provisional and open-ended. This is the modality of being of the creature as one who is contingent yet free. The creature stands before the Creator with his own distinct being and personhood to make his own decisions maturely in response to the life given it by the Creator. As a radically temporal being he is not bound back to some eternal pattern of being that fixes his possibilities. He exists precisely as Becoming. He is a distinct, nondivine reality responding to the work of the Creator by living responsibly in his own temporal frame of reference (1970:163).

In this context, Ruether interprets human sin as "the effort to abolish the free finitude of created being for divinization, to become 'like Gods.'" (1970:164). On this understanding, the emanational view of the universe, combined with social conservatism, represents the paradigmatic example of human sinfulness. Such a view delimits human freedom and openness while making idols of existing social arrangements.

In summary, Ruether's secular theology of the church puts the Biblical prophetic-liberating principle at the center. It is meant to designate her denial that sharp distinctions can be drawn between sacred and secular spheres such that the church is relegated to a private dimension of human existence and the salvation which it seeks is alienated from the human aspiration for the fulfillment of its essence, or the fulfillment of our highest aspirations for ourselves as human beings. Moreover, through its denial of what Ruether calls "an emanational view of the universe," her secular theology of the church represents a refusal to regard that aspirational horizon as already fulfilled in the present social structures. No such structures, either ecclesiological or "secular," can ever be regarded as perfectly mirroring the divine image or as being founded on human nature. The "aspirational horizon of meaning and value" is always an open horizon which must never be foreclosed.[10]

The terms of the distinction between church and world. How is the church distinguished from the world, on Ruether's view? In the Introduction, I distinguished three factors which deeply influence the way theologians draw the distinction between church and world, or three ways in which the distinction between church and world may be drawn. Each of those factors have implications for the church's distinctiveness in the world and for the posture toward the world which is regarded as appropriate for the church. The first factor is whether or not the church represents a unique epistemological perspective which enables it to have moral knowledge which is unavailable to the world. The second has to do with whether or not the same moral principles or values are regarded as valid for both church and world such that persons in each are held accountable to the same standards of conduct. The third has to do with the possibilities for the achievement of the norms and ideals which are regarded as valid. Even where church and world are regarded as knowing and being accountable to the same moral principles and rules, they may be distinguished with reference to the resources available to the church which enable living in conformity with those norms. On Ruether's account, the church is distinguished from the world primarily with reference to its embodiment of the full humanity which is the universal criterion by which human life and institutions are judged.

While Ruether consistently regards the church itself as subject to criticism from the perspective of the prophetic principle, or of the "aspirational horizon of meaning and value," she does not mean that the church's moral life is no different from that of the world. Or, to put the point in terms which explicitly draw the comparison between her perspective and that of Niebuhr, her "realism" with respect to the possibilities for realizing perfect humanity and perfect human community in history does not result in a view which minimizes (to the point of nearly eliminating, as in the case of Niebuhr) any distinction between the moral possibilities of the church and those of the world. On the contrary, the church is characterized by its embodiment of the ideal humanity which represents both our created essence and our future possibility. The church is "the avant-garde of liberated humanity" (1983a:193). It is "where the good news of liberation from sexism is preached, where the Spirit is present to empower us to renounce patriarchy, where a community committed to the new life of mutuality is gathered together and nurtured, and where the community is spreading this vision and struggle to others" (1983a:213). For Ruether, the church is distinguished by its greater embodiment of the full humanity which is possible for all persons than is evident in the world. The church experiences the first fruit of the human hope for the full harvest of human possibilities and struggles for a deeper experience of those possibilities while the world remains a barren wilderness.

Ruether shares with Hauerwas a sense that one's particular perspective determines what one sees or what norms one will regard as authoritative. This suggests a perspective like his which distinguishes church and world on epistemological grounds. However, for her, the privileged or authoritative perspective is not that which is characterized by its relation to the story of Jesus, (or not *just* such a perspective). Rather, for Ruether, as for liberation theology in general, it is the experience of oppression which provides the privileged hermeneutical or epistemological perspective. That experience and the authority of the norms drawn from it does not correspond to the sociological boundary between church and world. For Ruether, the norms drawn from the experience of oppression are visible from beyond the boundaries of the church and are applicable to the whole world. Thus, she rejects any perspective which refuses to seek the application of those norms beyond the boundaries of the particular community which regards them as authoratative, whether that community is the church or a non-religious liberation community. For example, she refers to an "eschatological feminism" which applies different moral norms to the church from those which it regards as authoritative in the world. Such a feminism "implicitly agrees that the subordination of women in society is unchangeable within history" but "insists on equality in the Church, for the Church belongs not to the world but to the transcendent sphere of redemption" (1983a:101). She also is critical of what she calls a "radical feminist" perspective that calls for the separation of women from men, denying the possibility of men's redemption. To the degree that Hauerwas' view is characterized by a sense that the norms drawn by the church from the story of Jesus are not normative in the world, Ruether's view is sharply distinguished from his. Of course, it is not that Hauerwas regards Christian norms as less than universally valid. He regards them as universally valid, but as requiring conversion to be seen as such. In the absence of such a conversion, individuals in the world are not regarded as accountable with reference to those norms. Ruether's view also requires a conversion, but it is to a dealienated consciousness which overcomes the false consciousness which fails to see the way human beings are interdependent with one another and with nonhuman nature rather than to the story of Jesus.

For Ruether, the same norm of liberation applies to both church and world. The content of such a norm is not drawn, as are Niebuhr's norms, from a universally valid conception of the human person, nor does it seem to be drawn from a perspective characterized by its relation to the story of Jesus, as for Hauerwas. It is not different norms or a unique epistemological perspective which seems to characterize Ruether's distinction between church and world. Finally, it is the greater possibilities for the embodiment of the norm of liberation as a result of "the Spirit" which has power there and the commitment of the community to the liberated life.

Eventually, however, even this distinction between church and world becomes ambiguous in Ruether's work. The church's record as a community which has embodied liberation is not an impressive one, to say the least. Moreover, she regards the church as only one community which has the possibility of embodying liberation in a way that distinguishes it from the world.[11] As we have seen with reference to her secular theology of the church, while she means to maintain a distinction between church and world, that distinction does not conform to the sociological distinction between the church and secular institutions. The church to which she refers in the distinction between church and world is wherever liberation is taking place and does not refer to the church as an institution. While the refusal to equate the church with ecclesiastical institutions or even with the body of those who profess faith in Christ has a long history in Christian thought, as in the case of Calvin's well-known distinction between the visible and the invisible church,[12] the church is usually regarded as a subset of those who profess faith if not of those who are affiliated with ecclesiastical institutions. Ruether's distinction between church and ecclesiastical institutions (and, one may guess, between church and those who profess faith in Christ) suggests that the church is both narrower and broader than the boundaries of the institution. It is commitment to liberation and participation in a community of liberation that apparently defines church for Ruether.

But how does she understand the relationship between such commitment and participation, on the one hand, and commitment to Jesus and participation in the Christian community, on the other? Ruether does affirm that "the centre of Christian theology," and presumably of Christian life, "is not an idea, but a person, a historical person, Jesus of Nazareth" (1983b:1). Charles Scriven's exposition of Ruether's thought says that it is "encounter with God" which makes liberation possible (Scriven 1988:109). Recall however, Ruether's insistence that "whatever diminishes or denies the full humanity of women must be presumed not to reflect the divine or an authentic relation to the divine, or to reflect the authentic nature of things, or to be the message or work of an authentic redeemer or a community of redemption" and that "what does promote the full humanity of women is of the Holy" (1983a:18–19). For Ruether, it is the full humanity of women or women's liberation from oppression which provides the key for identifying and understanding the divine. The usual Christian affirmation has been that Jesus of Nazareth provides the key for understanding the divine and for understanding what it means to be fully human and to have our essential humanity restored. It is not clear in Ruether's thought how Jesus of Nazareth functions to clarify either. Scriven finally says that despite Ruether's appeal to the story of Jesus in support of her own commitment to women's liberation, her attention to Jesus is highly selective. She ignores as much as attends to Jesus.

> Her selective ignoring of Jesus certainly suggests that however important the authority of Christ is for Ruether's exposition, it remains nevertheless a highly ambiguous authority.

> That this is so seems consistent with Ruether's overall account, according to which God is "the imageless one" whose Word is a constant challenge and surprise. But how, we may well wonder, does this relate to the

apparently opposite claim of the New Testament that affirms Jesus Christ as the very image of the invisible Father (Scriven 1988:115–116).[13]

A test case for Scriven, and certainly from Hauerwas' perspective, is Ruether's attitude toward violence. He regards her comments as an example of her selective attention to Jesus. He notes that, with reference to both Reinhold Niebuhr and to Latin American liberation theology, she shows a "sympathy for the use of violence in a just cause." He notes, however, that "[w]hen she does so, she does not invoke the Jesus story, nor even consider the New Testament's account of Jesus' own attitude toward political violence" (1988:115).

Scriven's comment here is on target. In *To Change the World*, Ruether speaks of "a situation of total violence" in parts of Latin American and notes that "there is no way to protest or struggle without evoking violence" (1983b:29). She also says, "Non-violent struggle is no protection against unjust violence in a system which is maintained by unjust violence" (1983b:28). Such comments are accurate, but, from the perspective of Jesus' authority over the lives of Christians, they are beside the point. The question is not whether Christians may evoke violence or put themselves at risk in a struggle for justice, but whether, in the light of Jesus example and teaching, they may use it. One may come to the conclusion that they may (indeed, many Christians, possibly the majority, have come to this conclusion), but if a relationship to Jesus is the defining element of the church, that is, if Jesus is at the center of the Christian life, then one has to account for the relationship between that judgment and Jesus' teaching and example. That Ruether does not provide such an account demonstrates the ambiguous role Jesus plays in her conception of the Church.

One wonders what is the relationship between violence and her judgment that

> Jesus' originality does not lie in his spiritualization of the kingdom, but rather in the fact that he saw the true fulfillment of its early hopes in a more radical way than many of his contemporaries. He did not see the struggle against injustice and oppression primarily as a holy war against the Romans. This does not mean that deliverance from oppression did not include deliverance from the Romans. But Jesus looked deeper than the oppression of Israel by Rome to the fundamental roots of oppression itself. . . . Unless this fundamental lust for domination is overcome, a successful war of liberation will only replace one domination with another. Jesus seeks to model, in his own life, a new concept of leadership based on service to others, even unto death. This is the model that he wishes to impart to his followers (1983b:15).

Interestingly, one of the more typical contemporary ways of arriving at a judgment that violence may be justified for Christians while still taking

Jesus' teaching and example as authoritative is not available to Ruether. Some have argued that Jesus' teachings were set in the context of an expectation of an imminent establishment of the Kingdom of God which rendered usual moral commitments (including those which require protecting the innocent by force) null and void. Once that expectation is seen to be false, the prohibition of violence is no longer valid. Paul Ramsey has taken such a view in his *Basic Christian Ethics* (1950:36ff, 66ff, and 165ff). Such an option is unavailable to Ruether because she argues against the literal conception of the relationship between eschatology and history on which such a view is based, and argues for the constant directive and critical importance of the idea of the Kingdom of God or the hope of restored humanity for the church's life.

None of this is to suggest that the commitment to human liberation (and the preferential option for those who are oppressed) cannot be justified on biblical grounds or with reference to Jesus' life and teachings. It is not to suggest that Ruether has failed to pay attention to the biblical resources for such a commitment. Nor is it meant to suggest that human religious commitment can exist apart from a sense that the object of that commitment is committed to the well-being and fulfillment of the human person and the human community. Christian faith holds not simply that God exists and that Jesus of Nazereth is the central revelation of the nature of God, but that the God who has become known to us in Jesus is good, is for us, and is worthy of our worship. Nor am I ignoring the hermeneutical problem which Ruether and liberation thought in general has so keenly recognized. I do not deny that our interpretation and understanding of Jesus is profoundly influenced by the concerns and commitments that we bring to the biblical text. Ruether is to be applauded for making her concerns and commitments clear, and Hauerwas can probably be faulted for having too much confidence that he is able to identify what Jesus' life and teaching mean for us and for paying too little attention to the hermeneutical problem.

What my comments do mean to suggest is that Ruether's ecclesiology can be faulted for not making clear how either the biblical witness or the person of Jesus who is at the center of the Church challenge and shape her conception of the full humanity of women. Liberation thought has insisted that theological insight arises out of a hermeneutical *circle*. The contemporary community brings its own commitments (and suspicions) to the text, but the movement is circular in that one's commitments are in turn challenged and informed by the text. There is to be a "fusion" of the horizon of the text with that of the contemporary community such that its own horizons are expanded and new insights gained.[14] At one level, Ruether's work may be understood as a masterful application of such a method. She has set up a dialogue between contemporary movements for social change and the eschatological hope expressed in scriptures; she has brought the biblical sense that the fulfillment of human hope is always finally an act of divine grace, and therefore can be identified with no particular human achievement, to bear upon to the sometimes self-righteous and unrealistic utopianism of contemporary revolutionary movements. My complaint is that Ruether has not made it clear how the biblical text, and in particular its witness to Jesus, informs and challenges and shapes our conception of the fulfillment for which we aspire.

Oppression and Liberation: From Dualism/Alienation to Integration/Reconciliation

For Ruether, the questions to which theology addresses itself arise out of the tension between the "facts" of human existence, especially the reality of human sinfulness and oppression, and the human aspiration for the fulfillment or realization of the good which is possible for human beings. That living out of our full humanity is made impossible by the evil which is characteristic of our human existence. The church is to be that community which has begun to experience redemption from evil and the fulfillment of the highest possibilities of human nature. Of course, this characterization of Ruether's philosophy of religion and her ecclesiology tells us nothing about her understanding of evil and human liberation. Our task in this section is to consider that understanding.[15]

Dualism as Alienation

Ruether's analysis focuses on the intellectual and symbolic patterns in human consciousness or thought that correspond to and accompany our oppression of each other and our exploitation of the earth in ways that thwart the achievement of our highest human possibilities. She believes she has discovered a common form in human consciousness which both reflects and perpetuates evil in our lives. Moreover, the social structures of oppression correspond to this same pattern.[16] Her conception of human liberation, and her understanding of the forms of consciousness, thought, and symbolization which may serve as vehicles for that liberation, also follow a common pattern.

Over and over again Ruether argues that the ideological and sociological structures of oppression follow a dualistic pattern in which aspects of thought and life which, on her view, ought to be seen as mutually or reciprocally related and of equal value, are separated, polarized, and hierarchically related such that one term of the dualism is inappropriately valued and the other inappropriately denigrated or under-valued. Her formal conception of the structures of liberation is one that requires the reconciliation of those forms of thought and life which have been so alienated such that they are recognized as mutually related and are valued together. Dualistic patterns of thought and symbolizations, particularly with reference to the divine or God, human nature, and the relationship between humanity and the natural world, are the mechanism in human consciousness which serves to justify evil in human life. She identifies dualistic patterns of thought which accompany an array of evils which are regarded as thwarting the human experience of our full humanity: sexism, racism, anti-semitism, ecological destruction, and economic and political exploitation.[17] On her view human liberation from such evils requires forms of human consciousness and social structures in which the dualistic patterns are replaced by those in which aspects of life which can be differentiated are related on equal rather than hierarchical terms.

Ruether's analysis of evil or oppression in terms of dualistic patterns of thought and social structures is similar to the use Marx and Feuerbach made of the concept of "alienation" which they had borrowed from Hegel.[18,19] Gajo Petrovic has defined alienation as "the act, or result of the act, through which something, or somebody, becomes (or has become) alien (or strange) to something, or somebody, else." He notes that alienation is often understood as equivalent to "reification," that is, "the act (or result of the act) of transforming human properties, relations, and actions into properties and actions of things which are independent of man and which govern his life" (1967:76). Petrovic's definition of reification indicates that the alienating act is an act of human consciousness whereby human properties or human creations come to be regarded as independent of people's conscious activity. That is to say, alienation is understood as a human act whereby properties, relations, and actions that are human come to be regarded as beyond human control and, as such, alien or strange from the human perspective. Thus, at its most basic level, alienation is self-alienation in a double sense. First, it is the action of a human self or human selves. It is something done *by* human selves and not *to* them. Secondly, it is to regard aspects of of ourselves which are properly human as alien or strange or as not subject to human control. Therefore alienation is *from* the human self. It is to treat that of which the human self is truly subject as an object over against the self. Alienation is usually understood as alienation of the self, from itself, through the self's own action or as a result of its own action.[20] It should also be noted that the reification of some aspect of the self, the mistaken regarding of it as an object over against the self as subject, is also accompanied by a denigration or devaluation of the reified term. Petrovic writes:

> Self-alienation is not simply a split into two parts that are equally related to the self as a whole; the implication is that one part of the self has more right to represent the self as a whole, so that by becoming alien to it, the other part becomes alien to the self as a whole (1967:79).

Petrovic's account of the concept of alienation as self-alienation or reification is applicable to Ruether's identification of the dualistic patterns of thought and symbolization which lie behind human evil. For Ruether, dualism involves the identification and separation of two aspects of human experience and the regarding of one of those as alien or strange. That identification and separation is a human act, an act of human self-consciousness. Moreover, though the identification and separation is an act of human consciousness, the dualistic pattern is regarded as "'natural,' inevitable or divinely given" (Ruether 1975b:xiv), and, as such, beyond human control. Finally, one term of the pair which is separated or polarized in human consciousness is falsely regarded as superior and the other inferior. In summary, the dualistic patterns of thought which Ruether employs to understand and explain the power of evil over us represent acts of human consciousness whereby aspects of our life which ought to be held in co-equal relation are polarized and placed in opposition or in hierarchical relation. Those dualisms are falsely regarded as natural or divinely ordained and therefore inescapable or beyond human control.

That alienation, for Ruether as for Marx, is fundamentally self-alienation is not to suggest that either used the term only with reference to what were regarded as defects of individual self-consciousness. For both, alienation has social dimensions, and even dimensions affecting the human relation to the non-human world. Petrovic has noted that, in the passage entitled "Alienated Labor" in Marx's *Economic and Philosophic Manuscripts*, "four forms of man's alienation" are suggested: "the alienation of man from the products of his activity, the alienation of man from his productive activity itself, the alienation of man from his human essence, and the alienation of man from other men" (1975b:78). He has also noted that Marx talked about other forms of alienation without carefully distinguishing and organizing those forms. Bertell Ollman also notes the various forms alienation takes in Marx (1976:133ff), and Allen Buchanan seems to regard the multiple forms of alienation to which Marx refers as a positive factor which makes the theory of alienation "rich enough to encompass the pervasiveness of exploitation in capitalism" (1982:42).

Ruether's conception of alienation is also multi-faceted. She speaks of alienation "as operating on three levels: 1) alienation from oneself, from one's body; (2) alienation from one's fellow person in the 'alien' community; (3) alienation from the 'world'; from the visible earth and sky" (1972:16–17). Despite an effort to organize and relate the various levels on which alienation works, she is, like Marx, capable of generating a seemingly endless list of dualisms which she employs to analyze evil and to suggest a vision of liberation. For example, in her earliest reference to dualistic patterns of thought which must be overcome if the movement from oppression to liberation is to occur, Ruether cites the dualisms of individual and collective, nature and grace, oppressor and oppressed, body and soul, subject and object (1972:7–22). In a recent book she refers to false dualisms between "faith and life, prayer and action, and daily work, contemplation and struggle, creation and salvation" which liberation theology attempts to overcome (1983b:19). In that same work she cites false dualisms between judgment and promise, particularism and universalism, law and grace, letter and spirit, old and new Adam, and history and eschatology which have contributed to Christian anti-Semitism (1983b:33–40).

Body-Soul and object-subject dualism as the fundamental expression of self-alienation. While Ruether can be criticized for failing always to organize and relate the various dualisms or forms of alienation which she identifies, it is possible with reference to Ruether, as with reference to Marx, to identify certain fundamental forms of alienation or the fundamental dualisms which characterize human oppression and the structures of consciousness which reflect and justify that oppression. For Ruether, the most basic dualistic patterns of thought which must be overcome are those which draw distinctions between body and soul and between subject and object. The dualism of body and soul became dominant in Christian thought, she says, through the influence of biblical apocalypticism (which divided history into eons of sin and redemption and the human race into damned and saved) as interpreted through the eyes of Gnosticism with its fundamental dualism of material and spiritual or body and soul. These twin influences, according to Ruether, "gave to classical Christianity a dualistic mode of moral, epistemological and ontological perception." She regards this classical Christian mode of perception as "substantially responsible for constructing the very world of alienation from which we seek liberation" (1972:16).

While Ruether sees the "anti-material spirituality" of classical Christianity as having been partially corrected in the empirical worldview of modern science, that correction was incomplete because the Cartesian epistemology on which modern science is based is grounded in a similar dualism of subject and object.

> Thinking and knowing were a process whereby a non-material thinking subject reduced all around him, including his own body, to the status of an object to be mastered. Reality was split into a "non-material thinking substance" and a "non-thinking extension" or "matter." Subject-object dualism and the objectification of "outer reality" has been the basis of modern science. So, although Renaissance man repudiated one aspect of classical Christian spirituality, modern scientific man preserved an analogous bias, in a dualistic perception of outward reality as "dead matter" (1972:17).

What makes dualistic patterns of thought evil or oppressive is not simply their identification of contrary aspects of human experience; it is, rather, the setting of those aspects into opposition, and the devaluation of one aspect over against the other, which is then regarded as superior or as representing the true essence of humanity, or as the sphere or realm in which human fulfillment is possible. What makes the dualism of body and spirit wrong, from Ruether's perspective, is that two aspects of human being which are both a part of the human essence and neither of which are overcome or negated in the fulfillment of that essence are set in opposition such that one, the body or material aspect of human existence, is devalued and the other, the spirit, is regarded as superior and the sole bearer of the human essence and the fundamental (if not exclusive) realm of human fulfillment.

We have already seen that Ruether regards alienation as operating on three levels: alienation from one's self, from others, and from the external world. From her perspective, in which it is fair to say not that one *has* a body, but that the human person is embodied, the setting of body and spirit into opposition and the devaluation of the body results in self-alienation because an aspect of one's selfhood, one's body, is regarded as alien or strange or as less representative of the human essence, and another aspect, the soul, is thought, as Petrovic says, "to represent the self as a whole." Moreover, the subject-object split, which is related to the soul-body dualism in that the soul is identified with the subjective quality of human existence and the body with the experience of the non-self as object, results in alienation from the external world. The "earth, air, water, plants and animals," which share the material qualities of the human body, "are not perceived as living 'beings' who form a single community of life" with the human person. Rather, "[t]hey are seen simply as 'objects to be used'" (1972:18).

Ruether is not as clear about how the subject-object dualism is mistaken as she is about how the dualism of body and spirit is mistaken. Along with the Cartesian epistemological perspective she wants to affirm the human person as subject. Yet, both the subject-object and soul-body dualisms are manifest as social oppression when some persons or groups are treated as objects, and their possession of those qualities which make autonomous subjectivity possible is denied, or when they are identified with the bodily rather than the spiritual qualities of human existence. But it is not clear how that which is objectified by human consciousness, and is thus split off from it and set in opposition to it, is properly related to the human subjectivity. For Marx, alienating objectification[21] occurred when the object was a creation of human subjectivity but was contrary to the interests of the self which brought it into being and/or was regarded as outside of human control as, for example, when the product of labor was not owned by the one whose labor brought it into existence, or when the value of the product was determined by supply and demand regarded as "natural" laws. Ruether seems to have something different in mind when she speaks of the objectification of the external world. The earth and sky are surely not human creations and are properly regarded as somehow independent of human subjectivity. What her comments suggest is that she regards their treatment as objects as alienating when such treatment results in a disregard for the interdependence of human life and the external world. While it is clear that treatment of the body as an object external to the self improperly regards as non-self or alien what, from Ruether's perspective, ought to be treated as an aspect of the self, the alienated earth and sky are not intended by Ruether to be regarded as aspects of the self. Rather, they are alienated by being seen as in opposition to the self rather than interdependent with it.

Self-alienation, male-female dualism, social oppression. Alienation from the body results, according to Ruether, in an inappropriate hatred of the body and fear of sensual pleasure and bodily feeling. Alienation from the "world" is at the root of the contemporary ecological crisis. But Ruether also wants to insist that the soul-body and subject-object dualisms are at the root of social oppression. "Social oppression in Western culture has operated out of a psychology which projects this same dualism of body and soul, subject and object into sociological alienation and oppression" (1972:18). Ruether's point is that those alien or devalued aspects of the self are projected onto or identified with those groups which come to be oppressed as a way of justifying their oppression. Moreover, it is denied that such groups have the spiritual qualities that are regarded as essentially human, or the qualities which make human subjectivity possible, or, if they have them that they have them to a degree that makes the oppressed group relevantly equal to the oppressing group. Lacking the qualities of subjectivity, they are treated as objects to be used for the purposes of the oppressing group.

A fundamental claim made by Ruether is that "sexual or male-female dualism was the original model for this social projection of psychic dualism" (1972:19). This claim does not mean that women are "the only ones to suffer from a social projection of psychic polarization." It suggests rather that

> we must see [the] sexual model as providing the basic model for all types of social oppression and its accompanying cultural appropriation and institutionalization. This same model of social projection of psychic dualism has been extended to each of the other rejected, subjugated groups in society (1972:20).

Or, as she put the matter in the opening pages of *New Woman/New Earth:*

> Sexual symbolism is foundational to the perception of order and relationship that has been built up in cultures. The psychic organization of

consciousness, the dualistic view of the self and the world, the hierarchical concept of society, the relation of humanity and nature, and of God and creation - all these relationships have been modeled on sexual dualism. . .

The male ideology of the "feminine" that we have inherited in the West seems to be rooted in a self-alienated experience of the body and the world, projecting upon the sexual other the lower half of these dualisms. As Simone de Beauvoir pointed out many years ago in her classic study, *The Second Sex*, in male-dominated societies it is always woman who is the "other," the antithesis over against which one defines "authentic" (male) selfhood. But a repressive view of the alien female was also the model for the inferiorization of other subjugated groups, lower classes, and conquered races. Subjugated groups are perceived through similar stereotypes, not because they are alike, but because the same dominant group (ruling-class males) are doing the perceiving. All oppressed peoples tend then to be seen as lacking in rationality, volition, and capacity for autonomy. The characteristics of repressed bodiliness are attributed to them: passivity, sensuality, irrationality, and dependency. The dominant race, class, and sexual caste, on the other hand, model their self-image after ego or consciousness. They are the true humanity or selfhood, possessing intrinsically the qualities of initiative, reason, capacity for autonomy and higher virtues (1975b:3–4).[22]

Ruether's claim about the priority of male-female dualism is derived from her study of the history of ideas and religious symbolization as it relates to women, and much of her historical analysis is dedicated to justifying this claim and explaining the historical process "whereby the female person, possessing a different but strong body and an equal capacity for thought and culture, was subverted and made to appear psychologically and intellectually inferior" (1975b:5).

Liberation as Overcoming Dualism and Alienation through Integration and Reconciliation

Integration and Reconciliation at the level of human consciousness. Just as Ruether's analysis of evil suggests that the structures of human consciousness follow a pattern whereby elements of human experience are separated and set in opposition, with one term of the pair elevated and valued over against the other, which is in turn suppressed, denied, used as means to some greater end, or undervalued, a liberated consciousness is one that reunites the polarized pair, recognizing their dialectical relation or their mutuality of relation rather than their opposition.

We have already seen this pattern in our discussion of Ruether's ecclesiology. Recall that Ruether sees the key ecclesiological dilemma as the relation of history and eschatology. She rejects those dualistic views which would draw a sharp distinction between the "fallen" or sinful historical existence of the church and the world, and the hope of an eschatological restoration of the human essence. It seems fair to suggest, using the terms we have used to describe the idea of alienation, that those who hold such dualistic views regard eschatology (the world to come, heaven, the Kingdom of God) as in opposition to (or in judgment over) history. Moreover, the eschatological dimension is of higher value and it is in its "triumph" over the historical dimension that salvation or the restoration of full humanity or the human essence is achieved. Ruether, on the other hand, sees history and eschatology as properly related in a dialectical synthesis in which the eschatological hope remains in constant tension with the history such that the restoration of full humanity stands in constant judgment over, even as it is partially realized in, history. Her rejection of a linear conception of the relation of history and eschatology, and its "flight to the unrealizable future," and her call for "conversion to the center, conversion to the earth and to each other," also follows the pattern of integrating and setting in dialectical or mutual relation elements of human experience which have been set in opposition or in hierarchical relation (1983a:255–6).

In her most systematic theological work, *Sexism and God-Talk*, Ruether provides the outline of liberated consciousness with reference to theological language, anthropology, and the relation of humanity to nature. Her vision of the social structures which accompany a liberated consciousness, which has always followed this pattern of integrating and mutually relating persons, groups of persons (distinguished by gender, race, or class), and traditionally distinguished spheres of life, is also restated there. With reference to language about God, conceptions of and myths about the divine which justify hierarchical relations or relationships of dominance and submission between human beings (especially males over females), and which reflect a sense of a differentiation and hierarchical relation between matter and spirit, or between the limited, physical dimension of human existence and the transcendent ego of the human self, are to be replaced by language drawn from the experience of women and other dominated groups which names the divine as ground of both material and spiritual being.

While calling for female images of the divine, Ruether rejects the use of such images to capture "the feminine side of God" while merely perpetuating "patriarchal gender hierarchy" (1983a:61). "Adding an image of God/ess as loving, nurturing mother, mediating the power of the strong, sovereign father, is insufficient" (1983a:69). She wants to affirm images of the divine which "include female roles and experience" (as well as the "images drawn from the activities of peasants and working people, people at the bottom of society"), but what she is seeking to avoid is alternative images (to those drawn from the experience of ruling class males) which merely add to the dimensions of the divine while maintaining the association of women or peasants with humility and nurturing roles. "God/ess language cannot validate roles of men or women in stereotypic ways that justify male dominance and female subordination" (1983a:69). Just as she rejects a romanticist response to western dualism (a response which accepts the dualistic differentiation while reversing its devaluation of the feminine and its regard for masculine characteristics),[23] it is fair to assume that Ruether would also reject female images of the divine which continue to associate the female with particular characteristics while reversing the valuation of those characteristics with relation to masculine characteristics. What Ruether seems to favor, then, is male and female images of the divine which suggest no hierarchical relation between characteristics regarded as masculine or feminine, nor even a complementarity of male and female characteristics.[24]

Her alternative to the theological language which conceives the divine as transcendent spirit over and above nature is the divine as "Primal Matrix" or "ground of being." "Feminist theology," she writes:

> must fundamentally reject this dualism of nature and spirit. It must reject both sides of the dualism: both the image of mother-matter-matrix as "static immanence" and as the ontological foundation of existing, oppressive social systems and also the concept of spirit and transcendence as rootless, antinatural, originating in an "other world" beyond the cosmos, ever repudiating and fleeing from nature, body, and the visible world. Feminist theology needs to affirm the God of Exodus, of liberation and new being, but as rooted in the foundations of being rather than as its antithesis. The God/ess who is the foundation (at one and the same time) of our being and our new being embraces both the roots of the material substratum of our existence (matter) and also the endlessly new creative potential (spirit). The God/ess who is the foundation of our being-new being does not lead us back to a stifled, dependent self or uproot us in a spirit-trip outside the earth. Rather it leads us to the converted center, the harmonization of self and body, self and other, self and world. It is the *Shalom* of our being (1983a:70–71).

Ruether suggests in this quotation that it is not the differentiation of body and spirit to which she objects, but the identification of the divine with only one term of the pair. For her, the divine must be imaged as the ground of our material and spiritual being.

Ruether's comments with reference to God-language suggest her alternative conception of the relation between human beings and nature and her alternative anthropology. Feminist theology, she says, "must question the hierarchy of human over nonhuman nature as a relationship of ontological value. It must challenge the right of the human to treat the nonhuman as private property and material wealth to be exploited" (1983a:85). Human beings, she insists, must see their unique capacities for transcendence and intelligence as in continuity with other forms of "the radial energy of matter." "We must respond to a 'thou-ness' in all beings" (1983a:87). We must see "the responsibility and necessity to convert our intelligence to the earth" (1983a:88–89), recognizing our "interdependence" with nonhuman nature. "The notion of dominating the universe from a position of autonomy is an illusion of alienated consciousness" (1983a:89).

Integration of public and private, work and home. We have seen that Ruether regards the self-alienation or alienated consciousness which is at the root of the whole structure of dualistic patterns of thought as correlated with the alienation between human beings and with alienated social structures. Oppressed racial minorities, the poor, and, especially, women have been identified with the lower terms in the basic dualisms of body-soul and subject-object and in the dualism between nature and humanity. Such groups have been assumed to possess high measures of those qualities associated with the body or nature and to be deficient in those qualities of spirit and subjectivity which are regarded as essentially human. This view has served to justify the inferior social status of women, non-white races, and the poor. It has also resulted in social structures which divide human life into separate spheres and the assignment of particular groups to roles within those spheres.

The most basic such separation, or the one on which Ruether's attention is most sharply focused, is the distinction between public and private, or domestic, spheres of life and the traditional association of women with the child-rearing and housekeeping roles of the domestic spheres. Ruether's understanding of liberation from this alienation of public and private spheres and from women's association with the lower or private sphere follows the pattern we have already seen. She rejects any alternative to this traditional mode of women's oppression which accepts the basic distinction between spheres. On her view, romantic, liberal, and Marxist responses to the traditional oppression of women are all guilty of such an acceptance.

She rejects the response of romanticism, despite its reevaluation of typically feminine characteristics and spheres, because it accepts the labeling of certain characteristics as male and others as female when, in fact, according to Ruether, there is no biological basis for such a distinction. An integrated human self-consciousness is one in which both traditionally male and female characteristics are affirmed and developed. She is especially critical when that romanticist reevaluation provides an additional argument for women's restriction to domestic roles.

She also rejects the liberal and the Marxist solutions. Liberalism, she says, "seeks to extend the rights of citizenship, suffrage, ownership of property, and access to political office, education, and all avenues of employment to women. It seeks to make women 'equal to men' within the public sphere" (1983a:43). While recognizing the significance of such a perspective, she regards the liberal solution as inadequate because the liberal perspective, while allowing women's access to the public sphere, continues to regard the "traditional male sphere as normative" and "offers no critique of the modes of functioning within it" (1983a:110). Moreover, it is often blind, she says, to the "double shift" of duties that women perform because of their continued disproportionate responsibilities in the domestic sphere, responsibilities which serves as a handicap to them in the public sphere.[25]

Marxism is more able to recognize the problem caused by the double shift, and Ruether praises typically Marxist measures such as "nationalized child-care centers, maternity leave with guaranteed re-employment, and communal kitchens" as "social preconditions for the equality of women in the economy which Western capitalist society is still not willing to accept" (1975b:175). Yet, she ultimately rejects the Marxist approach. While it "solves" the problem "by giving over female work to state agencies in order to integrate women into productive labor" (1975b:207), it does so in a way that only exacerbates the alienation of women from the exercise of their full potential. "If collectivism means state control, then an abolition of the home would be the total alienation of one's life to institutions external to one's own control and governed by a managerial elite" (1983a:226). Her own version of socialism, which she calls "communitarian," proposes a different solution. Her vision of a liberated society requires "transforming the relationship among power, work, and home."

> The strategy of a communitarian socialist society . . . would bring work back into an integrated relationship to self-governing living communities. Women's work is still communalized and professionalized, but control over these functions remains with families themselves who band together in groups on the level appropriate for particular functions. For example, a residential group would develop communal shopping, cooking, child care, cleaning, or gardening by collectivizing its own resources. The child is not taken out of the family into an impersonal state agency to free the mother for other activity. Rather, it gains a tribe while remaining rooted in the family (1983a:226).[26]

Once again Ruether proposes bringing into relationship spheres which have been divided and not just a simple reevaluation of the separated and hierarchically related spheres.

Reconciliation between persons. Self-alienation, on Ruether's view, is accompanied by alienation from one's fellow person. Ruling class males who define themselves in terms of the subjective, rational, or spiritual qualities associated with the transcendent ego are alienated from the women, racial minorities, and the poor which they associate with the alienated physical or bodily dimension of their own authentic selfhood. An integrated psyche is one in which the self has an integrated conception of itself such that both terms are regarded as human in their interrelation. Such an integrated conception of the human self corresponds with a conception of human relationships in which whole persons are related to one another non-hierarchically without preconceived notions of their unique natural characteristics based on race, gender, or class.

Ruether's conception of reconciliation in non-hierarchical relationships entails that all persons are liberated from the alienating relationships and not just those who are the victims of false dualisms. Just as Marx regarded communism as liberating the capitalist from the alienating relationships between persons in a capitalist society, Ruether sees the overcoming of false dualisms as enabling all persons, both male and female, oppressor and oppressed, to achieve their full humanity. She has included among her false dualisms one which would divide human beings into "children of light" and "children of darkness," along the lines of community of redemption vs. world or of oppressed vs. oppressor. Just as the church is always under the judgment of the Kingdom of God, the oppressed community seeking its liberation is always under the judgment of the vision of a fully reconciled community in which relationships of domination are overcome. Thus, even while she insists that "anger and pride . . . are the vital 'virtues' in the salvation of the oppressed community," and that "there is a sense where it is true that [the oppressed seeking their liberation] 'do not have the time' to be worried about the humanization of the oppressor" (1972:12–13), she quickly adds that they

> must also keep in the back of their minds the idea that the dehumanization of the oppressor is really their primary problem, to which their own dehumanization is related primarily in a relation of effect to cause. Therefore, to the extent that they are not at all concerned about maintaining an authentic prophetic address to the oppressors; to the extent that they repudiate them as persons as well as the beneficiaries of false power, and conceive of liberation as a mere reversal of this relationship; a rejection of their false situation of power in order to transfer this same kind of power to themselves, they both abort their possibilities as a liberating force for the oppressors, and, ultimately, derail their own power to liberate themselves. Quite simply, what this means is that one cannot dehumanize the oppressors without ultimately dehumanizing oneself, and aborting the possibilities of the liberation movement into an exchange of roles of oppressor and oppressed (1972:13).

Ruether has consistently maintained this refusal to divide human beings into final categories of good and evil, oppressed and oppressor. This sense that to dehumanize "the enemy" is to dehumanize oneself is behind her refusal to endorse what she calls a radical feminist approach which envisions males as beyond redemption and the redeemed community as one composed entirely of liberated women. "Separatism reverses male hierarchicalism, making women normative humanity and males 'defective' members of the human species. This enemy-making of males projects onto males all the human capacities for competitive relations and ego-power drives and hence denies that women too possess these capacities as part of their humanity" (1983a:231). This view, says Ruether, does not entail that "women's communes and collectives and lesbian families cannot exist as good human relationships, as well as experimental bases for an alternative humanity."Such communities," she says, must be "experiments on behalf of humanity, male and female" (1983a:231).[27]

Women's Liberation, Overcoming Alienation, and Liberalism

Liberalism and Women's Liberation

Ruether is capable of extending high praise to the political and theoretical project known as liberalism. Among its achievements, she says, are a renewal of the biblical tension between the transcendent hope of the achievement (or restoration) of full humanity and the historical reality of human life. She points to "the liberal doctrine of progress" as "a new secular version of the doctrine of the millennium that was to be brought within history and on this earth by the immanent workings of the forces of history" (1970:43). For Ruether, liberalism's combination of hope and historical political struggle represents a secular version of the proper dynamic relating of eschatology and history which she believes was lost in Roman Catholic ecclesiology.[28] Moreover, secular liberalism "restored that catholicity of salvation that had been lost through a narrowing interpretation of the saved community as solely historical Christendom and finally only the ecclesiastical community" (1970:44). As we have seen, Ruether rejects any conception of redemption that limits it to the ecclesiastical realm; the salvation of which the Jewish and Christian scriptures speak and for which the faith community longs is the redemption of the whole world. Liberalism, on Ruether's view, has believed that the hope it offers is available to everyone.

Related to this is Ruether's judgment that liberalism incorporates the sense of self-criticism entailed by a recognition of the tension between human hope and reality and the view that no historical achievement ever fully embodies that hope. Under the aegis of her discussion of the false dualism of oppressor and oppressed, she criticizes "modern revolutionary societies," including the Soviet Union, for having failed to assimilate "the fruits of liberalism that could provide a theory and an institutional base for on-going self-criticism and self-correction" (1972:14).

Yet it is from the perspective of women's experience of oppression and women's appropriation of what Ruether has called "the critical principle of full humanity" and "the prophetic-liberating principle of the scriptures" that liberalism must ultimately be evaluated. Is liberalism an adequate tool for the liberation of women? Ruether regards the contemporary feminist movement as having been inspired by liberalism and as working within a liberal framework for the most part. "Feminism itself arose in the late eighteenth century as a part of the ideology of liberalism," she writes (1975b:162). She refers to liberal feminism as "the classical ideology of women's rights, in the nineteenth century and today" (1983a:43). It has been an attractive ideology because it challenged the traditional identification of certain groups, including women, with the lower term of the alienated conception of the self or human nature which has characterized western thought. Liberalism, she says,

> broke down the naturalized orders of traditional hierarchical society that divided people into priests, lords, and serfs: head-people and body-people. An abstract equalitarianism, based on the possession by all "men" of practical rationality, united the human essence in a single definition. . . All social revolutionary movements that seek to overthrow the rule of the feudal and then the bourgeois classes, white domination and male domination, draw on this tradition of democratic, universal human nature (1975b:192).

As we have shown in the opening chapter, the liberal view of the human person emphasizes the capacity (or potential capacity) of every individual human being for autonomy or liberty as the defining element of human personhood. It is with respect to their having a capacity for autonomy that human beings are equal, according to liberalism, and it is the fact that they each have that capacity which makes all individuals sources of moral claims upon one another. Liberalism has been a tool for the liberation of all oppressed or dominated persons, including women, according to Ruether, because this core conviction breaks down the distinction between persons in terms of their association with one or the other of the two terms of the typically western conception of human nature: ruling class white men with the transcendent, autonomous, or spiritual term, women, the darker races, and the poor with the physical or material term. On the liberal view, all persons are defined by their capacity for autonomy and are thus deserving of equal liberty. Whereas on the traditional view, certain persons are naturally superior and therefore naturally in positions of authority or domination over others, on the liberal view, all persons are by nature equal, and whatever authority one has over another arises primarily as a result of a free contract between them.

Ruether is not hesitant to regard this view as an important contribution to the liberation of oppressed persons, including women. Liberalism, she says, testifies "to important truths that I wish to affirm" (1983a:109). She appreciates the fact that liberalism has regarded women as bearers of the rights it identifies. She notes with admiration that liberalism has been able to accommodate much of the agenda of feminism in the twentieth century.

> Twentieth-century liberal feminism has taken this quest for equal rights further [than the struggle to open the public sphere to women]: equal pay for

equal work, equal access to all levels of a profession once women are admitted to it, the breaking down of formal and informal structures of power by which women in professions are excluded from top leadership roles. . . .

Liberal feminism has also turned to the whole underside of male control over women's bodies which nineteenth-century feminists only began to question: women's rights to reproductive self-determination, sex education, birth control and abortion. It has focused on women's right to dignity and control over their sexual persons, against sexual harassment on the job, wife battering in the home, rape in the streets (or home), and pornography, which dehumanizes the cultural imagination about women. Lesbianism also has achieved its place in the liberal feminist agenda, although not without considerable stress (1983a:217).

In addition, Ruether identifies liberalism as one of several intellectual traditions which has opened the ordained ministry to women. The others are the tradition of historical criticism as applied to scripture ("which allows the antifemale passages in Paul and the pastorals to be put aside for more fundamental theological principles" (1975b:73)), and romanticism. But she regards liberalism as the most important.

Liberal feminism succeeds in opening up the ordained ministry to women. The liberal tradition reclaims the idea of women's equality in the *imago dei*, but secularizes it. . . . The arguments for women's ordination in the nineteenth century also draw on prophetic and romantic themes. The text of Acts 2:17–18, in which the gifts of the Spirit are said to be poured out on men and women alike, was constantly evoked to justify women's right to preach. Likewise it is said that women's altruistic and nurturing nature and her natural spirituality especially suit her for ministry. But these arguments carry weight only when combined with the liberal assumption that a just social order should grant equal rights and opportunities to all its members (1983a:198).

The Deficiencies of Liberalism

Despite this high praise for liberalism, Ruether ultimately regards liberalism as inadequate for providing the theoretical resources for the full emancipation of women and the movement toward an ideal society. She regards liberalism as inattentive to the economic factors that enable or prevent the effective exercise of that individual autonomy which liberalism seeks to protect, and shares with Marx the even more radical view that private property is inherently alienating. Of course, this critique of liberalism is not unique to Ruether. The more distinctive and interesting aspect of her critique is her view that the alienation of public and private spheres is essential to the liberal "project." There are two aspects of her critique of that distinction and its association with liberalism. We have already seen that she regards the distinction and separation of public and private spheres as falsely dividing elements of life that ought to be integrally related. Here we will examine in more detail her understanding of the way that distinction and separation contributes to the oppression of women. Particularly, we will consider her argument that this alienating split is an essential feature of liberalism. A second aspect of her critique of the distinction between spheres has to do with the view that modes of functioning within the public sphere, modes which she associates with males, are oppressive. She believes that, while liberalism is to be praised for opening the public roles to women, it has not been sufficiently critical of the modes of operation within the public sphere. Thus, liberalism assumes that traditionally male modes of acting are normative.

With regard to the first aspect of her critique of the relation between liberalism and the distinction between public and private spheres of life, I will argue that the separation which she regards as alienating is not the same as the liberal distinction between public and private based on liberal neutrality. The alienating separation which she identifies has more to do with industrial technology than liberal theory. Moreover, liberalism has been able to address the problems for women which Ruether identifies as caused by the distinction of spheres. Her critique of liberalism's failure to address oppressive modes of functioning within the public sphere seems to be more pertinent, but it is relatively undeveloped. It is stated, but not clearly explained or argued. I will suggest an interpretation of what she means by this critique and argue that this is the most fundamental and persuasive aspect of her critique of liberalism. That critique reflects a communal (or relational) and historical conception of human selfhood, and a conception of autonomy related to it, which is an alternative to the liberal conception we have described. It is with reference to this aspect of her thought that I will indicate some of the interesting parallels between her radical or Marxist critique of liberalism and Hauerwas' communitarian one.

Liberalism's misunderstanding of the economic basis of human autonomy and the critique of private property. Ruether has consistently argued the traditional socialist and Marxist view that liberalism, as an ideology of the rising middle and business classes of the 18th and 19th centuries, fails to address the problem of economic inequality which limits the ability of the poor to exercise their autonomy. For example, in *The Radical Kingdom*, she wrote of "the failure of liberal democracy to effect a more fundamental economic revolution for the benefit of the masses."

> Liberal democracy was exposed by socialism as a middle class ideology that rose in the struggle against feudalism on the part of the new economic class who wanted political power commensurate with their economic powers. It had little to say to those deprived of economic power. . . . This is why the have nots of the world are attracted to socialism rather than liberal democracy as the formula for change, because it gets at the fundamental economic injustices between classes that liberal democracy does not touch (1970:190–191).

In *New Women/New Earth*, she wrote that liberalism is "limited in its willingness to actualize" the "equalitarianism" of its conception of human persons as fundamentally equal. "It did not envision the restructuring of economic relations that would make equality meaningful for the poor" (1975b:192). More recently, she has written that liberalism "is hostile to any economic egalitarianism that touches private property" (1983a:41).

If Ruether's comments here are meant to indicate that liberalism is incapable of recognizing the impact of economic factors on the exercise of autonomy and to mount a convincing argument for the distributional adjustments which reflect that recognition, she is surely mistaken. Many liberals have argued for a positive conception of rights and for broad redistributional schemes. On the other hand, the idea that natural or general rights include positive economic rights remains highly controversial in the United States and has not been codified into law. Taxation and social welfare programs have been designed to have redistributional effects, but the fact that the arguments for such measures have generally avoided appeals to general rights claims contributes to the tentativeness and instability of those measures. While private property rights are often "touched" or overridden in our society, the strength of such rights and the relative lack of controversy with reference to their validity in liberal theory and among most persons in our culture, severely limits the ability of a liberal state to address the economic issues which liberal theory is capable of recognizing. Great economic inequality and grinding poverty continue to exist relatively unchallenged in our liberal society.

Of course, Ruether's reference to liberalism's failure to address "fundamental economic injustices between classes," or to "touch" private property, may indicate a much more profound sense of the inadequacies of liberalism. Even the recognition of positive economic rights and arguments, based on distributive justice, for a broad redistribution of wealth would not be sufficient if the very existence of the institution of private property represents alienated relationships between persons and classes. If this is what Ruether means, and Ruether's commitment to socialism indicates that it is, then, when she refers to liberalism's failure to touch private property, she has in mind its failure to do away with it, not the more questionable claim that it is incapable of overriding property rights in favor of claims based on positive economic rights or distributive justice.[29]

We have seen that Ruether calls her model of a dealienated society communitarian socialism. Socialism may be defined as an economic system in which productive property (or the means of production) is collectively rather than individually owned, and in which resource allocation and the distribution of economic goods are determined by a democratic political process (rather than by the uncoordinated results of free market exchanges between individuals). By *communitarian* socialism, Ruether means that the collectivity which owns or controls productive property is a small local community rather than a larger unit such as the national state. For example, she suggests that "restoring ownership of the means of production to the people" means that the ownership and management of factories and workplaces should be given "into the hands of local committees of workers, rather than making the workers employees of a state bureaucracy" (1983a:226–227). She also refers to "a communal family" as a basic unit of communitarian socialist society (1983a:227). She does suggest that larger units such as city, state, national, and international governmental organizations will have to be responsible for "planning, distribution, and enforcement of standards," but she insists that "these levels of government must be rooted in strong self-governing local communities" (1975b:207).[30]

Ruether's argument that a liberated society would be a communitarian socialist one suggests that she accepts Marx's view that the institution of private property is a fundamental social expression of self-alienation and a mechanism whereby self-alienation is related to alienation between persons. Of course, for Marx, private property seems to have been not *a* fundamental social expression of self-alienation, but *the* fundamental expression of it.[31] Whether Ruether regards it as so exclusively fundamental is not altogether clear.

In her most extended discussion of Marx on private property, Ruether notes the well-known relationship between Marx's conception of alienated labor and his critique of private property.[32] She argues that the turning point between Marx's early and later writings was "the discovery that alienated self-relationship empirically took the form of alienated social relationship" (1970:101). Once Marx saw that alienated labor or alienated productive activity manifested itself socially as class conflict (or the alienation of capitalists and the proletariat) through the medium of private property (the capitalist is defined as one who has private property rights over the means of production and the products of human labor, the proletarian as one who lacks such property rights),

> Thereafter Marx spoke no more of the problem of the alienation of the self as such, but only in its social form as class conflict between the proletariat and the capitalist. But this supercession of the problem of alienation by the problem of class conflict does not negate the former problem but merely transfers it to another level, namely, to the arena of its social manifestation (1970:101).

On Ruether's view, because Marx diverted his attention away from the root of all alienation in self-alienation, he was never able to answer the fundamental question he posed, "How does it happen, we may ask, that man alienates his own labor" (1970:109)? According to Ruether, he was aware, as many of his followers were not,

> that the mere conversion of the property relation into public property owned by all does nothing to change the servitude inherent in the property relationship itself. It merely turns the state into an abstract generalized capitalist and generalizes the servitude of all men relative to this public capitalist. . . .
>
> Rather, Marx insists that the emergence of true communism must go beyond mere socializing of property to the overcoming of the property relationship altogether, i. e. the self-alienation on which the property relation is based. Thus communism supposes a regeneration of man that abolishes all subservience of the world of things over the world of persons. We might express Marx's thought at this point in the language of Martin Buber by saying that the world of I-It relationships are overcome, and henceforth man and the world live in a direct communion of I-Thou relationships (1970:103).

Ruether contends that Marx's vision of the perfect or communist society "is scarcely less transcendent to the present historical condition of man's existence than biblical eschatology" (1970:104), which is to say that the overcoming of self-alienation in the perfect society can no more be associated with some particular form of social organization than can the Kingdom of God. Yet, by diverting his attention away from his fundamental concern with self-alienation to the social forms he saw as its manifestation, he came to suggest that by abolishing private property the fundamental self-alienation of man would also disappear. "Thus Marx ignored his earlier insight that the external alienation was based on the inner one, and believed that the inner one could be overcome by abolishing the external alienation" (1970:106). In effect, then, Marx "had no suggestion" as to how overcoming the inner alienation of the human being was to be accomplished (1970:107).

It is not clear precisely what Ruether's solution to Marx's dilemma is. She suggests that for Marx "to have pursued the question of why man alienates himself would have suggested that man is involved in a dilemma within his own nature that he therefore cannot abolish" (1970:106). This indicates the possibility that, in fact, overcoming alienation is impossible precisely because of some inherent contradiction in human nature, such as that upon which Reinhold Niebuhr's realistic approach to social change is based. But Ruether herself does not seem to regard human redemption as impossible on the basis of a conception of human nature. Indeed, her early work suggested that human redemption involved the fulfillment of the human essence and not overcoming it. While Ruether does argue for a permanent tension between history and the eschatological fulfillment or restoration of full humanity, that tension is not based on an inherent contradiction in human nature.

A more feasible possibility is that she does not regard alienated labor and its social manifestation in the institution of private property as the fundamental social manifestation of human alienation. For Ruether, it is the domination of men over women that seems to be the primary social manifestation of a self-alienated consciousness. In *The Origin and History of the Family, Private Property and the State*, which Ruether cites as "the basis for socialist doctrines of women's liberation" and a "primary text" for contemporary feminist reformers (1975b:167), Engels argued that the oppression of women derives from the institution of private property. On his view, primitive society was matriarchal with communal property and an egalitarian relation between men and women. There was also no monogamous marriage because "[w]ithout private property to inherit, there is no concern to differentiate legitimate from illegitimate children." When general wealth increased and private property was instituted, matriarchal society was overthrown. "Now the male wished only his own children, especially the male heirs, to be recognized. The woman then must be subjugated to the monogamous marriage as herself a piece of private property, strictly excluded from all other sexual relations, so that he can be sure that her children are his own" (1975b:168).

There are reasons to doubt that Ruether regards Engels' account of the oppression of women as accurate. She argues that it is mistaken to regard primitive culture as perfectly egalitarian. She regards the prevalence of distinct male and female roles and male dominance of the political realm as the earliest forms of female oppression (See 1975b:5–19). Therefore, even if she accepts Engels' account of the relation between private property and monogamy, she seems to regard female oppression as prior to both. This suggests that private property is not the fundamental social expression of an alienated consciousness. Thus, it seems fair to say that, while Ruether regards private property as a form of social alienation which will be overcome in a de-alienated society, its absence is not sufficient to assure that alienation has been overcome. Indeed, in her critiques of contemporary Marxist societies, she indicates that the collectivization of property under the control of the state is more alienating than private property arrangements in industrial capitalism.

> Socialist ideology seems to contain a fundamental contradiction: It has seen itself as restoring ownership of the means of production to the people, while at the same time it continues the process of industrialization, that is, collectivization of work outside the home. It has identified ownership by the people with ownership by the state and management by the party bureaucracy. The result has been a deepening of the alienation of people from their labor and the creation of a new ruling class, the party bureaucracy (1983a:227).

She notes that the burden imposed on women by the second shift of duties they fulfill in the home is a problem in socialist as well as capitalist societies. "It would seem that patriarchy plus industrialism is the cause of this pattern" (1983a:225). Both comments suggest that it is not private property which is the primary social manifestation of alienation. Rather, it is the distinction between public and private spheres (which is exacerbated by industrialization's concentration of technology outside the private or domestic sphere) which is its primary social manifestation. None of this should obscure Ruether's acceptance of the belief that the institution of private property is inherently alienating. The abolition of private property relations is a necessary condition, on her view, for the establishment of a fully human society. However, it does indicate both that she does not regard the abolition of private property as a sufficient condition for such an establishment and that its formal or legal abolition does not automatically destroy a private property relation.

Liberalism and the alienation of public and private spheres. Though the distinction and separation of public and private spheres which Ruether regards as alienated does not seem to be intimately related to private property, Ruether's critique of liberalism with reference to that split does not depend upon the relation of private property to it. Her description of the way that split affects women does not require reference to private property nor, as we have seen, does the impact disappear with the elimination of private property.

The problems created for women by the split between public and private have to do with their inferior status in the economic world which liberalism has opened to them, a status which is in part a result of the double work shift they perform as a result of their nearly exclusive responsibility for domestic duties. The result is that, despite the access to the public or economic sphere which liberalism wins for women, they are prevented from exercising (in relation to men) the equal liberty that liberalism promises. "Liberal feminism begins to analyze" these factors, but an adequate response to them "continually pushes the limits of liberalism itself" (1983a:227) and results in "the radicalization of liberal feminism." This radicalization refers to a move toward socialism and a call for the abolition of private property, for she says immediately that "Only socialist feminism provides the tools for analyzing these contradictions and envisions a new system that might solve them" (1983a:221).

Ruether has several things in mind when she refers to women's inequality in the economic hierarchy. First, she speaks of women as a marginal labor force, noting that historically women have been employed during times of expanding industrialization and during war, but that, "with a shrinking need for labor-intensive production" in advanced industrialism and during times of peace they are laid off. Secondly, she speaks of "a female job ghetto," describing the concentration of women in a few and lower paid professions (1983a:218). This marginalization of women as potential employees, and their concentration in a few low paying professions or work categories, is undergirded by the unequal burden women bear in the home. "Statistical studies of women's domestic work continue to show that when women work, they still do almost all the housework" (1983a:220). Ruether sees three links between this second or double shift of duties that women customarily perform and the unequal status on the job.

> First, the psychological and cultural model of women's work in the home creates a model of women's work on the job that makes men hostile to women's equality with them in the same type of work. Second, women's time commitments to domestic work prevent them from putting in extra time after hours for travel, education, and committee work, which advance people in the meritocracy. Third, the first two factors shut women out of the networks of communication that are used to compete on the job (1983a:220).

Ruether argues that these factors are inherent to liberal economic institutions. "[T]he economic structure of industrial capitalism is one of pervasive, structural discrimination against women," she says (1983a:219). Moreover, "[t]he ideology of equal rights obscures as much as it aids women's real equality" (1983a:219). Finally, she concludes that only "socialist feminism provides tools for analyzing these contradictions and envisions a new system that might solve them" (1983a:221).

Ruether's arguments here are neither internally consistent nor valid with reference to liberal theory. First, in the section of *Sexism and God-Talk* from which this analysis of the limitations of liberal feminism is taken, Ruether has already acknowledged that twentieth-century feminism, working within a liberal framework, recognized the problem and proposed solutions for women's unequal status in the economic sphere. She is correct. The major arguments against the doctrine of employment-at-will (which would justify the right of employers to hire and fire women as they choose), for affirmative action in hiring and promotions, and for comparable worth have all been set within a liberal framework.

Several examples illustrate the point. Patricia H. Werhane has argued against the doctrine of employment-at-will on the grounds that while the traditional view insists that the practice is justified because both employer and employee are free to enter or withdraw from the employment relationship in fact, employment at will "does not preserve equal freedoms because in most employment relationships employer-managers are in positions of greater power than employees," and because "when an employee is fired without sufficient reasons employers or managers place this person involuntarily in a personally harmful position unjustified by her behavior, a position that an employee would never choose. Thus the voluntary employment agreement according to which such practices are allowed is violated" (1988:268). The important point for our purpose is that Werhane's argument against employment at will is a liberal argument, that is, it is one couched in terms of the primary value attached to individual autonomy. Also, the classical arguments for affirmative action, either as aggressive measures to tear down formal barriers to the employment and promotion of women or minorities or as the preferential hiring or promotion of racial minorities or women, and for comparable worth (or equal pay for equal work) are liberal ones. The elimination of formal barriers to entry or promotion is relatively uncontroversial because such barriers represent a clear example of a failure to respect the equal liberty of all individuals to pursue the life plan, including the type of work or profession, they desire. Preferential hiring is somewhat more controversial, but those who seek to justify it usually do so in terms of a principle of compensatory justice which requires that victims of unjust discrimination receive compensation for their injuries. Both Judith Jarvis Thomson (1984) and Tom L. Beauchamp (1988) have made such arguments.[33] Helen Remick's account of the arguments for comparable worth indicate that advocates make arguments similar to those advanced by Werhane against employment at will.

> The goal of comparable worth policy is to pay a fair market wage to jobs historically done by women. . . . In other words . . . comparable worth advocates seek to disentangle and remove discrimination from the market. The laissez-faire doctrine underlying the free market ideology assumes that employers and employees bargain as equals. Comparable worth policy can contribute toward a more smoothly running marketplace . . . [and] removes a market imperfection (i.e., inequality between employers and some employees) that impinges unfairly on groups with less market power (1984:289).

Again, my point is a simple one: all of these arguments which address the problem of women's unequal status in the work place are liberal ones. Moreover, and this with reference to the consistency of Ruether's argument, she has recognized liberal feminism's ability to analyze the problem. What she has not done is to suggest why the proposed solutions are inadequate. None of this is to deny that there is internal disagreement among liberals on these issues nor that in practice the job structure in U. S. industrial capitalism remains highly discriminatory. It is only to suggest that this may be because U. S. capitalism isn't liberal enough, and not because it is liberal.

Ruether's association of liberalism with the problems created for women by the double shift of duties they perform depends upon two assumptions. First, it assumes that the particular split between public and private which Ruether identifies as alienating and which serves to limit women's equality is essential to the liberal enterprise. Secondly, it assumes that the split between public and private parallels the distinction between men and women, that is, it assumes that liberalism accepts the nearly exclusive identification of women with the private sphere which gives rise to the double shift of responsibilities they bear. Neither of these assumptions are correct. First, while liberalism claims to make a distinction which can be characterized as a distinction between public and private, it is *not* the distinction described by Ruether as alienating and as resulting in disadvantages for women. Secondly, as Ruether herself acknowledges in her praise of liberalism, liberal theory has been the primary agent of the disassociation of women and men with the various dualisms which have operated in western thought, including the dualism of public and private.

Liberalism's commitment to neutrality can be and has been understood in terms of a distinction between public and private morality. Liberal theory attempts to discover universally valid principles of right which both restrict the individual's pursuit of the good and protect her right to conceive the good however she might. Those principles lay down the terms of public interactions between and among persons and institutions. Liberal theory seeks to remain neutral about the various conceptions of a good life which individuals conceive and pursue. Their pursuit is a private matter in which the state or government, as the primary institution which defends rights while remaining neutral with reference to the good life, may not interfere. Now, this distinction between public and private is fundamentally different from the distinction between work and home which Ruether regards as alienating and, in combination with the association of women with the private and men with the public spheres, as working to the disadvantage of women. Ruether's distinction has primarily to do with a split between work and home, or between economic and domestic spheres.

The liberal distinction between public and private cuts across both economic and domestic spheres of life. On the one hand, both are, from a liberal perspective, fundamentally private. The home is regarded in liberal society as a sphere of life uniquely associated with our individual pursuits of the good life. Romantic, sexual, and familial relations are essential aspects of the good life which many in a liberal society pursue. Government intervention in such matters is likely to be regarded as intrusive. Certainly basic institutions, including government, can not require marriage or the raising of children on the grounds that such is essential to a good life. Rather, we are free to marry or to raise children if and when we choose consistent with our own conception of what makes life good or what additional obligations we have beyond those entailed by the rights of others. Of course, government does intervene in domestic life in a liberal society. Liberal theory requires that it does. Liberal theory must recognize as legitimate government interference to assure that marriage contracts are validly entered into and that individual rights are not abused in familial relationships. Thus, liberalism can be construed as regarding the formation of a marriage contract and the abuse of spouses or offspring as public acts which require government intervention.

The liberal distinction between public and private also cuts across the economic sphere as well. Ruether regards economic life as public, but since government is associated with the public sphere and a major impact of liberal theory and practice has been to separate economic enterprise from government control, it seems fair to say that, from the liberal perspective, the economic sphere (like the home) is fundamentally private. Private property rights as general or natural rights and the substitution of free market exchanges for governmental allocation of resources and governmental planning of production and distribution means that the economic sphere is fundamentally private. However, as with reference to the domestic sphere, government is regarded as having a role to play. Government is the necessary guarantor that exchanges are genuinely uncoerced. Liberals will disagree as to how far the government role extends beyond the enforcement of contracts into such areas as the regulation of advertising, product and worker safety standards, negative externalities such as pollution, and anti-competitive behavior. But even a laissez-faire liberal sees some public or governmental role in the economic sphere.

The distinction between public and private or between the domestic and the economic spheres as described by Ruether does not correspond to the public and private distinction which is related to liberal neutrality. Moreover, liberalism is surely not committed in principle to women's association with the domestic sphere, such that it leaves them hampered by the unequal burdens it sees them as justifiably bearing in the domestic sphere, even as it fights for their inclusion in economic roles. In making her argument that the contradiction between liberal equality and the realities of a gender-related job hierarchy and the double shift of duties borne by women in contemporary societies calls for the radicalization of liberal feminism, Ruether appeals to Zillah Eisenstein's *The Radical Future of Liberal Feminism*. Like Ruether, Eisenstein affirms that liberalism is committed to the split between the private and public spheres of life (conceived as a split between domestic and economic, political, and educational spheres) and the association of women with the private sphere. Liberalism, she says, is "a specific ideology seeking to protect and reinforce the relations of patriarchal and capitalist society." These "patriarchal underpinnings of liberal theory are indispensable to liberalism" (1981:6).

The division between the public and the private realms of social activity is
the starting point for [Locke's and Rousseau's] analysis, a division that
understands the realm of the family as the woman's sphere and the realm of
the public world as the man's (1981:6).

She argues "that women have been defined by their reproductive capacities
in Western society" and that the "reduction of women to mere biology is
at the core of Western liberal ideology" (1981:14).

Eisenstein supports her argument through extensive discussions of the
work of liberal theorists such as Locke, Rousseau, and Mill, and liberal
feminists such as Mary Wollstonecraft, Harriet Taylor, Elizabeth Cady
Stanton, and Betty Friedan. She attempts to demonstrate the way each
was constrained by the patriarchal underpinnings of liberalism. For
example, she shows that Locke does not deny that women are naturally
subject to their husbands in the conjugal relation. He "is simply denying
that this subjection should be used to justify the 'original grant of
government' or the 'foundation of monarchical power'" (1981:42).
Moreover, she argues that non-property owners, including women and the
laboring poor, were excluded from his conception of the rational or
autonomous individual, although she notes Locke made no distinction
between boys and girls in his theories of education. Wollstonecraft, who
was committed to the application to women of the liberal conception of the
human person and its corollary concept of natural rights, finally argued
that women must have access to the public sphere and education in
particular so that they could properly rear their children for the society in
which liberal freedoms prevailed. "As a result, Wollstonecraft has
redefined the aristocratic patriarchal vision of woman and replaced it with a
liberal patriarchal view: the rational, independent mother and wife"
(1981:107). She also points to the contradiction in Mill's *On the
Subjection of Women* between his view that it is impossible to know the
"nature of the two sexes as long as they have only been seen in their
present relation to one another" (Eisenstein, 1981:134, quoting Mill) and
his acceptance of what Eisenstein calls "the sexual division of labor"
(1981:135).

Now, while the survey and analysis of liberal theorists Eisenstein
presents is illuminating and demonstrates the influence of patriarchal ideas
in the work of liberals, including liberal feminists, it does not support her
contention that liberalism is essentially patriarchal. If the sexual
symbolism of gender division and hierarchy is as ancient and central to
our modes of perception as Ruether argues they are, one would expect that
even among liberals such patterns would still have their influence. What
one must show in order to conclude that liberalism is essentially
patriarchal is that the fundamental insights of liberalism are supportive of
those patriarchal conceptions. Neither Eisenstein nor Ruether provides
such a demonstration. Indeed, both argue that liberalism was in constant

conflict with those patriarchal conceptions rather than supportive of them.[34]

Ruether's argument that the contradictions experienced by working women in contemporary capitalist society indicate that feminism must move beyond liberalism to socialism is somewhat baffling, given her judgment that "although socialism has ameliorated the handicap of women in industrial society, it has not fundamentally altered it." She notes precisely the same alienation of domestic and economic spheres and the same impact on women in socialist societies as she has criticized in capitalist ones. "An analysis of women's work in socialist or communist societies shows that the same contradictions between unpaid domestic and low-paid wage labor continues." Her conclusion is that "patriarchy plus industrialism is the cause of this pattern" (1983a:225). Thus, it is the relationship between a view that regards women as subordinate to men and the industrial technology that has outgrown the home that is the root cause of these problems, and neither liberalism nor private property. Indeed, where liberalism and private property have been transcended, that is, in socialist societies, but where female subordination is accepted and industrial technology prevails, the pattern still exists.

The "maleness" of the public sphere and the liberal conception of the self. Ruether's critique of the split between public and private spheres of life includes another aspect which does represent an important attack on liberalism. Not only does Ruether regard the separating of public and private spheres as alienating, she also insists that "modes of functioning" within the public sphere are inadequate. As a result of their traditional restriction to the domestic sphere, women have developed alternative ways of acting and reasoning which Ruether regards as more adequate than those ways of acting and reasoning which males have traditionally utilized in the public sphere. Liberalism gains women access to the public sphere, but it does not allow them to challenge the traditionally male modes which dominate there.

> Liberal feminism too readily identified normative human nature with those capacities for reason and rule identified with men and with the public sphere. It claims that women, while appearing to have lesser capacities for these attributes, actually possess them equally; they have simply been denied the educational cultivation of them and the opportunity to exercise them. . . .
>
> There is important truth in this. Women, through the opening of equal education and political rights, have indeed demonstrated their ability to exercise the "same" capacities as men. But liberalism . . . assumes the traditional male sphere as normative and believes it is wrong to deny people access to it on the basis of gender. But once women are allowed to enter the public sphere, liberalism offers no critique of the modes of functioning within it (1983a:109–110).

How does Ruether understand "the modes of functioning" within the public sphere? And why ought such modes not be regarded as normative, that is, how are these modes deficient or incomplete?

Unfortunately, Ruether does not provide a detailed, systematic analysis and critique of the modes of functioning to which she refers. Her comments here and her analysis of human alienation do enable us to surmise that she has in mind competitive and hierarchical patterns of relationship between human persons and between persons and nonhuman nature which result in domination and exploitation. In *New Women/New Earth* she argues for changing "the self-concept of a society from the drive toward possession, conquest, and accumulation to the values of reciprocity and acceptance of mutual limitation" (1975b:204–205). Because males have been primarily, if not exclusively, responsible for establishing the terms of our self-understanding, she regards the possessive and competitive self-conception as a male conception. She also associates the alternative values or modes of operation, those which she characterizes as reciprocal and mutual, with females.[35]

The competitive patterns of relationship and the attendant drives toward possession, conquest and accumulation are, on Ruether's view, a reflection of the dualistic conception of the human person operative in western thought. It is a conception of human selfhood which emphasizes the capacities for individual transcendence and autonomous will while denigrating or denying the material and relational aspects of human selfhood. Her characterization of the dominant conception of the human person in our culture is consistent with the liberal conception I have described. Liberalism, as we have seen, regards the human capacity for transcending the limitations of one's historical and cultural particularity, and choosing one's own conception of the good and acting upon that conception within the limits of moral principles discovered from that transcendent perspective, as that aspect of the human person which is the source of our moral status.

Once again it is important to point out that liberals may disagree about the degree to which the human self is capable of achieving an autonomous or transcendent standpoint which is characterized by its independence from the influence of those others with whom one is culturally and historically related. What is fundamental to the liberal perspective is its commitment to the protection of that autonomous sphere and to institutional provisions which allow for its development and exercise by individuals. Ruether describes the dominant view in our culture as one that regards the autonomous or transcendent aspect of human selfhood as the essential self. One might claim that liberalism is not committed to such a description of the self. A liberal may in fact regard the self as integrated in the way that Ruether does. Liberalism, one might protest, does not deny that the human self is embodied and, therefore, limited.[36] What makes one a liberal is simply his or her commitment to the protection of that autonomous capacity.

While this complaint has a measure of cogency, it obscures the way in which a term such as "essential" functions both descriptively and normatively for Ruether. When she argues that the dominant conception of the self in western culture regards the transcendent or autonomous aspect as "essential," she means to say that our basic moral commitments and institutions are aimed at the protection of that aspect of human selfhood and its development and operation. Liberals surely recognize the physical, cultural, historical, and, therefore, limited aspects of human selfhood, and as a result it might be said that liberals are in no way committed to the view of the self which Ruether regards as the western view. However, Ruether might respond, and I believe it would be a fair response, that to the degree that a normative perspective makes an exclusive commitment to the protection, development, and operation of a particular dimension of human selfhood, it is fair to say that that perspective regards that dimension as essential. Her description of the dominant western view of the self as essentially spiritual or transcendent is therefore accurate with reference to the liberal perspective.

As we have seen, Ruether regards such a characterization of the human self as inadequate. She denies that the essential aspect of human selfhood is the capacity for transcendence and autonomous will, and argues that the result of a view that does not recognize the self's essential interdependence with others and with non-human nature is relationships of domination and subordination between persons and the exploitation of nature. While she does not deny that human beings, including women, have "psychic traits of intellectuality, transcendent spirit and autonomous will that were identified with the male," she does insist that when those traits are regarded as expressions of our human essence and therefore given exclusive protection, as they are in liberal society, where basic institutions are designed to protect the equal right of all to develop and act upon such traits, oppression is the inevitable result. Ruether also suggests that an undervaluing of relationships which limit one's sphere of autonomy also results. Therefore, she insists, "in order to play out the roles shaped by this definition of the male life style, the woman finds that she must either be childless or have someone else act as her 'wife' (i. e., play the service role for her freedom to work). Women's liberation is therefore *impossible* within the present social system except for an elite few" (1972:116).

On Ruether's view, the fruits of the victory that liberal feminism wins for women, the gaining of their acceptance into a public sphere operating under this male (and liberal) conception, can only be harvested by middle-class women

who are tempted to compensate for gender discrimination by using women
of the lower class to do their "women's" work, thereby freeing themselves
to compete as equals with men of their group. The dual-career family at
upper executive levels is made possible by the affluence that can hire the
housekeeper and the private secretary. This is then touted as the fulfillment
of the promise of liberal feminism, although actually the economic
position of the upper middle class is being reinforced against women and
men of lower classes and races. Such equality at affluent levels remains
token. Its visibility and acclaim only serves to disaffect poor women,
working-class women, minority women, and women as housewives from
feminism. The glitter of feminist "equality," as displayed in *Cosmopolitan*
and *Ms.*, both eludes and insults the majority of women who recognize that
its "promise" is not for them (1983a:222).

In summary, the liberal conception of the self, which regards the
capacity for autonomy as its essence and the source of its moral status,
emphasizes the independence of the individual both from nonhuman
nature and from others, with the result that nonhuman nature comes to be
regarded as something to be exploited or controlled for human persons,
and other persons are seen as in competition with the self, as threats to its
basic interests and its fulfillment. The result is both ecological crisis and
social relations built on domination. While we have discussed the
relationship in Ruether's thought between the dualistic conception of the
self and ecological crisis and social domination, what Ruether's discussion
and critique of liberalism makes clear is that those relationships of
domination are inevitable even when, as in liberalism, all persons are
regarded as possessing the traits associated with the autonomous
dimension of human experience. Liberalism may introduce an element of
fluidity in gender and race relations; to the degree that women and people
of color are now regarded as equally human, their autonomy equally
protected, and their competitive situation equalized through aggressive
measures to guarantee equal opportunity, women and people of color will
gradually be found in positions of leadership and moving up the economic
scale. Of course, given the resistance among those in groups traditionally
favored, such liberal measures may be slow in gaining acceptance and
their acceptance is often tentative. Moreover, debates within liberalism
with regard to whether and to what degree liberal rights require positive
measures to protect individual autonomy will also serve to slow the gains
of traditionally oppressed groups. But Ruether's fundamental point goes
even further. Even where the liberal insistence that the liberty of all
persons must be protected is unambiguously accepted, and even where
aggressive and positive measures to assure equal opportunity are in place,
relationships of domination, class relationships, will still prevail among
human persons. Since we are in fact both autonomous and bound, both
spiritual and physical beings with a capacity for independence which is
always limited by our essential interdependence with nonhuman nature

and with each other, where our capacity for autonomy and independence is provided exclusive protection, or is given highest value, those who are able to achieve a wide measure of that independence or who gain the widest sphere for its expression must always do so at the expense of others. Those at whose expense the independence of the few is gained will expend their energies in meeting their own physical needs and the physical needs of others, while those for whom liberal society works will be freed in large measure to develop and express the capacities for autonomy which belong to all of us.

Ruether's social conception of human selfhood and communitarianism

On Ruether's view, a more accurate conception of the self requires integrating the transcendent or autonomous aspect of human selfhood with its alienated material and relational aspects. This more accurate conception opens our eyes to the ways in which we are related, rather than distinguished, as selves, and places higher value on mutuality as opposed to competitiveness. This dealienated or integrated conception of the self is important for overcoming the domination of some persons by others. Where transcendence is regarded as the essential feature of human selfhood, or the protection of independence or autonomy is regarded as the most important function of basic institutions, or the achievement of such autonomy is regarded as the highest human value or good, the inevitable result is domination of those others with whom we are in fact interrelated as selves.[37] Moreover, because of its recognition of our interdependence with the natural world, this integrated conception of the self holds the key for overcoming the contemporary ecological crisis. Overcoming that crisis requires a view of our selves as part of nature, as interdependent with the natural world, rather than a view which distinguishes our nature from the natural world.

As these comments suggest, certain interesting parallels exist between Ruether's conception of an integrated self and the communitarian conception of the self. This suggests affinities between radical social thought (represented by Ruether) and communitarian thought (represented by Hauerwas) which have largely gone unnoticed. Judith Vaughan has outlined a conception of the self drawn from what she calls "radical social thought, and in particular the conflict tradition in the social sciences and from feminist writings," and regards Ruether's conception of the self as an example of that conception (1983:3). This conception emphasizes that human beings are "essentially social." On this view, persons "are constituted by one another and . . . achieve their identities through their relations with one another" (1983:7–8).

Apart from social interaction there can be no human person. Human nature and sociality are synonymous. This understanding of the individual as essentially social can be seen as part of a general social ontology which maintains that to be is to be interrelated. This view of reality "emphasizes wholeness, connectedness and interdependence, and a different consciousness of self, others, human society, and the natural world" (1983:80).

She distinguishes such an understanding from those which regard human sociality as referring "to the external relations of radically separate individuals,"[38] and from what she calls "collectivist" conceptions which "view society: (1) as an entity in itself, distinct from the individuals who compose it; and (2) as the whole for which the individuals exist only as parts" (1983:80). Moreover, she argues that Marx's conception of the person was essentially social in the sense described in the above quotation.

An important aspect of this social conception of the person is the conception of human freedom which is related to it. Freedom is not understood, as it is in liberal thought, as the ability to exercise one's autonomous capacity for choice, rather it is, Vaughan writes:

the capacity of persons to co-create themselves as well as the society, world, and cosmos of which they are a part; it is the ability to co-determine what reality becomes. Freedom is only realized interdependently. Shlomo Avineri states this principle in this way: ultimate freedom is based "on a universal recognition of man's dependence upon each other. The very alteration of circumstances [is] accomplished through co-operation with other human beings." . . . [H]uman beings become free in relationship with others (1983:83).

Individuals lose their freedom, they are dominated by others, when they are "in a situation that has been defined by another person or group," and are "forced to operate within this situation without being able to effect one's own definition." Dominant persons "deprive the dominated of their ability to determine, in relationship with others, what reality becomes . . . thus preventing self-realization through transformative activity. Relationships of domination are non-reciprocal, and therefore unfree" (1983:86). The human consciousness that is related to such relationships of domination is alienated and "false."

False consciousness, as it exists in Western capitalist society, dissolves the human world into a world of atomistic individuals in social classes confronting each other with mutual hostility. . . . People "do not know themselves and others as social beings whose needs demand mutual cooperation but as private and competing entities, an anarchistic galaxy of selfish worlds" (1983:97).

Vaughan is correct in her judgment that Ruether's anthropology is one which regards the human person as essentially social. Moreover, Ruether associates such a conception of the human person with women. Women, she says, "have traditionally cultivated a communal personhood" (Ruether, 1972:124). On Ruether's view, it is this sense of the essential sociality of the human person, and the cooperative models of human interaction associated with it, which liberalism does not allow women to bring with them as they function in the public sphere that liberalism opens to them. Vaughan's description of the basic components of the anthropology of radical social thought, and particularly her discussion of the meaning of freedom associated with it, is helpful in terms of clarifying what could be an important misunderstanding in Ruether's thought. Ruether repeatedly upholds the value of autonomy. For example, in *Liberation Theology*, she insists that even while women speak up "for a new humanity arising out of the reconciliation of spirit and body," this should not mean "selling short our rights to the powers of independent personhood. Autonomy, world-transcending spirit, separatism as the power of consciousness-raising, and liberation from an untamed nature and from subjugation to the rocket-ship male—all these revolutions are still vital to women's achievement of integral personhood" (1972:124).[39] In the context of criticizing romanticism's celebration of traditionally female virtues in *New Women/New Earth*, she insists that "women need to recover the rationality, autonomy, and self-definition which they have been denied as tools of male needs and negations" (1975b:29).[40] And, in *Sexism and God-Talk*, she criticizes an "overreliance of Christianity" on parental images for the divine because such images, she says, function to "prolong spiritual infantilism as virtue and to make autonomy and assertion of free will a sin" (1983a:69).

What Ruether does not always make clear is that the conception of autonomy which she means to affirm is fundamentally different from the dominant western and liberal conception which she so often criticizes as producing hierarchical relationships between persons and the human domination of nature. Vaughan's analysis is helpful in this regard. The alternative conception of freedom which she identifies in radical social thought alerts us to the possibility of a conception of autonomy which is consistent with it. There are indications that Ruether does indeed share the conception of freedom as co-creation with others of the self and its social world which Vaughan identified. Ruether describes such a capacity as a power. Ruether speaks of exercising one's powers of creativity and of being denied those powers by being forced into a silence that allows others to define one's self-conception. With reference to racism, she writes of power as the restoration of one's creativity, and associates that power with autonomy.

> Power is man restored to his integrity and creativity, so that his actions directly and effectively express his soul. Power is participation in the making of one's destiny. Power is effective action. Power is the ability to create autonomously. Power alienated from this integrity becomes

oppressive, but man's redemption is the restoration of human power from
alienation to self-directed and self-fulfilling creativity. In such a fashion
does Marxism speak of man's "fall" as his alienation from his "work,"
while the redeemed society would be one where man's alienation from his
power is overcome, and his creativity restored to an integrated self in
community with one's fellowmen and nature (1972:133).

She refers to women also as having been forced into a silence such
that their own self-images correspond to male definitions of them. In
male ideology, "woman is the one acted upon and defined by the male
perception and 'use,' and her own self-definition and perspective are never
heard or incorporated culturally. Women, as all oppressed people, live in a
culture of silence, as objects, never subjects of the relationship"
(1972:102). In *Sexism and God-Talk*, she again refers to "the reduction
of women to silence," and the "male monopoly on cultural definition,"
such that some become "the object rather than the subject of that
definition" (1983a:74). All of this suggests a conception of autonomy as
the capacity to participate in the social process of co-creation and self-
definition. Moreover, Ruether associates such a conception of autonomy
with the overcoming of relationships of domination such that persons
relate to one another as full human beings rather than as subject and object.
With reference to racial oppression and overcoming the dualism of
oppressor and oppressed to which we have referred previously, she says
that the oppressed race tends to "internalize" or accept as its own the
definition of them created by the oppressor. "The oppressor," she insists,

also is dehumanized by this false relationship, for he receives no authentic
communication from the oppressive role, but receives back only a mask
donned by the oppressed to reflect the demands of those in power. . . . The
rebel against oppression is demanding a true order based on the common
nature of all men. . . . Rebellion is the breaking of silence between man and
man: the initiation of true communication for the first time, based on two
autonomous selfhoods that can stand as "I" and "Thou" for each other. In
rebellion the rebel affirms a common human nature as the ground upon
which both he and the oppressor stand and the basis upon which the
oppressor must recognize the justice of his demands (1972:129–130).

In summary, while Ruether affirms autonomy, her conception of that
value is fundamentally different from the liberal conception. Therefore,
Ruether's consistent affirmation of autonomy should not lead to the
mistaken conclusion that hers is only a version of the liberal commitment.
Rather, the autonomy she values is grounded in a fundamentally different
conception of the human self. It is a conception which regards the self as
constituted in and by relationships with others and with nonhuman nature.
The self is not given apart from those relationships, nor is autonomy
conceived of as the transcendence of them. Autonomy is the power and
freedom to participate equally in the co-creation with others of the social

world. Autonomy, then, is the capacity to participate in a process of self-definition rather than to choose and pursue a conception of the good from the perspective of an already given self. Respect for autonomy is understood more in terms of allowing or enabling every person to have a voice in the process of self-definition rather than as allowing or enabling each person to choose his or her own conception of the good.

It is usually the case that the differences between critiques of liberalism which draw heavily on Marx and the recent communitarian critiques are emphasized. Amy Gutman, for example, in her discussion of communitarian critiques of liberalism, has pointed to the differences. Whereas both the radical and the communitarian critics "fault liberalism for being mistakenly and irreparably individualistic," they seem to suggest quite different political prescriptions. The implications of the "new communitarian criticism are more conservative" than those of the old radical, or Marxist inspired criticism.

> Whereas the good society of the old critics was one of collective property ownership and equal political power, the good society of the new critics is one of settled traditions and established identities. For many of the old critics, the role of women with the family was symptomatic of their social and economic oppression; for Sandel, the family serves as a model of community and evidence of a good greater than justice. For the old critics, patriotism was an irrational sentiment that stood in the way of world peace; for [Alasdair] MacIntyre, the particularistic demands of patriotism are no less rational than the universalistic demands of justice. The old critics were inclined to define deviations from majoritarian morality in the name of nonrepression; the new critics are inclined to defend the efforts of local majorities to ban offensive activities in the name of preserving their community's "way of life and the values that sustain it" (Gutman 1985:309).

While not attempting to respond to all the contrasts that Gutman draws here, I do want to suggest that she passes too quickly over her point that both radical and communitarian critiques of liberalism regard it as mistakenly individualistic. More recently, Marilyn Friedman has pointed to the similarities between feminist and communitarian thought and has suggested that "one might anticipate that communitarian theory would offer important insights for feminist reflection" (1989:276). Fundamental agreement about the inadequacy of an important aspect of liberal theory suggests the possibility of similarities between the radical and the communitarian critiques that Gutman leaves unexplored. Moreover, it suggests the possibility of constructive dialogue between the communitarian and radical or liberationist critics of liberalism. I want to point to some of those similarities as displayed in Stanley Hauerwas' communitarian critique and Ruether's radical one and suggest some of the poles around which a dialogue between the two perspectives might take place.

First, it is important to make clear the most fundamental sense in which both Hauerwas and Ruether regard liberalism as mistakenly individualistic. For both, the individualism of liberalism is rooted in its conception of the self as "given" apart from the social relationships and the historical context in which it finds itself, or as "ontologically prior" to those relationships and that context. While the liberal sense that the essence of the human self lies in that capacity for distancing oneself from one's relationships and one's history is related to the high value placed on individual independence and achievement as well as the view that social relationships are good primarily as a means for the achievement of more basic individual values, and while both Hauerwas and Ruether are critical of such values, the target of their attack is the individualistic conception of the self upon which those values are based.

Sharing a sense that the self is not given prior to its being in relation or apart from its own action and reflection on it, both Hauerwas and Ruether regard morality and ethics as having to do with a process of self-making or self-transformation. For both, ethics is not simply and not primarily critical reflection on what we should do. Rather, it is critical reflection on the kinds of persons and kinds of communities we ought to be. This suggests that, for both, the first virtue of basic institutions is not "justice" understood as a fair adjudication of the conflicting claims of autonomous selves. Rather, it is the capacity to shape good selves and good communities. For both, then, ethics is always teleological; it is fundamentally concerned about the movement toward an end or goal, and basic institutions are not, as in liberalism, to be neutral about such a telos. Instead the primary purpose of such institutions is to engage us in a process whereby the telos that is appropriately ours is discovered and a process for moving toward it is begun.

Let me also suggest that Hauerwas and Ruether both incorporate in their conceptions of the self and of the role of politics provisions which guard against the totalitarian or authoritarian implications which liberals often see where politics is conceived as fundamentally teleological or directed toward some particular conception of the good for selves or for communities. Liberals fear that, when basic institutions lose their neutrality, a particular conception of the good is imposed upon individuals in violation of the respect for liberty that is due them as persons capable of an autonomous choice of the good life or the goods of life. For both Hauerwas and Ruether, such fear is misplaced because there is no individual self to be respected apart from the conception of the good or the social relationships in which they are formed. Yet Hauerwas insists that everyone must be given a voice and allowed to participate in the adventure of discovery whereby the telos which is to shape the self- and community-making process is defined. And Ruether insists that a fundamental characteristic of oppression is the silence into which the oppressed are forced, such that they are prohibited from participation in the process of self-definition according to which they are to live. Such silence prohibits the formation of the I-Thou relationships or relationships of equality upon which true community must be based. For both Hauerwas and Ruether, authoritarian or totalitarian implications are avoided because no *a priori* conception of the telos of human life in community is the basis of their teleological conception of ethics and politics, and because each insists on the participation of all in the process of self-definition or in the discovery of the telos toward which human life is directed.

None of this is to suggest that profound differences do not exist between Ruether's radical and Hauerwas' communitarian suggestions of an alternative to liberal political theory. While both deny an *a priori* self and insist that the self is a social construct, Hauerwas emphasizes the way the self is shaped by the history and narrative of the communities of which the individual is a part, whereas Ruether is suspicious of the communities which have shaped the identity of women and envisions a revolutionary restructuring of human relationships as necessary for the coming to be of an authentic human self.

Marilyn Friedman's warning that "communitarian philosophy as a whole is a perilous ally for feminist theory" (1989:277) is appropriate here, although I think she may have overrepresented the threat of communitarian theory. She notes that, for communitarians, the communities which shape individual identity "have a kind of morally normative legitimacy." They often fail "to acknowledge that many communities make illegitimate moral claims on their members, linked to hierarchies of domination and subordination." The particular communities to which communitarians often look as having at least *prima facie* moral legitimacy—Friedman mentions family, neighborhood, and nation—"are troubling paradigms of social relationship and communal life" (1989:279).

First, it should be pointed out that, though communitarians point to the shaping influence of community, and even communities which may be horribly oppressive, this does not in principle entail that they make the normative judgment that every kind of shaping is right or good. Friedman herself quotes MacIntyre saying that "the fact that the self has to find its moral identity in and through its membership in communities such as those of the family, the neighborhood, the city and the tribe does not entail that the self has to accept the moral *limitations* of the particularity of those forms of community." She goes on to say, "Nevertheless, according to MacIntyre, one's moral quests 'must begin by moving forward from such particularity,' for it 'can never be simply left behind or obliterated'" (1989:279, quoting MacIntyre, 1981:205).

Friedman's "nevertheless" suggests that MacIntyre's communitarian point that the influence of one's given communities can never be left behind profoundly qualifies the previous claim that insisting upon the shaping influence of one's communal attachments does not entail being totally controlled by them. MacIntyre, and communitarians in general (including Hauerwas), would not regard the second claim as a profound qualification of the first. Friedman's judgment that it does points to one difference between communitarian and radical perspectives such as Ruether's. While both agree that communal or social attachments are constituitive of individual selfhood, Hauerwas envisions a continuity between past and present that Ruether tends to deny. Or, to put the matter another way, Ruether is much more inclined to envision the recreation of social relations *de novo*, whereas Hauerwas sees the transformation of community and self as a much more gradual and tentative process. Thus, Ruether presents a utopian vision for the reconstruction of human society and selves (a communitarian socialist utopia), whereas Hauerwas presents a process of discovery whose centerpiece is a commitment to the dialogue, forgiveness, and non-violence which prevents the process from becoming stagnant.

This difference may be one of style and it ought not be exaggerated. Recall Ruether's insistence on the interrelation of our analysis of oppression and our vision of an alternative and her sense that no human project is ever the perfect achievement of our essential humanity. Both elements of her thought suggest a continuity between past and future, or between those elements of our identity which are given and those over which we exercise control through our efforts to achieve our full humanity. That sense of continuity is consistent with the communitarian view expressed by Hauerwas. On the other hand, Hauerwas is not committed to the view that it is impossible for one to change communities or change stories or that one cannot exercise a measure of choice over one's identity. Recall his sense, borrowed from Aristotle, that we are responsible for our character. His view is that our various stories and communities overlap and influence one another. What he denies is that there is some storyless autonomous perspective from which to choose.

Marilyn Friedman insists that, while admitting "the important constitutive role played by social and communal relationships," feminists believe that there is no reason to regard "the moral claims made by the social and communal relationships" in which we are embedded and from which we gain our identity as normative. She suggests that we are capable of adopting "a standpoint independent of some particular subject" from which we are able to judge the moral claims made upon us by our communities (1989:281). That such a standpoint is available is precisely what the communitarians are denying is possible. A feminist view that sees its critical perspective as independent in this way has not abandoned the liberal paradigm. Ruether makes no such claim, however. Ruether (and liberation theology in general) claims that the perspective of criticism is a particular and not a universal or independent one: it is the perspective of the oppressed from which moral claims are critiqued.

Interestingly, then, the dialogue between Hauerwas and Ruether will return to the problem we addressed at the end of our discussion of Ruether's ecclesiology: the relationship between one's particular place in a community of liberation and the particular claim made upon us by the story of Jesus. For Hauerwas, perspectival or epistemological privilege is given to those who see and know from the particular standpoint of the community whose identity is shaped by the biblical narrative and, especially, by the story of Jesus. For Ruether, such privilege is assigned to the oppressed and, particularly, to women. For Ruether, the primary source of authority is women's experience in a liberation community, whereas for Hauerwas it is the story of Jesus.

Endnotes

[1]"By patriarchy," Ruether has written,

we mean not only the subordination of females to males, but the whole structure of Father ruled society: aristocracy over serfs, masters over slaves, king over subjects, radical overlords over colonized people (1983a:61).

[2] Ruether denies that regarding experience as a fundamental source of theology and full humanity as its critical principle is unique to feminist theology. Scripture and tradition, she says, "are themselves codified collective human experience." Moreover, "human experience is the starting point and the ending point of the hermeneutical circle. Codified tradition both reaches back to roots in experience and is constantly renewed or discarded through the test of experience" (1983a:12). Likewise, "the correlation of original, authentic human nature (*imago dei* /Christ) and diminished, fallen humanity provided the basic structure of classical Christian theology" (1983a:19). What is unique about feminist theology is that it uses *women's* experience as a source of theology and "that women claim this principle [of full humanity] for themselves. Women name themselves as subjects of authentic and full humanity" (1983a:19).

3Again, Ruether denies that regarding this prophetic principle as central to theology is unique to feminist theology. What is unique, she insists, is the appropriation of it for women. "Feminist theology claims that women too are among those oppressed whom God comes to vindicate and liberate" (1983a:24). She recognizes that the application of the prophetic principle to women is not common in the Bible itself. "Feminism appropriates the prophetic principles in ways the Biblical writers for the most part do not appropriate them," that is, as justification for a critique of patriarchal social structures. "Feminist readings of the Bible can discern a norm within Biblical faith by which the Biblical texts themselves can be criticized" (1983a:23).

4 Ruether's references to the human essence and the critical principle of "the full humanity of women" suggests some *a priori* or foundational conception of human nature from which the criteria of liberation may be derived. Rebecca Chopp says this language suggests a "humanistic method" which

> turns upon three basic assumptions: 1) that there is a structure expressive of human nature that stands behind history (history thought of as a collective singular), 2) that this structure is thought to be universal, and 3) that our words about human nature refer implicitly to this extrahistorical structure (1989:10).

Chopp protests, however, that Ruether's use of such a humanistic method "does not and cannot match the vision suggested in much of her recent work. That vision is radically open, pragmatic in character, pluralistic in style, and ready to form radically new ways of being and doing." Chopp contends that the humanistic method indicated by Ruether's references to human essence or full humanity "precipitates a wandering away from our real, concrete, historical experience" rather than attention to it (1989:10).

Chopp's point is somewhat insightful, yet I'm not sure that the contrast she draws between Ruether's references to full or essential humanity and a vision that is drawn from concrete experience and is radically open is valid. As I will show, Ruether has a conception of the human person which emphasizes our "essential sociality." (This terminology is borrowed from Judith Vaughan's book *Sociality, Ethics, and Social Change: A Critical Appraisal of Reinhold Niebuhr's Ethics in the Light of Rosemary Radford Ruether's Works* (Vaughan, 1983).) This conception of the human person gives a certain form to her conception of human liberation and a good society. However, because such a conception emphasizes that the human person is socially and historically developed it draws attention to and not away from concrete experience as Chopp suggests. Her conceptions of full humanity and of liberation are drawn from her analysis of the "real, concrete, historical experience" of women. Because this is so, it is impossible to describe the substantive content of this critical principle except after one has considered her analysis of the oppression and the ideology which has justified the structures of oppression.

With reference to her critique of liberalism it is interesting that she does not criticize its foundationalism as does Hauerwas. She does not suggest that no foundational perspective or no conception of the human person is possible. Rather she contends that the liberal foundation is mistaken. This should not obscure the similarities between her position and Hauerwas', however. She and Hauerwas share a conception of the self as a social and historical construct which requires attention to the particularities of human experience as the source of human insight.

5 Her earliest books, such as *The Church Against Itself* (1967) and *The Radical Kingdom* (1970), draw upon this prophetic principle and its application to the church. But it is not until *Liberation Theology* (1972) that the feminist theme become important. It is only from *New Women, New Earth* (1975b) onward that it becomes dominant.

6 Ruether does not refer specifically to the prophetic-liberating principle in *The Church Against Itself.* It is not identified as a methodological principle until *Sexism and God-Talk* (1983), but it is fair to say that she was employing it even in her first book.

7 She has in mind both the early or apostolic church and those Anabaptist communities of the Radical Reformation which regarded themselves as the first fruits of the eschatological restoration of humanity.

8 Ruether has difficulty explaining her conception of demythologized or dehistoricized eschatology in a way that escapes suggesting the historical literalism of the original apostolic understanding of Christian eschatology. She herself uses the language that suggests a literal historical future. "The eschatological event encounters the present, but always as a reality whose fulfilled essence lies in the future" (1967:61). Her use of the concept of *kairos* as opposed to *chronos* (in *The Church Against Itself*) with reference to Christian eschatology does suggest something other than a literal or linear conception of the eschatalogical future. For example, she writes:

> The church, in its true nature, is not detached from history, but vitally relevant to history and progress, and stands at the very heart of the creative ferment of history. It is wherever history is experienced as *kairos*, as the decisive moment of conversion and as the breakthrough of new powers and possibilities.
>
> This *kairos* is always eschatological in nature. By definition it transcends the actual situation and encounters man as the power of the new and the power from Beyond. Every *kairos* partakes of the Kingdom of God (1967:63).

In *Sexism and God-Talk* and *To Change the World*, Ruether explicitly argues against linear or literal language with reference to Christian hope. She writes that "the projection of human hope on one final era or system of redemptive relationships, to be sought (or given by God) through a single linear process, contradicts the possibilities of historical existence" (1983a:253). She regards the affirmation of the hope for a restored humanity at the end of human history as "a useful myth for keeping history itself open" (1983a:253). Moreover, when "this end point is not seen as something that can actually be achieved or can ever 'happen' on earth," it properly serves as a basis of criticism of secular revolutionaries who identify the restoration of human possibilities with a particular social revolution. Still, she says, such a linear view "has no roots" in a theology which sees "God/ess as ground of creation. There are no clues in that which is natural. This endless flight into the future idolizes change and fails to respect the relational patterns of our bodies as ground of holy being" (1983a:254). She proposes "conversion to the center, conversion to the earth and to each other, rather than flight to the unrealizable future" as "a model of change more in keeping with the realities of temporal existence" (1983a:255–6).

In *To Change the World*, she says that conversion as an alternative to views which stress an end point "suggests that, although there is no one utopian system of humanity that lies in a paradise of the past, there are certain ingredients of a just and liveable society" (1983b:68). Conversion also suggests a "model of messianic redemption" which is taken "from the Hebrew idea of Jubilee" (1983b:69).

[9]This attack on the separation of public and private spheres is exhibited later with reference to Ruether's consideration of liberalism as an ideology for the liberation of women. There she will argue that the distinction between public and private spheres is a characteristic of liberal thought which renders it inadequate from the perspective of the critical principle of the full humanity of women.

[10] In one of her most recent books, Ruether presents a theology and liturgical resources for what she calls "Women-Church." There she argues that many Christian women "are beginning to recognize the need for autonomous bases for women's theologizing and worship" (1985:4).

Previously, we have seen that Ruether regards her appeal to women's experience as the primary source and criterion of theology to be unique not because of its appeal to experience, but rather because it makes women's experience the primary source for theology. Likewise, she says that her use of the full humanity of women as the critical principle of theology is unique only in that she has claimed that principle for *women*; her critical principle shares with the prophetic-liberating principle of scripture a critique of all that is oppressive and an affirmation that God is active for the liberation of the oppressed, but it is unique in that it makes central the application of that principle to the oppression of women.

In a similar way it can be said that Ruether's defense of Women-Church is a feminist application of a secular theology of the church. It represents an effort to relate all aspects of women's lives to the sacred. The book includes liturgical rites to mark or celebrate a wide variety of experiences, many of which (though not all) are unique to women. For example, there are rites of covenanting, baptism, and sacramental sharing of food, as well as rites of healing from incest, wife battering, rape, abortion, and miscarriage, and rites for "coming-out" as a lesbian, for preparation for birthing, for the marriage of a lesbian couple, and to mark the arrival of menopause. Morever, Women-Church is understood as a community of liberation among women which exhibits a variety of forms and is open to constant reshaping in the light of new insights drawn from the experience of women's liberation.

[11] She says that "[t]he powers and principalities are still very much in control of most of the world. The nucleus of the alternative world remains, like the Church (theologically, *as* the Church), harbingers and experimenters with new human possibilities within the womb of the old" (1983a:234). This suggests that the Church is part of the nucleus of an alternative world, but not exclusively so.

[12] See *Institutes of the Christian Religion*, Book IV, Chapter 1, Section 7 (Calvin 1960:1021).

13 The quotation from Ruether here is in *The Church Against Itself* (1967:220).

14 The term "fusion of horizons" and the hermeneutical theory to which liberation thought appeals is developed in Hans-Georg Gadamer's *Truth and Method* (1975). An interesting use of Gadamer's method and its application to scripture and ethics is Thomas Ogletree's *The Use of the Bible in Christian Ethics* (1983).

15 Ruether's understanding of evil and her vision of human liberation cannot be treated separately because they are developed in dialectical relation with one another. Neither evil and oppression, nor good and liberation, are definable except in relation to and out of the experience of their opposites. Evil as a conceptual category designates that which stands over against our fulfillment; it is in terms of our vision of what that fulfillment might entail that the analysis of evil proceeds. Yet, our vision of liberation is also shaped by our analysis of evil. Ruether puts the point this way:

> Humans stand out against their environment and are able to imagine alternatives to what is. They are able to generate, mentally and culturally, ideals and projects of what might be, as something better than what is, and they can use this ideal to judge and change the existing situation. Human beings, then, stand in the existential dialectic between the "is" and the "ought." The two are interdependent. One can project "oughts" only in the context of what is. "What is" is, in turn, a construct shaped by one's perception of an alternative, better option. One cannot, for example, describe the present situation as patriarchy or capitalism until one has developed an alternative, feminism or socialism (1983a:160).

Such a view does not entail that "evil has no objective reality." It means simply rather "that the center of the drama is the human person situating itself in opposition to perceived falsifications of its own being in the name of a transcendent possibility of a good self" (1983a:159).

16 I have consciously chosen phrases such as "correspond to and accompany" and "reflect and perpetuate" in order to avoid the impression that the sociological structures are determined by consciousness, as according to an idealistic conception of the relation between thought and social structures. However, neither do I mean to suggest that for Ruether that consciousness is strictly determined by social structures, as according to a strict Marxist materialism. It seems to me that Ruether regards consciousness and social structures as dialectically related.

17 The association of conceptions which thwart human fulfillment with dualistic patterns that polarize dimensions which ought to be related dialectically has already been seen in our analysis of her ecclesiology. The error of the main conceptions of the church and its function has been their polarization of the historical existence and eschatological hope in such a way that the eschatalogical hope for a restored humanity loses its critical and motivational force in the historical life of the church. The apostolic and radical reformation communities erred in their almost exclusive focus on the fulfillment of eschatological hope in their own community. On

Ruether's view, both eschatalogical hope/historical reality, and church/world must be seen as dialectically related rather than polarized.

18 Hegel did not use the concept in an absolutely negative sense. On his view, the natural world is created by God (or Absolute Mind or Absolute Spirit) in an act of self-alienation. Man, for Hegel, is "the Absolute in the process of dealienation," or in the process of reconciling itself to the natural world. Every creative human act (and, the human person is regarded by Hegel as essentially creative) is an act of self-alienation which "can be overcome only in the sense of being adequately known." It is in this process of human self-knowledge that man serves as the medium for the process of dealienation or reconciliation in which God is engaged. "To the extent that he [man] does not perform this function, he does not fulfill his human essence and is merely a self-alienated man" (Petrovic 1967:76–77).

Feuerbach disputed Hegel's conception of human being as God in the process of reconciliation or dealienation. On the contrary he regarded God as a creation of the human person, a product of our own alienation from ourselves. Marx agreed with Feuerbach on this point, "but he stressed that the religious alienation of man is only one among many forms of man's self-alienation." He also denied the Hegelian view that all human creativity or self-expression represents alienation. That is, he "criticized Hegel for . . . having identified objectification with alienation" (Petrovic 1967:77).

19 Ruether's sense of the interrelatedness or interdependence between our analysis of the deficiencies of human existence and our conception of the human essence or the ideal forms of human life is another aspect of her thought which parallels characteristics of Marxist thought. Bertell Ollman has written of Marx's concept of alienation:

> Alienation can only be grasped as the absence of unalienation, each state serving as a point of reference for the other. And, for Marx, unalienation is the life man leads in communism. Without some knowledge of the future millennium, alienation remains a reproach that can never be clarified. An approach to grasping the "logical geography" involved may be made by contrasting the expressions "health" and "disease": we only know what it is to have a particular disease because we know what it is not to. If we did not have a conception of health, the situation covered by the symptoms would appear "normal." Furthermore, when we declare that someone is ill we consider this a statement of "fact" and not an evaluation based on an outside standard. This is because we ordinarily conceive of health and disease as internally related, the absence of one being a necessary element in the meaning of the other. Similarly, it is because Marx posits an internal relation between the states of alienation and unalienation that we cannot regard his remarks as evaluations. There is no "outside" standard from which to judge (1976:131–132).

In comparing Ruether and Marx, we will have more to say with reference to Ollman's characterization of Marx's thought as lacking "outside" standards.

20 Thus Petrovic can say that self-alienation for Hegel and Marx "is alienation *of* a self *from* itself *through* itself" (1987:78–79).

21 Recall that for Marx, as opposed to Hegel, not all objectification represented alienation.

22 Ruether's claim about the priority of male-female dualism is somewhat ambiguous. Sometimes, as in the quotation from *Liberation Theology* and at the beginning of the second paragraph of this quotation from *New Woman/ New Earth*, she suggests that the alienation of the self from itself in the dualism of body and soul is prior to the male-female dualism and that the sexual dualism is based on that self-alienation. On the other hand, the first paragraph of this quotation indicates that sexual symbolization of the male-female dualism shapes the experience of psychic dualisms as if the male-female polarity is that upon which the psychic split depends. Possibly the way to understand this apparent contradiction is in terms of a dialectical relation between consciousness and cultural symbols. On such a view, neither self-alienation nor male-female dualism is regarded as prior to the other, nor as that upon which the other depends or from which it derives. Rather, the male-female dualism of our culture's sexual symbolization represents the fundamental manifestation of psychic dualism and the primary mechanism for its continuation in human consciousness.

23 See her discussion of Romanticism in *New Woman/New Earth* (1975b:19–24) and *Sexism and God-Talk* (1983a:105–109).

24 Ruether praises ancient forms of religious consciousness in which male and female images of the divine are utilizied without suggesting "gender complementarity." "Gender division," she writes, was "not yet the primary metaphor for imaging the dialectics of human existence." Rather, she claims that "divine forces, male and female, are ranged on both sides of the dichotomies" (1983a:52).

25 We will have much more to say below with regard to liberalism and the public-private split as this is an important element of Ruether's critique of liberalism. At this point I am only concerned to show how her rejection of all those solutions which accept any sort of split between domestic and public spheres follows the pattern of liberation from alienation which is so evident in Ruether's work.

26 It could be argued that liberalism is capable not only of seeking women's equality in the public sphere, but also men's full participation in the private sphere in such a way as to prevent women from being disadvantaged by the "double shift." Later, Ruether suggests such an understanding but rejects it in terms of the integration of the public and private spheres. She writes with reference to the psychic integration to which we referred above:

> This means not just the integration of women into roles in the public
> sphere, defined by rational action, and the integration of males into
> domestic roles of caring and nurturing. These are indeed important
> beginnings, but the crossing of the psychic-social boundaries of the male

dualistic world leads women on to a further vision, a transformation of the relationship between the spheres of psychic capacities and social roles. . . .

Women, building upon psychic integration, seek a new sociological integration that overcomes the schizophrenia of mind and of society. Women want to integrate the public and the private, the political and the domestic spheres in a new relationship that allows the thinking-relational self to operate throughout human life as one integrated self, rather than fragmenting the psyche across a series of different social roles. Women want to tear down the walls that separate the self and society into "male" and "female" spheres. This demands not just a new integrated self but a new integrated social order (1983a:113).

[27]This view is in no way altered by Ruether's recent writing for the women-church movement. In her book *Women-Church*, Ruether argues that the establishment and empowering of women's liturgical communities is necessary because the oppression of women has included as an essential aspect "the repression of women . . . into silence; the deprivation of speech, of the capacity to articulate their own experience and communicate it." The formation of liturgical and other types of communities of women is necessary so that women can be enabled "to articulate their own experience and communicate it with each other" and "to form the critical culture that can give them an autonomous ground from which to critique patriarchy." She says that "this process of consciousness raising must necessarily have a separatist stage" (1985:59). But she is clear that it is only a first stage.

How Women-Church might be transcended in a redemptive community of both men and women liberated from patriarchy remains to be seen. I assume that it should happen as the fulfillment and culminating of a process in which Women-Church is one stage. One can see this begin to happen as women shape a sufficiently clarified critical culture so that some men feel compelled to try to understand it on its own terms and not simply to try to ridicule or repress it. What is required for the development of a new cohumanity of men and women liberated from patriarchy is that men begin to critique their own dehumanization by patriarchy and form their critical culture of liberation from it in a way that truly complements the feminist exodus and allows the formation of real dialogue. I assume the name for this liberated humanity would then no longer be "Women-Church," but simply "Church". . . (1985:61).

[28] It should be noted, however, that she associates the liberal theory of progress with the literal or linear conception of the relation between eschatology and history, which she has rejected in favor of a conception which sees the vision and hope of the fulfillment of the human essence as "at the center" of our existence rather than at the end (see 1983a:252–253).

[29] See Allen Buchanan's discussion of "The Marxian Critique of Justice and Rights" in his book *Marx and Justice: The Radical Critique of Liberalism* (1982:50–85). There he makes the claim that Marx's critique of liberal rights and justice has several implications, the most important of which, Buchanan says, are the following:

1) One of the most serious indictments of capitalism—and of all class-divided societies—is not that they are unjust or that they violate persons' rights, but that they are based on defective modes of production which make reliance upon conceptions of justice and rights necessary.

2) The demands of justice cannot be satisfied in the circumstances which make the conceptions of justice necessary; thus, efforts to achieve justice inevitably fail.

3) Conceptions of rights or justice will not play a major motivational role in the revolutionary struggle to replace capitalism with communism.

4) Communism will be a society in which juridical concepts—including the juridical concept of respect—have no significant role in structuring social relations.

5) The concept of a person as essentially a being with a sense of justice and who is a bearer of rights is a radically defective concept that could only arise in a radically defective form of human society.

While these implications of Marx's critique of liberalism are not all systematically displayed in Ruether's work, they do seem to me to be helpful in terms of understanding her critique. While she is capable of appealing to justice and rights, her conception of a good society is not so much a just one in which rights are respected as it is one in which alienation is overcome. Where such alienation is overcome, appeals to rights and distributive justice would seem to be unnecessary.

30 She refers in this context to a the principle of subsidiarity, apparently with reference to the concept, developed in Roman Catholic social teaching, that no responsibility should be left to a larger unit of governance that can be adequately handled by a smaller one.

31 Bertell Ollman says that private property "is Marx's most general term for the objects produced by alienated labor, and encompasses all the products that come out of a capitalist society. It *is* alienation viewed from the angle of the social product" (1976:158).

32 This relationship is the key link between self-alienation and private property in Marx's thought. As Ruether says of Marx's view: "Man is most specifically man, most specifically human, as creator, as maker" (1970:96). The root of human self-alienation is alienation from our productive activity, or alienated labor, that is, when human beings are not in control of our productive activity, when it is not an intrinsically valuable form of self-expression but is only instrumentally valuable as means to produce "things" of value, and when the product of our activity is the private property of another as in capitalist production.

33 Beauchamp, unlike Thomson, regards preferential hiring as reverse discrimination or a violation of the rights of those white males who are not hired or

are passed over for promotions in favor of minorities or women. He sees the principle of compensatory justice and the utilitarian benefits of preferential hiring as outweighing the violation of the rights of white males.

[34] Eisenstein, in fact, draws a diagram describing "Capitalist Patriarchy" which indicates supportive relationships between liberal individualism and capitalism and between male privilege and the patriarchal family, but a conflictual relationship between liberal individualism and both male privilege and the patriarchal family. Capitalism, according to her diagram, has the potential for both a conflictual and supporting relationship with male privilege and the patriarchal family. What her argument and her diagram confirm is that capitalism can (and does) display patriarchal features; it can accommodate itself relatively easily to a culture system which accepts male privilege and a patriarchal family, but those features are clearly in conflict with liberalism. The liberal underpinnings of capitalism account in part for its potential for conflict with the male privilege and patriarchy. Her central argument in the book is that the recent surge of married women into the workforce of industrial capitalism leads to their experiencing of the contradictions between liberal equality and their double shift of duties, their inferior position in the work place, and the possibility of the radicalization of liberal feminism, or a movement beyond liberalism. I would contend that the fact that the economic sphere has been opened to women is attributable in large measure to liberal ideology and that liberal commitments demand a response to the fact of their inferior status in the economic sphere and their double shift of duties. The experience of these facts as oppressive or unjust can be accounted for and responded to within a liberal framework and in no way indicates contradictions within liberalism which require moving beyond its framework. There may be other reasons for abandoning the liberal framework, but this isn't one of them.

[35] One ought not overemphasize her association of certain modes of reasoning and acting with males and others with females. She regards males and females as "naturally" or "inherently" distinguished only by minimal biological differences. The gender distinctions she makes with reference to modes of reasoning and acting have to do with the way men and women are socialized and with the spheres of activity in which they have traditionally operated. They are not natural differences.

[36] I have argued that it is the liberal recognition of the embodied quality of the autonomous self which accounts in part for its sense of the importance of private property.

[37] The contrast between the conception of the self which Ruether regards as dominant in western thought, with its corollary ethic based on the view that persons are fundamentally competitive, and her own integrated conception of the human self, with an ethic of cooperation as attendant to it, suggests comparisons to Carol Gilligan's distinction between an ethics of justice and an ethics of care (See Gilligan 1982 and 1987). Gilligan writes,

> From a justice perspective, the self as moral agent stands as the figure against a ground of social relationships, judging the conflicting claims of self and others against a standard of equality or equal respect (the Categorical Imperative, the Golden Rule). From a care perspective, the

relationship becomes the figure, defining self and others.   Within the context of relationship, the self as a moral agent perceives and responds to the perception of need. The shift in moral perspective is manifest by a change in the moral question from "What is just?" to "How to respond?" (1987:23)

Moreover, like Ruether, Gilligan identifies the justice perspective with males and the care perspective with females. In the case of both, I think it is fair to say that these identifications are in no way regarded as "natural" or permanent. Rather, they are regarded as products of the socialization of males and females in our culture and the association of males with public spheres and females with the private one. Gilligan's work is, of course, descriptive in nature.   Ruether is more concerned to make the normative point that the female perspective which emphasizes relationality and care ought to become operative in public spheres.

38 She makes what I would regard as an unhelpful distinction between those who hold this view and those who regard sociality as "essential for survival and fulfillment" while still regarding the individual as "prior (perhaps not temporally, but ontologically) to social life." She has already said of the first group that there is disagreement as to "the degree of animosity among individuals." The important distinction is between those who regard the self as "prior" or given apart from social relations (whether those selves exist in isolation, join together for instrumental purposes, depend upon one another for their survival, or are even quite friendly), and those who regard the self as essentially social.

39 Even here, however, Ruether warns that "[w]omen should not buy into the masculine ethic of competitiveness that sees the triumph of the self as predicated upon the subjugation of the others" (1972:124).

40 Later in the book she criticizes Freud for regarding the female "élan toward individuation and autonomous self-expression" as infantile, when the same traits in men are seen as a sign of maturity. She writes:

Freud is an accurate observer of phenomena. His mistake lies in confusing social phenomena with "nature," both biologically and normatively. His description of how one frustrates a woman's original sense of her own potency, how one gradually convinces her to give up her élan toward individuation and autonomous self-expression, labeling her very strength as weakness, her drives toward what would be regarded as maturity, if applied to a male, as "infantile," so that she finally is convinced to collapse as a self-initiating human being and becomes a tool of male power—all this accurately describes what goes on in the making of the "normative female" in male-dominated societies (1975b:149).

5
Roman Catholic Social Teaching:
A Qualified Affirmation of the United States

THE STORY of the Roman Catholic Church in the United States is a complex and difficulty one, as is the story of the various efforts of its adherents, leaders, and thinkers to find the church's place and define its social ethical responsibility in the liberal political culture of this country. Recent publications by David O'Brien, Bryan Hehir, and Avery Dulles point to this complexity.

O'Brien, for example, has identified three broad historical styles of public Catholicism in the United States—republican, immigrant, and evangelical—each of which continues to have strong support. What O'Brien calls the Republican style celebrates the liberal democratic experiment in the United States with its recognition of religious liberty and the separation of church and state. Its tendency is to accept the relegation of specifically Christian values and concerns to the private sphere.[1] The immigrant style, says O'Brien, is characterized by "group consciousness, defensiveness, willingness to use power to achieve concrete results" (1989:55). It often resulted in the organization of parish centered, ethnic associations "both to preserve Old World traditions and facilitate advancement in the new" (1989:6). Those relating to the wider world in the immigrant style often employed the techniques of interest-group liberalism, exerting political pressure in the public sphere to protect church needs and interests.[2] The evangelical style developed in the middle of this century and, according to O'Brien, is "in many ways the most dynamic and influential." The evangelical approach regards the republican style as "too secular, the immigrant style too selfish."

> Neither, it appeared, had much to do with Christianity or with the life and witness of Jesus. They could not be satisfied with the subculture that the church's leaders constructed in order to preserve the faith and insure institutional survival, but neither were they satisfied with the dualism of a republican tradition that, by the time industrial society arrived, tended to segregate religion from the rest of life and to reinforce the modern schism that historians have noted as part of the experience of Christianity in the modern world. Instead they sought a reintegration, personal, communal, and public, by means of a complete commitment to the gospel, expressed in

profound religious faith, an interiorization of the spiritual life, and a dedication to serving the poor and healing the wounds besetting society (1989:6).3

Avery Dulles has identified not three, but four current Catholic strategies for relating to the culture of the United States: traditionalist, neo-conservative, liberal, and radical. Traditionalists are "those Catholics who are highly critical of what they find in the dominant American culture and who wish to restore the more centralized and authoritarian Catholicism of the years before World War II" (1990:55–56). Neo-conservatives and liberals affirm the accomplishments of liberal democracy in the United States. "The neo-conservatives are confident that the Catholic Church, with its liturgical, personalist and communal heritage, and with its long tradition of moral reflection on the proper ordering of human society, has unique resources for the renewal of the American experience" (1990:56). The liberals focus less on what Catholicism can contribute to the political culture of the Unites States and more on "how Americanism can help to modernize the church. They propose to reform Catholicism along the lines of participatory democracy" (1990:56).[4] The radical Catholic strategy, represented by the Catholic Worker Movement and the Berrigen brothers among others, borders on the "sectarian" and has been, in some of its manifestations "relentlessly countercultural." On the view of Daniel Berrigen, "the cross and the world. . . can never meet otherwise than in conflict. Christ . . . cannot enter our sinful world except under a cloud that blinds the eminences and authorities." The radicals express "prophetic vehemence against capitalism, consumerism, militarism, racism and the genocide of native peoples" (1990:57).

Hehir has surveyed the same field as O'Brien and Dulles and contends that "three distinct proposals for a style of social ministry have been advocated in the United States in the past decade. They are an educational-cultural model, a legislative-policy model, and a prophetic witness model" (1991:66). According to the first, the church's social teaching in the United States should "concentrate on broad themes of public philosophy, personal character, and family value" on the grounds that "[t]he fundamental public task for the church . . . is to shape the religion-cultural conception of society" (1991:66). Hehir regards this model as having limited usefulness because of its insistence that it is normally inappropriate for the church to advocate or oppose specific policies and because of its "great faith in the ability to move from important but broad social principles held by a citizenry to the specifics of policy choice." Moreover,

the basic conception of virtue, rights, and common good, which animates this model, amounts to a fundamental challenge to existing patterns of policy discourse in American society. This fact is a very good reason for pursuing the fundamental themes, but also a good reason to question whether the educational-cultural model is an adequate style of social ministry. . . . In the short to middle range, this model may leave the Catholic voice out of public life (1991:67).

The legislative-policy model goes beyond the previous model to the actual advocacy of concrete policies. According to Hehir, the style of the U. S. Bishops' pastoral letters "is a mix of the exposition of principles espoused in the educational-cultural model, and an application of those principles in the concrete details of the policy debate" (1991:67).[5] The prophetic-witness model challenges the appropriateness of this role. It "seeks to create within the church a clear counterpoint . . . to existing society vision and policies. . . . The prophetic-witness model seeks transformation as the product of a prior conversion; without conversion, it believes the transformationist strategies will always fall short of what the kingdom requires" (1991:68–69). Hehir cites Stanley Hauerwas as an exemplar of this model, but it is safe to suggest that those Catholics who adopt O'Brien's evangelical style and Dulles's radical strategy are representatives of this prophetic-witness model.

This brief foray into three recent ways of classifying the Roman Catholic Church's effort to understand its relationship to liberal political culture in the United States serves several important purposes by way of introduction to this chapter. Maybe most importantly, it indicates the complexity of the Roman Catholic response to the issues to which we are attending in this work. It forewarns us that there is no single Roman Catholic understanding of how to be the Church in the United States. I will pay greater attention to official Roman Catholic social teaching than O'Brien, Dulles, or Hehir did in the works to which I have referred. Moreover, I will specifically focus on the understanding and critique of liberalism displayed in that teaching. (Neither O'Brien, Dulles nor Hehir adequately considers the way in which each group's assessment of liberal culture influence the posture or style of social ministry or public presence advocated.) We should not expect, however, that such attention will generate a single coherent understanding of the proper relationship of the church to a liberal world. Presumably, all those who represent the options identified can find at least some support in the official teachings of the Church. Still, the interpretation offered here—relying on the methodology I have used throughout this work—will indicate that some of the prominent contemporary Catholic strategies for relating church and world in the United States are not well-supported in the church's official teaching.[6]

The first section of this chapter will focus on ecclesiology. In this section, I will describe the move away from a traditional natural law methodology with the emergence of "historical consciousness" in the official documents since Vatican II. The natural law method has been replaced by what David Hollenbach has called a "dialogically-universalist" method in which the unique social ethical resources upon which Christian faith draws are brought into conversation with the insights of the various human cultures and sciences in order to develop a social morality which contributes to human fulfillment and unity. In this context we will consider Charles Curran's judgment that contemporary Catholic social teaching still envisions a single moral order, that is, it sees Christians and non-Christians alike as called to the same social ethical commitments. Curran's argument is interesting precisely because it suggests some distinction between church and world with reference to what I have been calling the moral factor, in spite of the fact that the new methodology employed in official teaching since Vatican II suggests the possibility of a sharp distinction at the epistemological level. It raises the question of precisely what distinctive moral contribution the biblical and theological appeals in contemporary social teaching make in their dialogue with the culture.

In this section I will argue that the ecclesiology of the official Catholic social documents remains somewhat confused or incoherent; it seems to be in a stage of transition the implications of which have not been fully understood. Drawing on Norbert Rigali's response to Curran's claim, I will contend that, in fact, the historical consciousness which has emerged in official Catholic teaching suggests that Christian teaching must begin with a sense of its own distinctiveness (and that of every other perspective). From its relatively distinct perspective it seeks to discern the prospects and dangers of dialogue and cooperation. This way of understanding the importance of historical consciousness suggests as well that the dialogue with the world is carried on fruitfully and faithfully only where the particular moral insights of the faith are given specific concrete embodiment. The importance of the church's own concrete embodiment of its distinctive moral insights is also suggested by the shift from an institutional model of the church to models which regard the church as a pilgrim people serving the world as a sacrament of unity, which Avery Dulles's work in comparative ecclesiology has identified. I will contend that official teaching has been slow to recognize and attend to the importance of this concrete embodiment.

The dialogically-universalist method which Hollenbach so ably describes indicates that the question of the church's posture or style of relating to any culture will depend upon the specific features of that culture. Continuing the assumption we have made throughout this work, that liberalism provides the best descriptive and normative account of the public political culture of the United States, the second major section of this chapter will outline the understanding and critique of liberalism developed in contemporary Roman Catholic social teaching.[7] For it is only in the light of that understanding and critique that we can develop fully the way of being the Church in the United States advocated in social Catholicism.

In that second section, I will show that social Catholicism has an anthropology that integrates a social or communitarian understanding of the human person (like that of Michael Sandel and Stanley Hauerwas) with an appreciation for the individual capacity for autonomous self-direction. Such a conception regards human dignity as encompassing both dimensions. This perspective appreciates liberalism's insistence that the essential moral truth about us, that in terms of which our dignity is defined, is our individual capacity for autonomous self-direction, but is critical because it insists that the capacity for autonomous self-direction is not *the* essential truth about the human person, but only *an* essential truth. I will show how a communitarian conception of the person is reflected in the Roman Catholic conception of human rights.

Building upon the basic understanding of the church-world relation developed in the first section of the chapter and the analysis of official Catholic teaching's understanding and critique of liberalism in the second, I will in a brief conclusion suggest the outlines of the particular concrete embodiment of Catholic moral insights which are called for by that teaching. That is to say, I will outline what I believe to be the appropriate way of being the Church in the United States which is suggested by contemporary Catholic social teaching.

Church and World in Roman Catholic Social Teaching

Historical consciousness in contemporary social teaching

The historically conditioned demands of human dignity. One of the most noticeable characteristics of Roman Catholic Social Teaching since Vatican II has been the way in which appeals to natural law have become less and less prominent. There has emerged a greater recognition of the historically-conditioned character of human knowledge, of pluralism in morality, and a greater dependence on claims grounded in the particular biblical and theological beliefs of Christians. This methodological shift was accompanied by a shift from an institutional model of the church to ones that emphasized the church as a pilgrim people of God, serving the world as a sacrament of unity.[8] The new approach does not represent a shift to an epistemological perspective that is radically historicist, relativist, or perspectival like that of Stanley Hauerwas; it is more subtle and our description of it must be careful.

The first step in that description is to note the recognition at Vatican II "that the demands of human dignity are historically conditioned ones." David Hollenbach has written that this was the Council's "most important contribution to the human rights tradition" (1979:69–70). This recognition of the historical nature of our moral knowledge is directly tied to the way in which our selfhood is historically and socially shaped. That is to say, it is directly related to the communitarian anthropology of social Catholicism. Hollenbach writes that on the view taken in *Gaudium Et Spes,* one of the most important and influential documents produced by the Second Vatican Council,

> it is impossible to specify the conditions of human dignity *a priori.* Any justification of particular claims which would grant them the status of rights involves a measure of historical judgment. Any appeal to the nature of the human person which is used to justify rights claims must take into account the fact that this nature is structured and conditioned both historically and socially (1979:70).

Hollenbach does argue that not all the rights affirmed in contemporary social Catholicism are equal with respect to the degree of historical contingency associated with their recognition and validity. Indeed, he draws a distinction between what he calls personal, social, and instrumental rights[9] which in part has to do with the degree of contingency associated with each one. While I do not find Hollenbach's distinction between the personal, social, and instrumental rights entirely cogent, what is important for our purposes is Hollenbach's argument that there is a greater degree of historical contingency associated with the social and instrumental rights than with the personal rights.

> The advantage of distinguishing the three levels of rights, however, is its acknowledgement of the differing degrees of historical contingency and variability which govern the three types of rights. While the core personal rights have been consistently defended in the tradition's documents, there have been major shifts in its understanding of the appropriate form for instrumental rights (1979:97).

Does such a statement suggest that the "core personal rights" have a more universal, more foundational, epistemological status? It seems that Hollenbach regards them as having a more basic epistemological status than the social and instrumental rights that are affirmed in social Catholicism. It should be noted, however, that in this context Hollenbach says only that the personal rights "have been more consistently defended" in the social Catholic tradition, and not that they are recognizable by reason apart from that tradition. Therefore, while the "core personal rights" have a more basic status, they are not absolutely free of historical contingency.

The radical understanding of pluralism. The recognition in social Catholicism of the way human knowing is historically conditioned has resulted in an increasingly radical understanding of moral pluralism. Hollenbach notes that *Gaudium et Spes* and later documents are characterized by "the radical seriousness with which the challenges of pluralism are viewed" (1979:122). For these documents:

> One of the primary causes of grief and anxiety in modern social life is a breakdown of basic patterns of meaning, a loss of coherence between the diverse forms of knowledge and technique which humanity has developed, and an increasing inability to conduct genuinely communicative social and political discourse (1979:119).

They recognize "a crisis of moral reason itself," because "[r]eason does not have a univocal meaning which is capable of providing univocal answers to the basic moral questions of society" (1979:122).[10] *Gaudium et Spes* sees this crisis of reason as a fundamental "sign of the times." It notes in an early paragraph:

> Although the world of today has a very vivid sense of its unity and of how one man depends on another in needful solidarity, it is more grievously torn into opposing camps by conflicting forces. For political, social, economic, racial and ideological disputes still continue bitterly, and with them the period of a war which would reduce everything to ashes. True, there is a growing exchange of ideas, but the very words by which the concepts are expressed take on quite different meanings in diverse ideological systems. . . (Second Vatican Council 1965, par. 4:181).

Hollenbach cites "the treatment of the relation of Christianity and culture in *Gaudium et Spes*" as "the clearest evidence" of the shift from an earlier natural law perspective, with its confidence in a universal human reason, to one which has a "more tentative understanding of [the power of reason's] scope," consistent with a recognition of radical pluralism. Hollenbach notes that in the earlier documents it was reason "which gives persons the power to make history, to understand their social relationships, to be self-determining and to be obedient to God's law without loss of personhood and freedom" (1979:124). In *Gaudium et Spes*, however, it is culture that is the source of the human ability to make history and to be self-determining and morally responsible agents in history.

Hollenbach correctly cites two "significant differences" in the shift from the language of "reason" to that of "culture." First, he notes that "culture is the possession of social groups in history, where reason is viewed as an individual characteristic of the person which can reach timeless truths." Second, there are "a plurality of cultures," as *Gaudium et Spes* recognizes, while the documents which employed the natural law methodology "speak in terms of a single reason possessed by all" (1979:124). At Vatican II, then, the Roman Catholic church adopted a methodology that recognized the culture- or tradition-bound status of all human achievement and knowledge. Another way to put the matter is to say that after Vatican II social Catholicism is communitarian through and through. Whereas it had always affirmed the social nature of the human person, it has now come to recognize that that sociality or relationality is radical; the human person is social in every dimension of his or her being and doing; we make history or exercise our agency, we achieve whatever fulfillment is available to us, we gain whatever knowledge we have, only in relationship with others.

A dialogically-universalist method. With the shift to a perspective that denies the existence of a univocal and universal human reason and recognizes the particularity of every cultural perspective, of necessity, specific theological warrants rise to the forefront of social Catholicism. "The uniqueness" of the new approach has to do with the fact that the role of "the religious and theological dimensions of human existence as interpretative keys for the understanding of the demands of human dignity in the face of cultural, social and intellectual pluralism has become both fully explicit and methodologically central." Hollenbach quotes *Gaudium et Spes:* "The truth is that only in the mystery of the incarnate Word does the mystery of man take on light" (1979:127; Second Vatican Council 1965, par. 22:197).

The contrast between the role of specifically Christian appeals in pre- and post-Vatican II methodologies should not be drawn too sharply. The natural law methodology did not deny the importance of a faith perspective, the scriptures, or of revelation. Hollenbach notes that while the methodology of the pre-Vatican II documents presupposed that "the theory of rights[11] rests on human reason and should be accessible to all reasonable people" (1979:113), this never meant that the Popes regarded proper reasoning about social matters as "independent of the influence of Christian doctrine." Reason always needed to be "enlightened by revelation" (1979:114), and a coherence between Christian doctrine and that which could be learned through the employment of reason was presupposed. This presupposition resulted in both negative and a positive functions for specifically Christian insights. Negatively it meant that "reason itself cannot contradict any of the ethical implications of fundamental Christian doctrine." Positively, "doctrine also helps to fill out the shape of the structure of human dignity" (1979:114). The implication seems to be that the basic shape of that structure was regarded as identifiable by reason alone. Moreover, Hollenbach says that Christian faith was regarded as providing "the standpoint" from which reason operates. The primary contribution of this standpoint was regarded as motivational, although it also was seen as bringing "into high relief" particular dimensions of the human person and social life.[12]

It should also be noted that the conciliar and post-conciliar documents do not deny the validity of knowledge and insight drawn from the various cultures and from those scientific disciplines which are a part of human cultures. Hollenbach notes that as dimensions of culture, those disciplines have their own "proper autonomy" (1979:123). Thus, the conciliar recognition of historically and socially conditioned character of social ethical knowledge and of radical cultural pluralism, while it means that explicitly theological and biblical appeals are brought to the fore in a new way, does not result in a rejection of the insights of the cultures and the various knowledge-producing disciplines within culture. One of the ironies of the shift from a type of natural law methodology that posited an univocal human reason to one that emphasizes the historically and perspectivally conditioned character of all human reasoning is that it has resulted in an approach that is significantly more open to, and in dialogue with, the sciences and with the various human cultures. This result is ironic, because the idea of natural law generally suggests confidence in the reason possessed by all human persons, whereas a perspective that recognizes the conditioned character of all human reasoning suggests that where one stands makes all the difference in the world. Thus, while Stanley Hauerwas emphasizes the epistemological privilege of the church and Rosemary Ruether emphasizes the epistemological privilege of the oppressed and particularly women, the Catholic recognition of cultural pluralism is coupled with a recognition of the epistemological validity of all perspectives.

Hollenbach labels contemporary Catholic social teaching "a *dialogically universalist ethic* rather than a natural law ethic."

> We might also call it an ethic of *pluralistic theological realism*. It is dialogic and pluralistic in its reliance on both the plural methods of the various human sciences and on the religious beliefs and doctrines of Christianity. It is theological in its ontological roots. And it is realistic and universalist in its epistemological claims to be seeking knowledge of the really existing structure of the dignity of every person and the ethical demands of this dignity (1979:131).[13]

Hollenbach's characterization seems fair.[14] Contemporary social teaching is explicit in affirming its openness to the insights of all human persons and cultures and the insights of the various human sciences. It envisions a process of mutual discovery in which all human cultures, the sciences, and the church have a contribution to make.

A basic ambiguity:
What specific contribution does faith make to social ethics?
    While it is clear that contemporary Catholic social teaching envisions a dialogue between church and world, a precise understanding of the contribution of each is not offered. What is particularly difficult to assess is precisely how the contribution of a Christian faith perspective or of uniquely Christian sources of knowledge and insight is understood.

Hollenbach says that what the Christian perspective provides is "a total view of human affairs" which focuses and provides a critical perspective on the insights of those disciplines. He writes:

> This claim to a total view of human affairs is not a claim to knowledge of all that there is to be known about social, economic, political and scientific matters. It is rather a claim that from the Gospel and the doctrines of the Christian faith, Christians possess the key by which the "signs of the times" can be properly interpreted. This totality is thus methodological, not substantive. Arrival at substantive conclusions depends on the full employment of the scientific and cultural resources which are available at any period in history. These resources are then to be organized, criticized and transformed in a dialectical way by the believer relying on the insights gained from the Christian faith (1979:128–129).

It is not immediately clear what Hollenbach means by saying that the total view of human affairs provided from a faith perspective is "methodological and not substantive." Does he mean to suggest that the faith perspective offers no unique or distinctive moral content? Is the Christian contribution to social morality still strictly motivational? If so, this does not distinguish it from the pre-conciliar approach.

Charles Curran's interpretation is less ambiguous, but, as we shall see, less accurate as a description of the social teaching since the Vatican II. In an important essay which is dedicated to assessing the current status of official Catholic social teaching, Charles Curran has asked, "Does official Catholic social teaching recognize one social moral order that is the same for all, or are Christians and Catholic called to do something different from what is required of others in trying to bring about a more just society" (1990:73)? His answer is a resounding and unqualified yes: "In my judgment, the answer to the question is there is only one social moral order and all humankind, including Christians, are called to work for the same social justice" (1990:74).

Curran's claim does not represent a blindness on his part to the methodological shift we have been describing. Indeed, the question he raises is set in the context of a recognition on his part of the emergence of a more explicitly theological and biblical methodology in Catholic social teaching.[15] Thus, Curran's claim that official Catholic teaching recognizes one social moral order does not mean that it does not draw significantly upon sources of authority that are distinctly Christian or that the faith perspective has no significant contribution to make to social ethics. The claim seems to be relevant in terms of what I have called the moral, rather than the epistemological factor. Yet, he insists that the distinctive sources and perspective from which the church makes its moral judgments results in no substantive distinction in social morality. With reference to Pope Paul VI's encyclical *Evangelii Nuntiandi,* but expressing a view which he seems to regard as descriptive of the entire post-conciliar social tradition, Curran insists that the teaching

> does not propose that Christians should do something different from what others are called to do in the service of justice and true human advancement. The church provides Christian liberation with the inspiration or faith, the motivation of fraternal love, and a social teaching. No specific mention is made of a special content for Christians which is different from the justice, human advancement, and social good for which all human beings are called to work (par. 38) (1990:77).

Hollenbach's position is more nuanced. Despite his reference to a methodological rather than substantive contribution from the perspective of faith, he does contend that reflection from a more explicitly religious and theological perspective has had significant impact on the content of Catholic human rights theory. He notes, for example, that the Christian norm of love has become "the foundation of a conception of mutual love and human solidarity that is richer than any philosophical or empirical discussion of the mutual obligations of human beings toward each other." As well, there has been a developing sense of the centrality of the social rights "which guarantee access of all to participation in the political, economic and cultural life of society" and of a "notion of community which especially emphasizes care for the weak and the needy" (1979:132).

The centrality of a biblical and theologically shaped understanding of human dignity as the source of social ethical norms in official Catholic social teaching since Vatican II, consistent with this claim of the Pastoral Constitution of the Church, is not difficult to illustrate. The theological foundation of the theme of development,[16] the sense of the close relationship between evangelization and social action,[17] the principle of solidarity,[18] and the growing respect for non-violent forms of social ethical involvement[19] are all examples of the impact of biblical and theological sources in contemporary Catholic social teaching on the content of morality.

It seems evident that Curran's judgment that no distinguishable Christian content is suggested by contemporary Catholic teaching is mistaken or at least not as carefully nuanced as it ought to be. It is interesting that the passage of *Evangelii Nuntiandi* to which he refers in suggesting a motivational, but not substantive Christian distinctiveness is not nearly as clear as his own statement. Discussing "The Specific Contribution of the Church," the paragraph says that the church

> is trying more and more to encourage large numbers of Christians to devote themselves to the liberation of men. She is providing these Christian *liberators* with the inspiration of faith, the motivation of fraternal love, a social teaching which the true Christian cannot ignore and which he must make the foundation of his wisdom and of his experience in order to

translate it concretely into forms of action, participation and commitment (Paul VI 1975, par. 38:274).

The question that is begged in Curran's reference to this passage is whether the "social teaching which the true Christian cannot ignore" suggests specific obligations for Christians which are different from those recognized as incumbent upon all others. Interestingly, the U. S. Bishops pastoral letter *The Challenge of Peace* explicitly suggests such a distinction in its discussion of the two styles of teaching it employs.

> The religious community shares a specific perspective of faith and can be called to live out its implications. The wider civil community, although it does not share the same vision of faith, is equally bound by certain key moral principles. For all men and women find in the depth of their consciences a law written on the human heart by God. From this law reason draws moral norms. These norms do not exhaust the gospel vision (United States Catholic Conference 1983, par. 17:10).

The letter's affirmation of Christian non-violence alongside its use of just war criteria suggests that non-violence may well represent a moral duty validly grounded in the specific perspective of faith and the gospel vision. Yet, the U. S. Bishops recognize that adherence to the criteria of just war and conscientious participation in war are also valid options for Christians.

One way to get at what is troubling about Curran's insistence that official Catholic teaching recognizes no distinctive Christian moral content and his claim that it recognizes one social moral order is to consider a distinction between ontology and epistemology. Curran's claim that social Catholicism recognizes one social order and no distinctive Christian ethical duties seems to conflate ontological and epistemological matters. That is to say, it fails to separate the question of the existence of a moral order from the question of access to or knowledge of that order. One may recognize only one valid moral order while denying that all human beings have equal access to that order. The rejection of a traditional natural law methodology with its confidence in a univocal human reason in favor of one that recognizes the plurality of cultures and the historicity of human reason may represent only an epistemological shift and not one that questions the existence of a single moral order. But, an implication of this is that while there may still be an acknowledgement of a single moral order, this does not preclude recognizing that different perspectives grant different understandings of the content of that order. Thus, a perspective that draws explicitly upon Christian theological sources and symbols may well have a different conception of the content of the social moral order than that of others, but to recognize this is not to deny that there is only a single moral order. Curran seems not to recognize this possibility. He seems to confuse the sense that there is a single moral order and that all perspectives allow some kind of access to it with the view that all perspectives will necessarily arrive at fundamentally similar conclusions. Thus Christian social ethics must have no distinctive content, if there is only a single moral order and all cultural perspectives have some kind of validity or their own "proper autonomy." But this does not follow.

By failing to distinguish the ontological or normative from the epistemological, Curran also may misconstrue the role of motivation or inspiration. Can moral motivation be separated from moral epistemology as he suggests? Can the motive or inspiration I have for fulfilling a moral claim be separated from my capacity to recognize the moral claim as valid? Consider the virtue of solidarity or the principle of non-combatant immunity. Is it the case that one can recognize the validity of these from any perspective and Christianity only provides the motivation to fulfill their demands? I would argue that the very motivation which Christian beliefs provide for living in solidarity with others and for refusing to attack non-combatants also creates the conditions of the possibility of recognizing these as part of the content of ethics.

A passage from *Solicitudo Rei Socialis* is noteworthy with regard to this question as to whether a faith perspective permits a particular and distinct understanding of the content of morality. The specific theme under discussion is integral development and the idea that such development is to be understood in moral rather than economic terms. The Pope wrote:

> One would hope that also men and women without an explicit faith would be convinced that the obstacles to integral development are not only economic but rest on *more profound attitudes* which human beings can make into absolute values. Thus one would hope that all those who, to some degree or other, are responsible for ensuring a "more human life" for their fellow human beings, whether or not they are inspired by a religious faith, will become fully aware of the urgent need to *change* the *spiritual attitudes* which define each individual's relationship with self, with neighbor, with even the remotest human communities, and with nature itself; and all of this in view of higher values such as the *common good* (John Paul II 1987, par. 36:40).

Notice here the lack of confidence in the capacity of persons "without an explicit faith" to recognize the very basis of the true development of the human person. The Pope can only hope that such a recognition is possible. Surely, on his view, the perspective of faith results in more than a simple added motivation to do what all are capable of recognizing as morally demanded. Rather, a mature and thoughtful faith perspective enables the recognition of the true foundation of social morality. Christian faith recognizes a distinctive content, if not an absolutely unique one.

Norbert Rigali believes that the whole question of "whether Christian faith makes any difference with regard to the material content of the moral life" (1990:80) is based on a false understanding of morality that is inconsistent with the historical consciousness that began to emerge at

Vatican II. The question of whether or not Christian faith changes the content of morality derives, he argues, from the "classicist" or traditional natural law assumption that "the norm of morality is human nature." By contrast, from an epistemological perspective that recognizes the historically conditioned character of morality, the norm of morality is

> the historical human person. . . . The heart of morality, consequently is the self-realization of the human person in history through virtue (vice), character, faith, world-view, community, friendship, commitment, political involvement, relationships, etc. as well as through the intellectual-volitional-affective activity and outward action that constitute the act of deliberate will. In a word, the realm of morality is concrete human persons as self-actualized in history (1990:85).[20]

From such a perspective, there is "no presupposition of a single morality,"

> for the oneness of moral law is directly derived not from the singleness of human nature but from the unity of the human race in history. A true morality is indeed based on objective human values, but it is based on objective human values as perceived from some historico-cultural perspective. Since human values, moreover, are naturally interrelated and correlative, they can be discerned only collectively, in relation to one another, and not discretely, as if they were individual entities unto themselves. In other words, human values are a perceived system of human values and a perceived system of human values is itself possible only in light of some world-view (1990:88).

Therefore, according to Rigali, the question is not whether Christian ethics adds something extra and distinct to more broadly human ethics. Rather, Christian ethics is "about one of the many modes of being-human . . . about the Christian way of being a human person in history" (1990:86). Or: "The question about Christian morality, therefore, is a question, not about whether Christ adds more norms to already existing ones, but about the normative way of life that originates in the value system of the world-view derived from the Christian story" (1990:89). Rigali concludes: "Starting from the historical fact of moral pluralism, [a historically-conscious methodology] finds specifically Christian morality—indeed moralities—as a given and wonders how it should be shaped in the contemporary world. For historical consciousness, therefore, the debate question is resolved by being dissolved" (1990:90).

It seems then that Curran understands his claim that Catholic social teaching recognizes a single moral order to mean that despite the recognition of the social and historical particularity of all human knowing and of the distinctive perspective of faith, it envisions no distinctive Christian conception of social ethics because of its confidence that all cultures and all the human disciplines are capable of recognizing the basic content of social ethics. On my view, Curran is mistaken. Rigali's argument is persuasive that presupposing a single moral order is inconsistent with the historical consciousness that emerged at Vatican II. Catholic social teaching does recognize the validity, or at least the potential validity, of all cultural perspectives and of the insights gained by the human sciences. Moreover, it does not regard the perspective of faith as absolutely self-sufficient, that is, as without need of the potentially valid insights of various cultures and sciences. The faith perspective and the unique sources of authority upon which faith draws does give it an epistemologically privileged position from which other sources are evaluated. This privileged perspective does suggest the possibility of a distinctive content and indeed contemporary teaching points to certain features of the present Catholic understanding of social ethics that distinguish it from non-Catholic or non-Christian social ethics. It regards this Christian social ethic as valid for all people, though at the same time it recognizes that all people do not acknowledge it as such. Rigali's comments do not indicate the complete abandonment of the idea of a single social moral order, however. Rather they suggest that a single social moral order is a concrete historical challenge rather than a presupposition. Such an order derives "not from the singleness of human nature but from the unity of the human race in history" (1990:88). Of course, that unity is more a matter of hope than reality; as *Gaudium et Spes* recognized, one of the signs of the times is the radical disunity of an increasingly interdependent world. (At the same time, The Pastoral Constitution identified the church as a sacramental sign of unity, as we shall discuss more fully below.) This suggests the possibility of a different understanding of Curran's claim that official teaching recognizes a single moral order: all are obligated to a social moral order that is becoming known, or most fully becoming known, only from the perspective of faith, in fertile dialogue with all cultures and all knowledge-producing disciplines.

The importance of all this for our purposes is the way in which it illuminates the three factors in terms of which the distinction between church and world is typically drawn: epistemological, moral, and human possibilities. This analysis suggests that contemporary Catholic social teaching does draw a distinction between church and world with respect to all three of the factors. First, it does recognize that the church has a distinct epistemological perspective or distinct sources of insight into the social moral order and a distinct set of practices and commitments that the world does not have. Moreover, a faith perspective provides an overview of the human situation and human dignity that is essential to a proper understanding of social morality. Thus faith provides a sort of epistemological privilege. Yet, this perspective does not deny the validity of a completely worldly or secular perspective. Because God is Creator and source of all that is, even those who stand outside the church and those disciplines which do not employ a specific faith perspective still have valid insights which the church itself needs. Second, with respect to the moral factor, the unique epistemological perspective of the church means that there will be a distinctive Christian ethic, though the distinction may or may not be sharp depending upon the particular aspects of the cultural world the church shares and the way in which the insights of that world are incorporated into the church's own vision of the social moral order. The distinction between church and world with respect to the moral factor is contextual. That is to say, the church may find itself able to cooperate more fully in some cultures than others and may find itself required to adopt a critical posture over against important basic features of certain cultures, but a less critical one in others. Again, the question is contextual, but the presumption seems to be that the church will find itself able to cooperate with, but required to instruct and critique, every culture. Most importantly, it seeks to incarnate itself in faithful ways in every culture. While the third factor, what I have called the moral possibilities factor, is of less relevance with reference to Catholic social teaching, it does seem fair to suggest that that teaching does indicate that faith provides inspiration and motivation which distinguishes Christian moral accomplishments from those of the world.

My basic disagreement with Curran regarding the idea of a single moral order should not be construed as suggesting that all this is unambiguous in the official documents. It is not. Passages can still be found in which natural law assumptions seem to prevail. Moreover, from the perspective of the interpretation I have given, the documents can be criticized for being overly casual about the ease with which the church's dialogue with the world can take place, especially given the clear recognition in *Gaudium et Spes* of moral and cultural pluralism and a breakdown in communication. The documents surely are not always explicitly about the specific content of Christian morality, the exact status of the norms which documents like *The Challenge of Peace* believe are valid for all, the reasons those beyond the church have for accepting such norms, and the relationship between these and those derived directly from a specifically Christian vision and worldview. Rigali has written, and I believe correctly, that "Catholic moral teaching is in a state of transition" deriving largely from its failure to recognize the implications of its new historical consciousness. He writes:

> Thrust by the council into an historically conscious era, it is undergoing radical transformation from a classicist discipline into contemporary science of Christian existence. And until this long, complicated process is accomplished and a new consensus of presuppositions created, the debate about specifically Christian morality will remain unresolved. In this respect moral theology in 1968 was, and today still is, unready for the question about specifically Christian morality (1990:86).

Becoming a "science of Christian existence" would require much greater attention on the part of Catholic social teaching to the nurturing of life in the church and the Christian community as a prerequisite for entering the dialogue with the world which it properly regards, it seems to me, as an important task of the church.

Models of the Church and the Church's social ethical contribution.
The Church as pilgrim people of God. The difficult and ambiguous matter of the conciliar and post-conciliar understanding of the church's specific social ethical contribution can also be viewed in terms of the mystical communion, servant and sacramental models of the Church which have been employed. According to Avery Dulles, the "principle paradigm" of the Church in the documents of Vatican II, following the lead of *Lumen Gentium*, is "the people of God" understood as "a Spirit-filled community, a fellowship of life, charity, and truth." This he associates with the idea of the Church as a mystical communion or the Church as the body of Christ. By way of contrast with an institutional model, which emphasizes the objective, visible, organizational elements of the Church as a society, the metaphors "people of God" and "body of Christ" stress that the Church is "a communion of men, primarily interior but also expressed by external bonds of creed, worship, and ecclesiastical fellowship" (1987:56).

Dulles notes that many Catholic thinkers since Vatican II have followed the councils lead by turning to "the sociological concept of community" suggested by the people of God paradigm "as a principle for the renewal of the church. They would wish to see the Church in our time become a place in which one can establish rich and satisfying primary relationships" (1987:57). Understanding the church as "people of God" suggests, then, that the church's own life represents a profound social ethical accomplishment which distinguishes it from the world. Dulles insists that under this model the Church goal remains "a spiritual or supernatural one." The Church is still understood as leading people "into communion with the divine." But this divine communion, which clearly has benefits in terms of interpersonal communion or unity, "is not simply the reward of a life well lived. To some extent it is given with the very existence of the Church" (1987:57).

The "to some extent" can be understood to refer to at least two aspects of Vatican II ecclesiology. The benefits of interpersonal communion and communion with God are realized "to some extent" in the present life of the Church in the sense that only eschatologically is this communion perfected. Thus, *Lumen Gentium* refers to the Church as a "Pilgrim Church" which "will attain her full perfection only in the glory of heaven" (Second Vatican Council 1964, par. 48:78). But, with regard to what might be called the strictly human, social ethical, or this-worldly benefits of Church life *Gaudium et Spes* suggests another respect in which human fulfillment is only partially given with the very existence of the Church. The *Pastoral Constitution* makes clear from the outset that the Church's pilgrimage toward its eschatological fulfillment creates an "intimate bond" between it and the world.

> The joys and the hopes, the griefs and the anxieties of the men of this age, especially those who are poor or in any way afflicted, these too are the joys and hopes, the griefs and anxieties of the followers of Christ. Indeed, nothing genuinely human fails to raise an echo in their hearts. For theirs is a community composed of men. United in Christ, they are led by the Holy Spirit in their journey to the Kingdom of their Father and they have welcomed the news of salvation which is meant for every man. That is why this community realizes that it is truly and intimately linked with mankind and its history (Second Vatican Council 1965, par. 1:178).

The document quickly notes that the most "eloquent proof" of the Second Vatican Council's "solidarity with the entire human family" is shown "by engaging with it in conversation" about the problems that frustrate human fulfillment on earth (par. 3:179). Thus, the Council suggests that it sees the Church as no perfect social ethical community, no community with all the answers to human problems. Rather it engages in conversation with the world from the perspective of Christian faith, expecting to contribute to the world's pilgrimage but also to be illuminated itself by that which those outside the church experience and discover.

Later, in speaking again of "The Church and the World as Mutually Related," *Gaudium et Spes* specifically includes a discussion of "The Help Which the Church Receives from the Modern World." There the council expresses gratitude for "the experience of past ages, the progress of the sciences, and the treasures hidden in the various forms of human culture." As a result of these "the nature of man himself is more clearly revealed and new roads to truth are opened" (par. 44:230). Therefore, the Church is a pilgrim community both because its fulfillment is eschatological and because it conjoined with the world in a pilgrimage of discovery of that which promises a nearer fulfillment of human social ethical possibilities.

The Church as Servant of the world. Clearly then, because the Church is envisioned as a *pilgrim* people of God, a people of God having not yet arrived, the idea of a sharply distinct social ethical contribution suggested by the idea of the Church as community of friendship or interpersonal communion is mitigated. The servant model is characterized by the same ambiguity or tension. The immediate conclusion one might draw from the idea of the Church as servant, that the Church has some distinct and possibly unique social ethical contribution to make to the world, is contrary to Dulles's understanding of the model. Indeed he specifically associates it with the dialogic theological method of the social documents which we have noted emphasizes the conversation between church and world in a mutual journey of social ethical discovery. Moreover, he associates the servant model with secular theologies of the church, like that we have seen in the work of Rosemary Ruether, ecclesiologies which emphasize the way in which Church and world participate in the same tension between the realities of human existence and that for which persons in community may hope or to which they aspire. On the servant model, as Dulles interprets it, the world is served by Church, not by its embodiment of a more perfect social life, but by hearing "from the Church a word of comfort or encouragement. . . . The special competence of the Church is to keep alive the hope and aspiration of men for the Kingdom of God and its values" (1987:97).

Dulles notes, correctly I believe, that a weakness of this model is that it leaves the church's distinctive contribution ambiguous. "The concept of service," he insists, "must be carefully nuanced so as to keep alive the distinctive mission and identity of the Church" (1987:102). Moreover, he notes that the servant model "goes astray if it seeks to set itself up in opposition to the kerygmatic," that is, in opposition to the Church's distinctive message of salvation in Jesus Christ (1987:102). "It may be convincingly argued, that the modern world very much needs something the Church alone can give: faith in Christ, hope in the ultimate coming of God's kingdom, and commitment to the values of peace, justice, and human brotherhood, all of which are dominant biblical themes" (1987:98).

The Church as Sacrament. The idea that the Church has a distinctive social ethical contribution to make may be suggested most clearly by the idea of Church as sacrament. Yet even here, the similarities between church and world are signaled. This model is suggested in the first article of the *Dogmatic Constitution of the Church*: "By her relationship to Christ, the Church is a kind of sacrament of intimate union with God and of the unity of all mankind; that is, she is a sign and instrument of such union and unity." (Second Vatican Council 1964, par. 1:15). *Gaudium et Spes* quotes this passage precisely in the context of explaining "The Help Which the Church Strives to Give to Society" (Second Vatican Council 1965, par. 42:216).

Avery Dulles has explained that in Catholic thought a sacrament is understood as "a sign of grace." He notes that "a sign could be a mere pointer to something that is absent, but a sacrament is a 'full sign,' a sign of something really present. . . . Beyond this, a sacrament is an efficacious sign; the sign itself produces or intensifies that of which it is a sign." He says further that a sacrament "is a socially constituted or communal symbol of the presence of grace coming to fulfillment" (1987:68). It is grace embodied, made concrete. In this sense, then, Christ can be properly referred to as the sacrament of God and the Church as the sacrament of Christ. Let me quote Dulles at some length here:

. . . In [Christ] the invisible grace of God takes on visible form. But the
sacrament of redemption is not complete in Jesus as a single individual. In
order to become the kind of sign he must be, he must appear as the sign of
God's redemptive love extended toward all mankind, and of the response of
all mankind to that redemptive love.

The Church therefore is in the first instance a sign. It must signify in
an historically tangible form the redeeming grace of Christ. It signifies
that grace as relevantly given to men of every age, race, kind, and
condition. Hence the Church must incarnate itself in every human culture.

The Church does not always signify this equally well. It stands under a
divine imperative to make itself a convincing sign. It appears most fully as
a sign when its members are evidently united to one another and to God
through holiness and mutual love, and when they visibly gather to confess
their faith in Christ and to celebrate what God has done for them in Christ
(1987:68).

But sacrament, as we have been saying, is a sign of grace realizing
itself. Sacrament has an event character; it is dynamic. The Church
becomes Church insofar as the grace of Christ, operative within it, achieves
historical tangibility through the actions of the Church as such (1987:69).

This indicates that the church most ably fulfills its proper function
when it provides a contrast model, when it uniquely exhibits unity and
peace. The idea of sacrament, however, represents a denial that the Church
is an absolute contrast to the world. What occurs paradigmatically there is
also happening beyond the Church. Dulles specifically raises the question
as to whether the grace of Christ is operative beyond the Church. His
answer is in the affirmative and, indeed, he cites the way in which the
Church as Sacrament points to this fact. He asks:

Does the grace of Christ operate beyond the borders of the visible Church?
What could this mean? If the Church is defined as the visible sacrament of
Christ's invisible grace, the question may be rephrased to read: Can the
grace of Christ be present and operative and yet fail to achieve its
appropriate corporate expression? The answer I suppose, is that the
expression is never fully appropriate. The Church never fully achieves
itself as Church, at least not in the conditions of this world. It is true
Church to the extent that it is tending to become more truly Church. On the
other hand, something of the Church as sign will be present wherever the
grace of God is effectively at work. The Christological and corporate
dimension of grace will assure a certain ecclesial quality to the life of grace
wherever it occurs (1987:71).[21]

This last comment points to the epistemological privilege of the Church
due to its sacramental imagination. The Church's distinctiveness, under
the sacramental model, is suggested in terms of its holding the key to
recognizing the concrete embodiments of God's grace wherever they may
appear. The Church knows and points where God is working in the world
because wherever God's grace is at work it will have an "ecclesial quality,"

which I take to mean that it will realize itself in human communion like that at the Lord's Table. Finally, Dulles says,

> Wherever the grace of Christ is present, it is in search of a visible form that adequately expresses what it is. In this perspective the Church may be defined as the association of men that palpably bear witness to the true nature and meaning of grace as God's gift in Jesus Christ. Grace disposes a man more and more to receive and process the gospel of which the Church is the historical bearer. Expressions of grace not historically linked with Christ will be—at least in that respect—more ambiguous (1987:71).

David Hollenbach has offered a similar comment:

> The kingdom is already present, even though not fully so. The shape (though not necessarily the extent) of this presence is given its clearest expression in the sacramental life of the church. Thus wherever the kingdom becomes visible it will have the shape outlined by this sacramental life. The claim that there is an analogy between the inner sacramental life of the church and the public life of society is not an argument for the reestablishment of Christendom. It is simply a claim that though neither church nor secular society is the kingdom, both can be *loci* in which the reality of the kingdom becomes visible and actual in human experiences. It is to maintain that the church and secular society can both be partial realizations in history of the kingdom of God. Whether this realization occurs in the ecclesiastical or political spheres it will have the same imaginative contours. Those contours are expressed in the sacramental symbols that give form to the church's life of worship (1988:195).

The Church, then, from the perspective of its own distinctive effort to stand as a sign of grace, as a sacrament of unity, gains the imagination for a proper identification of the signs of God's presence in the world.

The Roman Catholic Critique of Liberalism

We have seen that contemporary Catholic social teaching has developed an ecclesiological perspective which calls for a dialogical relationship between church and world. That dialogue is aimed at the mutual discovery of the social ethical norms necessary for life lived in solidarity and at generating the mutual effort to embody the unity which, contemporary social teaching suggests, both church and world are seeking. This perspective recognizes the distinctive and specific epistemological and moral significance of the church. The church draws upon unique sources of authority which enables it to be an "expert in humanity." From its epistemologically privileged perspective it engages in dialogue with other perspectives from which it expects to gain valuable insight. Moreover, it is a mystical communion and a sacrament of unity that uniquely embodies human unity and human communion with the divine. Yet this distinctiveness is not absolute because the divine grace which makes communion among persons and between persons and God possible is operative in the world as well as the church. While this draws the outlines of the church's relationship to the world, it indicates that the precise relationship of church and world is always contextual; it will depend upon the way in which the church understands the culture in which it finds itself. Cooperation and prophetic judgment are possible modes of relationship with every culture. Therefore, to understand what official Catholic social teaching points to in terms of the church's relationship to the liberal world of the United States requires an understanding of its critique of liberalism.

From the beginning the architects of modern social Catholicism have regarded their teaching as providing a sharp critique of liberalism. Leo XII in *Rerum Novarum* and Pius XI in *Quadragesimo Anno* envisioned a social order which represented a "third way" between the democratic capitalist order which liberal theory described and justified and the alternatives proposed by Marxism and Socialism. More recent teaching has abandoned the effort to impose a particular social order in favor of a theory of human rights regarded as applicable to and realizable in a variety of social orders.[22] Especially since the pontificate of John XXIII and the Second Vatican Council social Catholicism has shown a much greater appreciation for individual liberty and for the institutions associated with liberal societies.[23] Despite this emphasis on human rights and an appreciation for liberal institutions, the authors of Catholic social teaching still regard their views as representing a sharp critique of the liberal society and liberal political economy of the United States.[24]

There are two difficulties associated with any effort to speak of the Roman Catholic critique of liberalism. The first has to do with a question raised by John Coleman: "In what sense do the social encyclicals constitute a coherent unity of teaching" (1986:170)? Coleman tends to emphasize the discontinuities in social Catholicism noting that "various social teachings do not . . . entirely square with one another." Yet he does admit that "it is possible and legitimate to show a unity in the social teaching."[25] Moreover, he acknowledges that David Hollenbach in his *Claims in Conflict*, upon which much of my own analysis will rely, "shows the way toward this task" (1986:186).[26] My own task seems all the more difficult, and this is the second difficulty, because my focus is on anthropology and Charles E. Curran has argued that there is a "changing anthropological emphasis in this body of social teaching" (1986:188).

Despite these problems I believe it can be shown that it is possible to speak of the Roman Catholic critique of liberalism and even to regard that critique as grounded in a consistent anthropological perspective. Coleman himself acknowledges that when one's methodology is not historical, but philosophical or analytical, as mine is in this work, one is more likely to find continuity.[27] Furthermore, despite its title, Curran's discussion of "the changing anthropological bases of Catholic social ethics" focuses not on the anthropological base of the teaching, as much as the normative implications drawn from that base. Surely he is correct to note that "freedom, equality and participation" are supported in contemporary social Catholicism while "Pope Leo condemned the modern liberties" (1986:189). It seems to me, however, that these differences have more to do with changes in the understanding of society and the state than with changes in the basic anthropological perspective.[28] The anthropology of social Catholicism has consistently emphasized what may be called the social, relational or communitarian aspects of human personhood rather than focusing primarily on the dimensions of autonomy or independence which have characterized liberal theory.

Social Catholicism's Communitarian Anthropology

I have identified the basic anthropological conviction of liberalism as the view that every individual is a source of moral claims on the basis of the capacity for autonomous self-direction. Autonomy as self-direction refers to our individual capacity for at least some degree of transcendence over the particular aspects of our existence, the capacity for self-conscious reflection on the goals, values, or ends which shape human life. Our capacity for autonomous self direction means that every individual is capable of choosing the ends, goals, or values toward which his or her life will be directed, and the means for pursuing those ends, free from the absolute determination of those choices by human desires or passions and/or by the historically shaped values and practices of the communities of which the individual is a part. Liberalism is characterized by the view that this capacity is the essential or defining aspect of our nature. To respect human beings is to protect and allow expression to this capacity and the fundamental obligation of basic institutions is to assure that human persons are so respected.

By way of contrast, a communitarian conception of the human person, while not denying the existence of some capacity for autonomous self-direction, emphasizes the way in which both the moral norms which limit human conduct and the values or goods by or toward which human conduct is directed are discovered or shaped by our interactions with others in the communities of which we are part. For the communitarian, we are not primarily autonomous but "encumbered" selves, that is, we are persons whose identity, values, and choices are largely determined by our communities. On this view, there is no self that can be understood apart from the ends it seeks and the traits it possesses, no self that autonomously chooses certain values. Rather, we find ourselves as parts of various communities in which certain ends are valued and pursued; our identity, our sense of self, is inseparable from those communities and those ends. Respect for the moral claims made by the human peson or for the dignity of persons so conceived entails attention to the relationships in which various values, goods, or conceptions of human flourishing are conceived and realized. Such a conception regards the good or goods of human persons as common, that is to say, they are discovered, produced, distributed and enjoyed in relationship or in association with others.

Nowhere in Roman Catholic social teaching does one find sustained attention devoted to the development of a careful conception of the human person. Yet, several of its prominent features—including the insistence throughout that the person is by nature social, the attention to the social and institutional setting which makes the realization of human rights possible, the teleological framework in which the conception of human rights is set, the prominence of the idea of the common good, and the dramatic shift since Vatican II from a natural law methodology to one which emphasizes historical consciousness and the radical diversity of human moral perspectives—all suggest that the conception of the human person which is operative in social Catholicism is one which includes and gives prominence to the communitarian perspective which I have described.

A variety of commentators have referred to the Roman Catholic social teaching or Roman Catholic human rights theory as being grounded in or presupposing the view that the human person is social by nature and have noted that this view distinguishes social Catholicism from liberalism. For example, Curran has noted that "Catholic social ethics has consistently recognized the social nature of human beings. As a result Catholic social ethics looks upon the state as a natural society, for human beings are called by nature to live in political society" (1986:204). John Langan (1986),[29] Bryan Hehir (1980),[30] and Lisa Cahill (1980)[31] specifically contrast Roman Catholic and liberal anthropological perspectives in terms of the greater attention in Roman Catholic thought to the individual's integral relationship to community or society.

On my view, David Hollenbach provides the most satisfactory account of the distinction between liberal and Roman Catholic views.[32] According to Hollenbach, the primary concern of social Catholicism is "the preservation and promotion of the dignity of the human person" (1979:89). [33] The important point is that whereas a liberal conception of human dignity focuses on the capacity for autonomous self-direction as the source of that dignity and insists that the respect for dignity is primarily manifest through respect for individual liberty, according to the Roman Catholic view, human dignity "is not a concept which derives its meaning from a particular class or genus of human actions. It has reality in all situations, independent of the kinds of actions and relations which give them structure" (1979:90). Hollenbach's point is that respect for human dignity requires regard for more than freedom of human action. He distinguishes three fundamental aspects of human dignity: the first has to do with human needs, the second with freedom of action, and the third with the social or relational context of human selfhood. Thus, he insists that Roman Catholic human rights theory "has identified a number of characteristic needs, freedoms, and kinds of relationship which must be met or protected in the life of every individual person. To each of these areas of human existence corresponds a set of human rights which defend human dignity within that sector" (1979:94–95). In John XXIII's classic formulation of the Roman Catholic understanding of human rights, *Pacem in Terris*,[34] this concern to affirm human dignity in all its dimensions is reflected in the defense of a broad range of rights: the civil and political rights which are characteristic of liberal democratic societies, the economic rights affirmed by Marxist and socialist societies, and the social and cultural rights often appealed to by contemporary ethnic minorities and affirmed in the United Nations Universal Declaration on Human Rights. Moreover, it is this concern to maintain an understanding of the human person in all the dimensions of our activity and being that lies behind Paul VI's defense of what has been called "integral development" in *Populorum Progressio*. Because Roman Catholic theory is concerned to affirm and protect human dignity in all its dimensions, which Hollenbach sees as grouped around the poles of need, freedom, and relationship, Hollenbach refers to it as an "integral theory of rights" (1988:93).

Now, it is precisely within the context of his discussion of the integral conception of the human person that Hollenbach signals the fundamental error of both liberalism and Marxism from the Catholic perspective. The problem with both "has been the identification of a limited domain of human existence with the radical foundation of human rights" (1988:91). On Hollenbach's reading the problem with both is that their reading of human nature is too limited.[35]   Both take a part for the whole. Hollenbach's description of liberalism's truncated anthropology is not quite as carefully articulated as it ought to be. He says that the problem with liberalism is that its "foundation [for human rights] is limited to freedom negatively understood" (1988:91). His comment here suggests what I have identified as the fundamental anthropological claim of liberalism. On my interpretation, liberalism takes what I have called the individual capacity for autonomous self-direction as the fundamental if not the entire ground for regarding the human person as a source of moral claims and specifies the content of those claims with reference to that capacity. It is not necessarily the case, however, that those claims are specified negatively, as Hollenbach indicates. The fundamental anthropological claim of liberalism has been correlated with an argument for positive rights, that is, the view that respect for the individual capacity for autonomous self-direction may require positive actions on the part of others.

Still, he is not far off the mark. For the most influential versions of liberalism in the United States, it seems to me, are those which emphasize the negative dimensions of freedom. Even if positive duties are recognized, the negative ones tend to be regarded as more basic. Moreover, he has signaled correctly the fundamental difference between the liberal and Roman Catholic perspectives. The problem with liberalism, according to social Catholicism, is that there is a broader basis for the moral claims that persons make upon one another than our capacity for autonomous self-direction. There are other dimensions of our nature that are essential elements of our personhood and these too must be respected and protected if we are to grant human beings the respect they deserve. Hollenbach writes:

> The fundamental value that undergirds [Roman Catholic social teaching] is neither simply the liberty of the individual stressed in the liberal democracies nor simply the social participation and economic well-being stressed in various ways by Marxism and socialism. Rather the theory maintains that respect for freedom, the meeting of basic needs, and participation in community and social relationships are all essential aspects of the human dignity that is the foundation of all rights. The institutional protection of personal freedom is emphasized by liberal democracy. The fulfillment of human needs is stressed by the developing "basic-needs" strategies at the center of the North-South debate. And the restructuring of the social and economic order in a way that allows genuine communal participation in the corporate life of society is the program of socialist thought. Each of these ideologies links its fundamental understanding of human rights with a particular structural obstacle to the realization of human dignity. The contemporary Catholic understanding, however, refuses to tie its notion of human dignity to only one of these three spheres of life in which persons can be either violated or protected by the structure of the social order (1988:95).[36, 37]

Hollenbach's use of the word "ideologies" in the above quotation should be noted. On his view, liberalism and Marxism are ideologies precisely to the degree that they lift up only a single element of human nature and only the particular institutions which each regards as essential for protecting and giving expression to that particular aspect.[38]

As we have seen, the Catholic conception of human dignity attempts to integrate all dimensions of human being and doing, including the autonomous dimension. As a result, Roman Catholic human rights theory embraces the rights aimed at protecting individual liberty which are associated with liberalism. Moreover, especially in the encyclicals of John Paul II there is a notable appreciation for the benefits of a free economy. For example, in *Sollicitudo Rei Socialism*, promulgated in 1987 to mark the twentieth anniversary of *Populorum Progressio,* he cited "the right of economic initiative" (John Paul II 1987, par. 15:13) [39] and in *Centesimus Annus,* which marked the one hundredth anniversary of *Rerum Novarum* he noted that one cause of the demise of communism in Eastern Europe was "the inefficiency of the economic system, which is not to be considered simply as a technical problem, but rather a consequence of the violation of the human rights to private initiative, to ownership of property and to freedom in the economic sector" (John Paul II 1989, par. 24:10). Later in *Centisimus Annus,* he contends that "the free market is the most efficient instrument for utilizing resources and effectively responding to needs" (par. 34:14). Moreover, in the context of answering the question as to whether the demise of communism in Eastern Europe means that capitalism should be their goal, he writes:

> If by *capitalism* is meant an economic system which recognizes the fundamental and positive role of business, the market, private property and the resulting responsibility for the means of production as well as free human creativity in the economic sector, then the answer is certainly in the affirmative even though it would perhaps be more appropriate to speak of a *business economy, market economy* or simply *free economy* (par. 42:16–7).

Of course, these affirmations of liberal values and institutions are quickly and unmistakably qualified in John Paul II's encyclicals. For example, upon praising the free market as "the most effective instrument for utilizing resources and effectively responding to needs" he quickly adds:

> But this is true only for those needs which are "solvent" insofar as they are endowed with purchasing power and for those resources which are "marketable" insofar as they are capable of obtaining a satisfactory price. But there are many human needs which find no place on the market. It is a strict duty of justice and truth not to allow fundamental human needs to remain unsatisfied and not to allow those burdened by such needs to perish. . . (par. 34:14).

And his affirmation of capitalism as a praiseworthy model for Eastern Europe is followed by:

> But if by *capitalism* is meant a system in which freedom in the economic sector is not circumscribed within a strong juridical framework which places it at the service of human freedom in its totality and which sees it as a particular aspect of that freedom, the core of which is ethical and religious, then the reply is certainly negative (par. 42:17).

In the same context he notes that

> there is a risk that a radical capitalistic ideology could spread which refuses even to consider these problems in the *a priori* belief that any attempt to solve them is doomed to failure, and which blindly entrusts their solution to the free development of market forces (par. 42:17).

In the light of Hollenbach's analysis, neither the affirmation of liberty nor its qualification is surprising. Roman Catholicism's comprehensive and integral anthropology and conception of human rights affords it room for a deep appreciation of liberty and of the liberal institutions which provide its protection.[40] On the other hand, that same theory means that liberal values and institutions are not adequate to the full protection of human dignity in all its aspects both because it fails to attend sufficiently to human needs and to the social nature of human personhood. The Roman Catholic theory simply does not allow the *a priori* judgment that human liberty and its protection should have the priority status that liberalism assigns it. Admittedly, an abiding problem in Roman Catholic theory is the matter of priorities. Where human needs, freedom, and sociality are regarded as equal sources of human dignity and as equal sources of moral claims upon the individual and communities is problematic. Hollenbach, of course, is well aware of this problem. Indeed, his *Claims in Conflict* draws its title from this problem. There he raises the fundamental question:

> Has the theoretical inclusiveness of [the Roman Catholic] approach to rights been bought at the cost of abstract generality? Has the emphasis on the interconnection between all human rights made it impossible to establish priorities in a world where not all desirable goods are immediately and simultaneously realizable? Does the desire to reconcile and harmonize all the various human rights really betray an inability to admit the reality of conflict and the need for making hard choices (1979:14)?

Hollenbach attempts to draw some a sense of priorities from his analysis of Roman Catholic social teaching. He argues for three principles of priority:

> 1) The needs of the poor take priority over the wants of the rich.

> 2) The freedom of the dominated takes priority over the liberty of the powerful.

> 3) The participation of marginalized groups takes priority over the preservation of an order which excludes them (1979:204).

His conclusions are consistent with the "preferential option for the poor" which has been consistently affirmed in the social encyclicals. Even John Paul II, who may be regarded as having the most favorable view of liberal values and institutions, has suggested such priorities in the criticisms he raises.[41]

The Communitarian Content of Roman Catholic Human Rights Theory

Roman Catholicism's integral theory of human dignity and human rights means not only that it regards liberal theories, values, and institutions as inadequately attentive to the needs of the poor, it also means that liberalism fails to protect the social, relational, or communal dimension of human dignity. This is the communitarian dimension of Roman Catholic anthropology. A communitarian theory of human rights will have three basic characteristics which distinguish it from typically liberal understandings. All of these reflect that a communitarian anthropology emphasizes the relational dimension of human personhood in ways that liberal understandings do not. First, a communitarian theory of human rights will either recognize rights belonging to the community or communities which are constitutive of personal identity alongside those rights which are attached to persons as individuals, or, it will regard the exercise of individual rights as limited by the claims of communities in ways that liberal theory does not.[42] In social Catholicism this is primarily reflected in the way that individual rights are regarded as limited by the demands of the common good.

Secondly, a communitarian theory will set all human rights in a teleological framework. Rather than regarding human selfhood as independent of the ends or purposes it autonomously chooses as in liberal theory, on the communitarian view, the human person is "constituted" by ends, goals, purposes, or values which are a part of his or her socially formed identity. Thus, the right or rights are not thought of as prior to or independent of the good, but are understood in relation to the good. Indeed rights are regarded as individual and social protections which are essential to the realization of the good. The fact that the theory of rights is set in a teleological framework will give to rights claims certain formal characteristics which significantly distinguish them from the way rights claims function in the liberal framework which lacks such a teleology. To put it differently, there are important differences in the grammar of rights language in communitarian and liberal frameworks. In social Catholicism this manifests itself in terms of the idea that those who hold rights have a duty to exercise those rights in the pursuit of those goods or values in terms of which the right is justified. In addition, this teleological framework means that basic institutions will not be neutral, as liberal theory insists they must; rather, these institutions will be evaluated in terms of their ability to promote human flourishing. Once again, it is the importance of the idea of the common good which illustrates this dimension in Roman Catholic social teaching.

Thirdly, a communitarian theory of rights will have as its core concern the protection of every individual's capacity to participate in the social process of self-definition and in the social discovery, production, distribution, and enjoyment of the human good rather than the protection of individual liberty understood as autonomous self-direction. Even though a communitarian perspective may not result in a radically different set of human rights, it will have a different understanding of which rights are more basic and which take priority in the case of conflict between rights claims. Roman Catholicism's communitarian basis is reflected in the centrality of participation as reflected in the right to development affirmed since Vatican II and in its willingness to support the priority of the rights of the poor to basic needs over the liberty rights of those whose basic needs are more than met.

Individual rights limited by the claims of communities. The communitarian framework of Roman Catholic human rights theory is reflected more clearly in the way that theory sees human rights as limited by the claims of communities rather than in the list of human rights it affirms. That is to say, it neither affirms individual rights that liberalism is absolutely incapable of recognizing nor does it typically regard rights as belonging to communities.

The argument I am making here indicates some disagreement on my part with the account of social Catholicism provided by David Hollenbach. As we have already noted, contemporary Roman Catholic social teaching affirms a wide range of human rights. If I understand Hollenbach correctly, he sees the broad range of rights affirmed in social Catholicism as corresponding to the integral conception of human dignity which is foundational to it. Using the tripartite division of the dimensions of human dignity suggested by Hollenbach, it can be said that because human beings are recognized as physical beings with definite needs, they have a right to life and bodily integrity (which entails rights to the food, clothing, shelter, medical care, and social security which are necessary to preserve life), and to work. Because we are relational beings, rights to "social intercourse" are necessary if our dignity is to be respected. These include the rights to assemble and associate with others, to communicate with others (which requires being educated into the culture of which we are a part), and to form families. Finally, because there is a dimension of independence in all that we do, we have rights to self-determination which include political participation and the freedom to move about as we chose, even from nation to nation.[43]

This suggests that liberal theories, because they do not recognize the relational dimension of human dignity as social Catholicism does, do not recognize rights to assemble, associate, and communicate with others. This is surely false. Liberal theories are perfectly capable of recognizing that individuals often choose to form social relations which they regard as essential for the fulfillment of their autonomously chosen ends. Thus there is nothing illiberal about recognizing the right of individuals to form various associations, whether familial, professional, social, or political.

Social Catholicism's recognition of such rights does not distinguish it from liberal perspectives.[44] Indeed, it is confusion on this point that has lead some commentators to improperly identify and articulate the difference between liberalism and the Roman Catholic perspective.

What I have in mind is the way in which commentators understand the claim that Roman Catholic, and communitarian perspectives in general, regard the human person as social by nature, or essentially social, and liberals do not. The meaning of this claim is not that communitarians value community whereas liberals do not. It is not that communitarians see the forming of relationships as an aspect of human flourishing while liberals do not. We have already seen this in our discussion of Michael Sandel's articulation of the communitarian perspective. According to Sandel, the liberal perspective is "individualistic" not in the sense that it presumes that human beings are only motivated by self-interest or that they place no high value on social relationships. Rather, it is individualistic in the sense that the self or person is regarded as separable from its ends and values and the social relationships in which those ends and values may be discovered and realized. Thus to respect the person is to respect his or her capacity for independence from those relationships rather than to respect him or her in those relationships. Another way to put this matter is to say, that liberals are perfectly capable of recognizing that individuals value social relationships and therefore see it as fundamentally important to protect the right to form such relationships, but the formation of relationships is given no priority independent of the actual choices of individuals to form them. The liberal perspective is neutral with reference to those conceptions of the good life which include the forming of relationships and those which give such relationships low priority. But they are perfectly capable of recognizing and even affirming the fact that humans often do find their flourishing in relationships with others. That affirmation is not allowed to result, however, in a set of public or governmental rewards and punishments that shows preference for the forming of good human relationships. Thus, communitarians can claim that liberals don't value community highly enough, or that the liberal framework inadvertently undermines community. They may not legitimately claim, it seems to me, that liberals intend to undermine community, or that liberalism is intentionally biased against community because it fails to recognize the value of human relationships. The mistake of liberals, from the communitarian perspective, is that liberals see that value as one that just happens to be chosen by autonomous individuals, rather than as constitutive of our very selfhood.

There is one right or set of rights that Hollenbach associates with the relational dimension of human personhood that does seem to reflect the communitarian basis of Roman Catholic human rights theory and which may distinguish it from liberal theories. I am referring to what are called cultural rights. Indeed, it is precisely in this context that the idea of rights attached to communities has begun to emerge. As Hollenbach has pointed out, "culture" is a corporate or social achievement, not an individual one as "reason" is often understood to be (1979:124). The protection of the dignity of every human person within a communitarian framework requires sustained attention to the relationship of individual persons to the culture which shapes their identity, enables the recognition of certain values and disvalues,[45] and sustains the practices in which recognized values are produced and enjoyed. If we are concerned about the dignity of every human person and the human person is constituted or encumbered by the culture which provides her with language and practices, then a fundamental concern must be that every person have the opportunity to gain the skills necessary for using those cultural resources and for participating in their ongoing development.

Thus, under the heading of "Rights pertaining to Moral and Cultural Values," *Pacem in Terris* insists that every person has "the right to share in the benefits of culture, and therefore the right to a basic education and to professional training in keeping with the stage of educational development in the country to which he belongs" (John XXIII 1963,par. 12:127). [46] The importance of "a right to culture" is greater in the later documents where the cultural relativity of human knowing and doing is recognized in a way that it is not in *Pacem in Terris*. For example, *Gaudium et Spes*, which recognizes that persons "can come to authentic humanity only through culture, that is, through the cultivation of natural goods and values," (Second Vatican Council 1965, par. 53:232) affirms the necessity of "Recognizing and Implementing the Right to Culture:"

> The possibility now exists of liberating most men from the misery of ignorance. . . . [U]niversal recognition and implementation should be given to the right of all men to a human and civic culture favorable to personal dignity and free from any discrimination on the grounds of race, sex, nationality, religious or social conditions.

> Therefore it is necessary to provide every man with a sufficient abundance of cultural benefits, especially those which constitute so-called basic culture. Otherwise, because of illiteracy and a lack of responsible activity, very many will be prevented from collaborating in a truly human manner for the sake of the common good.

> Efforts must be made to see that men who are capable of higher studies can pursue them. . . . Thus all individuals and the social groups comprising a given people will be able to attain the full development of their culture, a development in accord with their qualities and traditions (par. 60:238–239).

The Document of the 1971 Synod of Bishops, *Justice in the World*, speaks of the people's right "to keep their own identity" in the face of the destructive consequences of modernization for more traditional communities. It suggests that modernization need not be destructive, however, if it is accepted in the context of the traditional cultural values and if people are in effective control of the necessary cultural adjustments. "If modernization is accepted with the intention that it serve the good of the nation, men will be able to create a culture which will constitute a true heritage of their own in the manner of a true social memory, one which is active and formative of authentic creative personality in the assembly of nations" (Synod of Bishops 1971:395).

Thus, while the growing attention to cultural rights and the rights of communities in such a context in social Catholicism does suggest that its communitarian framework can result in the affirmation of specific rights that liberal theories may not recognize, it seems to me that the primary way the difference between the Roman Catholic and liberal theories of rights is exhibited is that social Catholicism sees individual rights as limited by the claims of human communities in significant ways. In *Pacem in Terris* this sense that individual rights may be limited by the community is suggested in the concept of the common good.

The common good is defined by John XXIII in *Mater et Magistra* and *Pacem in Terris* as that which "embraces the sum total of those conditions of social living whereby men are enabled to achieve their own integral perfection more fully and more easily" (John XXIII 1960 par. 65:66; John XXIII 1963 par. 58:138). In *Pacem in Terris*, he insists that the "realization of the common good" is "the whole reason for the existence of civil authorities" and "[i]ndividual citizens and intermediate groups are obliged to make their specific contributions" to it. "One of the chief consequences of this is that they must bring their own interests into harmony with the needs of the community." (John XXIII 1963, par. 54:135). This seems to suggest that the exercise of individual rights is limited in some way by the concern to protect the communities or the social practices in which human goods are discovered, produced, distributed and enjoyed. *Pacem in Terris* does make it clear that the common good places a limit on the exercise of rights. For example, it says that one's "right to freedom in searching for truth and in expressing and communicating his opinions, and in pursuit of art" is set within "the limits laid down by the moral order and the common good" (par. 12:127). And, John XXIII found it "opportune to point out that there is a social duty essentially inherent in the right of private property" (par. 22:129), a theme which has been present in Papal teaching on property since *Rerum Novarum*. The community is not said to have rights of its own, but the common good does place limits on the exercise of individual rights and implies individual duties to the community.

It should be noted, of course, that the relationship of the common good to individual rights is not exclusively one of limitation. For *Pacem in Terris* also makes clear that the common good "is chiefly guaranteed when personal rights and duties are maintained," (par. 60:139) and "[o]ne of the fundamental duties of civil authorities," whose whole reason for existence is the realization of the common good, "is to coordinate social relations in such fashion that the exercise of one man's rights does not threaten others in the exercise of their own rights nor hinder them in the fulfillment of their duties" (par. 62:139). Here the emphasis is on balancing the conflicting rights claims of individual persons and their communities as an aspect of the common good rather than a conflict between human rights and that concern for the good of the community of humanity.

Lisa Cahill's summary of the relationship between rights and the common good in Roman Catholic social teaching is helpful. She writes:

> . . . [R]ights are not spoken of primarily as individual claims against other individuals or society. They are woven into a concept of community which envisions the person as a part, a sacred part, of the whole. Rights exist within and are relative to a historical and social context and are intelligible only in terms of the obligations of individuals to other persons. The essential correlativity of obligations and claims is insisted upon. Despite widely differing emphases, the encyclicals consistently retain natural sociality and the common good as a framework for the consideration of actual rights and duties (1980:284).[47]

While social Catholicism does not offer precise specification of the way in which the claims of the community or a concern to protect human communities and social practices limits individual rights, what is important for our purpose is its argument that rights are always set within this social or communal framework and limited by a concern to preserve that framework. This sharply contrasts Roman Catholic human rights with rights as understood in liberal theory; in liberal theories individual rights are limited primarily if not exclusively by the rights of other individuals. Where there is a recognition of the claim of the community or the nation over against the individual and his or her exercise of rights (as for example when a nation is at war or under some other threat to its existence), the validity of that claim against the individual is ultimately grounded in the necessity for the social or political preservation of institutions protective of individual liberty.

The teleological framework of Roman Catholic Social Teaching. A communitarian theory will provide a teleological context for human rights. This is so because a communitarian conception is based upon a view of the person as constituted by the communities of which we are a part and by the ends or values which we share with those communities. To respect the human person so conceived is to respect the relationships of which he or she is a part and to enable human flourishing with reference to the shared values realized in those relationships. This of course means that basic institutions which respect human dignity, cannot be neutral with regard to the human good as liberalism insists. Roman Catholic social teaching is clearly teleological in orientation. Its understanding of justice and rights is not prior to some conception of the human good but is set within the context of such a conception. In other words, its conception of the content and function of human rights and justice is tied to arguments about the ends, purposes, or values which define human being and allow our fulfillment or flourishing. Its conception of the way individual rights are limited by the common good suggests this teleological framework. For communities are regarded as limiting the individual in important ways precisely because it is in community that the goods which make human life worthwhile are realized.

The double correlation of rights and duties. In a teleological moral theory the ends toward which human action is to be directed are not regarded as purely optional. They are not simply a matter of autonomous choice; rather they have a normative claim upon the person. In such a framework, those contexts in which rights-claims arise, that is, those contexts in which a person may legitimately claim some protection or assistance in the pursuit of a worthy end or *telos*, are also contexts in which the person himself is under obligation with reference to that same end.

This is reflected in Roman Catholic human rights theory by the double correlation between rights and duties which is recognized there. Rights and duties are generally recognized as correlative; for every right there are certain duties the observance of which are necessary if the right is to be respected. It seems fair to say with reference to liberal discourse, that the duties correlative to rights belong to someone other than the rightholder. That is to say, if I have a right someone else has a duty to respect that right. In Roman Catholic human rights theory, in addition to this correlation between rights and duties, there is another which reveals the teleological framework of that theory: If I have a right, not only do others have a duty to respect that right, but I also have duty both to exercise the right and to exercise it in a manner that is consistent with the common good. Thus in *Pacem in Terris* "[t]he right of every man to life is correlative with the duty to preserve it; his right to a decent standard of living, with the duty of living it becomingly; and his right to investigate the truth freely with the duty of pursuing it ever more completely and profoundly" (John XXIII 1963, par. 29:130). John Langan notes that this correlation between the rights and duties which a persons possesses is based in

a recognition that the goods with which both are concerned are essential to human flourishing and are, at least in their most fundamental and universal forms, not optional for human beings. The consequence of this first

correlation is that the individual is not in a condition of pure liberty and
discretion with regard to these goods but remains under moral obligation
(1986:115).

The teleological framework of Roman Catholic social teaching is also
reflected in the fact, which we have already noted, that the "realization of
the common good" is "the whole reason for the existence of civil
authorities" (John XXIII 1963, par. 54:135). There is no sense that the
basic institutions of society are neutral with reference to the question of
what constitutes a good life and a good human society. Indeed, in the
teleological framework of Roman Catholicism the whole purpose of
government is to assist persons in the realization of those ends which are
essential to their flourishing.

The ethical and cultural content of "development" as expressions of
Roman Catholic teleology. An interesting illustration of the teleological
character of Roman Catholic social thought and the critique of liberal
neutrality implied therein is found in the insistence that the "development"
which is a proper goal of governmental and economic institutions has a
supremely   ethical and cultural content.   Development has been a
fundamental theme of international relations since the end of World War II.
The concern for world peace and the international consciousness that the
war had generated and the concern about communist expansionism in the
third world caused many governments and international organizations such
as the United Nations to attend to the problem of poverty among the
majority of the world's nations and people. Economic development was
thought to be essential to preventing the spread of communism and the
prevention of war. In 1967, Pope Paul VI addressed a social encyclical to
this theme. *Populorum Progressio (On the Development of Peoples)*,
recognized the important economic dimension of development, while
noting in its very first paragraph the church's special attention to "the
development of those peoples who are striving to escape from hunger,
misery, endemic diseases and ignorance" (PP, par. 1:313).

Quickly, however, the encyclical signaled several important themes of
papal reflection on the matter of development: "Development cannot be
limited to mere economic growth. In order to be authentic, it must be
complete: integral, that is, it has to promote the good of every man and of
the whole man" (PP, par. 14:317–318). For our purposes here, the
important point to emphasize is that development, for Paul VI, is not
primarily to be understood in quantitative, but in qualitative terms. That is
to say, it is not to make more available whatever human beings happen to
want, but it is to promote that which is truly good, truly consistent with
appropriate values. Of course, this view of development which connects it
to a proper conception of the good for the human person and community is
in sharp contrast to the tendency in liberal thought to measure development
in strictly quantitative terms given that the question of quality is eliminated

for the most part from public relevance on the basis of the conviction that basic public institutions must be neutral with regard to the question of the human good.

Populorum Progressio's understanding of development insists that the foundation of human good is to be found in a proper orientation toward God which may indeed be undermined by the inordinate concern for material well-being.

> Increased possession is not the ultimate goal of nations nor of individuals. All growth is ambivalent. It is essential if man is to develop as a man, but in a way it imprisons man if he considers it the supreme good, and it restricts his vision. . . . If further development calls for the work of more and more technicians, even more necessary is the deep thought and reflection of wise men in search of a new humanism which will enable modern man to find himself anew by embracing the higher values of love and friendship, of prayer and contemplation (PP, pars. 19–20:319).

This is not to be construed as a denial of the importance of economic development or of reducing the material impoverishment of the poor. Rather it reflects a broader, more complete moral context for that concern.[48]

According to John Paul II, in his encyclical *Sollicitudo Rei Socialis,* which celebrated the twentieth anniversary of *Populorum Progressio*, a first point of originality in the earlier document was its emphasis on "the ethical and cultural character of the problems connected with development" (John Paul II 1987, par. 8:7). He continues to express the themes already signaled by his predecessor: the inadequacy of a strictly economic conception of development, the relationship of development to a proper conception of the good for the human person and community, and the fundamental significance of a proper orientation toward God. He develops Paul VI's ideas on the dangers of attaching too great an importance to economic or material goods through his critique of what he calls "superdevelopment" and "consumerism."

> . . . In fact there is a better understanding today that the *mere accumulation* of goods and services, even for the benefit of the majority, is not enough for the realization of human happiness. . . . On the contrary, the experience of recent years shows that unless all the considerable body of resources and potential at man's disposal is guided by a *moral understanding* and by an orientation towards the true good of the human race, it easily turns against man to oppress him.
>
> A *disconcerting conclusion* about the most recent period should serve to enlighten us: side-by-side with the miseries of underdevelopment, themselves unacceptable, we find ourselves up against a form of *superdevelopment*, equally inadmissible, because like the former it is contrary to what is good and to true happiness. This superdevelopment, which consists in an *excessive* availability of every kind of material goods for the benefit of certain social groups, easily makes people slaves of

"possession" and of immediate gratification, with no other horizon than the multiplication or continual replacement of the things already owned with others still better. This is the so-called civilization of "consumption" or "consumerism," which involves so much "throwing-away" and waste. . . .

All of us experience firsthand the sad effects of this blind submission to pure consumerism: in the first place a crass materialism, and at the same time a *radical dissatisfaction*, because one quickly learns—unless one is shielded from the flood of publicity and the ceaseless and tempting offers of products—that the more one possesses the more one wants, while deeper aspirations remain unsatisfied and perhaps stifled. . . .

The evil does not consist in "having" as such, but in possessing without regard for the *quality* and the *ordered hierarchy* of the goods one has. *Quality and hierarchy* arise from the subordination of goods and their availability to man's "being" and his true vocation (par. 28:27–28).

The attack on "consumerism" is developed further in *Centisimus Annus*. The context indicates again that John Paul II's affirmation of freedom in the economic sphere cannot be construed as an affirmation of a liberal account of the basis and scope of such freedom. John Paul II, despite his deep appreciation for the merits of the free market, in no way affirms the moral neutrality which is at the heart of the liberal justification for free economic institutions. Having affirmed the free market as "the most efficient instrument for utilizing resources and effectively responding to needs" in the previous paragraph, the Pope goes on to affirm "the legitimate role of profit as an indication that a business is functioning well." However, he quickly adds:

But profitability is not the only indicator of a firm's condition. . . . In fact, the purpose of a business firm is not simply to make a profit, but is to be found in its very existence as a community of persons who in various ways are endeavoring to satisfy their basic needs and who form a particular group at the service of society. Profit is a regulator of the life of a business, but it is not the only one; other human and moral factors must also be considered, which in the long term are at least equally important for the life of the business (John Paul II 1989, par. 35:14).

The teleological character of "the human and moral factors" which are cited is evident in the discussion that follows this warning. The encyclical calls for "an existence which is qualitatively more satisfying" and continues:

The manner in which new needs arise and are defined is always marked by a more or less appropriate concept of man and of his true good. A given culture reveals its overall understanding of life through the choices it makes in production and consumption. It is here that the phenomenon of consumerism arises. In singling out new needs and new means to meet them, one must be guided by a comprehensive picture of man which respects all the dimensions of his being and which subordinates his material and instinctive dimensions to his interior and spiritual ones. If, on the contrary, a direct appeal is made to his instincts—while ignoring in various ways the reality of the person as intelligent and free—then consumer attitudes and lifestyles can be created which are objectively improper and often damaging to his physical and spiritual health. Of itself, an economic system does not possess criteria for correctly distinguishing new and higher forms of satisfying human needs from artificial new needs which hinder the formation of a mature personality. Thus a great deal of educational and cultural work is urgently needed, including the education of consumers in the responsible use of their power of choice, the formation of a strong sense of responsibility among producers and among people in the mass media in particular as well as the necessary intervention by public authority (par. 36:14–15).

This can hardly be regarded as anything other than a severe critique of important tendencies in the commercial culture of the United States and of the liberal theoretical perspective which serves to justify those tendencies. The following section will discuss important ways in which the sharpness of this "teleological" critique of liberal institutions is dulled. Without getting ahead of ourselves it is important to point out in the above quotation that the ethical and cultural task of getting one's conception of the human good in order is not primarily the task of economic institutions and public authorities. An orthodox liberal might have no quibble with the call for the education of consumers. The liberal will certainly regard it as appropriate for individuals to make consumer choices on the basis of their well-considered conception of the human good. More questionable is the sense that the media and producers and the "public authorities" also share an important responsibility for formation of morally appropriate human needs.[49,50]

Interesting with regard to the role of the state in the moral and cultural task is John Paul II's comment with reference to the church's appreciation of democracy in his discussion "State and Culture." After affirming that "the church values the democratic system" he immediately signals a rejection of the contemporary liberal justification of democracy.

Authentic democracy is possible only in a state ruled by law and on the basis of a correct conception of the human person. . . . Nowadays there is a tendency to claim that agnosticism and skeptical relativism are the philosophy and the basic attitude which corresponds to democratic forms of political life. Those who are convinced that they know the truth and firmly adhere to it are considered unreliable from a democratic point of view, since they do not accept that truth is determined by the majority or that it is subject to variation according to different political trends. . . (par. 46:18).

It seems fair to characterize liberal neutrality as based upon "agnosticism and skeptical relativism" with regard to the question of the human good, the question which social Catholicism puts at the heart of its understanding of development, justice, and rights, and at the heart of its justification for democratic and free economic institutions. Moreover, while Catholic social teaching is committed to dialogical process aimed at discovering the content of that human good, liberalism sees no necessity for such a dialogue.

Equally interesting is John Paul II's discussion of the relationship between consumerism and "the ecological question" (par. 37:15). While acknowledging the destruction of the natural environment, he quickly moves to what he regards as "the more serious destruction of the human environment." "[T]oo little effort," he insists,

> is made to safeguard the moral conditions for an authentic "human ecology." Not only has God given the earth to man, who must use it with respect for the original good purpose for which it was given to him, but man too is God's gift to man. He must therefore respect the natural and moral structure with which he has been endowed. . . (par. 38:15).

The Pope notes that "the first and fundamental structure for 'human ecology' is the family" (par. 39:15) and makes evident the state's responsibilities for the moral environment.

> It is the task of the state to provide for the defense and preservation of common goods such as the natural and human environments, which cannot be safeguarded simply by market forces. . . . [T]he state and all of society have the duty of defending those collective goods which, among others, constitute the essential framework for the legitimate pursuit of personal goals on the part of each individual (par. 40:16).

Subsidiarity, limited government, and religious liberty. Now, while the teleological framework of Roman Catholic social thought surely represents a fundamental challenge to the liberal perspective, there are aspects of social Catholicism which serve to dull a bit of the sharp edge of critique that this teleological conception of the role or government represents to liberalism. These aspects also may serve to mitigate the potential authoritarianism of this teleological political theory. The first has to do with the Roman Catholic principle of subsidiarity which was first elaborated specifically by Pius XI in the encyclical *Quadragesimo Anno*. The second has to do with John Courtney Murray's crucial distinctions between society and the state and between the common good and public order, distinctions which enabled him to develop a persuasive argument for a Roman Catholic affirmation of religious liberty but which have implications well beyond that important issue. Another important consideration to note here is the following: with an increased recognition that there are a variety of perspectives from which values are discovered and understood the possibility of a process of dialogue and mutual discovery of values is envisioned rather than the imposition of the values of some particular elite.

The following statement from *Quadragesimo Anno* states what has been regarded in the social Catholic tradition as the principle of subsidiarity.

> Just as it is gravely wrong to take from individuals what they can accomplish by their own initiative and industry and give it to the community, so also it is an injustice . . . to assign to a greater and higher association what lesser and subordinate organizations can do. For every social activity ought of its very nature to furnish help to the members of the body social, and never destroy and absorb them (Pius XI 1931, par. 79:68).

The point is that whereas the state or government is obligated to provide "help" (which translates the Latin term *subsidium* from which the principle takes its name[51]) it ought not do what lesser associations are capable of doing. The principle recognizes, course, that governments do have an important and positive role to play. Indeed the following paragraph of *Quadragesimo Anno* suggests that one of the reasons for allowing lesser associations to fulfill their tasks is that as a result "the state will more freely, powerfully, and effectively do all those things that belong to it alone because it alone can do them: directing, watching, urging, restraining, as occasion requires and necessity demands" (Pius XI 1931, par. 69:80).[52] It is usually regarded, however, as a warning against government whose role has become too large. Indeed, Hollenbach says that more important than its recognition of the helping role of government is its insistence that "the family, the neighborhood, the church, and both professional and labor groups all have a dynamic life of their own which must be respected by government" (1979:157). He notes that the principle "defends institutional pluralism while also granting a limited role to the government in the economic sphere" (1988:69).

This idea that the role of the civil authorities is a limited one (even though their whole reason for existence is the realization of the common good) is further developed by John Courtney Murray in the arguments he mustered to gain Roman Catholic approval of the idea of religious liberty. Hollenbach has explained what he calls the integralist argument for the government enforcement of Catholicism (and this the denial of the validity of religious liberty and separation of church and state) in the following syllogism:

> -The Roman Catholic faith is the true religion
> -It is good for people to believe what is true
> -The state is obligated to promote the common good.
> -Therefore, the state is bound to promote Catholic belief, and wherever possible Catholicism as the religion of the state (Hollenbach, 1988:102).

Murray challenged this argument in a variety of ways, according to Hollenbach. He challenged the first premise because his "knowledge of the dynamic nature of Christian tradition prevented him from adopting the view that *all* truth has been exhaustively enshrined once and for all in Catholic doctrine and teaching" (Hollenbach, 1988:102). Still the brunt of his argument was directed toward the idea that the state is obligated to promote the common good. First, he argued that the common good has both temporal and spiritual dimensions and that the government "is fundamentally incompetent in matters touching the eternal destiny of human beings." Secondly, Murray distinguished between society and the state. Hollenbach's explanation of this distinction suggests Pius XI's principle of subsidiarity.

> Society is made up of many diverse communities and forms of association. .
> . . The state is just part of society, with a limited role within it. The denial
> of these limits, whether in principle or in fact, is what is meant by state
> absolutism, and it leads to totalitarianism. Good government is the servant
> of society, not *paterfamilias* to the nation, much less dictator. This is the
> core principle of constitutional government (1988:103).

Finally, on Murray's view, a distinction is to be drawn between "the common good of society, which all persons and communities that make up society are morally bound to pursue, and the narrower juridical notion of public order, which is the proper concern of government." The public order includes justice, public peace, public morality, and public prosperity. "Only when one or more of these fundamental prerequisites of social existence is violated should government intervene. Otherwise freedom is to prevail" (Hollenbach, 1988:103). [53]

Finally, of course, we should note the consistency between Murray's view that "not *all* truth has been exhaustively enshrined once and for all in Catholic doctrine and teaching" (Hollenbach, 1988:103), and the growing historical consciousness of social Catholic tradition and its recognition of radical pluralism and the relative autonomy of the various cultural alternatives. All of this suggests that there is no single set of goods or social practices that can be finally identified as essential to human flourishing. The order advocated by social Catholicism, like that which liberalism affirms, will be one in which a pluralism is respected.

Clearly, the principle of subsidiarity, the arguments of John Courtney Murray which lie behind Vatican II's official acceptance of the principle of religious liberty, and the recognition of cultural autonomy all point to a role for government that is more limited than what seems to be indicated by the view that the sole justification for government is the realization of the common good. This in itself tends to reduce the gap between the practical implications of Roman Catholic human rights theory and those of liberalism. It does not eliminate them entirely however. Hollenbach is right, it seems to me, in his challenge to Michael Novak's (1984) view that the idea of economic rights must be abandoned because the affirmation of such rights suggests a role for government that violates Murray's distinction between the full common good and the public order.[54] He is right, it seems to me, when he says that "[i]ndividuals, families, and a variety of mediating institutions in society have an obligation to see to it that people do not go hungry, homeless, or jobless. Nevertheless, when the problem exceeds the power of these persons and groups, government can and should intervene in ways carefully guided by political prudence" (Hollenbach, 1988:106). More important than the merits of this particular case is the fact that the principle of discrimination for determining when and what sort of government action is appropriate will not be individual liberty but the individual and social pursuit of the temporal goods that are available to it. The government will legitimately intervene, not when individual liberty is threatened, but when persons are not empowered for participation in the processes whereby the common good is discovered, produced, distributed and enjoyed.

Particpation as opposed to individual liberty as the defining value or central focus of Roman Catholic human rights theory. Contemporary Roman Catholic Social Teaching's emphasis on the person as a communal and historical being (while not ignoring the capacity for individual independence which is at the heart of liberal theory) is reflected in the way in which the concept of "participation" functions as a summary term for all that rights are intended to protect. Whereas in liberal theory rights are aimed at protecting individual autonomy or liberty, in contemporary Roman Catholic Social Teaching rights and justice are understood as protecting the individual's capacity for participation in the social and historical process in which individual and public goods are discovered, produced, distributed and enjoyed. [55] Hollenbach notes that in *Justice in the World ,* it is

> a fundamental right to participation which integrates all the other rights with each other and provides their operational foundation. Violation of dignity is regarded primarily as lack of influence on and participation in the shaping of the social forces which determine the limits within which human agency is effective (1979:87).[56]

The recent pastoral letter on the U. S. Economy promulgated by the Bishops of the United States has also employed the concept of participation as an organizing and integrating theme or function for all the human rights they regard as valid. "Basic justice," they wrote, "demands the establishment of minimum levels of participation in the life of the human community for all persons" (United States Catholic Conference 1986, par. 77:39). Hollenbach himself wants to affirm the identification of participation as the integrating norm or fundamental value in social

Catholicism as is indicated by the title of his essay "Justice as Participation." [57]

With such an understanding of the central focus of human rights, Hollenbach says, "marginalization or lack of participation thus becomes a primary criterion for judging if human dignity is being violated" (1979:86). Indeed, upon affirming minimum levels of participation, the U. S. Bishops write: "The ultimate injustice is for a person or group to be actively treated or passively abandoned as if they were nonmembers of the human race. This can take many forms, all of which can be described as varieties of marginalization, or exclusion from social life" (United States Catholic Conference 1986, par. 77:39). Notice, the fundamental evil is not the inability to exercise one's autonomy, but to be excluded from social life.

The idea of participation as the central value in Roman Catholic human rights theory and its conception of justice is related to the sense that many of the goods which are essential for human flourishing are public goods, that is to say, they are not only discovered as good in a shared cultural process; they are also produced and enjoyed socially.

> There are goods or values necessary for the realization of human dignity which transcend the sphere of private interaction and contract which is the concern of commutative justice. . .. No one creates a polity, an economy or a culture in private. Individuals come to share in these goods in a way that is mediated by political, economic and cultural structures.
>
> Such goods, in other words, are essentially public. . . they are not created by any individual person acting alone. . . . These goods are essentially relational. If they are to exist at all they must exist as shared (Hollenbach, 1979:147).

The relationship of the individual to such goods when his or her dignity is duly respected is not one in which the individual is left free to choose and pursue such goods. Rather human dignity is respected when one's participation in the social process of discovery, production, and enjoyment is facilitated. Thus Hollenbach writes: "Claims on these goods are claims to be permitted or enabled to participate in the life and activity of the communities which make their existence possible" (1979:147–148). Moreover, he notes that to have a claim on these public goods is to have a right to "access to and participation in social value." It is not a matter, as when goods are conceived of as autonomously chosen, of "obtaining a 'piece' of it" (1979:149). Distributive justice, which is concerned with adjudicating the various claims upon such public goods, "means equality of opportunity for entry into the social, economic, cultural and political relationships which constitute the common good" (1979:149). [58]

The idea that the recognition of a just claim on goods properly seen as public or social requires more than simply "obtaining a 'piece'" of such goods is implicit in the theology of work articulated by Pope John Paul II in his 1981 encyclical *Laborem Exercens*. That encyclical argues that "human work is a key, probably the essential key, to the whole social question" (John Paul II 1981, par. 3:294). Moreover, it argues that "work is a fundamental dimension of man's existence on earth" and that the human person "is the image of God partly through the mandate received from his creator to subdue, to dominate, the earth" (par. 4:295). Most significant in terms of the centrality of the idea of participation is the document's distinction between the objective and subjective sense of work. The objective sense refers to the various techniques, tools, and institutional arrangements which human beings employ in their work, as well as the 'things,' the material and external goods produced by such work. The subjective sense has to do with the fact that the human person is

> a subjective being capable of acting in a planned and rational way, capable of deciding about himself and with a tendency to self-realization. As a person, man is therefore the subject of work. As a person he works, he performs various actions belonging to the work process; independently of their objective content, these actions must all serve to realize his humanity, to fulfill his very humanity (par. 6:298).

Laborem Exercens insists that "[t]he sources of the dignity of work are to be sought primarily in the subjective dimension, not in the objective one" (par. 6:299).

John Paul II connects this emphasis on the subjective sense of work to important themes which have been present throughout the development of social Catholicism. He points to "the danger of treating work as a special kind of merchandise or as an impersonal force needed for production" (par. 7:300) and notes that this concern and the creation by "the liberal sociopolitical system" of such a state of affairs was the impulse behind *Rerum Novarum* (par. 8:302). In the same context he affirms the fact that "[w]orkers can often share in running businesses and in controlling their productivity, and in fact do so. Through appropriate associations they exercise influence over conditions of work and pay, and also over social legislation" (par. 8:302). As Gregory Baum has pointed out, *Laborem Exercens* "demands that in an ever increasing measure workers participate in the policy-making of their industries" (1986:237). John Paul II summarizes his teaching it terms of the principle of "the priority of labor over capital," (John Paul II 1981, par. 12:308) for it is precisely capital that represents work in its objective dimension. It is primarily by attending to the way work affects the worker himself, the way it enables her to participate in the creation of the common good and to express herself as a human being, that work is understood and its organization and institutionalization properly carried out.

David Hollenbach has captured the essential dimensions of the theology of work implicit in the social Catholic tradition and articulated in *Laborem Exercens*. He has written that "work in its created wholeness and healed redemption is an energetic contribution to the common life of society, an active form of human participation in human community" (1988:59) . For Hollenbach this theology of work is an expression of the centrality of participation.

> The realization of human dignity requires that one participate in social life. The dignity of the person is the dignity of a social being. Therefore both the possibility and the actuality of social participation are crucial to human dignity (1988:65).

Hollenbach sees several points as important for understanding the relationship between justice-as-participation and the question of the jobs in which persons work. First, he says that "justice in the employment sphere means that persons should have the opportunity to contribute to society through economic activity in concert with others" (1988:66). From such a perspective it makes sense to talk of "a right to employment" and to "insist that the creation of institutions for the enhancement of economic participation is of the highest priority" (1988:65–66). Consistent with the view that rights entail obligations not only for others and for society as a whole, but also for the rightholder, Hollenbach says that there is a

> moral obligation which calls on persons to contribute to the generation of the public good by aggregating their activity, to the extent they are able, with that of others in a productive way. This is the active meaning of justice-as-participation. It helps us see that justice in employment is as much a matter of creating the public good of a society as it is a matter of distributing it (1988:66).

Secondly, it means that the generation of a higher Gross National Product is not the sole measure of the moral value of the organization of human labor. "The organization of production also has very important effects on employment levels, patterns of discrimination, and environmental quality" (Hollenbach, 1988:67). John Paul II's perspective seems also to require consideration of the "quality of work" itself. Finally, because work is an essential dimension of participation it is not enough simply to guarantee all persons an income. Jobs are socially created goods which provide an organized, institutional framework through which such participation is possible. Distributive justice then concerns not just the distribution of income but also of jobs. Therefore,

> the demands of distributive justice will not be met simply by proposing some form of income policy such as a negative income tax, guaranteed annual income, or other welfare reform proposals, essential as these surely

are. . . . Such transfers are called for in justice in the cases of those with special needs such as the ill, the aged and the handicapped. . . . However, in the case of persons who through no fault of their own have been placed in a seriously disadvantaged position by socially correctable maldistribution of opportunity and power, transfers are at best a palliative for injustice (Hollenbach, 1988:68).

The intrinsic value of work entails that full employment is not justified on purely utilitarian grounds, or because it may serve to maximize production, nor as a means to a more just distribution of income. The opportunity to make one's contribution through a job that contributes to the common good is a necessary dimension of justice-as-participation.

Participation and marginalization in social Catholicism, on Hollenbach's reading, are related to questions of human agency and responsibility. As was the case with reference to Hauerwas, the understanding of agency and responsibility which Hollenbach's discussion suggests denies that they are to be understood entirely with reference to the autonomous or independent dimensions of human selfhood. For social Catholicism as for Hauerwas, agency is exercised in community with others and we are responsible not because we are capable of autonomous choice, but because we are participants in a social process of discovery and action toward those ends commonly regarded as worthy of human pursuit.

Hollenbach's analysis of social Catholicism suggests that the understanding of human agency and responsibility which is evident in those conciliar and post-conciliar documents in which the theme of participation has been developed is rooted in a sensitivity to a deep tension in human experience. That tension is described this way in *Gaudium et Spes:*

The truth is that the imbalances under which the modern world labors[59] are linked with that more basic imbalance rooted in the heart of man. For in man himself many elements wrestle with one another. Thus, on the one hand, as a creature he experiences his limitations in a multitude of ways. On the other, he feels himself to be boundless in his desires and summoned to a higher life. (Second Vatican Council 1965, par. 10:185–186, quoted in Hollenbach, 1979:72).

Hollenbach notes that there are two basic temptations associated with this tension: the first involves an idolatry which assigns transcendent value to a limited historical achievement; the second involves "a complete or premature withdrawal from historical engagement."[60] What is most important and interesting with reference to our concern here about the question of agency is Hollenbach's comment about the relationship of this tension to the human capacity to "make history." He writes:

The tension within the person described here, however, is both the positive source of the personal ability to make history and the result of this ability. More accurately, it is impossible to imagine a being conscious of his own participation in historical growth and change who would not be subject to such a tension. Historical existence demands the presence of the two poles of this tension: the pole of involvement in the limited and conditioned on the one hand and the pole of transcendence into the new, the unlimited and the absolute on the other. It is on this basis that the Council's acceptance of historicity leads it to an unequivocal reaffirmation of the dignity of the human person. Finite beings in which the tensions of historicity are not present are dumb, brute, unconscious—in short, they are things. Beings in which such tensions are present are human persons. They are neither things nor pieces in a social machine. Neither are they gods.

Within this framework it becomes evident that the limits and conditions of historical existence are not the enemies of human dignity. Rather the limited conditions of nature and history are the context in which personal dignity is realized. . . (1979:72–73).

It would of course be too indiscriminate to say that liberal thinking about human dignity does not see "the limited conditions of nature and history" as the "the context in which personal dignity is realized." However, it would not be off the mark to say that liberalism tends to see human dignity as rooted in our capacity for transcending those limits. They may not be regarded as "the enemies of human dignity," but surely neither is our rootedness in those limits a source of our peculiar dignity as human beings. Moreover, liberals tend to regard us as responsible agents in history precisely to the degree that we are able to transcend that rootedness. This is not the case in social Catholicism with its communitarian conception of human personhood. The Hollenbach quotation indicates that from such a perspective, our capacity to make history and to be conscious of ourselves as makers of history, that is our status as responsible agents, depends upon the tension between our encumbered and our autonomous dimensions, not our ability to take transcendent flight from it.

From such a perspective, Hollenbach can say that where the fundamental right of all persons to minimal levels of participation in the social process in which the goods essential for human flourishing are discovered and produced, it is the human capacity for responsible agency which is undermined. He writes that whereas the right to participation is the basic right that integrates all others

[v]iolation of dignity is regarded primarily as lack of influence on and participation in the shaping of the social forces which determine the limits within which human agency is effective. Indeed, the Synod's analysis of present social patterns [in *Justice in the World*] indicates that this circle of agency is shrinking to the vanishing point for a very large segment of the human race (1979:87).

Thus, the point is that for human beings to exercise their proper responsibility more than a regard for our autonomous dimension through measures to protect individual liberty is required. As well, measures must be in place to guarantee that we have access to the material resources necessary to meet our basic physical needs and that we have the opportunity to share in the cultural resources that are the particular tools in the hands of our communities for discovering the goods we shall seek together. Liberal theory, with its undue emphasis on individual liberty, its toleration of high levels of poverty and unemployment, its generation of labor-management relations in which worker participation in decision-making is minimal, and its failure to appreciate the importance of cultural rights, inadequately creates the institutions and practices which enable individual participation in the social process whereby goods are discovered, produced, distributed, and enjoyed.

Summary and Conclusions

Earlier I described what David Hollenbach has called the dialogically-universalist method envisioned and employed in contemporary Catholic social teaching. That method seeks to bring the distinctive and specific insights of a biblical and theological vision of social morality into conversation with the insights generated by all human cultures and sciences. These cultures and sciences are regarded as having their own proper autonomy, that is to say, they are regarded as sources of valid moral insights apart from any specific faith perspective. The validity of the cultures and sciences is derived from a confidence (from the perspective of faith) that their fundamental origin is in God. The goal of this dialogically-universalist method is overcoming or transcending the crisis in human reason which was recognized in *Gaudium et Spes*, a crisis which has the practical effect of generating division and hostility between nations, classes, racial and ethnic groups, and ideological camps. The dialogue which Catholic social teaching envisions and models is intended to generate a larger and larger measure of social moral consensus such that the unity which is God's intention for human persons and the Church's eschatological hope might be more nearly realized.

The method coheres with the vision of church and world in a common struggle or pilgrimage toward liberation, justice, peace and unity which is so powerfully expressed in the opening paragraph of *Gaudium et Spes*. It envisions, I have suggested, a relationship of cooperation between church and world, while acknowledging that the precise terms of that cooperation must be contextually determined. The church will draw upon the insights of every culture and attempt to embody itself in every culture. At the same time, however, it is recognized that the Church, as an expert in humanity and with its total vision of human affairs, may adopt the mode of prophetic denunciation in its dialogue with particular cultures, or rather, particular aspects of every culture. The precise nature and tone of the church's dialogical relationship with culture is contextual.

While the general terms of the church world relationship are clear, I argued that contemporary Catholic social teaching is ambiguous about the specific contribution that faith makes. It suggests that there is a distinctive faith perspective which generates a specific Christian understanding of social morality. However, in its desire to demonstrate openness to the insights offered by the cultures and sciences, to address all people of good will, and to arrive at moral consensus, it often leaves unclear which of its prescriptions derive from the total view of human affairs provided by Christian faith and what the relationship is between these and the norms thought to be shared by the human cultures and sciences which develop their insights independent of a faith perspective. Moreover, I contended that Catholic social teaching has failed to grasp some of the more profound implications of the historical consciousness that emerged at Vatican II and of the radical pluralism that was recognized there. Specifically, I argued that it fails to appreciate the way in which historically and culturally particular human reason is embedded in or related to particular practices and institutions. Further, I contended that Catholic social teaching is insufficiently attentive to specifically Christian practices and institutions which provide both the origin and the proving ground for the distinctive vision of human affairs that teaching offers. Finally, I argued that the models of the Church employed since Vatican II, particularly the idea of the Church as sacrament of unity, suggest that the church has a unique social ethical responsibility to embody or make concrete in distinctive institutions and practices its total vision of human affairs. The Church will only be an efficacious sign of the unity which is its eschatological hope if it embodies or concretizes in specific though surely imperfect ways that very unity.

What does our survey of the Catholic critique of liberalism suggest about the church's posture toward a liberal public world? First, we should note the way in which contemporary Catholic social teaching shows the impact of its dialogue with liberalism. The emergence of an appreciation for the political institutions of liberal democracy and for the role of freedom or human subjectivity in the economic sphere and the identification of the autonomous dimension of the human person as an essential dimension of its moral anthropology (which provides the grounds for its affirmation of democratic political institutions and free market economic ones) demonstrate the impact liberalism on social Catholicism. Thus, Catholic social teaching is a part of the overlapping consensus about human nature which, on John Rawls's account, makes liberal culture possible. The Catholic Church, then, has come to feel at home in the United States.

Yet, we would be remiss not to note the multitude of ways in which the principles identified by and the policies advocated in Catholic social morality indicate a large place for prophetic denunciation and a sense of alienation from liberal culture. Following David Hollenbach, I have argued that these critical perspectives are grounded in an integral anthropology that identifies two dimensions of human nature other than the autonomous one which are equally basic or, in some respects even more basic, and with reference to which human dignity must also be defined. The first dimension of human nature to which liberalism inadequately attends, according to the Catholic perspective, is its being made concrete in a body with definite and fundamental needs. Because of liberalism's failure to appreciate the way in which access to basic human needs is essential to human dignity it is too casual about and tolerant of the existence of poverty. Indeed, with its emphasis on freedom and its grounding of property rights in freedom (as opposed to human need) it tends to generate inequality and, ultimately poverty. The compassion, love or solidarity regarded as a basic norm of Christian social ethics demands giving priority to the needs of the poor. This sets Catholic morality at odds with liberal culture and requires prophetic denunciation on its part, even as it appreciates the way liberalism's unleashing of freedom in the economic sphere has contributed to the unprecedented economic growth which makes meeting human needs possible.

The Catholic sense that liberalism fails to appreciate the social or communitarian dimensions of human selfhood is also the source of a basic tension between Catholic and liberal social morality. From the Catholic perspective, liberalism is insufficiently attentive to the ways in which individual rights are limited by the common good or by the claims of the communities in which individuals find their identity. Moreover, liberalism is mistaken in its belief that human dignity is protected when basic institutions which structure public life are neutral about what constitutes a good human life. For Catholic social morality, a valid conception of justice and rights, that is, of the norms in terms of which public institutions are evaluated, is grounded in a valid understanding of the human good. Thus, the concept of development cannot be understood as the provision of more and more of whatever human beings can be induced to want (so long as their autonomy is respected), but must include a moral or cultural dimension that enables a true identification of the human good. Finally, and related to its failure to appreciate the fundamental nature of the individual claim to that which is essential to meeting his or her basic needs, liberalism insufficiently provides for every person's participation in the social, cultural, and dialogical process whereby human goods are discovered, produced, distributed, and enjoyed. Liberal culture does not generate sufficient concern for or solidarity with the majority of persons who are marginalized or shut off from full participation. Indeed, in important respects, liberalism generates such marginalization.

Catholic social morality represents a prophetic denunciation of much that is commonplace in liberal culture: consumerism, high unemployment rates, significant numbers of persons without sufficient access to health care, workplaces which fail to appreciate the fundamental subjective dimension of work and thus allow workers no important role in decision-making, laying off of workers without warning or notification, foreign policy goals that are aimed at protecting national economic and military security rather than contributing to genuine human development. It indicates that the church will live in fundamental tension with major elements of the public culture of the United States. This tension will require that its address to the culture will have a deep critical edge and that it will concern itself with the development of alternative public institutions that are operated in ways more respectful of all the dimensions of human dignity and in which Christian virtues of solidarity and compassion are exercised and nurtured. None of this is to deny, however, that the church will find itself part of a relatively narrow overlapping consensus which makes cooperation and friendly dialogue possible at a number of points.

My critique of Catholic ecclesiology indicated that I regard it as insufficiently appreciative of the importance of the church's own concrete embodiment in practices and institutions that are alternatives to "worldly" ones, a role for the church which is, however, suggested, especially in the idea of the church as a sacrament of unity. At this point, let me indicate the way in which the importance of this particular social ethical task is signaled by a specific aspect of the Catholic social morality: the combination of its insistence that justice is teleological in character or rooted in a valid conception of the good for human persons and its awareness that society and state are distinguishable. The Catholic insistence that the responsibility to respect human dignity in all its aspects does not reside with state or government alone, but with all the institutions of culture and, indeed, through the principle of subsidiarity, its insistence that lower or smaller levels of organization are to be preferred to larger ones, suggests that its understanding of the demands of human dignity are directed as much to corporations, labor unions, political parties, schools, hospitals, community organizations, etc., as to governments. For those of us whose imaginations have largely been shaped by the presuppositions of a liberal culture, this is easy to miss for we are prone to assume that talk of rights and public responsibilities is directed primarily to governments. But the teleological character of Catholic social teaching represents a denial of a liberal understanding of the distinction between public and private.

Thus, for example, the prescriptions of *Economic Justice for All* have as many or more implications for the management of large economic enterprises and other public institutions (and even family is in some sense a public institution, according to the Catholic understanding) as it does for governmental policy. Presumably, there are many Catholic Christians involved in the management of corporations, hospitals, and schools who are also participants in community organizations and labor unions. Moreover, it seems safe to say that the understanding of how those institutions ought to be operated so as to respect human dignity derives from certain distinct and specific Christian convictions. The Catholics or Christian managers of corporations, for example, have reasons to recognize and respect the demands of human dignity as understood in Catholic social teaching, that others presumably do not. Moreover, those managers and their institutions provide the concrete experience out of which the distinctive Catholic or Christian understanding of the demands of human dignity arise and in which they must be tested. This suggests that Catholic social teaching ought more specifically to be directed toward and to reflect the insights of Catholic Christian experience in economic institutions. Of course, the practices of those institutions in which Catholics and other Christians participate in the United States are more shaped by liberal than Catholic or Christian convictions and Catholic mangers would have much to contribute to an understanding of the precise challenges of reforming those institutions along the lines indicated by Catholic social teaching than do the Popes and Bishops (and their advisors) who write them. Moreover, I suspect the average Catholic Christian manager is largely unaware of the content of Catholic social teaching and of the gap between that teaching and the ordinary practices of those institutions.

I also suspect that were they aware of the teaching they would regard its implementation as largely impossible in most of the enterprises in which they are involved. This suggests not only that Catholic teaching ought to be directed more explicitly toward Catholic Christians who work in the institutions of a liberal society and draw more on their experience, but also that convincing non-Catholics or non-Christians, even those of good will, of the legitimacy of the Catholic conception of human dignity will require their knowledge and experience of the successful operation of institutions guided by those principles (admitting, of course, that the very idea of success is probably different). Let me cite an example. The U. S. Bishops' Pastoral on the U. S. economy draws heavily upon John Paul II's analysis in *Laborem Exercens*. It affirms that "employment is a basic right" (United States Catholic Conference 1986, par. 137:69) and calls for stronger "institutional protection" for workers in firms and on farms. It looks favorably upon a variety of arrangements that enable workers to have a greater role in the economic decisions that effect their lives, such as profit sharing by the workers in a firm; enabling employees to become company stockholders; granting employees greater participation in determining the conditions of work; cooperative ownership of the firm by all who work within it; and programs for enabling much larger number of Americans, regardless of their employment status to become shareholders in successful corporations (par. 300:148).

It then insists that these reforms "can enhance productivity, increase the profitability of firms, provide greater job security and work satisfaction for employees and reduce adversarial relations" (par. 300:148–149). Accepting the claim that such procedures do not threaten the long-term stability of the firm and economic productivity is one that requires demonstration. Thus, I am insisting that official Catholic teaching should not only more explicitly address itself to Catholic Christians but also that it should also more clearly recognize the importance of generating alternative institutional practices that are guided directly by Catholic social moral norms. This is not to insist that the dialogue with the world should be abandoned, but, rather that it may be engaged in more effectively and persuasively.

The conclusion which I am drawing from the survey of social Catholicism's ecclesiology and critique of liberalism may best be illuminated by way of reference to Brian Hehir's effort to categorize the various styles of social ministry to which we alluded at the beginning of this chapter. Hehir is critical of what he calls the educational-cultural style of social ministry primarily because of the difficulty of moving from broad moral values and principles to the formulation of specific policy proposals. Recall also his concern that

the basic conception of virtue, rights, and common good, which animates this model, amounts to a fundamental challenge to existing patterns of policy discourse in American society. This fact is a very good reason for pursuing the fundamental themes, but also a good reason to question whether the educational-cultural model is an adequate style of social ministry. . . . In the short to middle range, this model may leave the Catholic voice out of public life (1991:67).

Hehir's reference to "the basic conception of virtue, rights and the common good which animates this model" does not make clear enough that this basic conception is the conception most prominently displayed and developed in official Catholic teaching. His fear is that one cannot speak the language of "virtue, rights, and the common good" as developed in Catholic thought and at the same time hope to have any major impact on governmental legislation. My argument is that the epistemological and ecclesiological perspective of official Roman Catholic social teaching point to a social ministry whose primary contribution is the *concrete embodiment* of the church's distinct moral or cultural values in an alternative community rather than their *translation into particular legislative proposals*. That suggests something more like the radical or evangelical style, but with the immigrant Church's concern for building institutions identified by David O'Brien. To the degree that official teaching fails to recognize and concentrate on this implication of its analysis, that teaching remains largely incoherent and largely ineffective in directing the church toward its most faithful and effective relationship to liberal culture. I am hopeful that contemporary Roman Catholic social teaching is in a state of transition or flux on the way toward finding its proper voice.

Endnotes

[1] O'Brien writes:

The paradigm of this style, to use a modern term, was the relatively successful middle-class Catholic laity, so faithful to the church that they could not understand themselves apart from it, but fully at home, or at least wishing to be fully at home, in their community, their nation, and their world. At times, as when facing persecution or its threat, or when caught up in the heady experience of economic and social advancement, the republican Catholic rigidly segregated religious and civic loyalties, urged the church to stick to religion, and engaged in economic and political life with no direct and little indirect reference to religious faith. At its best, the republican tradition recognized the tension between religious and civic allegiances and attempted to mediate between them, asking what America had to teach the church and what the church could offer America (1989:5).

[2] The immigrant style has not disappeared, according to O'Brien. "In fact, it has experienced a revival among newer immigrants, most notably Hispanics, but is also reaching a growing number of Asians" (1989:247).

[3] According to O'Brien, the recent U. S. Bishops' pastoral letters on war and the economy demonstrate their adoption of the republican style through their employment of two styles of teaching.

One, addressed to members of the church, begins with the message of Jesus and explores the responsibility of Christians and of the church. The second, aimed at the general public, is intended to contribute to the development of the public moral consensus, to influence public opinion, and to help shape the public debate about policy by clarifying its moral dimension. Here the language is that of natural law, human dignity, and human rights (1989:249).

At the same time, O'Brien sees the influence of the evangelical style in both recent U. S. Bishops' pastorals, *The Challenge of Peace* by "emphasizing the dramatic demands of the gospel, affirming nonviolence as an option for individuals, and calling their people to discipleship in a 'society increasingly estranged from Christian values'" (1989:245).

The fact that O'Brien finds evidence of both the republican and the evangelical styles in recent pastorals of the U. S. Bishops indicates that these styles are not absolutely mutually exclusive. Of course, as I will suggest later, one could also argue that the presence of these two styles and the two types of language employed indicates the profound ambivalence or, still worse, incoherence of much contemporary Roman Catholic social teaching.

[4] Dulles notes the influence of Catholic liberalism on the the U. S. Bishops. Their recent pastorals "have introduced a dialogic method that promises to transform the Catholic Church into an open 'community of discourse'" (1990:56).

[5] Hehir's comment that the basic social ethical perspective of the educational-cultural style represents "a fundamental challenge to existing patterns of policy discourse" in the United States suggests that the legislative model which seeks to move into that very policy discourse represents a risk to the fundamental integrity of the basic Catholic perspective. Once we turn to the specifics of the Catholic critique of liberalism we will see more precisely why this is so.

[6] For example, I will contend that papal and episcopal teaching is significantly more critical of liberalism than O'Brien's republicans or Dulles's neo-conservatives and liberals, but not so much so as to support the position of the traditionalists.

[7] My concern is not primarily to trace the history of the appraisal of liberalism advanced by social Catholicism, but to provide an understanding of the perspective it provides on liberal society in its contemporary manifestations. I will concentrate particularly on the documents since *Pacem in Terris* and Vatican II.

[8] According to Avery Dulles, whose book *Models of the Church*, provides a broad analysis of modern ecclesiologies, an institutional model of the church was dominant in Catholic theology from the "late middle Ages to middle of the present century" (1987:34) and "reached its culmination in the second half of the nineteenth century. . . the Dogmatic Constitution of the Church prepared for Vatican Council I" (1987:36). Such a model identifies the church with its "institutional element," that is, "its visible structures, especially the rights and powers of its officers [priests, bishops, and Pope]" (1987:34). The Church so conceived is regarded as having three basic powers or functions, says Dulles, teaching, sanctifying, and governing. "In each case the Church as institution is on the giving end, so these authors say: The Church teaches, sanctifies, and commands, in each case identifying the Church itself with the governing body or hierarchy" (1987:37).

The institutional Church was regarded as *societas perfecta*. Bryan Hehir has noted that the meaning of this phrase was that the church was "'complete,' not morally impeccable." It meant that "the church possessed all the power and capacities needed for it to achieve its specific objectives as a religious community" (1991:56–57). He adds that the function of the idea "was to support the independence—hence the right and competence—of the church, then secondarily to seek an area of collaborative activity for church and civil authority, both of which were obligated to serve the person" (1991:57). We should note the relationship between the institutional model and the classicist or traditional natural law methodology of Catholic social teaching prior to Vatican II. The natural law was in principle accessible to all people of reason and in it was contained all that was necessary for the achievement of the human person's natural end. The Church was the guardian and source of the grace necessary for the salvation or the fulfillment of the human person's supernatural end. Still the Church saw itself, that is, principally the clerical hierarchy, as a competent teacher of the natural law. Ironically, during the period in which the institutional model was most dominant, the Church saw itself as in a relatively hostile relationship to the world, despite the accompanying employment of a natural methodology which suggests a very cooperative relationship between church and world at the level of social ethics. This ironic result is produced at least in part by the fact that during this period the Church's interpretation of the natural law varied sharply from the emerging modern or liberal interpretation.

9 This distinction is made on the basis of the fact that "rights can be differentiated according to the way content is mediated by society and social institutions." Personal rights refer to the basic needs, freedoms, and relationships that are "characteristics of every truly human person." He lists "life, bodiliness, self-determination, sociability, the need and ability to work, sexuality, family life, and some form of religious or philosophical convictions." Social rights reflect "the necessity of providing for the realization of these personal rights in societal interaction and communal life" (1979:96). The are "conditions for the preservation of the well-being of persons." at least part of which has to do with the degree of contingency associated with each. An instrumental right

> can be distinguished according to the kind of social interaction involved in its definition and protection. . . . Personal dignity is mediated not only by the realities of social interdependence but also by the way these realities are institutionalized. Thus the tradition has come to affirm a number of conditions which must be present in these macro-institutions if human dignity is to be preserved (1979:96–97).

Later we will see that he distinguishes between the various "needs, freedoms, and kinds of relationships" that must be attended to if all the dimensions of human selfhood are to be respected. To each of these dimensions corresponds particular sets of rights. The distinction between personal, social, and instrumental rights cuts across the previous one. That is to say, each of the rights that are related to the various dimensions of human dignity also represent one of three levels: personal, social, and instrumental. For example, the right to life and bodily integrity relates to the fact that physical need is one dimension of our dignity. It is also a personal right. Related to that same dimension is the right to food, which Hollenbach regards as a specification of the right to life at the social level. The right to social security is a further specification of the basic personal right at the instrumental level. (This is drawn from a chart presented in Hollenbach, 1979:98.)

10 These comments are suggestive of Alasdair MacIntyre's vivid argument in *After Virtue* that the Dark Ages are already upon us because moral arguments in contemporary liberal societies are interminable as a result of our lack of a tradition of reason that might enable us to reach agreement. As we shall see, however, social Catholicism is committed to an engagement in such "genuinely communicative social and political discourse" which suggests that ultimately its perspective is more

consistent with the view expressed by Jeffrey Stout in *Ethics After Babel*. According to Stout, moral disagreement in our pluralistic society is not so radical as to eliminate all agreement; even our ability to express understandable disagreement presupposes some basic level of mutual agreement or understanding. Moreover, he stresses "a language's capacity for hermeneutical enrichment" that is, its ability to change and grow in confrontation with new experiences and alien cultures or languages (See Stout 1988, especially 191–219).

[11] It would be more accurate to say "the understanding of society and government" rather than "the theory of rights." Social Catholicism was not explicitly a theory of rights prior to John XXIII's *Pacem in Terris*.

[12] The full quotation from which this summary is taken is worth having before us:

> The relation between reason and revelation in the pre-Vatican II ethic is the relation of differentiated, analytical thinking about the dignity of the person and about the concrete relationships between persons on the one hand and the standpoint from which this thinking proceeds on the other. The Christian standpoint or perspective provides motivation for moral behavior and shapes the attitudes which are characteristic of the Christian moral agent. Within this perspective, dimensions of the person and of social life are brought into high relief and are shown to be definitive of human dignity and, thus, of moral obligation. The non-instrumental value of the person, the centrality of freedom, the importance of building all order and unity in society on a communion of persons rather than on the suppression or subordination of the person to the group, the special claims of the poor and the oppressed, the goodness of the material conditions such as the body, food, shelter, work, property, the family and the state—all these central affirmations of the Roman Catholic rights theory are brought into the foreground by the doctrinal and symbolic background of Christian faith.
>
> It is this relationship between reason and revelation which explains the fact that the neo-scholastic tradition simultaneously maintained that Christian faith makes a radically important contribution to the moral existence of persons in society, and that the basic claims presented in the tradition can be known without explicitly adherence to this faith. The relation of religious doctrines and symbols to the claims formulated as rights and duties does not have the form of a deductive logic. The documents do not start with a theological doctrine or religious symbol and then, by a form of strictly syllogistic reasoning, conclude to a particular kind of concrete moral obligation. The connection between rights and duties on the one hand and doctrines and symbols on the other derives from the power which these latter have to evoke a coherent and living vision of the relation between persons in society, a vision of the structure of human dignity (Hollenbach 1979: 116–117).

[13] Avery Dulles has a similar understanding of the theological method employed at Vatican II and since. He labels the method

"secular-dialogic": secular, because the Church takes the world as a properly theological locus, and seeks to discern the signs of the times; dialogic, because it seeks to operate on the frontier between the contemporary world and the Christian tradition (including the Bible), rather than simply apply the latter as a measure of the former (1987:92).

Moreover, he associates this with secular theologies of the church and with the model of the church as servant which is distinguished from the alternative models Dulles has identified—church as institution, mystical communion, sacrament, and herald—by its refusal to follow their lead in giving "a primary or privileged position to the Church with respect to the world. . . . In all these models [other than Church as servant] the Church is seen as the active subject, and the world as the object that the Church acts upon or influences" (1987:89).

[14] And it is superior to Curran's suggestion that two methods, one scriptural and the other grounded in natural law, exist side by side in contemporary social teaching.

[15] Curran is not blind to this shift, but this is not to say that he has fully grasped the implications of it. As we will see below, it does not seem that he has. At this point, it is important to notice that while Curran notes in his essay the emergence of more explicitly biblical and theological warrants he does not associate this with or even recognize what may be called "historical consciousness" that emerged at Vatican II, or the historically conditioned character of human dignity. One result is that he speaks of "two different approaches," one biblical and theological, and the other based on natural law, standing side by side and raises the question of their relationship (1990:73). He does not explicitly recognize the way traditional natural methodology has been significantly revised.

[16] Pope Paul VI's 1967 encyclical *Populorum Progressio* (On the Development of Peoples), began papal reflection on the theme of development which John Paul II has significantly developed. *Populorum Progressio* offered a "Christian Vision of Development." In the context of his insistence that "development cannot be limited to mere economic growth" and that "to be authentic, it must be complete: integral, that is, it has to promote the good of every man and of the whole man," he indicates that human development points finally to the human relationship to God.

Just as the whole of creation is ordained to its Creator, so spiritual beings should of their own accord orientate their lives to God, the first truth and the supreme good. . . . By reason of his union with Christ, the source of life, man attains to new fulfillment of himself, to a transcendent humanism which gives him his greatest possible perfection: this is the highest goal of personal development (Paul VI 1967, par. 16: 318).

John Paul II has carried on this theme in his encyclicals, especially in *Sollicitudo Rei Socialis* and *Centisimus Annus*. A fuller discussion of his thoughts will be presented in the context of considering the Catholic critique of liberal neutrality.

[17] Both the 1971 Synod of Bishops' document, "Justice in the World" and Paul VI's encyclical *Evangelii Nuntiandi* (On Evangelization in the Modern World) display the increased reliance on specifically Christian sources through their effort to understand the integral connection between the church's evangelical mission and its social ethical responsibilities. In a formulation whose precise significance is much debated, the synod of bishops declared: "Action on behalf of justice and participation in the transformation of the world fully appear to us as a constitutive dimension of the preaching of the Gospel, or, in other words, of the Church's mission for the redemption of the human race and its liberation from every oppressive situation" (Synod of Bishops 1971:391). The same letter also displays the social ethical relevance of specifically Christian moral convictions in its insistence that "Christian love of neighbor and justice cannot be separated. For love implies an absolute demand for justice, namely a recognition of the dignity and rights of one's neighbor. Justice attains its inner fullness only in love" (Synod of Bishops 1971, :398).

Paul VI offers a slighly different statement of the relationship between evangelization and social responsibility in *Evangelii Nuntiandi*. Using an even more ambiguous phrase, he writes of the "profound links" between the two. Exegeting the exact meaning of either "constitutive dimension" or "profound links" is not essential to our present task, which is simply to illustrate the way in which the specifically Christian has come to be central to the understanding of social ethical responsibility. Paul VI's explanation of the "profound links" between social action and evangelism offer further illustration. He writes: "These include links of an anthropological order, because the man who is to be evangelized is not an abstract being but is subject to social and economic questions. They also include links in the theological order, since one cannot disassociate the plan of creation from the plan of Redemption" (Paul VI 1975, par. 31:271).

[18] The theme of solidarity as core principle and virtue of social ethics which has been prominent in post-Vatican II social teaching is also illustrative of the way in which biblical and theological sources are basic to contemporary social teaching. John Paul II's understanding of solidarity demonstrates both its importance for social ethics and its fundamental theological character. The importance of solidarity is signaled by his insistence that "genuine development must be achieved within the framework of *solidarity* and *freedom*," (John Paul II 1987, par. 33:35) a theme which Donal Dorr correctly notes is a part of his insistence that development is a fundamentally *moral* as opposed to economic category (1989:146). Soon, the Pope makes explicit the fundamental theological character of solidarity.

Solidarity helps us to see the "other"—whether a person, people, or nation—not just as some kind of instrument with a work capacity and physical strength to be exploited at low cost and then discarded when no longer useful, but as our "neighbor," a "helper" (see Gn 2:18–20), to be made a sharer, on a par with ourselves, in the banquet of life to which all are equally invited (par. 39:41).

Dorr correctly notes the connection between the Christian character of solidarity and "the aspect of generous self-sacrifice" in the Pope's explanation of solidarity. Dorr writes that the Pope "goes on to say that, for the Christian, the ultimate inspiration for solidarity comes from a unity that is even deeper than any unity based on natural and human bonds; this is a *communion*, a reflection of the unity of the three Persons in one God" (1987:152–153).

19 *The Challenge of Peace*, the 1983 pastoral letter from the U. S. Conference of Catholic Bishops is noteworthy in this regard. Even after it affirms and explains the traditional just war criteria it includes a section on "the value of nonviolence" which notes the pacifist tradition in the Church and the Pastoral Constitution's call for legal protection of conscientious objection. The bishop wrote:

> As Catholic bishops it is incumbent upon us to stress to our own community and to the wider society the significance of the support for a pacifist option for individuals in the teaching of Vatican II and the reaffirmation that the popes have given to nonviolent witness since the time of the Council (United States Catholic Conference 1983, par. 119:53).

An important question to raise is how the Bishops understood the relationship of pacifism to the just war criteria. An early paragraph in which "two complementary but distinct styles of teaching" is affirmed may hold the key.

20 While Rigali draws a contrast between human nature and the historical human person, some who recognize the historically conditioned character of moral knowledge still speak of human nature. Recall Hollenbach's way of putting the matter above: "Any appeal to the nature of the human person which is used to justify rights claims must take into account the fact that this nature is structured and conditioned both historically and socially" (1979:70).

21 David Hollenbach makes a similar point in an article entitled "A Prophetic Church and the Sacramental Imagination." He notes that

> each sacrament points to the world beyond the sanctuary. . . . Each of the sacraments has a social relevance that arises from the universality of the grace it bears. The sacramentalizing of God's grace that occurs in the church is not solely for the benefit of the internal life of the Christian community but also for the whole world (1988:97).

22 John Paul II, In *Sollicitudo Rei Socialis,* has specifically rejected the idea that Roman Catholic social teaching represents a third way: "The Church's social doctrine is *not* a 'third way' between *liberal capitalism* and *Marxist collectivism*, nor even a possible alternative to other solutions less radically opposed to one another: rather it constitutes *a category of its own"* (John Paul II 1987, par. 41:45).

23 As a result, some students of social Catholicism seem to believe that Catholic social teaching no longer provides a critical perspective over against the institutions and practices of liberal society. For example, Michael Novak has said that "the liberals of the late Eighteenth century set in motion the sorts of institutions that would with high probability realize" the common good as understood in contemporary Catholic teaching (under the influence of Jacques Maritain) (Novak, 1987:234). And, he writes that John Paul II's "concerns about the ordering of private property to the common good," concerns shared by the entire corpus of Catholic

social teaching, "are already observed in a multitude of institutional ways" in the contemporary economy of the United States (Novak, 1984:156). Similarly, but somewhat less forcefully, Dennis McCann argues that "the common good, as commonly understood [in Roman Catholic Social Teaching], does not provide a very helpful perspective for challenging the American political economy." This is true in part because the concept has been stretched so as to reflect "the church's growing appreciation for the virtues of the modern, democratic state" (1987:159).

[24] There is a certain parallel here between social Catholicism and the thought of Reinhold Niebuhr. As we we have seen, Niebuhr came to appreciate liberal institutions even as he remained an incisive critic of the theoretical justification for those institutions provided by liberal theorists. The same could be said of contemporary social Catholicism, although I believe it can be shown that Catholic teaching suggests an even greater challenge to liberal practice than did Niebuhr.

[25] Coleman further specifies by saying that "it is legitimate to show the particular Catholic teaching on social issues captured, for example, in key principles and concepts such as human dignity, solidarity, subsidiarity, the right to integral development, participation, the ultimate subordination of economics and politics to human fulfillment" (1986:186).

[26] Although Coleman quickly adds, parenthetically, that even Hollenbach "in places makes the unity stronger than the historical evidence will warrant" (Coleman 1986:186).

[27] Coleman writes:

In general, Catholic commentaries assume a unity in the teaching, are not critical of the economic or political foundations of papal teaching and often eschew a historical for a philosophical approach. Non-Catholic commentaries find it less easy to sustain the notion that the encyclicals comprise a unity, are often, even when sympathetic, critical and see the encyclicals in a historical context (1986:171).

While mine is a non-Catholic commentary, it's method is primarily philosophical rather than historical. Thus, if Coleman's account is correct, it seems that my emphasis on unity is not outside the mainstream of philosophical commentaries.

[28] Curran himself notes that in Leo "there is not the distinction between society and the state" which is crucial for Pius XII's famous "principle of subsidiarity," for John Courtney Murray's argument for religious liberty, and for the contemporary emphasis on participation. Furthermore, while Curran says that "freedom, equality, and participation are the significant *characteristics of anthropology* " (emphasis added) (1986:189), I would contend that these are not so much "characteristics of anthropology" as principles or values related to a particular anthropology. One's understanding of the human person can surely remain the same at some fundamental level while the principles or values one sees as related to that understanding change. It is my contention that modern social Catholicism's understanding of the human person has remained relatively stable at this fundamental level.

29 Langan says that "the Roman Catholic understanding of human rights in its classical form differs from the dominant varieties of liberalism, especially in Anglo-American culture, in its distrust of individualism and its emphasis on community. This is a matter of both the underlying anthropology and the moral restraints that affect the exercise of freedom in society" (1986:116).

30 Hehir draws the contrast with reference to Locke.

For the Christian position, the person is *social by nature*; in the Lockean position, the person is *social by necessity*. This means that in the Christian view the person can arrive at full human development only within a social context described in terms of family, society, and state, which are 'natural institutions.' For the Lockean social contract position, the person is by nature self-sufficient, devoid of intrinsic social bonds or responsibilities; the person enters the framework of society and the state, not as a 'natural setting' in which human development occurs through social interchange, but only because the protection of life, liberty, and property is too arduous outside some social setting (italics added) (1980:8).

31 Cahill says that in the modern papal encyclicals

. . . [R]ights are not spoken of primarily as individual claims against other individuals or society. They are woven into a concept of community which envisions the person as a part, a sacred part, of the whole. Rights exist within and are relative to a historical and social context and are intelligible only in terms of the obligations of individuals to other persons (1980:284).

She argues that the "fundamental difference" between this perspective and the liberal natural rights tradition is that "while both root some fundamental right or rights in the nature of the person as human, the natural law tradition emphasizes that the person is *essentially* social" (1980:285).

32 It will become evident below that I regard even his account as flawed. I don't believe he has made clear precisely how the Roman Catholic idea that persons are naturally social distinguishes it from liberal theories.

33 Hollenbach notes that John XXIII in his first major social encyclical, *Mater et Magistra*, had identified human dignity as providing the "the thread of continuity" which binds social Catholicism. John wrote:

The cardinal point of this teaching is that individual men are necessarily the foundation, cause and end of all social institutions. We are referring to human beings, insofar as they are social by nature, and raised to an order of existence which transcends and subdues nature. Beginning with this very basic principle whereby the dignity of the human person is affirmed and defended, Holy Church, especially during the last century. . . has arrived at clear social teachings whereby the mutual relationships of men are ordered (quoted in Hollenbach 1979:43).

[34] It is classic in that it gives clear expression to the full range of rights that social Catholicism has wanted to affirm and defend. It is a classic example of the natural law methodology employed in social Catholicism prior to Vatican II. But it is precisely its employment of this methodology which requires a qualification of its status as a classic document. Since Vatican II, social Catholicism has, for the most part, abandoned natural law in favor of a moral epistemology that emphasizes historical consciousness and radical cultural diversity. (See Hollenbach 1979: 107–133.) In this sense, *Pacem in Terris* is no longer a classic statement of the Catholic position.

[35] Hollenbach also suggests that their error may have to do with faulty strategic understanding of the historical and institutional conditions that are necessary for protecting human dignity. Thus the problem is strategic as well as fundamental. He has written:

. . . Disagreements [between Marxists and liberals] are in large part the result of *divergent* historical readings of the mechanism of social and economic interaction. Both liberal and Marxist thought propose the "ordering" of human rights they do, largely because of their conclusions about how the social system works. Their disagreement is a reflection of their desire to propose normative priorities which are strategically relevant to the social system as they interpret it.

Recent Roman Catholic criticism of liberalism and Marxism have been directed chiefly at the way their strategic concerns tend to be collapsed into normative theoretical prescriptions of the full content of human dignity and human rights. When this happens strategic morality becomes ideology—a mode of thought which narrows its normative description of the human person in the interest of strategic action. . . . The Catholic critique of these two contending approaches to the institutionalization of rights is aimed primarily at the narrowness of their normative "concepts of man" (1979:190).

[36] Hollenbach says that *Octogesima Adveniens* ,

is critical of those forms of both Marxism and liberalism which programmatically deny the fullness of integral development whether on ideological or strategic grounds. Each of these political and economic systems, if raised to the level of a complete social program, denies dimensions of personal and social development which are integral to human dignity (1979:83).

The most important texts from the encyclical with reference to liberalism and Marxism are the following.

Therefore, the Christian . . . cannot adhere to the Marxist ideology, to its atheistic materialism, to its dialectic of violence and to the way it absorbs individual freedom in the collectivity, at the same time denying all transcendence to man and his personal and collective history; nor can he adhere to the liberal ideology which believes it exalts individual freedom by withdrawing it from every limitation, by stimulating it through exclusive seeking of interest and power, and by considering social solidarities as more or less automatic consequences of individual initiatives, not as an aim and a major criterion of the value of the social organization (Paul VI 1971, par. 26:366).

. . . [A]t the very root of philosophical liberalism is an erroneous affirmation of the autonomy of the individual in his activity, his motivation and the exercise of his liberty (par. 35:370).

[37] John Langan is sensitive to the way in which the communitarian perspective of social Catholicism is critical of liberalism while not denying the partial validity of its anthropological and political wisdom. As a result,

there are still unresolved elements in the church's struggle with modern individualism and liberalism. At a fairly deep level within Catholicism there lives a desire for a more unified, more cohesive, and more disciplined form of society than prevails in the secularized West. There is also a view that liberalism errs in giving too much room to individual freedom at the expense of the common good and the needs of the disadvantaged, that its doctrine of rights leads to a neglect of duties, that liberal societies have lapsed into a resentful and self-protective consumerism, and that liberalism involves both the denial of a normative structure of goods for human beings in society and serious errors in anthropology. All this is, of course, apt material for future debate and dialogue. It does not indicate that Catholicism will abandon its human-rights doctrine; . . . But it does indicate that institutional Catholicism and Catholic political movements and actors may make significantly different choices about which human rights to struggle for in the political arena and which rights to accord priority to (1986:120–121).

[38] Again there is a certain ambiguity in Hollenbach at his point. The quotation in footnote 13 suggests that liberalism and Marxism may be characterized by institutional and social strategies which focus on protecting particular dimensions of human dignity. They become ideologies when that strategic focus is "collapsed into" a conceptual framework or anthropology that regards the autonomous dimension and expression of human nature as the sole essential foundation for human dignity, or the sole basis for the respect that is owed to the human person.

The distinction between the strategic and the conceptual or theoretical does suggest that the Catholic view as Hollenbach understands it could result in a strategic alliance with liberalism in particular contexts. Or, in certain contexts, the theoretical foundations of social Catholicism could result in a strategy that places emphasis on the protection of individual liberty and the rights and institutions that liberalism characteristically defends.

[39] The full quotation is as follows:

It should be noted that in today's world, among other rights, *the right of economic initiative* **is often suppressed.** Yet it is a right which is important not only for the individual but also for the common good. Experience shows us that the denial of this right, or its limitation in the name of an alleged "equality" of everyone in society, diminishes or in practice absolutely destroys the spirit of initiative, that is to say *the creative subjectivity of the citizen.* As a consequence, there arises not so much a true equality as a "leveling down." In the place of creative initiative there appears passivity, dependence and submission to the bureaucratic apparatus which, as the only "ordering" and "decision-making" body—if not also the "owner"—of the entire totality of goods and the means of production, puts everyone in a position of almost absolute dependence, which is similar to the traditional dependence of the worker-proletarian in capitalism.   This provokes a sense of frustration or desperation and predisposes people to opt out of national life, impelling many to emigrate and also favoring a form of "psychological" emigration (John Paul II 1987, par. 15:13).

40 It should be pointed out that this does not distinguish it from the communitarian anthropological perspective which I have associated with Stanley Hauerwas and have described by drawing upon the work of Michael Sandel.   To recognize or even stress the significance of the social, relational, or communitarian aspects of our selfhood is not to deny that we have a capacity for transcendence or autonomy.   Nor is it to deny the validity and importance of individual liberty and the rights and institutions which protect that liberty.   Recall our discussion, in the chapter on Hauerwas, of the political implications of the communitarian perspective as presented by Sandel.   There I pointed out that Sandel recognizes the importance of a liberal conception of justice and rights.   Of course, if a capacity or autonomy or independence over the social relations in which our total personhood is shaped is a perennial dimension of who we are, we will never be able to know ourselves well enough to do away with liberal justice entirely.   A communitarian conception of human personhood and the communitarian politics which coheres with it does not deny this.   What it insists upon, however, is that any political theory which ignores the relational aspect of our being or which relegates or limits concern about that dimension to the private sphere is an impoverished one which, in the language of social Catholicism, is threatening to the full dignity of the human person.

41 Most interesting may be his specific association in *Centisimus Annus* of liberalism with inattention to the needs of the poor.   Commenting on *Rerum Novarum,* he writes:

> . . . Liberalism is not the subject of a special section, but it is worth noting that criticisms of it are raised in the treatment of the duty of the state. The state cannot limit itself to "favoring one portion of the citizens," namely the rich and prosperous, nor can it "neglect the other," which clearly represents the majority of society. Otherwise, there would be a violation of that law of justice which ordains that every person should receive his due. "When there is question of defending the rights of individuals, the defenseless and the poor have claim to special consideration" (John Paul II 1989, par. 10:6).

42 In his important essay, "Assessing the Communitarian Critique of Liberalism," Allen Buchanan distinguishes radical and moderate communitarian views. His distinction is similar to the one I am drawing here. Ultimately, however, I think he confuses the matter somewhat and further distinction of the type that I am drawing is more helpful. According to Buchanan, the radical communitarian view

> rejects individual civil and political rights out of hand and seeks to replace references to individual rights either with teleological talk about the goods of communities or with talk about group rights. The moderate communitarian, in contrast, acknowledges individual civil and political rights but denies that they have the sort of priority the liberal attributes to them (1989:855).

Buchanan's distinction has two parts. First, the radical communitarian rejects individual rights whereas the moderate communitarian accepts them. Secondly, the radical communitarian either does away with rights talk altogether or replaces individual rights with the rights of groups or communities whereas the moderate communitarian, while regarding individual rights as lacking the priority that liberals assign them, does not employ the concept of group rights.

My complaint with regard to Buchanan's distinction is the following: while the distinction between communitarians who accept individual rights and those who reject them seems helpful (and clearly social Catholic communitarianism is of the moderate variety), it seems that either the radical or the moderate might choose to employ or not employ the language of group or community rights. He recognizes this with regard to radicals but not moderates. Moderates might challenge the priority of individual rights by listing group rights alongside individual ones and regarding the decision as to which have priority as a contextual one. On the other hand, they could also challenge that priority simply by regarding the exercise of individual rights as always limited by the claims of the community.

Interestingly, if James F. Childress' definition of rights as justified claims is correct, it makes no real difference whether the communitarian assigns rights to communities or not; if the communitarian believes that communities have justified claims against individuals they are saying the same thing as saying that communities have rights. To put the matter another way, if individuals have obligations to communities, it would seem to be consistent with the way the language of rights is used in moral discourse to say that communities have rights.

Childress, as far as I know, has not applied this argument about rights as justified claims and obligations as implying rights to the question of community rights. I am suggesting this implication of his argument on the basis of an argument from an essay on rights to health care. Childress is critical of the report of the President's Commission for the Study of Ethical Problems in Medicine and Biomedical and Behavioral Research, *Securing Access to Health Care*, for its careful avoidance of rights language. Rather than arguing for a right to health care, that report spoke of a societal *obligation* to provide equitable access to health care. Childress says that whatever rhetorical significance the language of rights may have, rights and obligations appear to have the same moral strength in much of the moral life. . . . [W]hen the Commission argues for a strong societal obligation to provide equitable access to health care, this obligation appears to imply a right on the part of citizens to equitable access to health care. Second, if rights are justified claims against others, they are justified by appeals to principles and rules in the same way obligations and duties are justified. The critical arguments hinge on principles and rules, by which both rights and obligations are justified. . .

The fear of the language of rights appears to stem in part from uneasiness about the relative strength and scope of rights against obligations; for example, a right to health care may appear to be both stronger and broader than a societal obligation to provide health care. But problems about content and scope, weight and stringency, are as serious for obligations as for rights (1984:48–49).

[43] This paragraph represents an effort to associate the basic categories of rights affirmed in *Pacem in Terris* with the dimensions of need, relationship, and freedom identified by Hollenbach. Hollenbach himself never actually shows the exact correspondence between the two sets of categories though he suggests that it can be done. Of course, there is an element of artificiality in my effort, because it could be said with reference to each category of fundamental right that the dimensions of need, freedom, and relationality are relevant. It does seem that each category of rights can be related most directly to one of Hollenbach's three dimensions of human dignity as I have done.

[44] Although, as we shall see below, there is an important formal characteristic of these and all other rights in a communitarian perspective such as that represented in the Roman Catholic social teaching that distinguishes the way specific rights which may be shared in both liberal and communitarian theories function differently.

[45] This particular way of understanding part of what culture makes possible, the recognition of certain values and disvalues, reflects the argument of Jeffrey Stout in the first section of his book *Ethics After Babel* that what moral languages (language representing the most fundamental cultural achievement) do is make available to those who use them "sets of candidates for truth and falsehood" about moral matters such as what is good or valuable and what is right (Stout 1988).

[46] For those nurtured in a foundationalist moral language, the qualification of a basic human right by the phrase "in keeping with the stage of educational development in the country to which he belongs" seems odd. If this is a human right, that is, a right that pertains to all human beings by virtue of their status as human beings independent of the particular relationships in which they find themselves, how can the right be relative to the country to which the person belongs? From the communitarian perspective it makes only limited sense to speak of the status of a human person independent of particular relationships, for it is precisely their relationship to a particular culture, community, or people that constitutes a fundamental dimension of who we are as persons. On such a view, the right to an

opportunity to develop the skills necessary to use cultural resources is, of course, relative to the particular culture (or country).   Of course, as cultures become increasingly interdependent, such a distinction becomes increasingly meaningless. An aborigine in Australia, whose life is increasingly influenced by the impact of an alien industrial capitalist culture would seem thereby to gain the right to an opportunity to learn the skills necessary to use the resources of that culture to his or her benefit.

[47] Consistent with what I have said above about the absence of specific rights attached to communities, Cahill does not suggest here that communities have rights. Hollenbach does use such an expression in attempting to articulate the Roman Catholic understanding of the relationship between the individual and the community.

The rights which protect human dignity, therefore, are the rights of persons in community.   They are neither exclusively the rights of individuals against the community nor are they the rights of the community against the individual (1979:65).

[48]   The concern about both material and spiritual well-being is explicit in Paul VI's specification of less and more human conditions.

Less human conditions: the lack of material necessities for those who are without the minimum essential for life, the moral deficiencies of those who are mutilated by selfishness. Less human conditions: oppressive social structures, whether due to the abuses of ownership or to the abuses of power, to the exploitation of workers, or to unjust transactions. Conditions that are more human: the passage from misery towards the possession of necessities, victory over social scourges, the growth of knowledge, the acquisition of culture.   Additional conditions that are more human: increased esteem for the dignity of others, the turning toward the spirit of poverty, cooperation for the common good, the will and desire for peace. Conditions that are still more human: the acknowledgement by man of supreme values and of God their source and their finality. Conditions, that, finally and above all, are more human: faith, a gift of God accepted by the good will of man, and unity in the charity of Christ. . . (Paul VI 1967, par. 21:319–320).

Commenting on *Populorum Progressio* David Hollenbach says: "The human personality is multifaceted.   The protection of human dignity, therefore, requires respect for the multiple social, economic, intellectual, interpersonal and religious conditions of personal development" (1979:78–79).

[49] For example, Milton Friedman's concept of corporate social responsibility surely indicates that for a manager of a corporation to fail to respond to expressed needs if such were to result in reduced corporate profits would amount to stealing from stockholders and a failure to respect the individual liberty of consumers. Admittedly, less radically neutral conceptions of corporate responsibility can also be developed within a liberal framework. More importantly however, is that an observation of the U. S. economy suggests that producers and the media show little regard for

considering the moral value of the needs they form and respond to.   One can hardly imagine a successful corporate manager reporting to his or her stockholders that "it is therefore necessary to create lifestyles in which the quest for truth, beauty, goodness and communion with others for the sake of common growth are the factors which determine consumer choices, savings and investments."   Or, justifying investment decisions arguing that "the decision to invest in one place rather than another, in one productive sector rather than another is always a moral and cultural choice" (John Paul II 1989, par. 36:15). Again, it is important to understand that within the framework of liberal thought such a consideration of moral value is itself regarded as morally dubious.

50 While John Paul II is clear that the state shares responsibility with all the elements of society, he does not always make it clear what the "necessary intervention of the public authorities" with regard to the necessary educational and cultural work entails. His discussion in paragraph 48 of *Centisimus Annus* strikes a much more neutral chord that the comments here cited.

51 See Hollenbach 1979:157.

52 Indeed, John XXIII did not place the emphasis on the principle which Pius XI had given it in part because he wanted to emphasize the importance of the role of government as a result of the increasing interdependence of persons and groups. In *Mater et Magistra* (1961), Pope John XXIII cautioned against a too restrictive interpretation of the principle, especially in view of the "the multiplication of social relationships, that is, a daily more complex interdependence of citizens" (John XXIII 1960, par. 59:65). His concern, appropriately, is that the principle would be appealed to in order to argue against state activism when in fact individuals through their intermediate communities are unable to achieve for themselves what is required by the dignity derived from their human nature. Moreover, in *Pacem in Terris* the principle is appealed to in order to argue that problems associated with the realization of "the universal common good" cannot be solved by "the public authorities of individual states" but by "worldwide public authority" (John XXIII 1963, par. 140:158).

53 For a fuller discussion of Murray's views on this matter that is consistent with Hollenbach's presentation, see Coleman, 1982:97–102.

54 It seems to me that Novak consistently underestimates the gap that remains between social Catholicism and liberalism in his work.   (See especially Novak 1984).

55 The idea of participation seems to me to reflect a continued awareness of the individual capacity for independence even as the moral relevance of it is diminished as compared to liberal theory.   Without that capacity persons would not be able to participate as individuals at all in the process of historical and social self-definition. That that capacity is not absolute and that it is not the aspect of our selfhood that is assigned primary moral relevance means that *only* participation (or co-participation) in a process of identifying the values that shall define us and our common good is possible rather than autonomous individual choice of those values.

56 In *Justice in the World* participation is regarded as a fundamental dimension of "a right to development," which seems itself to be seen as the most basic norm of social, political, and economic life. This right, it says, "must be seen as a dynamic interpenetration of all those fundamental human rights upon which the aspirations of individuals and nations are based" (Synod of Bishops 1971:393). In the context of discussing this right, the synod of Bishops speak of "a development composed of both economic growth and participation" and conclude that "[p]articipation constitutes a right which is to be applied both in the economic and in the social and political field" (Synod of Bishops 1971:394–395).

Hollenbach also lumps participation and the right to development together. He says,

> Both the "right to development" and the "right to participation" are shorthand ways of affirming the interconnected rights of those deprived of development and excluded from economic and political participation. These two "synthetic" rights are in the best tradition of the Catholic bias to say: *both* political liberty *and* basic human needs (1988:98).

57 There is an element of ambiguity in Hollenbach's interpretation of social Catholicism and the role of participation as a unifying or fundamental norm. For while he sometimes suggests that participation serves this function, at least at one point he suggests that participation is but one of three fundamental norms which correspond to the three dimensions of human dignity.

> The fundamental value that undergirds [the Roman Catholic commitment to human dignity] is neither simply the liberty of the individual stressed in the liberal democracies nor simply the social participation and economic well-being stressed in various ways by Marxism and socialism. Rather the theory maintains that respect for freedom, the meeting of basic needs, and participation in community and social relationships are all essential aspects of the human dignity that is the foundation of all rights. The institutional protection of personal freedom is emphasized by liberal democracy. The fulfillment of human needs is stressed by the developing "basic-needs" strategies at the center of the North-South debate. And the restructuring of the social and economic order in a way that allows genuine communal participation in the corporate life of society is the program of socialist thought. Each of these ideologies links its fundamental understanding of human rights with a particular structural obstacle to the realization of human dignity. The contemporary Catholic understanding, however, refuses to tie its notion of human dignity to only one of these three spheres of life in which persons can be either violated or protected by the structure of the social order. . . (1988:95).

Now, despite the apparent implication here that to regard participation as a single basic or unifying norm would be to lift up one dimension of human dignity at the expense of other equally valid ones, it is in this precise context that Hollenbach says that the right to participation is a "synthetic" right that enables the Catholic human rights theory to affirm both the civil and political rights which correspond to the independent or autonomous dimensions of human being and the economic rights which correspond to our physical nature. Thus, he does seem to regard participation as the most basic norm which unifies the other norms which Catholic human rights theory affirms.

[58] Earlier, Hollenbach has said that "[t]he aggregate set of all such public goods, considered in their interrelatedness and mutual dependence, constitutes what the tradition calls the common good" (1979:147). This doesn't seem quite accurate with reference to the concept of the common good in social Catholicism. I would argue that it goes beyond what Hollenbach calls the public goods with which distributive justice concerns itself. Hollenbach correctly identifies a sphere of commutative justice which "is concerned with the relationships which bind individual to individual in the sphere of private transactions" (1979:146). My quibble with his identification of public goods with the common good, is that his recognition of a sphere of commutative justice suggests that there is a sphere which involves private as opposed to public goods. Moreover, there are rights associated with that sphere. As we have already noted, *Pacem in Terris* said that the common good "is chiefly guaranteed when personal rights and duties are maintained" (John XXIII 1963, par. 60:139), and that "[o]ne of the fundamental duties of civil authorities," whose whole reason for existence is the realization of the common good "is to coordinate social relations in such fashion that the exercise of one man's rights does not threaten others in the exercise of their own rights nor hinder them in the fulfillment of their duties" (John XXIII 1963, par. 62:139). Both comments suggest that the common good has to do with regulating and relating the rights associated with all the spheres of justice including those concerned with more or less private goods. This would mean that public goods are an element of the common good, but the common good is more than an aggregation of these public goods.

None of this is to deny that even the goods associated with the sphere of commutative justice are enjoyable only in a social context in which institutional arrangements for the protection of the rights associated with it are in place. In this sense even these goods are social goods. But if this is how Hollenbach's comment about the public good and the common good is to be understood then the sphere of social justice totally incorporates the sphere of commutative justice and the distinction between them becomes almost meaningless.

[59] The document has previously identified imbalances between the specialized practical fields of knowledge (which modern persons have mastered) and "a comprehensive view of reality" that would synthesize and order these various fields and shape human conscience (which we seem to lack), between rich and poor nations, and between the desire for peace and the desire to "propagate one's own ideology" (Second Vatican Council 1965, par. 8:184).

[60] The description of the tension in human experience in *Gaudium et Spes* (and Hollenbach's account of the temptations associated with that tension) is reminiscent of the thought of Reinhold Niebuhr. Hollenbach himself notes this in a footnote (1979:105).

6

On Being the Church in the United States:
Some Conclusions

MY PURPOSE in this study has been to understand how several contemporary Christian theologians, representing diverse theological perspectives influential in the United States, conceive the relation between the church and the world, particularly the relation between the church and the liberal political culture which dominates politics in the United States. How and to what extent does liberal political culture provide an appropriate framework in which Christians may build up their own community, bear witness to their faith, and faithfully exercise their social ethical responsibilities and their concern for the neighbor? How and to what extent is the liberal political polity of the United States not just an appropriate framework for the exercise of Christian moral concern, but actually a vehicle of that concern and of the Christian hope for a divine reign of justice and peace? In other words, what liberal political values and institutions are consistent with and even grounded in Christian faith? And, alternatively, what critical perspective on the liberal political culture of the United States does Christian faith provide? In the light of their understanding of the general relationship between church and world and their theological analysis of liberalism, what posture should the Christian community adopt toward the political culture of the United States: uncritical involvement in all roles and aspects of public life which it provides as a primary mechanism for exercising Christian concern for the neighbor in faithfulness to God? Selective involvement in those aspects which are not inconsistent with Christian ethical insights while placing primary emphasis on the unique tasks of Christian people? Total separation or non-involvement and disinterest in public life as defined by liberalism? Selective involvement and detachment with an eye toward revolutionary change of the liberal culture? Total detachment with an eye toward revolutionary change?

In the introdcution, I developed an account of three factors in terms of which a theological account of the general relationship between the church and the world is understood. The epistemological factor has to do with the particular theologian's understanding of the sources of social ethical knowledge and their relationship. If the church is thought to draw upon unique sources of authority for understanding its social and political responsibilities, the possibility of sharp distinction exists. The moral factor has to do with whether or not the theologian regards the Christian community as having moral obligations which are distinct from those to which those outside the church are bound. Where the same principles and values are thought to apply to both, or at least where there is a significant overlap, it is likely that the distinction between church and world will not be sharply drawn, and that the posture of church toward the world will be one of broad cooperation and full participation in the major institutions and roles in the culture. The human possibilities factor has to do with whether or not the church has motivation or inspiration which enables it to achieve higher moral accomplishments than those outside the church. The distinction between church and world may be sharply drawn on the basis of the church's greater moral possibilities with reference to principles and values held more generally. Such a distinction may result in a posture of selective cooperation, since participation in some institutions and roles may be regarded as inappropriate for Christians because they represent compromises with the lesser moral achievements of those outside the church. Or, some institutions and roles may be thought as inappropriate to the church's own life, given that those compromises are unnecessary there. The conception of the church/world relation and the postures which Niebuhr, Hauerwas, Ruether, and Roman Catholic social teaching advocate for the church over against the liberal political world of the United States reflect their various judgments on these matters.

A major assumption of this work is that the theologian's account of the relationship between church and world is contextual in nature. That is to say, the posture that he or she advocates toward the world will depend upon the particular social and political culture which has shaped the theologian and in which the church for which the theologian writes exists. This is particularly relevant with reference to the moral factor. The distinction between church and world with reference to it will depend upon the conception of social and political morality which is dominant in the world and the degree to which it is consistent with what the theologian regards as Christian social and political responsibility. A second major assumption is that liberal theory provides the best account of social and political morality in the United States. Therefore, the task of the first chapter was to develop an account of liberal moral and political theory. That account focused on liberalism's insistence that individual human beings are equal sources of moral claims or owed equal respect on the basis of their capacity for autonomous self-direction, that is, their capacity to develop and pursue a conception of the good human life developed in independence of the social and historical factors which shape human life. The respect which every individual is owed on the basis of that capacity is respect for his or her liberty as an individual, where liberty is understood not as license, but as independence. On the basis of this fundamental anthropological claim, I showed the way in which liberal theory has developed a conception of human rights in which civil and political rights understood negatively have primary place and positive economic rights gain tenuous recognition. In addition, I showed the relationship between this basic anthropological claim and the contemporary liberal insistence that basic public institutions must be relatively neutral with regard to various conceptions of the human good. Finally, I provided brief accounts of the liberal justification for democratic political institutions and free market economic ones.

Reinhold Niebuhr: The Public Church

For most of their history the mainline Protestant churches have maintained a relatively cooperative and friendly posture toward the liberal democratic-capitalist public culture of the United States. Indeed, until recently those churches played a dominant role in defining the public culture; those churches enjoyed *de facto* establishment despite official, constitutional or *de jure* prohibition of the establishment of an official religion. It is not unfair to suggest that mainline Protestant churches for the most part embraced and contributed to the developments in political theory that provided the motivation and justification for a liberal culture. There were, of course, elements of conflict in the relationship and the churches often generated reform movements which were to a greater or lesser degree in tension with the liberal ethos. Still, for the most part, the mainline Protestant churches regarded the liberal public culture as consistent with Christian social ethical obligations. They were quite comfortable modeling a Public Church posture, providing a theological justification for the fundamental practices and institutions of the public culture, seeing no contradiction between Christian responsibilities and performing the roles public institutions provided, engaging comfortably in public debates in the terms provided by that culture, and attempting to influence public policy and reforming it as needed.

Reinhold Niebuhr probably has provided the most sophisticated theological rationale for a liberal public culture and the Public Church posture. He drew no sharp distinction between the church and the liberal political world of the United States. Indeed, it is not unfair to say that for Niebuhr the United States was his church. Niebuhr did not distinguish the exhortation he gave to those engaged in public roles from that which he gave to the church. No separate language or set of appeals was necessary. There was no sense that political responsibility of Christians differed from that of any other citizens. He seemed to regard all important societal roles and functions as appropriate for Christians.

Niebuhr's sense that no sharp distinction between church and liberal world need be drawn was based largely on his judgments with regard to the three factors which I identified in the introduction. First, Niebuhr shared with liberal theory the view that the fundamental source of social ethical knowledge was human nature itself. Moreover, his account of human nature was largely compatible with the liberal view I have described. Niebuhr's understanding of the transcendent or spiritual dimension of human nature includes the liberal understanding of autonomy as self-direction. He understood that spiritual dimension as being a source of individual worth (or dignity) and as justifying a wide range of liberty. While Niebuhr's conception of the human person was more complex than the liberal view I have described—emphasizing as it does not the way in which the human person is always rooted in the limitations of our physical nature and our contingent relations to particular communities and historical experiences—the critique which he derived from this does not shatter liberalism's basic commitments. The Niebuhrian view that attention to organic factors must remain significant for an overall theory of justice because of the limited scope of individual autonomy can be absorbed into the liberal perspective. However, it suggests a liberal perspective that is much more tentative, much less certain of its universal validity than has been characteristic of foundationalist versions of liberal theory. It suggests that the principles of justice and the basic rights upon which liberalism seeks to base itself must be seen as extremely general in nature, requiring the wisdom of experience for their understanding. It suggests an appreciation of traditional norms and structures of authority that liberalism sometimes lacks. Moreover, the absorption of the Niebuhrian sense of the ongoing importance of organic factors would certainly result in a liberalism that is "realistic" about the prospects for achieving justice in society, in the sense that it would recognize the constant need for a pragmatic strategy for maintaining a balance of power between the various vitalities present in a pluralistic society. Yet, none of this is fundamentally inconsistent with contemporary versions of liberalism like those of John Rawls or Michael Walzer.

Niebuhr's sense that liberal conceptions of human nature do not "do justice to the height of human self-transcendence" (1941:123) represents a more fundamental critique of the liberal perspective, though even here it is necessary to distinguish an aspect of that critique which is overdrawn from another which is an accurate portrayal of the essential liberal spirit. On the one hand, Niebuhr meant by this charge that liberalism fails to recognize that the capacity for autonomy entails a radical freedom which invalidates any order which is discoverable in nature or by reason. Once again, this implies a tentative and open quality to the interpretation and application of the basic norms that are to guide society in the reform of its basic institutions toward an order that more closely approximates perfect justice. I have argued that contemporary liberal conceptions of universal order are less comprehensive and more flexible, and therefore more like his own conception, than Niebuhr suggests. Which is to say that liberalism is capable of absorbing such a challenge.

On the other hand, Niebuhr's argument that liberalism fails to recognize that the very autonomy which it seeks to protect and enhance promises universal and indeterminate manifestations of human evil is on target and represents a more fundamental challenge to the liberal enterprise. Niebuhr's sense that human evil is rooted in the transcendent or autonomous aspect of human nature means that he is more willing than liberals tend to be to appeal to traditional structures of order and authority as a check upon that evil. Thus, Niebuhr regarded organic communal factors as morally relevant because of the limitations on the human capacity to transcend such factors, because of the natural moral sentiments which are nurtured in community, *and* because they are an absolutely essential element of control over the evil potential in human freedom. This last is Niebuhr's most compelling reason to appreciate the communal and historical factors which shape human life. He regarded the liberal ignorance of this aspect of human autonomy as the most fundamental source of its optimism and sentimentality. It meant that liberalism built its understanding of politics on the idea of "an essentially harmless individual" (1944:18). According to liberalism, if individuals were set free from the traditional authorities, and if their pursuit of happiness as they conceive it were controlled only by the principles of right which their autonomous reason can discover independently of those traditional authorities, then their capacity for evil would be greatly diminished. But for Niebuhr, that autonomous reason rooted in the spiritual dimension of the human person is as prone to the distortions of human evil as are the traditional sources of authority, if not more so. The struggle between autonomous reason and traditional authority was not, for Niebuhr, a struggle between good and evil. That human beings were capable of using their radical freedom in indeterminately evil ways meant that the restraint imposed by traditional authorities was an important and necessary contribution to justice.

Despite this basic challenge to liberal anthropology, Niebuhr did not draw a sharp distinction between church and liberal world with reference to the moral factor. The norms which are regarded as relevant in the liberal framework and which liberals have derived from their understanding of human nature are not inconsistent with the ones which Niebuhr regarded as applicable to Christians. While Niebuhr's primary moral principle was love, his understanding of that norm was drawn more from his account of human nature than from scripture or the teaching and example of Jesus. It was for him the "law of life," the observance and fulfillment of which fulfilled our nature. Moreover, though love plays no fundamental role in liberal political theory, the principles of justice, liberty, and equality, which Niebuhr thought necessary to mediate the demands of love in a sinful world, are similar to liberal principles of justice. Niebuhr's understanding of love as self-sacrifice, which does seem to be drawn from specifically Christian sources and require Christian appeals for its justification, does not serve to sharply distinguish the political life of Christians from other citizens in a liberal polity for four reasons: 1) its requirements are seen as going beyond or above the requirements of justice and not as contradicting them, 2) it serves more as a critical rather than as a guiding principle for human life, 3) its fulfillment is considered impossible even for the church, and 4) to live according to it would render Christians ineffective and irresponsible in the public or political realms of life. Moreover, Niebuhr apparently regarded Christians as no more able to live according to the "higher" requirements of self-sacrifice than others. He rejects the idea of a "realized eschatology," which would contend that in its own historical existence the church is beginning to experience and embody the first fruits of the triumph of transcendence and eternity over the limitations and anxiety caused by human rootedness in historical existence. Thus, whatever differences exist between Christian love and liberal justice are mitigated by the fact that Niebuhr did not draw a sharp distinction between Christian moral possibilities and worldly ones. All are subject to sin's limitations and the achievement of liberal justice may be the best to which any of us may aspire in our public lives.

I have indicated that Niebuhr was mistaken in his belief that the liberal reading of human nature and the norms which it derived from that reading were consistent with his own reading. Niebuhr's conception of love has a teleological character; it sees human life as directed toward a perfect relation of the self to God, to others, and to itself. Surely such a conception violates liberal neutrality. Even if liberal neutrality is limited, even if liberalism defends a thin theory of the good or has its own partial or its own conception of the minimal requirements of a good society, that limitation on liberal neutrality is in terms of a commitment to individual autonomy or liberty and not to a situation where interpersonal relations are ones in which "one individual penetrates imaginatively and sympathetically into the life of another" (1953:156). Surely it is not one in which an individual's proper relation to God is thought of as a fundamental aspect of human flourishing which liberal institutions must promote. Niebuhr overestimated the degree to which a liberal culture is one in which such love is nurtured.

Moreover, while Niebuhr's conception of justice shares with liberalism a fundamental commitment to individual liberty and to the basic equality of every human person, I have argued that he overestimated the overlap between his own interpretation of what love requires and liberal commitments. There are important differences between his understanding of human freedom and its moral relevance and that of liberalism, differences having to do with Niebuhr's sense that communities as well as individuals require liberty and that our freedom is the source of our universal sinfulness. In addition, Niebuhr's commitment to equality is fundamentally different from the liberal commitment. It is not understood with reference to liberty, but rather with reference to that ultimate *telos* to which love directs us. Also, Niebuhr's understanding of the relationship between equality and liberty is fundamentally different. For Niebuhr, the commitment to equality is limited by liberty in the sense that the recognition of the claims of the neighbor which love requires must be given freely; constrained or coerced equality, equality required and enforced by law, lacks this important aspect of what love demands. In liberal thought, equality is understood with reference to liberty. The equal claim that we make upon one another is respect for liberty. Even where liberals have regarded that respect as requiring positive assistance to others in the exercise of liberty, that positive assistance is limited by the fact that it is required limits the liberty of those obligated to provide the assistance. There is no such built in limit to what equality requires for Niebuhr. Thus, Niebuhr's conception of justice is significantly more egalitarian than even that of a fairly egalitarian liberal such as Rawls.

All of this suggests that the tensions between Niebuhr's perspective and the liberal framework are so great as to justify a more heightened sense of the distinction between church and world than Niebuhr's work suggested. Niebuhr's judgment in the middle of this century that liberal institutions in the United States had served the cause of justice well, despite what he regarded as the deficiencies of liberal theory, was a provisional one, and there are reasons to question both that judgment (because of the great racial and economic inequality that remained despite the achievements made during the Roosevelt administration) and that he would have maintained it even now. The reasons for raising these questions in part have to do with the fact that working within the Niebuhrian framework requires the always controversial judgment as to whether the particular structure of justice which exists is the greatest possible one given the limitations which arise from human sinfulness and the balance of vitalities present in the society. An even more fundamental reason (internal to the Niebuhrian framework) for suggesting that the tension between church and liberal political culture may be greater than Niebuhr suggested has to do with the fact that his conception of justice was significantly more egalitarian than the liberal conception. Niebuhr, it seems to me, underestimated that tension.

Stanley Hauerwas: The Peaceable Church

The reasons just suggested for drawing the distinction between church and liberal world more sharply than Niebuhr did are internal to his own framework. There are other reasons for doing so which require moving beyond the structure of his thought. The work of Stanley Hauerwas illustrates some of those reasons. In his many publications over the past two decades, Hauerwas has drawn a sharp distinction between the church and the world and has emphasized the church as an alternative to the secular liberal political polity of the United States.   He has challenged what he regards as the majority view among Christian ethicists "that Christianity and democracy are integrally related" (1988:175).   For this majority, he says, "the subject of Christian ethics was America" (1985:31).   Hauerwas' philosophical and theological convictions compel him to stand outside this mainstream.   He regards the church, rather than the nation and its government, as the primary subject of Christian social ethics.   He does not regard a liberal democratic polity as hospitable to fundamental Christian convictions and the preservation of Christian identity.   Moreover, while his responses to questions about abortion, health care, poverty, justice, and war have focused on how the life of the Church ought to be shaped in relation to such important social ethical issues, he has, for the most part, refused to address questions of public policy related to those same issues.   He has generally avoided a resort to the language of rights, the primary idiom in which public policy discourse is carried on in the United States.   He has challenged the appropriateness of Christians serving in the police or the military, and he questions whether liberalism provides an appropriate account of the way in which many other roles are to be morally exercised.   He argues that fulfilling its social ethical responsibilities in a liberal world requires the church to embody a peaceable alternative to the liberal public polity; it fulfills its social ethical responsibility primarily by being a Peaceable Church.

Hauerwas draws his sharp distinction between church and world with reference to all three of the factors we have identified.   He draws the distinction at the epistemological level by way of his insistence that all ethics is narrative-dependent.   At the moral level he draws a sharp distinction by way of his claim that the church has a commitment to peaceableness or non-violence which distinguishes it from all other non-church or worldly perspectives.   With reference to the moral possibilities factor, Hauerwas insists that the church's distinct commitment to peaceableness is achievable—it is a real possibility for the church, because in Jesus the Kingdom of God has come among us and in him the fulfillment of human eschatological possibilities has been made concrete and real.

The distinction that Hauerwas draws at the epistemological level is crucial to his understanding of the distinction between church and world. For Hauerwas, there is no universal ethical perspective.   Every morality is embedded in a tradition which is shaped by particular historical and social experiences and the narratives by which every community interprets and displays its distinct perspective.   Thus, Christian morality, as every other, is distinctive, in this case in terms of the particular perspective incorporated in the biblical narrative and especially the narrative of Jesus' life.   That is, the principles, values, and virtues by which life is interpreted and guided are grounded not in human nature but in the particular narratives or stories by which people are formed and by which they understand the *telos* toward which their life is directed. In principle, therefore, the ethics of every community is sharply distinguished. While there may be certain common human experiences and even certain formal characteristics shared by every particular conception of ethics, these are not an adequate basis for the identification of common principles and values upon which institutions and roles appropriate and valid for all can be established. Hauerwas' position represents the view that the church has a unique epistemological perspective which gives it moral knowledge unavailable to the world. Because the church understands itself (and the world) with reference to the story of Jesus, the principles, *telos*, and virtues by which it directs its life are distinct from those by which the world directs its life. The church knows what the world cannot know. The world will have other stories with reference to which its principles, *telos*, and virtues are understood.

Hauerwas' argument for drawing a sharp distinction between church and world with reference to the epistemological factor is persuasive. It suggests another reason for the inadequacy of Reinhold Niebuhr's idea of the Public Church. We have seen that Niebuhr justified his understanding of the basic norms of love and justice from the study of human nature rather than by virtue of appeals to distinctly Christian convictions (though he regarded Christian convictions as confirming those insights). On the other hand, he emphasized that humanity, both individually and collectively, is radically free, and, as a result, he regarded as mistaken any attempt to discover fixed moral norms in the regularities of nature or in the coherence that human reason is able to give to human existence. Moreover, he pointed to the positive moral relevance of the particular historical community or communities of which the individual is a part and which shape both our identity and our moral understanding. There is an inconsistency between Niebuhr's justification of his principles of love and justice in human nature and both his critique of natural law and his emphasis on the importance of historical tradition. The fact that his own understanding of the norms he thought were to be drawn from human nature is so different from the understanding which is typical of liberals, who also regard their understanding as drawn from certain convictions about universal human nature[1] suggests that his understanding was much more influenced by distinctly Christian sources than he thought or indicated. It suggests that ethics is narrative-dependent in a much more profound way than Niebuhr made clear—though his own sense of the importance of community and tradition in shaping human understanding points in this direction.

While Hauerwas' claim that ethics is narrative dependent suggests that a distinction between church and world will exist, it does not indicate the precise nature or degree of that distinction, nor does it suggest what the posture of the church will be toward the world in which it finds itself.

That requires an analysis of that world itself and the story or stories which shape its life. Hauerwas' argument for the posture that the church should adopt toward our liberal political culture depends upon his understanding of its story and the principles, *telos*, and virtues which it regards as appropriate to that story. That is to say, we must attend to what I have called the moral factor. Hauerwas' view that the church should see itself as an alternative to liberal politics is based on his judgment that there is a sharp contrast between the liberal story and the principles, *telos*, and virtues appropriate to the Christian story.

I have suggested that a fundamental reason for the sharpness of Hauerwas' critique of liberalism is that he regards it as a strategy for dealing with the fact of our plural conceptions of the good that is an alternative to his own: pacifism and openness to the stranger. Interestingly, both the liberal strategy and Hauerwas' Christian perspective are efforts to deal with the fact of our pluralism in ways that prevent resorts to violence. The development of the liberal theory of the state was in part an effort to find a way to stop the seemingly interminable religious wars that plagued the political life of Europe for several centuries. And the judgment that it made an important contribution to that end seems justified. That the wars it sought to end were largely motivated by Christian religious convictions is all the more reason to suggest that a Christian critique of liberalism ought to begin with no small measure of contrition and an appreciation for the contributions liberal society has made to the prevention of religious strife. This is not to deny that the record of liberal societies with respect to the Jews is hardly a proud one.[2] Nor is it to deny that the liberal effort to secure agreement around a set of basic rights provides a mechanism for justifying coercion and violence and that the liberal attempt to secure peace falls short of requiring the measure of toleration which Hauerwas' construal of the Christian obligation to non-violence and openness to the stranger requires. It is not intended to deny that liberal states have been capable of imperialistic wars and that Christians have been wrong in lending their support to such wars. I am only contending that there is a more positive relation between liberal and Christian commitments than Hauerwas suggests, and that historically Christians have seen liberalism as an ally and even a vehicle of the Christian commitment to peaceableness.[3] While the relation between the church and liberal politics requires a more nuanced treatment, Hauerwas does provide an important corrective to the conviction among many Christians in the United States that some version of liberal politics can be equated with Christian politics.

Moreover, Hauerwas' commitment to pacifism offers another important corrective to Niebuhr's sense of the basic compatibility of liberal political culture with Christian convictions. This sense of compatibility was made possible because of Niebuhr's rejection of pacifism, because of the various ways he mitigated the potential of love as self-sacrifice for defining a distinctive Christian political ethic, and because of his understanding of politics or political responsibility. Niebuhr suggests that living self-sacrificially, or living according to what love demands under the condition of human sin, is impossible even for the church. He draws no sharp distinction between church and world with reference to the greater capacity the church might have for living according to such a norm. Moreover, according to Niebuhr, living self-sacrificially, which would include the disavowal of the use of violence in one's own defense, results in political ineffectiveness and irresponsibility, as does a broader commitment to refrain from violence (which would also preclude the use of violence in the defense of others). Both his view that the church cannot be distinguished by its greater capacity for conforming its life to the demands of love and his view that pacifism is politically irresponsible seem dubious.

Niebuhr's refusal to distinguish between church and world in terms of the church's capacity for conforming its life to self-sacrificial love seems inconsistent with his claim that self-sacrifice requires a religious justification. Moreover, he conflates two separable claims: that love as self-sacrifice cannot be justified "historically," that is, apart from specifically religious appeals, and that it cannot be fulfilled historically. The church is characterized, if by nothing else, by the fact it finds religious justifications for its way of life compelling. More particularly, because its *religious* claim is that Jesus of Nazareth and the way of life he taught and embodied (a way of life which included a willingness to sacrifice one's interests and even one's self or life) is a unique disclosure of "the contours of God's grace, purposes, and power as well as the contours of the sort of human life that is genuinely responsive to God" (Ottati 1989:73), the church is that people who finds compelling reasons that "the world" may not for being willing to sacrifice the self and its interests. Even if such sacrifice requires religious justification, that does not mean that it is impossible for it to be fulfilled historically. The way of life taught by Jesus can be embodied historically because, as Hauerwas has pointed out, it was so embodied by Jesus. Moreover, it is known to be an historical possibility because it has been so embodied by Christian martyrs and others from the first century until our own.

Yet these historical facts are so evident that Niebuhr could not have ignored them, and they evidently do not count against what he meant by the claim that living self-sacrificially is an historical impossibility. He must have meant that living according to a principle of self-sacrifice and without the use of violence was an impossibility for a community that intended to maintain itself historically and to exercise political responsibility—both of which are apparently regarded by Niebuhr as appropriate intentions for the church. Niebuhr did not regard as heretical a Christian pacifism which understood itself as a witness to the divine judgment upon all human achievements of justice (based as they must be

on coercion and violence) and to the eschatological expectation that God
will finally transmute "the present chaos of this world into its final unity"
(1960:135). But such witness represents, for Niebuhr, a refusal to live
according to a responsible political ethic, and he apparently regarded the
church as more obligated to exercise political responsibility than to bear
witness to its hope.

One need not render judgment about the church's primary
responsibility under the terms laid down by Niebuhr. The choice between
witness and political responsibility is made necessary only if one accepts
Niebuhr's rather narrow conception of politics. For him, politics has to do
with power and its exercise by individuals and groups. Moreover, power
necessarily takes physical form (as violence or coercion) from time to time.
Politics is the art of organizing power in such a way that a tolerable balance
of power between competing individuals and groups in a society is
achieved and maintained. (See Niebuhr 1943: 256–259.)[4]

But one need not see the refusal to use physical force as a withdrawal
from politics if one has a broader understanding of the nature of politics.
Hauerwas has suggested, for example, that an adequate conception of
political life must recognize the effort of a community or group of
communities to identify and experience the common good. On such a
view, our conception of politics is impoverished when we see it primarily
as a matter of balancing the claims of various individuals and groups (and
balancing the power that is behind those claims) and ignore the effort to
deal with those "goods" of life together that all individuals and groups
share. When the concept of common good is at the center of our
understanding of politics the physical dimensions of power become less
important. "Violence," says Hauerwas,

> is necessary not as the essence of community [or government, or politics],
> but when community is no longer sustained by the common wills of those
> that make it up. True authority does not need violence as it is the
> recognition and obedience given by the citizen to the governors who
> legitimately lead in accordance with the common good of that society.
> This does not mean that power is excluded from the state, but it is a
> power that is nonviolent in the sense that the individual is directed to the
> good of the society in the context of his own wider loyalty to the society.
> For power is the essence of the state, not simply because some refuse to
> obey from evil intention, but because of the richness of the various visions
> of the good that must be directed toward the whole of the common good
> (1974:218–219). [5]

According to such an understanding of politics, a pacifist stance does
not entail a refusal to engage in politics. Pacifism is consistent with a
viable political ethic because the essential political task—the discovery of
the common good—is one to which violence is not necessarily related.
The judgment that living self-sacrificially and/or without the use of

violence (or, at least, with a weighty presumption against its use) is possible for Christians and is incumbent upon them does not entail a withdrawal from politics or an irresponsible denial of the church's responsibility to address political issues. Or, to put the matter in terms of the distinction between church and world, the view that the church is sharply distinguished from the world because it has compelling reasons, that the world does not have, for living self-sacrificially or non-violently does not entail that the church eschews any engagement in politics or denies that it has political responsibilities.[6]

In addition to his conviction that the Christian story provides a pacifist alternative to liberalism's manner of dealing with moral pluralism, Hauerwas' argues that the church should form an altnernative polity because of his conviction that the liberal story represents an effort to deny or escape our boundedness to the stories and traditions of the communities of which we are a part. Liberalism, on his view, defends and promotes a false understanding of human freedom and responsibility and, to the degree that it is successful in making such freedom possible, it prevents us from developing the virtue and experiencing the freedom and responsibility which is possible for us. That is to say, its basic anthropological perspective undermines the capacity of any tradition or any moral community to inculcate the virtues that are essential for the realization of the human good as that tradition or community sees it.

My acceptance of Hauerwas' basic epistemological framework (and his conception of politics) does not entail an uncritical assessment of his overall account of the proper relation between the church and the liberal world. Regarding the discovery of moral knowledge as fundamentally an historical rather than a foundational enterprise, or regarding ethics as narrative-dependent, means that one must approach the question of the church's relation to the world with a measure of suspicion. It is to begin with the presumption that, because the church has a particular story that shapes its fundamental identity and worldview, it is likely to have a conception of the norms by which its life is directed which is fundamentally different from the conception of those whose identity and worldview is shaped by different stories. Of course, that the story of Jesus is not the only story that shapes the lives of Christian people, though it is its authoritative and distinctive one, and that there are certain common human experiences and common features which every ethos shares, should also alert us to the possibility that there is a basis for cooperation and agreement between church and world. Therefore, from Hauerwas' own epistemological perspective, the question is whether he has adequately attended to and construed the distinctions and commonalities between the church's manner of life and that which liberal political culture promotes. As Michael Quirk has suggested, "As long as church and world share at least *some* beliefs in common, a dialogue between them can take place. . . . A quantum of incommensurability between the Christian and the secular paradigms does not preclude the possibility of their rational comparison and practical judgment about their comparative worth" (1987:85). Thus, Hauerwas' emphasis on the church as a separated community and his concern for the maintenance of its integrity must be evaluated in terms of his critique of the particular world or culture in which it finds itself. In terms of the church in the United States, this finally hinges on the validity of Hauerwas' critique of liberal culture.

Is liberalism as profoundly mistaken about the nature of our selfhood as Hauerwas contends, and does the liberal framework and the translation of Christian convictions into its idiom represent as profound a threat to Christian integrity as Hauerwas imagines? Quirk suggests, correctly it seems to me, that the chasm between church and the liberal world may not be as great as Hauerwas indicates. If Hauerwas is to make his argument compelling he must attend more carefully to the historical relationship between Christianity and liberalism in the west. As Quirk contends, Hauerwas' argument needs to be "supplemented by an understanding of the ways in which the history of Christianity has affected the fortunes of the secular world" (1987:83).

Accepting Hauerwas' basic epistemological standpoint while recognizing an important historical relation between liberalism and Christianity suggests a somewhat different way of posing the question of Christian separation from our culture. If Hauerwas' epistemological perspective, including its sense that ethical notions are teleological in character, is correct, then the conversation between liberal and Christian ethics has to do with the question of what constitutes a worthy end for human life. This suggests the possibility of the Hauerwasian Christian community playing a fundamental role in society in terms of its participation in a conversation about the nature of the good. Such conversation is possible if there are any points of commonality, any shared sense of what constitutes a good human life. Given the intimate historical relation between Christianity and liberalism, one suspects that the possibility of conversation is great. Early in his career, Hauerwas indicated that the church had an important contribution to make to democratic society in terms of contributing to the discovery of "a substantive notion of the common good within a democratic framework" (1974:229). Now, Hauerwas is apparently pessimistic about the prospects for such a discovery.

There are reasons to believe that such pessimism is not justified. The fact that the Roman Catholic Bishops of the United States have been able to address public policy issues from a teleological perspective and engage others in meaningful dialogue suggests that such an approach remains fruitful. Hauerwas would seem to have a stake in increasing the impact of what Robert Bellah and his colleagues identified in *Habits of the Heart* as the biblical and civic republican traditions in American life. Hauerwas has denied that civic republicanism has ever had the influence which Bellah attributes to it. But there are reasons to believe that many of the moral fragments which continue to influence us in the United States could be made sense of if they were provided a context in an ethos dedicated to the discovery of a common *telos*. Hauerwas might resist the suggestion that the church has a role to play in a liberal polity, in terms of a restoration of a teleological approach to political ethics and the conversation about the common good which such an approach requires, on grounds apart from his judgment that liberal theory is so dominant that such an approach and such a conversation is currently impossible. He might argue that such a tack represents merely another way to delude the church into thinking that it has a stake in the continued existence of democratic nation-states, a stake important enough to justify Christian participation in wars of defense. Yet there is no reason in principle why a Christian commitment to non-violence need be compromised simply because Christians are willing to participate in our society by addressing questions of public policy and practice in the idiom of the common good.

I have indicated that Hauerwas' communitarian critique of liberalism shares much with the critique raised by Michael Sandel. If I am correct about this, there is a basis for cooperation and participation in liberal society that Hauerwas seems to ignore. Sandel's conclusion (suggested by the title of his book) is not that the liberal framework is invalid, but that it is limited in its applicability and is not the sole measure of the virtue of basic institutions. "Justice finds its occasion," he wrote, "because we cannot know each other, or our ends, well enough to govern by the common good alone. This condition is not likely to fade altogether, and so long as it does not, justice will be necessary" (1982:183). Liberal justice remains relevant because we are not without a capacity for individual independence from those communities and ends which constitute us and that capacity merits respect and protection. It is not the exclusive source of our humanity, not that alone which gives us dignity and makes us sources of moral claims, but it is a part of who we are that our basic institutions ought to respect. The challenge for communitarian politics is to identify political principles and institutions that enable both our discovery of a broad common good (and which enhance our realization of that good) and our recognition of the degree to which we always remain separate persons, always strangers to each other, with disagreements about what is good for us and with true conflicts of interest. This suggests that there is a basis for cooperation and participation in the public dialogue about policy, even in the terms set by the liberal framework, which Hauerwas does not acknowledge.

In summary, Stanley Hauerwas has made an important contribution to our understanding of the relationship between the church and the liberal world. It is an important corrective to those views which have tended to see the United States as a more important agent of what God is doing in the world than the church. Even without committing oneself to his (apparently) absolute commitment to non-violence, Hauerwas' work can be regarded as an important challenge and corrective to the much too casual acceptance of Christian participation in war and to the view that a refusal to use or condone violence, or a weighty presumption against violence, renders us politically irresponsible. His broad understanding of politics can prod us to imagine more creative ways to deal with conflict and to appreciate that the way in which the Christian community shapes character through its worship and its telling of the story of Jesus is an important political task. Moreover, he has made a profound contribution by demonstrating the way the thinly teleological or neutral language of liberal rights does not allow a communication of the full way of life in which Christian commitments are embedded. Our playing the political game on liberal terms often results in failure to faithfully address both our primary responsibility to bear witness to the human *telos* as it is understood through its proleptic disclosure in Jesus Christ and our eschatological hope for its fulfillment. Hauerwas properly warns us that talking about justice and rights as they are understood in a liberal society may in fact represent a failure of witness.

Rosemary Ruether: The Radical Church

For Rosemary Ruether, the most important way in which the distinction between church and world is drawn is with reference to the third of the three factors we have identified. On her view, the church is to be characterized by its more perfect embodiment of the human aspiration for liberation than any other community. While Ruether consistently regards the church itself as subject to criticism from the perspective of what she calls the "aspirational horizon of meaning and value," which is a universal human characteristic, she does not mean that the church's moral life is no different from that of the world. While she is "realistic" in the sense that she is aware that the church remains always and ever sinful and falls short of realizing the perfect humanity and perfect human community for which we yearn, she does, in contrast to Niebuhr, draw a distinction between the moral possibilities of the church and those of the world. The fundamental characteristic of the church, for Ruether, is its embodiment of the ideal humanity which represents both our created essence and our future possibility. The church, she insists, is "the avant-garde of liberated humanity" (1983:193). It is "where the good news of liberation from sexism is preached, where the Spirit is present to empower us to renounce patriarchy, where a community committed to the new life of mutuality is gathered together and nurtured, and where the community is spreading this vision and struggle to others" (1983:213). The church experiences the first fruits of the human hope for the full harvest of human possibilities, and struggles for a deeper experience of those possibilities while the world remains a barren wilderness.

Ruether also draws an important distinction with reference to the epistemological factor. The judgment that the church is distinguished from the world primarily with reference to the degree to which the church embodies *universal* human aspirations should not obscure the way in which her perspective shares with Hauerwas a sense that one's particular perspective determines what one sees or what norms one will regard as authoritative. The distinction she draws, however, is not between church and world but cuts across both. For Ruether, the privileged or authoritative perspective is not that which is characterized by its relation to the story of Jesus. Rather, as for liberation theology in general, it is the experience of oppression which provides the privileged hermeneutical or epistemological perspective. That experience and the authority of the norms drawn from it does not correspond to the sociological boundary between church and world. For Ruether, the norms drawn from the experience of oppression are visible from beyond the boundaries of the church and are applicable to the whole world. Both church and world are under obligation to the moral perspective of the oppressed.

Drawing the human possibilities and epistemological distinctions in this way leaves the distinction between church and world ambiguous. The ambiguity arises because she regards the church as only one community which has the possibility of embodying liberation in a way that distinguishes it from the world. She does not make clear how she understands the relationship between the Christian community and those non-Christian communities of liberation. Nor does she make clear how one's commitment to Jesus or one's participation in the Christian community shapes one's understanding of human liberation or full humanity. The usual Christian affirmation has been that Jesus of Nazareth provides the key for understanding the divine and for understanding what it means to be fully human and to have our essential humanity restored. It is not clear in Ruether's thought how Jesus of Nazareth functions to clarify either. Her attention to Jesus and to the gospel accounts of his life is fairly selective. She displays serious attention to the gospel in her commitment to reconciliation and to non-hierarchical relationships, but her discussions of the use of violence in the struggle for liberation is inadequately informed by a distinctly Christian perspective. Most importantly, Ruether's ecclesiology does not make clear how the biblical witness and the person of Jesus who is at the center of the Church informs and challenges her conception of the fulfillment of our essential humanity. Thus, Ruether's insistence that women's liberation provides the sole theological and moral criterion seems to exclude the roles of scripture and Jesus as loci of revelation and in so doing undermines the integrity of the church.

This is not to deny that the integrity of the church is also undermined when it fails to commit itself to and embody human liberation and when it excludes the voice and vision of the oppressed as it develops its sense of the nature of human liberation and fulfillment. Indeed, Ruether's work provides an important corrective to Hauerwas' epistemological perspective, for despite his formal concern that the Christian community remain always open and hospitable to the stranger, his interpretation of Christian social ethical responsibilities does not demonstrate adequate attention to and appreciation of the insights generated by the perspective of the poor and the oppressed. They remain "strangers" within the version of Christian social life which Hauerwas envisions.

Still, for the church to retain its historic identity as the body of Christ, that voice and vision must be kept informed by scripture. The "hermeneutic circle" which characterizes much Christian liberation theology captures this sense of the dialogical relationship between the scriptures and the experience of oppression. Ruether does not provide adequate account of that dialogue, nor does her own ethic adequately display its results.

With reference to the moral factor, Ruether does provide an important analysis and assessment of liberalism. The question for Ruether is, of course, whether or not liberalism provides an adequate intellectual framework for aiding women's struggle for liberation. Liberalism has been an attractive ideology for women because the liberal view of the human person emphasizes the capacity (or potential capacity) of every individual human being for autonomy or liberty as the defining element of human personhood. Liberalism has been a tool for the liberation of all oppressed or dominated persons, including women, according to Ruether, because this core conviction breaks down the distinction between persons in terms of their association with one or the other of the two terms of the dualistic conception of human nature which is typical in the western world: ruling class white men with the transcendent, autonomous, or spiritual term, women, the darker races, and the poor with the physical or material term. Ruether is not hesitant to regard this as an important liberal contribution to the liberation of oppressed persons, including women.

Still, Ruether regards liberalism as unsatisfactory. The most cogent and persuasive aspects of her critique have to do with her judgment that liberalism has failed to aggressively pursue the individual's rights to those economic means necessary to render their liberty effective, and with her analysis of liberalism's conception of the autonomous self.

Ruether regards liberalism as unable to translate its commitment to the equal protection of the liberty of all persons into a commitment to the economic egalitarianism necessary to render that equal liberty effective. Certain liberals have, of course, interpreted the liberal commitment to equal liberty as requiring broad redistributional schemes that have tended to weaken private property rights. Some liberals go so far as to argue for positive economic rights meant to protect the access of all individuals to at least minimum levels of such basic needs as food, housing, and health care. Yet, her critique in this respect is not invalid. Though some liberals have made such arguments, they have not been the dominant voice within liberalism. The idea of positive economic rights as human rights has not become dominant in the United States, and their institutional and legal protection is not provided. Even though taxing and spending policies have been used for redistributive purposes and large welfare programs have been enacted, their justification has not been based in the idea of a universal right to an economic minimum.

Ruether's critique of liberal economics is more radical, however, than the simple challenge that it has not been consistent enough in its commitment to equal liberty or that it has not recognized the material or economic basis of human liberty. She accepts Marx's view that private property is inherently oppressive or alienating. Ruether envisions an ideal society or ideal human relations in which persons relate to one another non-hierarchically. Where human relations are mediated by the institution of private property, that is, where some have large property holdings and others have much less or none at all, such mutuality is impossible. Ruether does not give quite the central place to private property in her conception of alienation as did Marx. She is critical of Marx for forgetting his essential insight that the root of all alienation is an alienated self-conception. On Ruether's view, property relations, or alienated relationships that result from property relations, are but one of the social manifestations of self-alienation. Gender differentiation, or the association of different capacities and roles with women and others with men, is for Ruether the fundamental social manifestation of self-alienation. Thus, she is clear that the elimination of private property is not a sufficient condition for the achievement of ideal social relations. This judgment should not obscure the fact that she shares with Marx the idea that ideal human relations are impossible where there is private property. Her socialism is what she calls "communitarian," which is to say that the collectivity which owns or controls productive property is a small local community rather than a larger unit such as the national state. Her concern is to assure that every individual shares control over the economic resources that are necessary for his or her life and welfare. That control is absent both where there is private property and where property is controlled by an inaccessible state bureaucracy.

Another important contribution in Ruether's critique of liberalism has to do with her view that the liberal conception of the self obscures the way in which persons are interdependent and results in relationships of domination between persons. The dualistic conception of human selfhood which she identifies with western thought regards the transcendent or spiritual dimension of human selfhood as its higher or essential dimension. For classical versions of the Christian faith it is in that dimension, through escape or redemption from human finitude and materiality, that human salvation or fulfillment is to be found. While liberalism is neutral with reference to the question of ultimate human fulfillment, it too celebrates the transcendent or autonomous dimension of human selfhood through its commitment to the protection of that dimension and the allowance of the widest possible expanse for its expression.

Ruether denies that the transcendent or autonomous aspect of human selfhood is that aspect which merits exclusive protection. That capacity, on her view, is not the source of our worth and dignity as human beings. Moreover, when it is so regarded and it is allowed the widest possible expression, that is, when our normative anthropology does not recognize the interdependence of the self's two dimensions, and the self's essential interdependence with others and with non-human nature, relationships of domination and subordination between persons and the exploitation of nature is the result.

With a dualistic rather than interdependent conception of our selfhood, nonhuman nature comes to be regarded as something to be exploited or controlled for human persons, and other persons are seen as in competition with the self, as threats to its basic interests and its fulfillment. The result is both ecological crisis and social relations built on domination. Relationships of domination are inevitable even when, as in liberalism, all persons are regarded as possessing the traits associated with the autonomous dimension of human experience. Liberalism introduces an element of fluidity in gender and race relations; to the degree that women and people of color are now regarded as equally human, their autonomy equally protected, and their competitive situation equalized through aggressive measures to guarantee equal opportunity, women and people of color will gradually be found in positions of leadership and moving up the economic scale. However, since we are in fact both autonomous and bound, both spiritual and physical beings with a capacity for independence which is always limited by our essential interdependence with nonhuman nature and with each other, where our capacity for autonomy and independence is provided exclusive protection or is given highest value those who are able to achieve that independence or who gain the widest sphere for its expression must always do so at the expense of others. Those at whose expense the independence of the few is gained will expend their energies in meeting their own physical needs and the physical needs of others, while those for whom liberal society works will be freed in large measure to develop and express the capacities for autonomy which belong to all of us.

Rosemary Ruether makes several important contributions to our understanding of the relationship between church and liberal world. First, she provides a reminder that the church does not exist for itself but for all humanity. Its attention should be directed to the liberation of the human community and not the preservation of its own institutional structure. If the Hauerwasian perspective focuses our attention on those aspects of the church which make it distinctive, and emphasizes a concern to maintain the integrity of the church as that community characterized by its allegiance to the story of a particular human person, Ruether reminds us that an important aspect of that story is its illustration of the truth that the community which would gain or guard its or her life loses it or misses its point, while pouring it out for others is the way of finding life's abundant *telos*. Secondly, she reminds us that when the church is faithful to its task it is about the business of making possible and exhibiting in its own life the closing of the gap between what human life is and what she has called its "aspirational horizon," or what the life of all can be at its best. She reminds us that the church must be distinguished from the world by its more perfect embodiment of the features of that divine commonwealth toward which Christian eschatological hope points. She also makes an important contribution by reminding us that the church always remains under the judgment of that hope, even as the world is always under that judgment. In this she maintains the best insights of Niebuhr's realism without allowing that realism to result in complacency or pessimism.

Another way of expressing the contribution that Ruether makes is with reference to an important theme in Hauerwas' work. Hauerwas insists that the church must always be hospitable to the stranger. Ruether's work represents a sustained effort to make us aware of the ways in which the church (and the liberal world) has made the poor and women strangers it refuses to receive with hospitality. Her work is a sustained effort to make sure that the church becomes more hospitable by being willing to listen to the voices of female and impoverished strangers. Those voices, as Ruether interprets them, have served to remind the church of the ways in which liberalism has served to create a human household in which women, particularly, but even the poor to some extent, are welcomed with hospitality, but also of the ways in which it has welcomed them only as household servants. Her work suggests a posture toward the liberal world which is both appreciative and supportive of its contributions, but critical of its shortcomings. Her insights are particularly valuable toward illuminating the way in which the liberal framework contributes to profound material inequality between persons and the abuse of the environment. Because liberalism seeks to respect our individual independence and allow its broadest expression when, in fact, we are interdependent with both the physical world and other selves, the independence it gains for some will be bought at the price of both great abuse to our physical environment and the material impoverishment and oppression of others. This insightful and illuminating critique of liberalism reminds the church that even if many, including many in the church, have been the beneficiaries of the freedom and prosperity which liberalism has helped to create, it cannot remain complacent about the cost of that achievement if it is to be hospitable to the poor and a steward of the creation. Ruether properly reminds the church in the United States that the wealth and freedom it enjoys in a liberal society may have caused it to lose the integrity of its witness to and proleptic embodiment of a life of shalom in which all enjoy the fruits of the richness of God's good creation and in which humanity and the created order coexist in a mutually supportive relationship.

Despite these significant contributions, I have suggested that Ruether's understanding of the relation of church to liberal world is ambiguous because she has failed to make clear how one's commitment to Jesus or one's participation in the Christian community shapes one's understanding of human liberation or full humanity. Christian claims seem to justify and provide motivation for the human aspiration for fulfillment and liberation while the content of that aspiration is finally determined by the insights of women and the poor. Despite my criticism, this ambiguity in Ruether's thought may be one with which a church that is true to the scriptural witness and to Jesus will have to live. Even the ambiguity may be a contribution that serves to guarantee the church's attitude of self-criticism and its openness to the criticism that comes from the stranger. The church should appreciate such guarantees and see them as a sign of the continuing presence of Christ in its midst, for Christ reminded us that when we are hospitable to the stranger and to the poor we are hospitable even to him.

Roman Catholic Social Teaching: The Church as Sacrament of Unity

At Vatican II, Roman Catholic social teaching shifted from a natural law methodology that assumes that autonomous human reason has access to universal truth to an epistemological perspective that recognizes the historically conditioned quality of human knowledge. Accompanying this shift was more concentrated attention to scripture as a source of authority for Christian social ethics. These methodological innovations signaled the possibility of sharp distinction between church and world as it suggests that all knowledge is relative to the perspective in which one stands and that the church draws upon a source of authority that the world does not share. The possibility of a sharp distinction at the epistemological level has not become a reality, however, because the new perspective has insisted on the "proper autonomy" of the human sciences and of diverse cultural perspectives on truth, based on their ultimate source in a common creator. Thus, while recognizing the radical pluralism of cultures and that deep ideological and moral conflicts are an important feature of modern life, the social encyclicals have employed a method that recognizes the possibility of dialogue between a biblically based faith perspective and various human cultures, a dialogue which moves toward the common discovery of ways of living together that contribute to human flourishing.

One of the uncertainties in this new methodology has to do with the precise status and role of explicitly theological and biblical perspectives in relation to knowledge drawn from the sciences and to the perspectives of cultures not shaped by the biblical story and faith. In this respect it shares an ambiguity which is characteristic of Rosemary Ruether's work. David Hollenbach has written that, in post-conciliar social teaching, "the religious and theological dimensions of human existence" function as "interpretative keys for the understanding of the demands of human dignity in the face of cultural, social, and intellectual pluralism" (1979:127). Yet he also suggests that the distinct faith perspective is "methodological and not substantive" (1979:128). Hollenbach goes on to suggest ways in which the faith perspective does make a substantive social ethical difference, however. His ambiguity mirrors the ambiguity of the social teaching he is attempting to explain. Thus, we can say that, while the distinct resources of faith, or the distinct biblical and theological sources of authority for faith, are intended to have some sort of priority in this dialogue, the idea of "epistemological privilege" employed in liberation theology with reference to the poor and the oppressed is too strong a term for the status of the faith perspective in the recent social encyclicals. Clearly, the historicism of those encyclicals does not result in the sort of combative or conflictive dialogue with the world which Hauerwas' rhetoric suggests. At least in terms of the tone of their address to the world, the Catholic social encyclicals do not regard their historicist epistemological perspective as necessitating the sort of sharp distinction between church and world that Hauerwas describes.

We should not overestimate the difference between Hauerwas and post-conciliar social teaching at this point. While Hauerwas' tone with reference to what he calls "the world" is strident, a cornerstone of his social ethic is openness to the stranger, which suggests the kind of dialogue that *Gaudium et Spes* specifies. Moreover, for both, the epistemological method they employ only suggests the possibility of a sharp distinction between church and world. The actual distinction is contextually drawn at the moral rather than the epistemological level. That is to say, the specific terms of the relationship between church and world depend upon the actual norms and values to which the world outside the church declares its loyalty and with reference to which it builds and reforms its institutions. With reference to this moral factor, while Hauerwas' language is significantly more strident than that employed in the social encyclicals, their moral critique of liberalism remains sharp-edged.

The Roman Catholic critique of liberalism, like Hauerwas', is rooted in a communitarian anthropology. On the Roman Catholic view, liberalism is based upon a truncated anthropology that takes a part of that which is essential to human nature, our capacity for autonomy, and makes it the exclusive source of our dignity. According to the Catholic view, a proper respect for the dignity of the human person must also recognize that human beings are bodies with definite and concrete human needs and that we are social or relational beings. Thus, the social encyclicals recognize basic positive human rights to economic necessities and are critical of liberal cultures for their toleration of great inequality and massive poverty. In the face of the domination of liberal economies, the social encyclicals have borrowed liberation theology's commitment to a preferential option for the poor. Moreover, the encyclicals recognize rights to culture and rights to cultural identity which are grounded in the social nature of the human person. The recognition that human beings are persons in community with others means that alongside rights belonging to individuals is the recognition of the basic claims of the community itself, also expressed in the language of rights. The idea of participation, which is also related to the social or relational nature of the human person, provides the key or unifying theme for the entire package of rights in the same way that individual liberty functions in liberal theories of rights.

The Catholic perspective is also critical of the degree of moral and cultural neutrality which is operative in liberal societies. The Catholic conception of human rights is grounded in a teleological framework; that is, rights are those protections and guarantees essential to human flourishing or essential to the realization of the good for the concrete human person in community. From such a perspective, the Catholic encyclicals are highly critical of the crass, materialistic values that seem to flourish in liberal cultures like the United States. Therefore, they are critical of conceptions of development which are attentive only to economic progress, to producing more and more goods, without attention to the human good. Moreover, the Catholic conception of the human *telos* recognizes the way in which the good for the human person is discovered, produced, distributed, and enjoyed in community with others. Drawing upon the biblical command to love and the unity of the three persons of the Trinity, it calls for an intense solidarity between persons as the foundation of social ethics. From such a perspective it is critical of the individualism and social alienation that liberal cultures seem to produce.

The relationship of Catholic social teaching to liberalism is not entirely critical, of course, and it would be a mistake to draw the distinction between liberal and Catholic social morality too sharply. There is a deep respect in postconciliar Catholic social teaching for individual liberty and the institutions which protect and give expression to that liberty in a liberal society. Since the second Vatican Council, Catholic social teaching has recognized the validity of religious liberty, the separation of church and state, democratic government limited by the rights of the individual, and market economic institutions. Moreover, the practical impact of the critique of liberal neutrality is mitigated a great deal by the principle of

subsidiarity and the distinction between the common good and the more
limited idea of the public order which is the immediate concern of
government. As a result, the Catholic concern for a full conception of the
human good as the foundation for social ethics is directed to all the public
institutional actors in a culture and not just to government. In this respect,
the Roman Catholic critique of liberalism is superior to that of Stanley
Hauerwas. It displays that more careful and nuanced analysis of the
relationship between Christian convictions and liberal ones that I have said
is lacking in Hauerwas' work.

On the other hand, it has much to learn from Hauerwas' attention to
the social and political life of the church itself. On my view, the most
important weakness of Roman Catholic social teaching has to do with the
degree to which it has failed to understand an important implication of the
methodological shift that took place at Vatican II. Drawing upon the work
of Norbert Rigali, I have argued that the shift from a natural law to an
historicist methodology requires greater attention to the concrete
embodiment of a distinctive way of life than official Catholic teaching has
yet displayed. That attention and concern is a significant characteristic of
Stanley Hauerwas' work. Yet, the idea of the Church as Sacrament of
unity suggests the very attention to the church as church, to the importance
of the church's own embodied life as an important social ethical
contribution, which that method indicates. Indeed, in my judgment the
model of the Church as Sacrament, drawn from Roman Catholic thought,
provides the best heuristic device for coming to terms with the church's
relationship to a liberal polity. It suggests the unique social ethical
contribution of the church itself which is a characteristic of the thought of
Stanley Hauerwas. It indicates that something of social ethical significance
is occurring when the church embodies a distinctive way of life that is
consistent with its fundamental convictions about God's way in and with
the world. Yet, at the same time, a sacrament is characterized by the way
in which it instills distinctive meaning in ordinary human events, like
washing with water or sharing food and drink. The idea of the church as
sacrament suggests that the distinct thing of social ethical significance that
is going on in the church is not absolutely distinct. It captures therefore
the positive aspects of Rosemary Ruether's secular theology of the Church
and overcomes the weakness of Hauerwas' too sharply drawn distinction
between church and world as a result of his insistence that God does
something absolutely unique in the formation of the church as a social
ethical community. The idea of the church as sacrament also suggests the
privileged status of, or the priority assigned to uniquely Christian sources
of social ethical insight. It suggests that it is in the church's sacraments
and especially at the Lord's table that the church gains the hermeneutical
skill necessary to identify where God's redemptive activity is efficacious
even beyond the boundaries of the church. It draws our attention to our
own distinctive contribution as a holy community, alerts us to the ways a

Christian way of life stands in sharp contrast with the ways of the wider world, including a liberal one, while indicating the conviction that God's activity is not entirely absent even there. It metaphorically reflects the complex combination of appreciation and criticism which Roman Catholic social teaching appropriately displays toward a liberal polity. It suggests that the question of the church's relationship to a liberal polity will require an ongoing process of discernment which will be faithful only if Christian vision is focused by the eucharist and baptism.

Endotes

[1] This difference in understanding, despite the fact that both Niebuhr and liberals regard their judgements as having been drawn from human nature, is but another example of the disagreement among those who claim that their conclusions are universally accessible to human reason.   Such disagreements always cast doubt on the validity of any such method.

[2] See Hauerwas' essay "Remembering as a Moral Task: The Challenge of the Holocaust" in *Against the Nations* (1985).

[3] J. Robert Nelson, for example, has written that "[n]either the Lutherans nor the Calvinists but the 'left wing' Christians of the Reformation of the sixteenth century were the direct predecessors of the most energetic movements for freedom from oppression by princely and prelatic power" (1979:2). It is interesting that the "left wing" of the Protestant Reformation produced the most direct theological contribution to the development of liberal theory and, also, important examples of pacifist communities from which Hauerwas draws inspiration.   What is the relation between these two facts?

[4] Power is a perennial aspect of politics, according to Niebuhr, because of two basic anthropological considerations:

> The one is the unity of vitality and reason, of body and soul. The other is the force of human sin, the persistent tendency to regard ourselves as more important than any one else and to view a common problem from the standpoint of our own interests (1943:258–259).

These "facts" of nature entail that power and its physical manifestations are inescapable aspects of political life.   The rejection of their use by an individual or group implies, then, a withdrawal from politics.

[5] Hauerwas is not referring to Niebuhr in these comments, but to John Howard Yoder (who Hauerwas says sees violence "as the essence of the state").   Indeed, Niebuhr recognized a distinction between power and violence as does Hauerwas. However, Niebuhr sees the relationship between power and violence as so intimate that the willingness to use one seems to entail a willingness to use the other, and since politics involves the organizing and balancing of all the forms that power

takes, it necessarily involves the use of violence. As importantly, for Hauerwas, though Niebuhr does recognize the settling of disputes through spiritual power rather than violence, what he does not envision is a political effort to arrive at a common conception of the good. Politics, for Niebuhr, is simply managing the conflicts that arise from competing concepts of the good. Thus, Hauerwas says that Niebuhr "has failed to see the significance of community for political behavior" (1974:235).

[6] I am not claiming that the refusal to use violence—in the defense of innocent others, for example—is never politically irresponsible. I am only claiming that the refusal to use violence does not entail a refusal to be political or to accept that one has political responsibilities. Consider Miscamble's claim that "Hauerwas effectively removes the church from the life and death policy issues of the human community" (1987:73). If this judgement is based upon Hauerwas' pacifist position it is surely mistaken. Such a commitment does not remove the church from life and death policy issues. Whether or not it makes the manner of the church's engagement in politics irresponsible in particular cases is another question.

Works Cited

Abott, Walter M., ed.
1966   The Documents of Vatican II.   New York: The American Press.

Ackerman, Bruce
1980   *Social Justice in the Liberal State.* New Haven and London: Yale University Press.

Barber, Benjamin
1984   *Strong Democracy: Participatory Politics for a New Age.* Berkeley, Los Angeles, and London: University of California Press.

Barker, Ernest, ed.
1962   *Social Contract.* New York: Oxford University Press.

Baum, Gregory
1986   "John Paul II's Encyclical on Labor." In *Readings in Moral Theology No. 5: Official Catholic Social Teaching.* See Curran, Charles E. and McCormick, Richard A, 1985.

Baum, Gregory and Ellsberg, Robert, eds.
1989   *The Logic of Solicarity.* Maryknoll, New York: Orbis Books.

Beauchamp, Tom. L.
1988   "The Justification of Goals and Quotas in Hiring." In *Ethical Theory and Business,* 3rd Edition. See Beauchamp, Tom L. and Bowie, Norman E., eds., 1988.

Beauchamp, Tom L. and Bowie, Norman E., eds.
1988   *Ethical Theory and Business,* 3rd Edition. Englewood Cliffs, New Jersey: Prentice Hall.

Beauchamp, Tom L. and Childress, James F.
1983   *Principles of Biomedical Ethics;* 2nd Edition. Oxford: Oxford University Press.

Beckley, Harlan
1981   "A Social Ethic Emphasizing Church and Family." *Interpretation* 36: 298-301.

1985   "A Christian Affirmation of Rawls' Idea of Justice as Fairness: Part I." *The Journal of Religious Ethics* 13.2 (Fall): 210-242.

Bedau, Hugo Adam
1980   "Human Rights and Foreign Assistance Programs." In
                       Human Rights and U. S. Foreign Policy. See Brown, Peter
                       G. and Maclean, Douglas, eds., 1980.

Bennett, John C.
1984   "Reinhold Niebuhr's Social Ethics." In *Reinhold Niebuhr:
                       His Religious, Social and Political Thought.* See Kegley,
                       Charles W., ed., 1984.

Brown, Peter G. and Maclean, Douglas, eds.
1980   *Human Rights and U. S. Foreign Policy.* Lexington,
                       Massachusetts and Toronto: D. C. Heath and Co.

Buchanan, Allen E.
1982   *Marx and Justice: The Radical Critique of Liberalism.*
                       Totowa, New Jersey: Rowman and Allenheld.

1989   "Assessing the Communitarian Critique of Liberalism." In
                       Ethics 99 (July): 852-882.

Burtt, Edwin A., ed.
1939   *The English Philosophers from Bacon to Mill.* New York:
                       Random House.

Byers, David, ed.
1985   *Justice in the Marketplace: Collected Statements of the
                       Vatican and the U. S. Catholic Bishops on Economic
                       Policy, 1891-1984.* Washington, DC: United States
                       Catholic Conference, 1985.

Cahill, Lisa Sowle
1980   "Toward a Christian Theory of Human Rights." *Journal of
                       Religious Ethics* 8.

Calvin, John
1960   *The Institutes of the Christian Religion.* McNeil, John T.,
                       ed. and Battles, Ford Lewis, trans. Library of Christian
                       Classics, Volume XXI. Philadelphia: The Westminster
                       Press.

Childress, James F.
1984   "Rights to Health Care In a Democratic Society." In
                       Biomedical Ethics Reviews. See Humber, James M. and
                       Almeder, Robert T., eds., 1984.

Chopp, Rebecca
1989   "Seeing and Naming the World Anew: The Works of
                   Rosemary Radford Ruether." *Religious Studies Review* 15
                   (January): 8-11.

Coleman, John A.
1982   *An American Strategic Theology*, New York: Paulist Press.

Coleman, John A., ed.
1991   *One Hundred Years of Catholic Social Thought:
                   Celebration and Challenge.* Maryknoll, New York: Orbis
                   Press.

Cooper, John W.
1985   *The Theology of Freedom: The Legacy of Jacques Maritain
                   and Reinhold Niebuhr.* Macon, Georgia: Mercer University
                   Press.

Cort, John
1988   *Christian Socialism.* Maryknoll, NY: Orbis Books.

Cranston, Maurice
1967   "Liberalism." In *The Encyclopedia of Philosophy.* See
                   Edwards, Paul, ed., 1967.

1983   "Are There Any Human Rights?" *Dædalus* 112 (Fall): 1-18.

Curran, Charles E.
1985   "The Changing Anthropological Bases of Catholic Social
                   Ethics." In *Readings in Moral Theology No. 5: Official
                   Catholic Social Teaching.* See Curran, Charles E. and
                   McCormick, Richard A, 1985.

1991   "Catholic Social Teaching and Human Morality." In *One
                   Hundred Years of Catholic Social Thought: Celebration and
                   Challenge.* See Coleman, John A., S. J. ed., 1991.

Curran, Charles, ed.
1990   *Moral Theology: Challenges for the Future: Essays in
                   Honor of Richard A. McCormick.* New York: Paulist
                   Press.

Curran, Charles E. and McCormick, Richard A., eds.
1985   *Readings in Moral Theology No. 5: Official Catholic Social
                   Teaching.* New York: Paulist Press.

Damico, Alfonso J., ed.
1986   *Liberals on Liberalism..* Totowa, NJ: Rowman and
                       Littlefield.

De Lue, Stephen M.
1986   "The Duty to Justice in Ideal Liberal Theory." *Liberals on
                       Liberalism.* Alfonso J. Damico, ed. Totowa, NJ: Rowman
                       and Littlefield.

Dorr, Donak
1989   "Solidarity and Integral Human Development." In *The
                       Logic of Solidarity.* See Baum, Gregory and Ellsberg,
                       Robert, eds., 1989.

Dulles, Avery
1987   *Models of the Church: Expanded Edition.* Garden City,
                       New York: Doubleday and Company.

1990   "Catholicism and American Culture: The Uneasy
                       Dialogue." *America* 162/3: 54-59.

Dworkin, Ronald
1978   "Liberalism." In *Public and Private Morality.* See Stuart
                       Hampshire, ed., 1978.

1977   *Taking Rights Seriously.* Cambridge, Massachusetts:
                       Harvard University Press.

Edwards, Paul, ed.
1967   *The Encyclopedia of Philosophy.* New York: Macmillan
                       and Company, Inc. and The Free Press.

Eisenstein, Zillah R.
1986   *The Radical Future of Liberal Feminism.* Boston:
                       Northeastern University Press.

Fitch, Robert E.
1984   "Reinhold Niebuhr's Philosophy of History." In *Reinhold
                       Niebuhr: His Religious, Social and Political Thought.* See
                       Kegley, Charles W., ed., 1984.

Fox, Richard Wightman
1985   *Reinhold Niebuhr: A Biography.* San Francisco: Harper
                       and Row.

1986   "Reinhold Niebuhr—The Living of Christian Realism." In *Reinhold Niebuhr and the Issues of Our Time*. See Harries, Richard, ed., 1986.

Friedman, Marilyn
1989   "Feminism and Modern Friendship: Dislocating the Community." *Ethics* 99 (January): 275-290.

Gadamer, Hans-Georg
1975   *Truth and Method*. New York: The Seabury Press.

Gajo, Petrovic
1967   " Alienation." In *The Encyclopedia of Philosophy*. See Edwards, Paul, ed., 1967.

Galston, William
1982   " Defending Liberalism." *The American Political Science Review* 76: 621-629.

1986   " Liberalism and Public Morality." In *Liberals on Liberalism*. See Damico, Alfonso J., ed., 1986.

Gaus, Gerald F.
1983   *The Modern Liberal Theory of Man*. London and Canberra: Corrom Helm.

Gill, Emily
1986   "Goods, Virtues, and the Constitution of the Self." In *Liberals on Liberalism*. See Damico, Alfonso J., ed., 1986.

Gilligan, Carol
1982   *In a Different Voice: Psychological Theory and Women's Development*. Cambridge: Harvard University Press.

1987   "Moral Orientation and Moral Development." In *Women and Moral Theory*. See Kittay, Eva Feder and Meyers, Diana T., eds., 1987.

Gray, John
1986   *Liberalism*. Milton Keynes, England: Open University Press.

Gustafson, James
1975   *Can Ethics Be Christian?* Chicago and London: The University of Chicago Press.

1985   "The Sectarian Temptation: Reflections on Theology, the
                  Church, and the University." *Proceedings of the Catholic
                  Theological Society* 40: 83-94.

Gutman, Amy
1985   " Communitarian Critics of Liberalism." *Philosophy and
                  Public Affairs* 14:308-322.

Hampshire, Stuart, ed.
1978   *Public and Private Morality.*

Harries, Richard, ed.
1986   *Reinhold Niebuhr and the Issues of Our Time.* Grand
                  Rapids, Michigan: Eerdmans.

Hart, H. L. A.
1961   *The Concept of Law.* Oxford: Oxford University Press.

1970   "Are There Any Natural Rights?" In *Human Rights.* See
                  Melden, A. I., ed., 1970. (Originally published in *The
                  Philosophical Review*, Vol. 64, (1955)).

Harvey, A. E.
1982   *Jesus and the Constraints of History.* Philadelphia:
                  Westminster Press.

Hauerwas, Stanley
1974   *Vision and Virtue.* Notre Dame, Ind.: University of Notre
                  Dame Press.

1975   *Character and The Christian Life: A Study in Theological
                  Ethics.* San Antonio, Texas: Trinity University Press.

1977   *Truthfulness and Tragedy.* Notre Dame, Ind.: University of
                  Notre Dame Press.

1981   *A Community of Character: Toward a Constructive
                  Christian Social Ethic.* Notre Dame, Ind. and London: The
                  University of Notre Dame Press.

1983   *The Peaceable Kingdom: A Primer in Christian Ethics.*
                  Notre Dame, Ind. and London: University of Notre Dame
                  Press.

1985a   *Against The Nations: War and Survival In a Liberal Society.*
                  Minneapolis, Chicago, and New York: Winston Press.

1985b   "Introduction." *Character and the Christian Life: A Study
                 in Theological Ethics*. San Antonio, Texas: Trinity
                 University Press.

1986a   "Should Christians Talk So Much About Justice?" *Books
                 and Religion* 14 (May/June): 3,15-16.

1986b   *Suffering Presence: Theological Reflections on Medicine,
                 the Mentally Handicapped, and the Church*. Notre Dame,
                 Ind. and London: University of Notre Dame Press.

1987   "Will the Real Sectarian Stand Up?" *Theology Today* 44
                 (April): 87-94.

1988   *Christian Existence Today*. Durham, NC: Labyrinth Press.

Hehir, J. Bryan
1980   "Human Rights from a Theological and Ethical
                 Perspective." In *Moral Imperatives of Human Rights: A
                 World Survey*. See Thompson, Kenneth W., ed., 1980.

1991   " The Right and Competence of the Church" in Coleman,
                 John A., ed., *One Hundred Years of Catholic Social
                 Thought: Celebration and Challenge* . Maryknoll, New
                 York: Orbis.

Hobbes, Thomas
1968   *Leviathan*. C. B. MacPherson, ed. Middlesex, England and
                 New York: Penguin Books.

Hoffman, W. Michael and Moore, Jennifer Mills, eds.
1984   *Business Ethics: Readings and Cases in Corporate Morality*.
                 New York: McGraw-Hill.

Hollenbach, David
1979   *Claims in Conflict: Retrieving and Renewing the Catholic
                 Human Rights Tradition*. New York: Paulist Press.

1988   *Justice, Peace, and Human Rights: American Catholic
                 Social Ethics in a Pluralistic Context*. New York:
                 Crossroad.

Humber, James M. and Almeder, Robert T., eds.
1984   *Biomedical Ethics Reviews*. Clifton, New Jersey: Humana
                 Press.

Hume, David
1962   "Of the Original Contract." In *Social Contract*. See Barker,
                       Ernest, ed., 1962.

Jewett, Paul
1975   *Man as Male and Female*. Grand Rapids, Michigan:
                       William B. Eerdmans Publishing Company.

John XXIII
1960   *Mater et Magistra*. In *Renewing the Earth: Catholic
                       Documents on Peace, Justice and Liberation*. See O'Brien,
                       David and Shannon, Thomas A., eds., 1977.

1963   *Pacem in Terris*. In *Renewing the Earth: Catholic
                       Documents on Peace, Justice and Liberation*. See O'Brien,
                       David and Shannon, Thomas A., eds., 1977.

John Paul II
1981   *Laborem Exercens*. In *Justice in the Marketplace: Collected
                       Statements of the Vatican and the U. S. Catholic Bishops
                       on Economic Policy, 1891-1984*. See Byers, David, ed.,
                       1985.

1987   *Sollicitudo Rei Socialis*. In *The Logic of Solicarity*. See
                       in Baum, Gregory and Ellsberg, Robert, eds., 1989.

1989   *Centesimus Annus*. In Origins: Catholic News Service
                       Documentary Service; Vol 21, No. 1.

Jones, L. Gregory
1988   " Should Christians Affirm Rawls' Justice as Fairness? A
                       Response to Professor Beckley." *Journal of Religious
                       Ethics* 16 (Fall): 251-271.

Kant, Immanuel
1948   *The Groundwork of the Metaphysic of Morals*. H.J. Paton,
                       trans. New York: Harper and Row. (The parenthetical page
                       number refers to the standard Royal Prussian Academy
                       edition.)

1965   *The Metaphysical Elements of Justice*. John Ladd, trans.
                       Indianapolis: Bobbs-Merill. (The parenthetical page
                       number refers to the standard Royal Prussian Academy
                       edition.)

Kegley, Charles W., ed.
1984   *Reinhold Niebuhr: His Religious, Social and Political
                Thought.* New York: The Pilgrim Press. (Originally
                published in 1956.)

Kittay, Eva Feder and Meyers, Diana T., eds.
1987   *Women and Moral Theory.* Totowa, New Jersey: Rowman
                and Littlefield.

Lacquer, Walter and Rubin, Barry
1979   *The Human Rights Reade.* New York: The New American
                Library.

Langan, John
1979   "Human Rights in Roman Catholicism." *Journal of
                Ecumenical Studies* 19.

Laslett, Peter
1960   "Introduction" to John Locke's *Two Treatises of
                Government.* New York: The New American Library.

Lindbeck, George
1984   *The Nature of Doctrine: Religion and Theology in a
                Postliberal Age.* Philadelphia: Westminister Press.

Little, David, and Twiss, Sumner B.
1978   *Comparative Religious Ethics: A New Method.* San
                Francisco: Harper and Row.

Livingston, James C.
1971   *Modern Christian Thought From the Enlightenment to
                Vatican II.* New York: The MacMillan Company.

Lloyd-Thomas, D. A.
1988   *In Defence of Liberalism.* Oxord and New York: Basil
                Blackwell.

Locke, John
1954   *Essays on the Law of Nature.* W. von Leyden, ed. Oxford:
                Clarendon Press.

1955   *A Letter Concerning Toleration.* Indianapolis, Indiana:
                Bobbs-Merrill/Library of Liberal Arts.

1960   *Two Treatises of Government.* Peter Laslett, ed. New
                York: The New American Library.

MacIntyre, Alasdair
1981   *After Virtue*. Notre Dame, Ind.: University of Notre Dame
                         Press.

1988   *Whose Justice? Which Rationality?* Notre Dame, Ind.:
                         University of Notre Dame Press.

Macpherson, C. B.
1977   *The Life and Times of Liberal Democracy*. Oxford and New
                         York: Oxford University Press.

McCann, Dennis
1987   "The Good to be Pursued in Common." In *The Common
                         Good and U. S. Capitalism*. See Williams, Oliver F. and
                         Houck, John W., eds., 1987

Melden, A. I., ed.
1970   *Human Rights*. Belmont California: Wadsworth Publishing
                         Company, Inc.

Merkley, Paul
1975   *Reinhold Niebuhr: A Political Account*. Montreal and
                         London: McGill-Queen's University Press.

Mill, John Stuart
1939a   " On Liberty." In *The English Philosophers from Bacon to
                         Mill*. See, Burtt, Edwin A., ed., 1939.

1939b   "Utilitarianism." In *The English Philosophers from Bacon
                         to Mill*. See, Burtt, Edwin A., ed., 1939.

Miscamble, Wilson D.
1987   "Sectarian Passivism?" *Theology Today* 44 (April): 69-77.

Nelson, Paul
1987   *Narrative and Morality: A Theological Inquiry*. University
                         Park and London: The Pennsylvania University Press.

Niebuhr, Helmut Richard
1951   *Christ and Culture*. New York: Harper and Row.

Niebuhr, Reinhold
1932   *Moral Man and Immoral Society*. New York: Charles
                         Scribner's Sons.

1935   *An Interpretation of Christian Ethics.* New York: Harper
                and Brothers, New York. (Page references are to the New
                York: Seabury Press paperback edition of 1979.)

1940   *Christianity and Power Politics.* New York: Charles
                Scribner's Sons.

1941   *The Nature and Destiny of Man: A Christian Interpretation,
                Volume I: Human Nature.* New York: Charles Scribner's
                Sons.

1943   *The Nature and Destiny of Man: A Christian Interpretation,
                Volume 2: Human Destiny.* New York: Charles Scribner's
                Sons.

1944   *The Children of Light and the Children of Darkness: A
                Vindication of Democracy and a Critique of Its Traditional
                Defense.* New York: Charles Scribner's Sons.

1952   *The Irony of American History.* New York: Charles
                Scribner's Sons.

1953   *Christian Realism and Political Problems.* New York:
                Charles Scribner's Sons.

1955   *The Self and the Dramas of History.* New York: Charles
                Scribner's Sons.

1957   "Christian Faith and Natural Law." In *Love and Justice:
                Selections from the Shorter Writings of Reinhold Niebuhr.*
                See Robertson, D. B., ed., 1957.

1960   *Reinhold Niebuhr On Politics.* Davis, Harry R., and Good,
                Robert C., eds. New York: Charles Scribner's Sons.

1984   "Intellectual Autobiography of Reinhold Neibuhr." In
                *Reinhold Niebuhr: His Religious, Social and Political
                Thought.* See Kegley, Charles W., ed., 1984.

Novak, Michael
1982   *The Spirit of Democratic Capitalism,* New York: Simon
                and Schuster.

1984   *Freedom with Justice: Catholic Social Thought and Liberal
                Institutions .* San Francisco: Harper and Row.

1987   "Free Persons and the Common Good." In *The Common
                        Good and U. S. Capitalism*. See Williams, Oliver F. and
                        Houck, John W., eds., 1987

Nozick, Robert
1974   *Anarchy, State, and Utopia*. New York: Basic Books, Inc.

O'Brien, David
1988   *Public Catholicism*. New York: Macmillan Publishing
                        Company.

O'Brien, David and Shannon, Thomas A., eds.
1977   *Renewing the Earth: Catholic Documents on Peace, Justice
                        and Liberation*. Garden City, New York: Doubleday.

Ogletree, Thomas W.
1980   "Character and Narrative: Stanley Hauerwas' Studies of the
                        Christian Life." *Religious Studies Review* 6 (January):
                        25-30.

1983   *The Use of the Bible in Christian Ethics*. Philadelphia:
                        Fortress Press.

Ollman, Bertell
1976   *Alienation: Marx's Conception of Man in Capitalist Society*
                        (2nd Edition). Cambridge: Cambridge University Press.

Ottati, Douglas F.
1989   *Jesus Christ and Christian Vision*. Minneapolis: Fortress
                        Press.

Outka, Gene
1980   "Character, Vision, and Narrative." *Religious Studies
                        Review* 6 (April): 110-118.

Pannenberg, Wolfhart
1967   "The Revelation of God in Jesus of Nazareth." In *Theology
                        as History*. See Robinson and Cobb, eds., 1967. New
                        York: Harper and Row.

Pius XI
1931   *Quadragessimo Anno*. In *Justice in the Marketplace:
                        Collected Statements of the Vatican and the U. S. Catholic
                        Bishops on Economic Policy, 1891-1984*. See Byers,
                        David, eds. 1985.

Paul VI
1967   *Populorum Progressio*. In *Renewing the Earth: Catholic
                Documents on Peace, Justice and Liberation. See O'Brien,
                David and Shannon, Thomas A., eds., 1977.

1971   *Octogesma Adveniens*. In *Renewing the Earth: Catholic
                Documents on Peace, Justice and Liberation. See O'Brien,
                David and Shannon, Thomas A., eds., 1977.

1975   *Evangelii Nuntiandi*. In *Renewing the Earth: Catholic
                Documents on Peace, Justice and Liberation. See O'Brien,
                David and Shannon, Thomas A., eds., 1977.

Quirk, Michael J.
1987   "Beyond Sectariansim?" *Theology Today* 44 (April): 78-
                86.

Ramsey, Paul
1950   *Basic Christian Ethics;* Chicago and London: The
                University of Chicago Press.

1962   *Nine Modern Moralists*. Englewood Cliffs, New Jersey:
                Prentice Hall, Inc.

Rawls, John
1971   *A Theory of Justice*. Cambridge: Harvard University Press.

1985   "Justice as Fairness: Political Not Metaphysical."
                Philosophy and Public Affairs 14 (Summer): 223-251.

Remick, Helen
1984   *Comparable Worth and Wage Discrimination: Technical
                Possibilities and Political Realities*. Philadelphia: Temple
                University Press.

Reynolds, Charles H. and Norman, Ralph V., eds.
1988   *Community in America: The Challenge of Habits of the
                Heart*. Berkeley, California: University of California Press.

Robinson and Cobb, eds.
1967   *Theology as History*. New York: Harper and Row.

Ruether, Rosemary Radford
1967   *Church Against Itself*. New York: Herder and Herder.

1970   *The Radical Kingdom*. New York: Harper and Row.

1972   *Liberation Theology: Human Hope Confronts Christian History and American Power.* New York: Paulist Press.

1974   *Faith and Fratricide.* New York: Seabury Press.

1975a   "Misogynism and Virginal Feminism in the Fathers of the Church." In *Religion and Sexism: Images of Women in the Jewish and Christian Traditions.* Rosemary Radford Ruether, ed. New York: Simon and Schuster.

1975b   *New Woman/New Earth: Sexist Ideologies and Human Liberation.* New York: Seabury Press.

1983a   *Sexism and God-Talk: Toward a Feminist Theology.* Boston: Beacon Press.

1983b   *To Change the World: Christology and Cultural Criticism.* New York: Crossroad.

1984   *Women-Church: Theology and Practice.* New York: Harper and Row.

Rigali, Norbert
1990   "The Uniqueness and Distinctiveness of Christian Morality and Ethics." In *Moral Theology: Challenges for the Future: Essays in Honor of Richard A. McCormick.* See Curran, Charles, ed., 1990.

Robertson, D. B., ed.
1957   *Love and Justice: Selections from the Shorter Writings of Reinhold Niebuhr.*

Sandel, Michael
1982   *Liberalism and the Limits of Justice.* Cambridge: Cambridge University Press.

Schlesinger, Arthur, Jr.
1984   "Reinhold Niebuhr's Role in Political Thought." In *Reinhold Niebuhr: His Religious, Social and Political Thought.* See Kegley, Charles W., ed., 1984.

Scriven, Charles
1988   *The Transformation of Culture: Christian Social Ethics after H. Richard Niebuhr.* Scottdale, Pa.: Herald Press.

Second Vatican Council
1964   *Lumen Gentium*. In *The Documents of Vatican II*. See
                        Abott, Walter M., ed., 1966.

1965   *Gaudium et Spes*. In *Renewing the Earth: Catholic
                        Documents on Peace, Justice and Liberation*. See O'Brien,
                        David and Shannon, Thomas A., eds., 1977.

Simmons, A. John
1979   *Moral Principles and Political Obligations*. Princeton, NJ:
                        Princeton University Press.

Smith, Adam
1981   *The Wealth of Nations*. In *Anglo American Liberalism:
                        Readings in Normative Political Economy*. See,
                        Waligorski, Conrad, and Hone, Thomas, eds., 1981.

Spragens, Thomas
1986   "Reconstructing Liberal Theory: Reason and Liberal
                        Culture." In *Liberals on Liberalism*.. See Damico,
                        Alfonso J., ed., 1986.

Stone, Ronald H.
1972   *Reinhold Niebuhr: Prophet to Politicians*. Nashville and
                        New York: Abingdon.

Synod of Bishops
1971   *Justice in the World*. In *Renewing the Earth: Catholic
                        Documents on Peace, Justice and Liberation*. See O'Brien,
                        David and Shannon, Thomas A., eds., 1977.

Stout, Jeffrey
1988   *Ethics After Babel*. Boston: Beacon Press.

Thompson, Kenneth W., ed.
1980   *Moral Imperatives of Human Rights: A World Survey*.
                        Washington: University Press of America.

Thomson, Judith Jarvis
1984   "Preferential Hiring." In *Business Ethics: Readings and
                        Cases in Corporate Morality*. See Hoffman, W. Michael
                        and Moore, Jennifer Mills, eds., 1984.

Troeltsch, Ernst
1981   *The Social Teaching of the Christian Churches*. Chicago
                        and London: University of Chicago Press.

United States Catholic Conference
1983   *The Challenge of Peace: God's Promise and Our Response.*
                       Washington, DC: United States Catholic Conference

1986   *Economic Justice for All.* Washington, DC: United States
                       Catholic Conference

Vaughan, Judith
1983   *Sociality, Ethics, and Social Change: A Critical Appraisal
                       of Reinhold Niebuhr's Ethics in the Light of Rosemary
                       Radford Ruether's Works.* Lanham, MD: University Press
                       of America.

Waligorski, Conrad, and Hone, Thomas, eds.
1981   *Anglo-American Liberalism: Readings in Normative
                       Political Economy.* Chicago: Nelson Hall.

Walzer, Michael
1983   *Spheres of Justice: A Defense of Pluralism and Equality.*
                       New York: Basic Books, Inc.

Werhane, Patricia
1988   "Employee and Employer Rights in an Institutional
                       Context." In *Ethical Theory and Business,* 3rd Edition. See
                       Beachamp, Tom L. and Bowie, Norman E., eds., 1988.

Williams, Daniel D.
1984   "Niebuhr and Liberalism." In *Reinhold Niebuhr: His
                       Religious, Social and Political Thought.* See Kegley,
                       Charles W., ed., 1984.

Williams, Oliver F. and Houck, John W., eds.
1987   *The Common Good and U. S. Capitalism.* Lanham, Md.:
                       University Press of America.

Yack, Bernard
1988   "Does Liberal Practice Live 'Down' to Liberal Theory?
                       Liberalism and its Communitarian Critics." In *Community
                       in America: The Challenge of Habits of the Heart.* See
                       Reynolds, Charles H. and Norman, Ralph V., eds., 1988.

Yoder, John Howard
1971   *The Original Revolution.* Scottsdale, Pa.: Herald Press.

1984   *The Priestly Kingdom.* Notre Dame, Ind.: University of
                       Notre Dame Press.

n. a.   *"Christ and Culture* : A Critique of H. Richard Niebuhr."
                     Unpublished.

Index